Reynard the Fox

Polygons: Cultural Diversities and Intersections
General Editor: Lieve Spaas, Professor of French Cultural Studies, Kingston University

Volume 1
Reynard the Fox: Social Engagement and Cultural Metamorphoses in the Beast Epic from the Middle Ages to the Present
Edited by Kenneth Varty

Volume 2
Echoes of Narcissus
Edited by Lieve Spaas in association with Trista Selous

Volume 3
Human Nature and the French Revolution: Communities of Faith: From the Enlightenment to the Napoleonic Code
Xavier Martin
Translated from the French by Patrick Corcoran

Volume 4
Secret Spaces, Forbidden Places: Rethinking Culture
Edited by Fran Lloyd and Catherine O'Brien

in preparation

Volume 5
Beyond Language and Culture: Communication across Boundaries
Edited by Magda Stroinska

Volume 6
Expanding Suburbia
Edited by Roger Webster

REYNARD THE FOX

Social Engagement and Cultural Metamorphoses in the Beast Epic from the Middle Ages to the Present

studies by
Elaine C. Block, Jean Dufournet,
Jan Goossens, Jill Mann,
Jean-Marc Pastré, Wilfried Schouwink,
Roger Stephenson, Jean Subrenat,
Elina Suomela-Härmä, Rik van Daele,
Kenneth Varty and Paul Wackers

Edited by Kenneth Varty

Berghahn Books
New York • Oxford

First published in 2000 by

Berghahn Books
www.BerghahnBooks.com

Editorial offices:
604 West 115th Street, New York, NY 10025, USA
3 NewTec Place, Magdalen Road, Oxford OX4 1RE, UK

© 2000 Kenneth Varty

All rights reserved.
No part of this publication may be reproduced in any form
or by any means without the written permission
of Berghahn Books.

Library of Congress Cataloging-in-Publication Data

Reynard the Fox : engagement in the beast epic from the
Middle Ages to the presnet / studies by Elaine C. Block ... [et
al.] ; edited by Kenneth Varty.
    p. cm. — (Polygons ; v.1)
Includes bibliographical references and index.
ISBN 1-57181-737-9
   1. Reynard the Fox (Legendary character) in iterature. I.
Block, Elaine C. II. Varty, Kenneth. III.
Series.

PN57.R48 R49 2000
809'.93374—dc21
                                        00-059873

British Library Cataloguing in Publication Data
A catalogue record for this book is available
from the British Library.

Printed in the United States on acid-free paper.

ISBN 1-57181-737-9 (hardback)

Contents

List of Illustrations	vii
Acknowledgements	xi
Introduction Kenneth Varty	xiii
1. The Satiric Fiction of the *Ysengrimus* Jill Mann	1
2. Rape and Adultery: Reflected Facets of Feudal Justice in the *Roman de Renart* Jean Subrenat	17
3. Morals, Justice and Geopolitics in the *Reinhart Fuchs* of the Alsatian Heinrich der Glichezaere Jean-Marc Pastré	37
4. Medieval French and Dutch Renardian Epics: Between Literature and Society Paul Wackers	55
5. The Printed Dutch Reynaert Tradition: From the Fifteenth to the Nineteenth Century Paul Wackers	73
6. The Flemish *Reynaert* As An Ideological Weapon Rik van Daele	104
7. The Ill-Fated Consequence of the Tom-Cat's Jump, and Its Illustration Jan Goossens	113

8.	Choir-Stall Carvings of Reynard and Other Foxes *Elaine C. Block* and *Kenneth Varty*	125
9.	Reynard in England: From Caxton to the Present *Kenneth Varty*	163
10.	Hartmann Schopper's Latin *Reinike* of 1567 *Wilfried Schouwink*	175
11.	The Political Import of Goethe's *Reineke Fuchs* *Roger H. Stephenson*	191
12.	Paul Weber's Satirical Use of Reineke in Cartoon Form *Kenneth Varty*	209
13.	The Death and Resurrection of the *Roman de Renart* *Kenneth Varty* and *Jean Dufournet*	221
14.	The Fox and the Wolf in the Well: the Metamorphoses of a Comic Motif *Kenneth Varty*	245
15.	The Fox and the Hare: An Odd Couple *Elina Suomela-Härmä*	257
Notes on Contributors		269
Bibliography		273
Index		283

List of Illustrations

Figure 4.1	Reynaert teaching Kuwaert the hare the Creed. Marginal illustration in a *Lancelot* manuscript. Yale 229, f. 133v. (Randall 1966, fig. 195).	69
Figure 4.2	Reynaert teaching Kuwaert the hare the Creed. Marginal illustration in a Latin psalter, probably owned by Gwide of Dampierre, Brussels, Royal Library, 10607, f. 86r. (Randall, 1966, fig. 194).	69
Figure 5.1	Prose incunabulum: Prologue. The Hague, Royal Library, 169 G 98, f. 3r.	78
Figure 5.2	Prose incunabulum: Impressum. The Hague, Royal Library, 169 G 98, f. 113r.	79
Figure 5.3	Rhyme incunabulum: first leaf of fragment (f. h2r). Copied from Breul 1927, 2.	80
Figure 5.4	*Reynaert de vos* ... Plantijn, Antwerp, 1556. Title page.	81
Figure 5.5	*Reynaert de vos* ... Plantijn for Peter van Keerbergen, Antwerp, 1564. Freiburg, University Library, E 7963 (Rara), f. A3v–A4r.	83
Figure 5.6	*Reynaert de vos* ... Plantijn, Antwerp, 1566, f. B1v–B2r.	83
Figure 5.7	*Van Reynaert die Vos* ... Schinckel, Delft, 1589, f. A2v–A3r.	84
Figure 5.8	*Reynaert den vos* ... Verdussen, Antwerp, c. 1700, pp. 8–9.	84
Figure 7.1	Tibert castrates a village priest. Misericord, Bristol Cathedral, c.1520. Photograph by Elaine C. Block.	114

Figure 7.2	Tibert jumps up castrated priest's back. Misericord, Bristol Cathedral, c.1520. Photograph by Elaine C. Block.	115
Figure 7.3	Tibert castrates a village priest. Woodcut, c.1495 from a copy of *The History of Reynard the Fox*, c.1560–85, owned by W. Grauwels.	115
Figure 7.4	Tibert attacks a village priest. Woodcut from *Reynke Voss de olde*, Rostock, 1539.	117
Figure 7.5	Tibert attacks a village priest. Woodcut from *Van Reyneken Vosse dem Olden*, Frankfurt, 1550.	117
Figure 7.6	Tibert castrates a village priest. Etching by Allart van Everdingen (1621–75).	118
Figure 7.7	Tibert castrates a village priest. Etching by Wilhelm von Kaulbach, 1846.	119
Figure 7.8	Tibert castrates a village priest. Etching by J.H. Ramberg, 1826.	120
Figure 7.9	Tibert attacks a man's nose. Drawing by Rie Kooyman, 1968.	122
Figure 7.10	Tibert attacks a man's upper leg. Drawing by Willem Backer, 1929.	122
Figure 7.11	Tibert leaps to attack a naked man's private parts. Drawing by Bert Bouman, 1979.	123
Figure 7.12	Tibert attacks a naked man. Drawing by Dolf de Rudder, 1985.	123
Figure 8.1	Bruin caught in a half-split log. Misericord, Bristol Cathedral, c.1520. Photograph by D.R. Maxted.	127
Figure 8.2	Bruin caught in a half-split log. Woodcut from *Reynke de vos*, Lübeck, 1498.	128
Figure 8.3	Reynard mounts the gallows ladder. Misericord, Bristol Cathedral, c.1520. Photograph by D.R. Maxted.	130
Figure 8.4	Reynard mounts the gallows ladder. Woodcut from *Reynke de vos*, Lübeck, 1498.	132
Figure 8.5	Reynard mounts the gallows ladder. Woodcut, c.1495 from a copy of *The History of Reynard the Fox*, c.1560-85, owned by W. Grauwels.	132
Figure 8.6	Bruin and Isegrim dance. Misericord, Bristol Cathedral, c.1520. Photograph by Elaine C. Block.	133
Figure 8.7	Centre: fox with cock chased by woman with distaff. Left: cowled fox preaches to hens and a cock; right: man with stick about to join in fox	

List of Illustrations ix

	chase. Misericord, Ely Cathedral, 1338. Photograph by Kenneth Varty.	135
Figure 8.8	Fox with goose chased by woman with distaff. Misericord, St Botolph, Boston, 1390. Photograph by D.R. Maxted.	136
Figure 8.9	Fox with duck or goose chased by woman with distaff. Misericord, Norwich Cathedral, 1480. Photograph by J.C.D. Smith.	137
Figure 8.10	Fox with goose watched by woman with distaff. Misericord, Beverley Minster, 1520. Photograph by Elaine C. Block.	138
Figure 8.11	A fox preaches to a group of ducks. Misericord, Wells Cathedral, c.1330. Photograph by D.R. Maxted.	141
Figure 8.12	A seated fox-bishop, attended by an ass-priest, holds a cock by the neck. Misericord, St Botolph, Boston, 1390. Photograph by D.R. Maxted.	142
Figure 8.13	Two cowled foxes on either side of a goose lectern. Misericord, Beverley St Mary, 1445. Photograph by Elaine C. Block.	146
Figure 8.14	A fox-monk faces a monk. Each places a hand on a book held between them. Misericord, Chester Cathedral, 1390. Photograph by D.R. Maxted.	147
Figure 8.15	A fox, shot through by an arrow, consults an ape-doctor. Misericord, Beverley St Mary, 1445. Photograph by Elaine C. Block.	150
Figure 8.16	Centre, a fox feigns death; left and right, foxes dressed as Franciscans, one with prey, the other with a bow and a flask. Misericord, St Mary, Nantwich, 1390. Photograph by Kenneth Varty.	151
Figure 8.17	Centre, geese hang a fox. To the right of the gallows, geese with a crucifix and a mace. Misericord, Beverley Minster, 1520. Photograph by D.R. Maxted.	152
Figure 8.18	An ape grooms a fox. Misericord, left supporter. St George's Chapel, Windsor Castle, c.1480. Photograph by Elaine C. Block.	154
Figure 8.19	A sick lion is attended by a fox-physician holding a urinal. Misericord, Gloucester Cathedral, 1345. Photograph by Kenneth Varty.	156

Figure 8.20	Apes steal equipment from a sleeping pedlar. Misericord, Manchester Cathedral, 1508. Photograph by D.R. Maxted.	157
Figure 8.21	Fox with man dangling from a shouldered stake behind him. Misericord, Castle Hedingham, probably late fourteenth century. Photograph by Kenneth Varty.	160
Figure 12.1	Eulenspiegel cuddles Reineke. *Die Geduldigen*. Lithograph, 1935, by Paul Weber.	211
Figure 12.2	Reineke as jester. Drawing for the cover of a book, 1966, by Paul Weber.	212
Figure 12.3	Reineke preaches. Drawing from J. Mähl's *Reineke Voss*, 1986, p. 108. Made by Paul Weber, 1924.	214
Figure 12.4	Reineke preaches. *Busspredigt*. Drawing, 1960, by Paul Weber.	215
Figure 12.5	Reineke offers reading glasses to an ass. *Die bessere Brille*. Lithograph, 1960, by Paul Weber.	216
Figure 12.6	Reineke awards medals. *Dekoration*. Drawing, 1960, by Paul Weber.	217
Figure 12.7	Reineke and dancing hens. *Tanz der Hennen*. Lithograph, 1960, by Paul Weber.	217
Figure 12.8	Reineke ferries a boatload of rabbits. *Die Überfahrt*. Lithograph, 1960, by Paul Weber.	218
Figure 12.9	Reineke the conductor. *Gänse... marsch*. Lithograph, 1960, by Paul Weber.	219
Figure 12.10	Reineke the cannon-breaker. *Schluss!* Lithograph, 1960, by Paul Weber.	219
Figure 12.11	Reineke confronts an armed horde. *Die Entscheidung*. Lithograph, 1976, by Paul Weber.	220
Figures 13.1 to 13.3	Three pages of drawings, 1976, by Jean-Louis Hubert for *Le Polar de Renard*.	239–241

Acknowledgements

Warm thanks are due to all the contributors to this volume for letting me have their essays in good time, and for responding so positively to the suggestions I made for amendments here and there. Special thanks are due to the contributors who composed their essays in English, a foreign language for them; namely, Wilfried Schouwink, Rik van Daele, and Paul Wackers (for his second essay).

For their freely rendered services, special thanks are also due to two translators in particular. Jean Subrenat records his gratitude to Gloria Cigman for her translation of his essay; Jan Goossens, Jean-Marc Pastré and Paul Wackers (for his first essay) record their gratitude to Hety Varty for her translations from both French and German. And Jean Dufournet and Elina Suomela-Härmä have offered me their warm thanks for my translations of their contributions.

I am also grateful to both Gloria Cigman and Hety Varty for word-processing their translations, and to Hety for proofreading ten of these essays for first submission to the general editor and the publisher. Jennifer Feller's advice on revising the entire manuscript following the copy editor's work on it, and in particular her help with problems posed by the second chapter, are much appreciated. The advice, help, and encouragement of the general editor, Lieve Spaas, have been invaluable.

For the use of their copyright photographs, we gladly thank Elaine C. Block, D.R. Maxted and J.C.D. Smith; and we thank Wilfried Grauwels for copies of woodcuts in early printed books which he owns.

We also thank the librarians and the staff of libraries for allowing us to reproduce drawings from manuscripts and incunabula in their keeping; in particular, the Royal Library in Brussels, the Royal Library in The Hague, the University Library, Yale and the A.Paul Weber Museum in Ratzeburg.

Kenneth Varty

Introduction

The Itinerant Fox

The fox we call Reynard has had a long life and has wandered far and wide in the world of fiction. At the beginning he was a high-ranking baron in the Animal Kingdom where he served, when it suited him, the Lion-King. Even in his early days he travelled considerable distances across numerous boundaries, often leaving behind him offspring whose descendants lived through stirring times, adapting their name to the language of the new culture which they had made their own, adjusting to new religious creeds and political systems, practising numerous professions and fitting into different social classes as they and their new masters (poets and storytellers, critics and commentators) thought fit.

Reynard saw the light of day, it seems, in Ghent in 1149 or thereabouts. Although this was then, as now, in Dutch-speaking territory, his first words were in Latin and he was known as Reinardus. From Ghent he travelled in the 1170s into French-speaking lands where he was called Renart. At that time the French for a fox was *goupil*, and he was *Renart le goupil*, Renart being his personal name just as Noble was that of the lion (*Noble le lion*), and Fière that of the lioness. His immense popularity in medieval France was to bring about, eventually, the death of the word *goupil* and its replacement by *renard*. About twenty years later, in the 1190s, he turned up in Alsace with the name Reinhart, but soon he returned to Flanders and, as Reynaert, spoke Dutch. While he lingered there, one of his French descendants made an excursion, at the end of the thirteenth century, into Italy where he established himself as Rainaldo. The Dutch-speaking Flanders fox's first foray abroad was to cross the Channel in 1481 in the company of William Caxton who named him Reynard and helped him found, in Westminster, what was to be a long-lived English branch of the family. Not long back in Flanders, in 1498, he made for Lübeck where he established another thriving branch of the family, one which spoke Low German and made famous the name Reynke. About fifty years later he moved south, to Frankfurt am Main, spoke High German and came to be known as Reinicke but, since Goethe, as Reineke. Further afield, in the sixteenth and seventeenth centuries, he crossed into Denmark and Sweden first as Reynicke, then, in Sweden only, as Reinick and Reninge. Lastly, in the nineteenth century, he made for Luxemburg where he is celebrated as Renert.

In six or seven different cultures which share just four languages, generation after generation of Reinardus's offspring have played central roles in poems, stories, historiated sculptures and drawings: French in France and francophone Belgium; Dutch in Flanders and the Netherlands; English in England, Scotland and, more recently, North America; German in Germany, Austria and parts of Switzerland. And it is chiefly from Reynardian texts in these languages that, through translations and adaptations, the Beast Epic fox's fame has been noised abroad. For example, parts of the medieval French *Roman de Renart* have been rendered into Portuguese, Romanian, Russian and Japanese.

The Main Objective

The chief aim of this volume of essays is to give some telling examples of the metamorphoses of the Beast Epic fox as he travelled through time and space entertaining people (rather like the travelling minstrel he once pretended to be in the *Roman de Renart*), and of his involvement in some of the basic problems and issues men and women have faced in many different kinds of society.

The Beast Epic

The title *Beast Epic* is given by literary historians to a genre which depicts an animal kingdom of the feudal kind ruled by a lion-king. In the medieval French model his name is Noble, and that of his queen is Fière (who, from time to time, reveals her amorous feelings for Renart). One of the most powerful barons at Noble's court is the wolf, Ysengrin (as his name suggests, a man of iron, but not a very clever one). He has a notoriously lascivious wife, Hersent. (The Latin for a she-wolf is *lupa*, slang for prostitute). In one of the very first stories of the many that make up the *Roman de Renart*, she seduces Renart, and soon afterwards, when Ysengrin knows about her adultery with Renart, the fox rapes her in full view of her helpless husband: hence the never-ending hatred of the wolf for the fox, and their enduring enmity. Hermeline is Renart's long-suffering wife, mistress of their castle-den, Malpertuis, and they have three sons (Malebranche, Percehaie and Rovel) who appear in just a few of the Beast Epic stories. Renart's only effective ally in all these tales is his first cousin, the badger Grimbert; but the monkey Cointereau is also a friend and, over time, he (or another of his tribe) plays a bigger and bigger role as a companion in mischief. The fox also has a love-hate relationship with the cat, Tibert (ancestor of all our tibby or tabby cats). They respect each other's stealth and cunning, and often form short-term alliances which lead to a conflict of interests in which Reynard usually comes off the worse. Other animals who play a major role invariably opposed to Renart are the clumsy, gullible bear, Brun; and the pompous cock, Chantecler (who has a wise wife called Pinte and many less-wise sisters-in-law, chief of whom is Couppée (who gets her head cut off by Renart's teeth). All these animals are portrayed as high-ranking barons who owe allegiance to Noble and (with the exception of Grimbert and Cointereau) have, sooner or later, grounds to complain to him about Renart.

In the essays which make up this volume, the Latin, Dutch, English and German equivalents of the French names just given are usually easily recognised. Occasionally they are totally different (in the *Ysengrimus*, the lion is Rufanus, the cock Sprotinus) but when that is so, the authors make clear who is who.

The Beast Epic context of the essays in this volume

The Ysengrimus

As mentioned above, it was as Reinardus that Reynard the Fox made his literary début in one of the finest masterpieces of all time, the *Ysengrimus*, a Latin verse epic of over 6,500 lines, composed in 1148-49, in a clerical milieu in Ghent. The narrative focuses on a strong but not-so-bright wolf named Ysengrimus. His main opponent and tormenter is a cunning little fox, his nephew, Reinardus. It is here that, for the first time in a literary work of art, the antagonism between a named wolf and a named fox becomes the animating force which drives a story from beginning to end, and in this case a fiercely critical, satiric and wonderfully comic story which targets, in particular, monk-bishops. This, appropriately, is the topic of the first essay here, by Jill Mann.

The Roman de Renart

The *Ysengrimus*'s fox becomes Renart le Goupil in the forty-odd tales which make up the twenty-six branches and nearly 30,000 lines of the French *Roman de Renart*. They were mostly composed as separate, only loosely-linked narrative poems, over a period of about seventy years, beginning in the 1170s. At one point in the *Ysengrimus*, as mentioned above, the fox first commits adultery with, then rapes, the wolf's wife and it is this more than any other crime or insult which lies at the heart of their enmity, and it is this which seems to have inspired a Frenchman known as Pierre de Saint Cloud to compose and to put together the first group of narrative poems in French centred on the fox. Since the publication in the 1870s of the first scholarly edition of the *Roman de Renart*, this is known as Branch II, and tells of Renart's brushes with a cock called Chantecler, an unnamed titmouse, a crow called Tiécelin, and a cat called Tibert, before climaxing with an account of his adultery with, then rape of Hersent. The author of this exceptionally entertaining, artistically splendid and earliest branch was careful not to resolve the quarrel between the fox and the wolf, and to leave the situation open so that their story might be continued. And so it was, first by the branch known as *Le Serment* (Reynard's Solemn Oath) in which Ysengrin complains to the king chiefly about Reynard's criminal violation of his wife, and the fox is brought to court to answer the charges made against him. This is one of several of his court appearances. At all of them he wins the day by verbal dexterity, trickery, lying and bribery. Within the next few years, and probably by 1180, this first *Roman de Renart* quickly attracted seven or eight more individual or little groups of tales, the best of which by far is Branch I, *Le Plaid* (Reynard's Trial). For the second time, Reynard is brought to trial at the king-lion's court, this time on a charge of murder, the murder of Chantecler's close relation, Couppée. Prior to this the wolf has once more brought the charge of rape, and other animals have brought other charges. The royal emmissaries, Brun and Tibert, are deceitfully received and shamefully treated, but Grimbert finally persuades Renart to come to court where, eventually, after much entertaining and intriguing debate, Renart is condemned to death. But he gets off. Easily the most successful and artistically accomplished of this early group of branches (as these stories are labelled), and although one of the later ones, it was placed first in most medieval French anthologies of Reynardian tales, and was to inspire the composition of other branches (especially of the juridical kind), as well as long narrative poems, beast epics in their own right, in other languages. It is to these juridical branches, to the administration of justice and in particular for the crime of rape in northern, twelfth-century France, that the second essay in this volume, by Jean Subrenat, draws our attention.

Reinhart Fuchs

The renown of Renart was such that, very soon after the composition of the first seven or eight branches, and in particular after Branch I, Reynard's Trial, he made his first appearance in German. Called Reinhart, he repeats many a crime and commits many a new one in the 2,260-odd lines of the German-speaking Alsatian Heinrich der Glichesaere's *Reinhart Fuchs*, probably composed around 1191. Especially in the opening sections of his epic, Heinrich selected much of his material from those first branches of the *Roman de Renart*, but then went on to add new material and mould it into a well-unified whole. His poem is one of the truly great satirical works of medieval German literature, and one of the most interesting of the Beast Epics. Jean-Marc Pastré's essay concentrates on the questionable administration of justice along with moral values and geopolitics in a region which seems to reflect parts of the territories of the twelfth and thirteenth centuries belonging to the Holy Roman Empire.

The Roman de Renart, Van den Vos Reynaerde, Reynaerts Historie

The fox's next known appearance in another foreign literature is as Reinaert in the thirteenth-century, 3,500-line Flemish Beast Epic entitled *Van den Vos Reynaerde*, better known as *Reynaert de Vos*. The story-line of this masterpiece is much the same as that in Branch I of the *Roman de Renart*, to which it owes a great deal. It survives in two complete manuscripts, the Comburg manuscript and the Dyck manuscript, both of which were copied in the fourteenth century. Later in that same century, or early in the fifteenth, a new version appeared, chiefly made by the addition of a substantial new ending which sometimes incorporates non-*Roman-de-Renart* material, and sometimes repeats material already present in the earlier part. This longer rehandling of the epic is entitled *Reynaerts Historie*. For simplicity, scholars and literary historians sometimes refer to the earlier one as *Reinaert I*, and to the later one as *Reinaert II*. Although so much of the story-line of the French Branch I, of *Reynaert de Vos* and of *Reynaerts Historie* is very similar, the authors of these three versions of the Beast Epic had considerably different readerships in mind, and different expectations in their readers' understanding and reactions. It is to these that Paul Wackers addresses himself in his first essay.

The Metamorphoses of the Dutch Reynaert Tradition in Print from the Middle Ages to the Nineteenth Century

It is in Dutch-speaking territory that the Beast Epic was created as early as 1150; and it is in Dutch that it has the longest, continuous history and appeal, where it still lives as nowhere else. But its authors have constantly adapted their material (mostly found in *Reynaerts Historie*) to changing circumstances and to new readers, as this second chapter by Paul Wakers shows.

Reynaerts Historie: *An Ideological Weapon*

In almost every language and period in which the Beast Epic has appeared, sooner or later the theme of conflict and war is treated, usually slanted by the author to make a sociopolitical point. In this essay, after looking over his shoulder at a few examples from the Middle Ages, Rik van Daele concentrates on this theme and the ways in which it has been treated in twentieth-century Flanders.

Reynard, Tibert, and the Misfortunes of a Village Priest

One of the most entertaining episodes in the Beast Epic is that in which Reynard tricks the cat Tibert so that he gets caught in a snare meant for himself, a snare which a village priest had set in a hole in his barn wall through which the fox was wont to go looking for poultry. Alerted by noises coming from his barn in the middle of the night, the priest rushes from his bed, armed but naked, together with his concubine and some of his sons. In the dark they attack their prisoner who, in self-defence, counter-attacks with teeth and claws and bites off one of the priest's testicles. This episode is first recounted in Branch

I of the *Roman de Renart*, and is repeated in almost every version of the Beast Epic from the Middle Ages to the present day, but it gets modified (both in words and pictures, for it has often been illustrated) to suit the sensibilities of the perceived readership. It is to these changing sensibilites that Jan Goossens addresses himself in this illustrated essay.

Choir-stall Carvings of Reynard and Other Foxes

Foxes have been carved on choir-stalls all over medieval Europe, along with many other animals, some of them imaginary, some real, almost all having a symbolic or moral value. In a small minority of cases, these foxes can be identified as Reynard in one or other of his adventures; others may well be him; others have been absorbed into his History. Elaine C. Block has examined and photographed every known set of misericords in situ apart from the ones in Funchal, Madeira. This illustrated essay, in which Elaine C. Block is joined by Kenneth Varty, concentrates on misericord carvings of the fox, and it reveals some interesting regional varieties and variants in the themes depicted. The only ones which can be identified with certainty as Reynard are to be found in England, whilst others which are at least very closely related to him are also only in England.

Reynard in England: From Caxton to the Present

It was in 1479, in Gouda, that Gheraert Leeu published a prose version of *Reynaerts Historie* which he called *Die Hystorie van Reyaert die Vos*. This is the text which William Caxton translated into English in 1481. Leeu also published another, illustrated edition in Antwerp between 1487 and 1490, and it was the illustrations in this edition which the artist who made the series of woodcuts for Wynkin de Worde's c.1495 version of Caxton's text closely imitated. Both Caxton's text and Wynkyn de Worde's woodcuts had a long history in England, often modified, sometimes subtly, sometimes boldly. Eventually they were replaced by new Reynard stories and pictures intended for different groups of people. This illustrated essay by Kenneth Varty traces the fortunes and characteristics of the English descendants of the Dutch Reynaert.

Hartmann Schopper's Latin Reinike of 1567

The Beast Epic in Latin is something of a rarity. We have the *Ysengrimus* of c.1150 (the only truly original Beast Epic in Latin); the *Reynardus Vulpes* of 1279 (an abbreviated translation and adaptation of the Dutch *Van den Vos Reynaerde*); and Schopper's translation and adaptation of a High German text which descended from the first Low German version of the Beast Epic *Reynke de Vos* (1498), which was a translation of the Dutch *Reynaerts Historie*. Schopper's text was composed when religious controversy and conflict raged fiercely, and in his essay Wilfried Schouwink brings this out, as well as certain characteristics due chiefly to the author's military experiences and the Latinisation of the story.

Goethe's Reineke Fuchs *of 1794*

Perhaps the most famous Beast Epic composed on German soil is Goethe's, which also goes back, but via a different route from that taken by Schopper's, to *Reynke de Vos* and to *Reinaerts Historie*. Goethe's most immediate source was a translation into High German (by J.C. Gottsched in 1752) from the Low German (as edited by F.A Hackmann in 1711). But he also had in his library several other versions of the Epic, including Schopper's and a 1780 adaptation in German of a popular Dutch *Reynaert* published by Plantijn in Antwerp in 1564, as well as the 1564 edition itself. He composed his *Reineke* in the wake of the French Revolution when he and his readers were very much aware of its consequences in France, and of social unrest, often fearful, often hopeful about their own political future. This is why Roger Stephenson has chosen to write about the political import of Goethe's *Reineke Fuchs*.

Paul Weber's Satirical Use of Reineke in Cartoon Form

One of Germany's finest book illustrators and political cartoonists, Paul Weber (1893-1980) came to admire Reineke when he illustrated, in 1924, Goethe's Beast Epic. Subsequently he took the fox out of his History and used him as one of his principal cartoon characters, some aspect of which are examined in this illustrated essay by Kenneth Varty.

Metamorphoses of the Roman de Renart *in the Nineteenth and Twentieth Centuries in France*

While the Beast Epic flourished in many forms in medieval France, the finest of which were some of the branches of the *Roman de Renart*, it went underground from the end of the Middle Ages until the nineteenth century. When it reappeared above ground in the nineteenth century, a number of distinguished scholars, talented literary artists, enterprising publishers and a mixture of mediocre and good book-illustrators revived its fortunes, bringing about some marked changes in style, content, purpose and presentation when compared with the *Renarts* of old. In this illustrated essay, Kenneth Varty focuses on Paulin Paris's version (1861); while Jean Dufournet concentrates on that of Albert-Marie Schmidt (1963), and then on that of J.-L. Hubert and G.J. Imbar, *Le Polar de Renart* (1973).

The Fox and the Wolf in the Well

Many literary artists from different cultures have treated in several literary forms, over a long period of time, for quite different publics, and with different objects, the way the fox gets into and out of a well at the wolf's expense. Concentrating on their comic qualities, this essay by the editor looks at two Jewish fables from before the *Roman de Renart*, which may well have been sources of two distinctly different branches in the French epic and probably intended for clerical audiences; then at these two branches, and at a thirteenth-century English parallel to the French branches; and finally at the modern negro American version by R. Chandler Harris in which the rabbit replaces the fox (and the fox replaces the wolf), which leaves us well placed to appreciate the topic of the final essay.

The Fox and the Hare:
the Peregrinations and Adventures of an Odd Couple

The final essay treats the fox, and in particular the fox and the hare in the folklore of northern Europe, more especially in Scandinavia and in Finland where so much pioneering scientific work was done in this field. The Beast Epic, and especially the *Roman de Renart*, fed on folklore, contains parallels with well-attested folktales, and very probably contributed to folktales. Elina Suomela-Härmä leads us eventually to the rape of the vixen by the hare, and reminds us of the rape recounted in the very first Beast Epic, the rape which inspired the author of Branch II, then the author of Branch I (composed after Branch II) and from which almost all the rest followed.

◈ CHAPTER 1 ◈

THE SATIRIC FICTION OF THE *YSENGRIMUS*

Jill Mann

The *Ysengrimus* is a Latin beast epic of more than 6,500 lines, which was written in the middle of the twelfth century, probably in Ghent.[1] It is at once one of the most important and the most neglected works of medieval literature. It is neglected mainly because it is very hard to read; not only is its Latin unusually difficult, but the peculiarly compressed and contorted nature of the poet's wit often makes his thought difficult to follow. It is important, first of all, because it initiates a major literary tradition. It stands at the head of the long line of medieval beast-literature – the line that includes the *Roman de Renart, Reinhart Fuchs, Van den Vos Reinaerde*, and a whole host of others. It is the first work to make the undying hostility between the fox and the wolf into the dynamic force of a full-length narrative, and the first to invest them with fictional personalities by giving them the now familiar names of Reynard and Ysengrimus. But the importance of this Latin poem is not merely historical; it is also important in its own right as a literary masterpiece. Ernst Voigt, the editor of the only critical edition of the poem, called it the 'comprehensive, systematically planned, wittily and artfully executed work of one of the greatest poets of the Middle Ages' (Voigt 1884). The *Ysengrimus* merits the title 'epic' not simply by virtue of length, but above all because it realises an autonomous fictional world, a world constructed on coherent laws which express a central satiric vision. It is the nature of this satiric vision that is the main concern of this essay. To understand the subtlety and originality of this poem, we need both to identify the features of the poet's contemporary society which are the objects of his attack, and to analyse the narrative fictions in which he embodies his vision of social disorder.

The *Ysengrimus* follows the classic epic structure; it begins *in mediis rebus*, and later recapitulates a sequence of earlier events. Book I opens with the only episode in which the wolf gets the better of the fox: the 'bacon-sharing', in which Ysengrimus devours the whole of a ham that Reynard has won from its peasant owner by trickery. The fox takes his revenge in the fishing episode, in which the wolf loses his tail after it is frozen fast in the river, and the field-division episode in Book II, in which the wolf attempts to cloak his predatory designs on four sheep by pretending to mark out the boundaries of their field, but is then battered senseless when they all charge at him. Book III describes the assembly of the animals at the court of the lion, who wants them to advise on a cure for his sickness: the fox persuades the lion that he will be cured if he is wrapped in the skin of a wolf, and Ysengrimus is flayed in order to provide the skin in question. The court is then entertained by hearing the relation of previous adventures, which make up an 'inset narrative' (Books IV–V): first, we hear of the pilgrimage of eight animals, which the wolf attempts, unsuccessfully, to join (as usual, he is beaten within an inch of his life by his intended victims). We then hear how the fox, too, was twice outwitted by the cock. Reynard next persuades the wolf to enter a monastery, which is named as 'Blandinium' – that is, the monastery of St Peter's in the town of Ghent – but the wolf is soon thrown out and beaten yet again, as a punishment for having drunk all the wine in the monks' cellar. This episode concludes the inset narrative, and the main narrative resumes with an account of the departure of the skinless wolf from the lion's court; attempting to claim a replacement skin from the horse Corvigarus, and then to devour the sheep Joseph, he is kicked senseless by the former and pulverised by the latter (Books V–VI). When the wolf's skin has grown again, Reynard organises a hunting expedition in which they are joined by the lion; when the wolf proposes that their spoils should be equally divided, the enraged lion, with one swipe of his paw, tears off his skin for the second time. Next, the fox persuades Ysengrimus to swear an oath on some 'relics', which turn out to be a trap, and he is forced to bite off his foot in order to free himself. In Book VII, the hapless wolf meets his end; he is eaten alive by the massive sow Salaura and sixty-six other pigs.

It is evident that the wolf is not very successful as a predator. The episodes of the poem, although not linked into a tightly organised plot, nevertheless follow a clear trajectory as they chronicle his progressive mutilation, torture and death at the hands of the animals he plans to make his victims. The epic arrangement of the narrated events means that after the bacon-sharing episode, in which he enjoys a brief triumph, it is downhill all the way. Gruesome as the descriptions of the wolf's torture are, the spirit which animates this relentless sequence of destruction is not a simple delight in sadistic violence. Rather, it is driven by a satiric impulse which transforms the apparently arbitrary features of each episode into a meaningful structure. The target against which this satiric impulse is directed will become clearer if we examine more closely the central figure of the wolf.

The wolf's dominating characteristic is his greed. He is always ready to eat, and his stomach and jaws are of monstrous size. His stomach is metaphorically equated with the pit of hell ('baratrum', 'Gehenna', 'Avernus'); it is also referred to, for example, as a lodging-house, a whirlpool, or a vaulted hall. His jaws are so huge they take on a life of their own. The wolf refers to them as a gaping doorway which he invites the fox to enter. When the wolf clashes them together, we are told that they resound like the banging of a weaver's combs, or like a sheet of metal being hammered on an anvil. On hearing the noise, the fox asks if someone is cutting down trees. The teeth inside these jaws are said to cut through bones like a knife through butter; they are described as pick-axes, or as scythes. When the fox throws over to the wolf a plate with eight pies on it, Ysengrimus swallows the lot in one gulp without even noticing that he has done so.

The wolf is not, however, a symbol of greed pure and simple; as his entry into the monastery indicates, he represents the greed of a monk. The satiric purpose of the poem is here clearly evident. But we do not have to wait until the monastery episode in Book V to perceive it. In the very first episode of the poem, Ysengrimus refers to his earlier profession as a monk, and explains that its effect was to intensify his natural rapacity, for he now unites the greed of a monk to that of a wolf.

> 'For when a monk sees any wealth on offer, he falls on it like the flash of lightning produced by a stormy sky. Should a twofold Charybdis acknowledge a limit, when a single one doesn't?

Holy ardour spurs me on from one side, and my destructive urges from the other. A monk's kindness is more savage than a wolf's cruelty; I say "that's enough" when I'm full, while a monk still says "that's not much". In the old days I used to be guilty of sin whenever I committed violence, and my depredations were not granted pardon, but once I had taken on the holy cowl, and the good brothers had taught me their example, both lawful and unlawful things were immediately permissible to me, and nothing is forbidden me except that I should go without.' (I 639–50)

The author's satiric target is not, however, monks in general; his aim is more specific, as becomes clear if we look at two important passages, in each of which the poet presents a contemporary cleric in a very unflattering light. The first of these clerics is Anselm, bishop of Tournai, who is mentioned by Reynard when he is cursing his teeth for having let go of the cock he held in his mouth; he should never have been so foolish, he says, as to forget to place profit above all other considerations. He cites the pope as an excellent example of someone who pursues profit in total disregard of morality and religion. But an even better example is provided by Bishop Anselm.

'In the pursuit of this virtue, Rome is outstripped by Tournai, the city blessed with Bishop Anselm. This good shepherd of Tournai himself shears off the fleeces from sheep and goats alike down to the living flesh. If only he were one of my teeth! He'd give his brothers a lesson in biting. He prowls around the churches as a hungry lion does the sheepfold, leaving only what he can't find. Whoever offers him less than he is told to (whether it's within his power or not) is compelled on his obedience to leave off reciting the holy offices. It's as if he bristles with as many robbers as he has teeth, and he doesn't allow the shorn fleeces to grow again; he gets in first, and would take, if he could, more than he finds – what a pity that he *can't* take more than he finds! He is sorry that he can't alter the limit to taking, and is sure that this is the only thing wrong with plunder. This is the bishop I hold up to you for imitation. What does that rag-wearer from Clairvaux know about anything? He's a straw-plaiter, someone who looks for knots in sedge, a pebble-peeler – let him go and milk cranes! You should imitate the excellent behaviour of this bishop, who devours like Satan and holds like Hell!' (V 109–30)[2]

Anselm was appointed bishop of Tournai in 1146, and died in 1149. He had not much time, therefore, to practise financial extortion in his diocese, but it is of some importance that he visited Ghent in 1147, to consecrate the leper-chapel belonging to the abbey of St Bavo's; what he did there, we do not know, but it seems to have been responsible for the poet's unfavourable impression of Anselm's character.

The second passage that contains an unflattering picture of a contemporary cleric occurs at the very end of the poem, and it too emerges abruptly from an animal monologue. After the death of the wolf, the sow Salaura rejects the suggestion that he should be buried. The only money that would be fit to pay for his burial, she says, is 'the cash for which the crafty pope sold Christians to the duke of Sicily'. She then breaks into incoherent cries of grief:

> 'Oh, disgrace to heaven! grief to the world! laughter in hell! One feeble monk has overthrown two kingdoms! Ah, woe is me! How lamentable is the tale I have heard, which is the cause of my loosening the bridle on my tongue in this way!' (VII 465–70)

When the sow is asked to explain herself, it becomes clear that she is referring to the Second Crusade, which took place in 1147–49, and ended in complete disaster for the Christian armies. The 'two kingdoms' she mentions are France and Germany, the participants in this Crusade; the 'one wretched monk' who has overthrown them is Pope Eugenius III, who launched the Crusade, with the backing of St Bernard of Clairvaux. Reynard the fox spells out the implied accusation against the pope: that he was bribed by Roger, Duke of Sicily, to send the crusaders by land to the Holy Land instead of by ship from Sicily, and thus to expose them to the disasters that befell them.

> 'I already know what you're thinking: you want to condemn the Bishop of Rome for wrongdoing and deception, treacherous swine. You're going to say that the duke of the volcanic region was afraid to let the Christians pass through his realm on their way to Jerusalem, so the pope, seduced by the gold and silver of the duke, persuaded the people to take the road through Greece, and one feeble monk overthrew two kingdoms, giving them up to hunger and misfortunes and the cunning of the Greeks. Besides those who were destroyed by the fury of the sea and the pestilence-laden air and the deceit of the Argolids, two thousand men perished through sleep and a storm, in a closed valley, surrounded by hills on all sides.' (VII 665–76)

These two historical figures – Anselm of Tournai and Pope Eugenius III – are the two principal real-life villains identified by the *Ysengrimus*, and they provide the key to its satiric fiction. For they have one important thing in common: both of them were monks who had taken office in the secular clergy. Anselm, before being appointed bishop of Tournai, had been abbot of the abbey of Saint-Vincent in Laon. Eugenius was a former monk of Cîteaux and a disciple of St Bernard of Clairvaux; at the time of his election as pope he was abbot of the monastery of Saints Anastasius and Vincent in Rome. The objects of attack, therefore, are not just a bishop and a pope, but a monk-bishop and a monk-pope.

When we look closely at the titles given to the wolf Ysengrimus in the poem, we see that he is not only called 'monk' ('monachus'), but also 'abbot' and 'bishop' ('abbas et presul'/'pontifex'). Scholars for a long time failed to notice both the *consistency* with which these two titles are applied to the wolf, and also the fact that they are not alternatives (that is, the poet is not attacking bishops at one moment and abbots at the next), but are to be taken together as a composite title indicating a dual role. If we grasp the fact that it is the monk-bishops who are the object of satiric attack, we shall immediately be able to understand how this aim determines the form of the fictional narrative in its two most important episodes – the court episode and the monastery episode. For, in each of them, the physical torture which the other animals inflict on the wolf is mockingly interpreted as an episcopal consecration. In the scene at the lion's court, Ysengrimus is, as elsewhere in the poem, represented as a monk – for example, he claims to be able to cure the sick lion because he has learned medicine in the cloister – and the other animals likewise refer to him as 'abbot'. When the bear flays the wolf, he slices the skin with such rapidity that he leaves some pieces of skin behind; there remains a strip of skin on his head, running between his ears, and little 'socks' of skin on each of his front paws. The sheep mockingly interprets these pieces of skin as the mitre and *suralia* (hose) which formed part of the distinctive insignia of a bishop (known as the pontificals). 'Take off the mitre, Bruno!', he says, 'If you don't take it off, he'll be called a fop; take the mitre off, Bruno!' (III 991–2). The wolf is already an abbot, he continues; is he now to be made a bishop as well? Why should all the honours go to wolves? (III 1,000–01) This central episode of the poem thus represents the wolf as an abbot who is consecrated bishop by a grotesquely parodic ceremony.

The monastery episode, too, climaxes with a sadistic parody of an episcopal consecration. The wolf, having complained of thirst, is taken to the wine cellar and left to his own devices. He samples the wine in every barrel, but does not bother to turn off the taps, so that the monk who comes to see what he is doing finds him swimming in a sea of wine. Incensed at this outrage to monastic property, the monks seize whatever weapon they can find and set off to punish the wolf. Terrified at the sight of this threatening crowd, the wolf tries to excuse himself by claiming that he was trying to prove his suitability to be a new kind of bishop, a monk-bishop. Bishops drawn from the secular clergy practise rapine, it is true, but only half-heartedly; what is needed is a new order of bishops, drawn from the ranks of monks. Their depredations will make the secular clergy look like mere amateurs.

> 'I'll tell you my idea. From the company of our order [monks] the majority of bishops are to be chosen, men whose life is publicly approved, and who shall demonstrate with how much tenderness they care for their sheep, and with what pure reverence they fear God. They shall decide that everything possessed by the people, the clergy, or the cloister, is legitimately to be seized for themselves, by force, by persuasion, by lawsuits, by simulation, by deceit, by threats, and whatever means are alien to order, morality, or moderation. This rule is only partially familiar to the bishops chosen from the secular clergy, and they observe it only partially, as they have learned it. They don't gulp down everything, but sip in half-mouthfuls; appeased by what they have grabbed, they allow many things to get away from them. So the more foresighted sections of the clergy must elect holy monks, whose practice is to leave nothing, and who may first gobble, then scrape, and finally lick. Truly, to them is the whole rule of virtues disclosed. I, hoping to become a high priest of these rituals, am giving an advance demonstration of my zeal: I devour, plunder, swallow. I have accomplished the work of numberless days in a single heroic act, in emptying the vessels of their gushing wine. Rumour usually travels far and fast once some notable subject-matter has set it going. Therefore I wanted to commit an outstanding deed, desirous of making my greed known at once, so that if any bishop is perhaps to be got rid of because his ravages are too restricted, I might fitly be appointed in his place.' (V 995–1,022)

The monks respond to the wolf's attempts at exculpation with the mocking claim that his wishes are about to be fulfilled: he is to be 'consecrated' with the implements they carry. The sacristan empties over him an incense-casket full of fleas, claiming that he is 'anointing him with oil'. Another monk breaks an earthernware pot over his head, claiming that he is 'setting the mitre in place'. A horse-collar is wrapped around his neck in place of the bishop's pallium. And so on.

As these two episodes show, the satiric attack in the *Ysengrimus* is relentlessly and ruthlessly directed against the type of cleric with whom the wolf here associates himself: the monk who leaves his monastery and takes office as a bishop. Since the beginnings of monasticism, monks had been elevated to the rank of bishop. The hybrid state of monk-bishop had caused difficulties for the canonists, who had to define the extent to which the new bishop was dispensed from the obligations of monastic life. It also aroused great hostility in certain quarters: Peter Abelard, for example, denounced the monk-bishop as a monstrosity, a man who had abandoned his monastic profession for the sake of soft living. The author of the *Ysengrimus* was, it appears, at one with Abelard in his dislike of and contempt for the monk-bishop.

This dislike appears not only in the two episodes we have just examined; features of the satiric fiction in other episodes of the poem are precisely moulded to fit the object of the satiric attack. Apparently arbitrary or gratuitous details turn out to be brilliant imaginative strokes which both identify the monk-bishop as the satiric target represented by the wolf and inflict a fitting punishment on the monk-bishop's crimes. The clearest example of this is in the pilgrimage episode. The wolf arrives at the house where the animal-pilgrims are spending the night and obtrudes himself on the company, to whom he is an unwanted guest. They pretend, however, to be delighted at his arrival, and Reynard sends the sheep to the larder in the next room to fetch some food. The sheep protests that all there is to eat is a pile of wolf-heads. The fox says they will serve the purpose very well. The sheep has in fact only *one* wolf-head, which the animals had earlier removed from a house-gable (where it had been nailed to ward off evil spirits). He offers it to the fox for approval, saying it was the head of 'an old Angevin'. The fox, however, rejects it as not good enough, and sends the sheep away for another. The sheep takes the head away, tears out its hair so as to give it a 'tonsure', and brings it back to the fox, saying it was the head of 'an English abbot'. Reynard rejects this one also, and orders the sheep to fetch the huge head in the corner, the one that has its mouth propped open by a stick. The sheep asks if he means the one belonging to 'a Danish bishop', which the goose accidentally pecked off his shoulders as he lay asleep in the grass, and then hissed so hard that he blew it all the way to the house? Yes, says the fox, that is the one he means. The sheep goes away and tears off all the hair and the ears as well from his one wolf-head and props open its jaws with a stick; then he returns and offers it to the wolf.

> Its drawn-back lips gaped in a horrible grin. The old man stiffened at the sight and turned his face aside; his hunger was shaken off, driven away by great fear. Then for the first time it was obvious that Fortune was not playing games; never before had he experienced fear to the same degree. 'What devil', he said, 'led me to these lupicides? Oh, misery, is the day tied by a rope, that it drags so slowly? Why this horned army? This Gerard – not content with having murdered unfortunate wolves – is said to have blown off his hair and ears and to have rolled his head here with hissing! Can I endure this without losing my mind?' The goose replied: 'Do you reckon this is something new, Ysengrimus? Truly, this has happened to me more than once. If I wanted, I could blow eight heads from wolves bigger than this one – and yours too, sir hermit! Do you think I haven't come out of my mother's egg yet?' – and he emitted an enormous noise from his hissing throat. When he heard it, the wolf cried 'Aaagh!' three times, and suddenly losing consciousness, fell flat on his back; for a long time he thought his head had been blown off and he had lost it, and that it had bounced away over the snows of Germany. (IV 312–32)

The point of this comic scene is that the wolf is terrified by an image of *himself*. The three versions of the head (as 'old Angevin', 'English abbot', 'Danish bishop') correspond to the three aspects of the wolf, as he is characterised in the text. He is old: the poet tells us he is 160 years old, and he is constantly referred to as *senex*, 'old man', throughout the poem. He is an abbot, and in addition, he is a bishop. The fact that it is the *same* head that is brought back every time in a different guise is precisely designed to make clear that it represents three different facets of the same wolf. The series of three reaches its climax with the last head, which has its mouth propped open by a stick, and which thus presents a compelling picture of the wolf's all-devouring greed. The wolf is confronted with a mirror-image of himself, with his own gaping jaws, symbolising the terrifying greed of the aged abbot-bishop.

In this episode, the arch-devourer is offered himself to devour. His punishment, that is, is determined by a law of comic reversal – 'the biter bit', 'the trickster tricked'. This principle underlies all the narrative episodes of the poem (Mann 1977); in every case, the predator is outwitted by his victim, the stronger animal is defeated by the weaker. Thus the wolf is beaten by the sheep, the fox is outwitted by the cock. The horse is tricked by the stork; the wolf is in turn tricked by the horse. Only in the bacon-sharing episode does the predator manage to fulfil his customary role: the wolf outwits the fox and devours the whole bacon. But this apparent exception only proves the rule, if we set this opening episode in the context of the whole poem. For we then see that the last episode of the poem precisely reverses the first: the wolf who began by devouring pork ends up being eaten by pigs.

If we look again at the central episode of the poem, we shall see how this vision of a 'world-upside-down' serves the satiric purposes of the poet. First, we may notice that the court episode contains a strange echo of the passage on Anselm of Tournai. As the bear prepares to flay the wolf, Reynard suddenly rushes forward with the plea that he should 'take no more than he finds' – because, says the fox, the wolf himself always acted on this principle.

> 'I make one small request – let there be room for it – grant it – and I'll show myself deserving: that you shouldn't take more than you find! He himself never took more than he found. It's right to take away what someone has, but wrong to take away more than that!' (III 931–4)

The fox's plea exactly echoes what is said about Anselm of Tournai: that he does not take more than he finds. (Naturally, this is merely an ironic way of saying that he takes everything he *can* find – a way of representing his greed as 'mercy'.) This verbal echo draws attention to the fact that the Anselm passage also contains a parallel to the flaying: the bishop does not shear his flock, which would allow the shorn fleeces to grow again; instead he 'fleeces' them, cutting down to the living flesh. The flaying of the wolf – who is the fictional representative of the 'abbot-bishops' – is thus an appropriate punishment imagined for the real-life abbot-bishops, who themselves 'flay' their flock.

The animals talk as if the wolf's skin was only a garment, easily and painlessly removed. Once it has been stripped from him, and Ysengrimus (still alive) is covered only by an inner membrane, dripping with scarlet blood, Reynard pretends to be indignant that the wolf has insulted the court by covering this splendid scarlet 'robe' with an ugly wolf-skin. This fiction raises the horrifying possibility that the fox is about to insist that this 'robe' too must be removed – that the flaying is to be repeated. Once again, the point is not simply gratuitous cruelty. In the first place, the fiction of the double garment is perfectly matched to the monk-bishops, who did not discard their monastic robes when called to the episcopacy, but wore their episcopal robes on top. Secondly, the notion that the wolf has a *series* of garments, each of which may be removed without killing him, corresponds to the absurd notion of bishops such as Anselm of Tournai, that their flock may be endlessly 'fleeced' in the same way.

This same notion finds a reflection in the fact that when the wolf is flayed he does not die, but on the contrary, grows another skin. No sooner has this happened than he loses it again; this time the fox lures him into making division of the booty won in their hunting expedition with the lion, and the lion, offended by the wolf's proposal that the shares be equal, removes the wolf's skin with one blow of his paw. The recrudescent power of the wolf's skin is reminiscent of the world of the cartoon, where the cat who is squashed flat by a steam-roller, say, is restored to three dimensions in the next frame. But the *Ysengrimus* does not indulge in such fantasies for their comic effect. The fiction that the skin will grow again is the counterpart of the fantastic belief which governs the behaviour of the monk-bishops – that their 'flock' is able to grow an endless series of skins which they can endlessly remove. Reynard's words to Ysengrimus, after he has lost his skin for the second time, are clearly directed at the real-life bishops rather than the fictional wolf:

> 'A sheep is better sheared than skinned, and even when skinned is some good, but is utterly useless when destroyed.' (VI 325–6)

In the flaying episode and its sequels, the poet therefore adopts the illusory belief of the monk-bishops as one of the fictional rules of his poem, but he does so *only* in order to make it the basis for a never-ending series of tortures on the wolf who represents those monk-bishops. The poet creates a whole fictive world on the principles of the real-life predators, and then imprisons them within it.

I have said that the *Ysengrimus* confronts us with a 'world-upside-down', but in fact the world is turned upside down not once but twice. For the poet sees the real world as *already* a 'world-upside-down'. The bishop should be a shepherd to his flock; if he preys on them – acting instead as a wolf – he is inverting the natural order of things. In the poem, this order of things is inverted a second time: the wolf is no longer the predator but the victim. We have already seen that in the pilgrimage episode it is the sheep who terrifies the wolf by confronting him with an image of his own head; the four sheep in the field-division episode also turn the tables on the wolf, battering him to a pulp. Later, when Ysengrimus makes an attempt to eat the sheep Joseph, Joseph pretends to be entirely willing to let the wolf eat him, and suggests that Ysengrimus should support his back against a post, open his mouth wide, and let him rush straight into his jaws. When the wolf does as he is told, the sheep charges straight at him and smashes his head to pieces. This epsiode presents an intensely concentrated expression of satiric paradox: it is the very act of (attempted) devouring that destroys the devourer. The wolf's punishment is frequently connected with the idea of eating; the animals pretend to be offering him a 'banquet', in which each blow is represented as an item of food or a cup of wine. As Mikhail Bakhtin has shown, the linking of food with violence is characteristic of Rabelais and of the comic-grotesque tradition of medieval literature in general. But nowhere else do we find a parallel to the neatness with which in the *Ysengrimus* the destructive aspects of eating are turned back on the devourer: in the sheep's charge, it is *the food itself* that inflicts destruction on the devourer.

At the end of the poem, the sow Salaura describes a 'world-upside-down' whose inversion heralds its own approaching end. Winter, she says, has turned to summer, and summer to winter. Floods have turned land to sea, and sea to land (VII 621–34). This apocalyptic scenario will culminate in the Last Judgement, in which the world turned upside-down by the monk-bishops will be inverted yet again, and the destroyers will be finally destroyed. Since the poem anticipates this final judgement by its fantasy punishment of the monk-bishops, in the person of the wolf, it is fitting that apocalyptic features are found throughout the poem. The imaginative kernel around which it appears to have been constructed is a biblical text which is linked with the prophecies of the end of the world – that is, Christ's warning in the gospel of Matthew (7: 15): 'Beware of false prophets, who come to you with the clothing of sheep, but inwardly they are ravening wolves'. Later in Matthew's gospel (24: 11), these 'pseudoprophetae' are represented as one of the signs of the approaching end; Christ tells his disciples that 'many false prophets shall rise, and shall deceive many'. Ysengrimus is both 'ravening wolf' and 'false prophet'; before his death, he asks for a brief respite so that he may utter a prophecy (a rather undignified one in which he bestows the curse of farting on pigs and human beings who resemble them). The very form of his death is determined by his role as a 'false prophet', since being eaten by pigs was the fate suffered by Mohammed, according to medieval legend. Ysengrimus thus fits neatly into the apocalyptic scenario outlined by Salaura, playing the role of the false prophet who heralds the imminent end of the world.

The traditional features of the apocalyptic vision supply one more important motif in the narrative fiction of the *Ysengrimus* – the motif of peace. The Sibylline prophecies which formed an important part of the eschatological literature of the Middle Ages foretold that the second coming of Christ would be preceded by the appearance of an Emperor, whose reign would bring about a Golden Age. All hostility would cease, lions and calves would stand together at the manger; the wolf would not seize the lamb. The prophecies of Isaiah likewise use images of peace in the animal kingdom (the wolf feeding alongside the lamb) to indicate the peace that will follow God's final judgement of the world. Vergil's Fourth Eclogue does the same. In the *Ysengrimus* we have a comic travesty of this apocalyptic peace in the animal kingdom. The word 'pax', in various meanings, is woven into the narrative. There is the simple conventional greeting 'Pax vobis'; there is the 'kiss of peace' which forms part of the ceremony of the Mass. There is also the 'peace of God', a legal peace proclaimed by ecclesiastical or secular authority, which guaranteed the safety of the weak and defenceless. The word 'pax' is constantly on the lips of predators in the *Ysengrimus*. In particular, the wolf habitually offers peace to his intended victims. He approaches the animal-pilgrims, and likewise the sheep Joseph, with the greeting 'Pax vobis'. When he joins the band of animal-pilgrims, he pretends to be a hermit who travels around spreading 'peace and justice' (pacem justitiamque). The fox tries to deceive the cock by exploiting the idea of the 'peace of God': he pretends that he has a charter guaranteeing a legal 'peace', so that the cock need have no fear of him. In the final episode, the wolf greets Salaura with his usual 'Pax tibi', and offers, as a priest, to give her the 'kiss of peace'. When he sinks his teeth in her ear, only to see a furious herd of sixty-six pigs galloping to her rescue, he fears, the poet says, that they intend 'to administer to him just the same sort of peace he had come to impart himself'. When he is finally disembowelled, the pigs mockingly pretend that no 'peace' could have been proclaimed, because the wolf had swallowed the items necessary to publicise it – charter, seal, and herald's trumpet – that is, his liver, heart and windpipe.

As all these examples show, the 'universal peace' between predator and victim in the animal world has not yet arrived; the peace that is so much talked about by the animals of the *Ysengrimus* is only a sham, a cloak under whose cover they can practise even greater rapacity. From the Old Testament we learn that such false proclamations of peace are characteristic of 'false prophets'. Jeremiah, for example, complains that 'from the prophet even to the priest, all are guilty of deceit ... [They said] Peace, peace, and there is no peace' (Jer. 6: 13–14; cf. 8: 10–11). Ezekiel too speaks of the prophets who see visions of peace, 'and there is no peace' (Ezek. 13: 16). These false prophets found a place in the reflections of twelfth-century writers on the Second Crusade. An annalist in the town of Würzburg, when reflecting on the failure of the Crusade, suggested that its instigators were 'pseudoprophets'. (He does not name St Bernard or the Pope, but it would be easy to identify them as the 'pseudoprophets' in question.) St Bernard himself, when writing the treatise *De Consideratione*, addressed to Eugenius III, immediately after the Crusade, consciously casts himself and the Pope in the role of false prophets by echoing the words of Jeremiah (6: 14; 14: 19): 'We have said "Peace", and there is no peace; we have promised good things and behold there is confusion'. So, in the *Ysengrimus*, the monk-bishops' false promise of peace is punished by the creation of a world in which their travestied peace is shown for what it really is, and the other animals imitate them by also using it as a cover for aggression. The 'pax' which the wolf is finally given is not the universal peace of the apocalyptic vision, but the 'pax et requies' of the burial service.

Yet if the *Ysengrimus* unmasks this false apocalyptic promise, it also substitutes for it its own version of the apocalyptic vision – the comic realisation of a 'world-upside-down' which provides the context for an imaginary destruction of the destroyers. The poet creates a comic apocalypse in which he can anticipate the Last Judgement – in which evil is unmasked and punished. But this punishment takes a wittily appropriate form: the monk-bishop is punished by being imprisoned in a fictional world which operates on exactly those laws that govern his own behaviour. Since he seems to imagine that his 'flock' can grow new fleeces even when they have been 'sheared' down to the living flesh, he is imprisoned in a world where a skin *will* grow again after it has been torn off – but where the consequence is that he becomes vulnerable to the infliction of ever-new tortures. Since he devours, he is devoured. Since he defines 'peace' as 'aggression', this is the kind of peace he is given.

Finally, it is the comedy of this satiric vision that should be emphasised, since it is this that saves the poem from narrow vindictiveness. The mock-solemnity of Salura's prophecy cannot disguise the zest and relish with which the poet inverts the ugly realities of the everyday world, replacing it with a fictional world in which the fantasy of liberation from established structures of power can be acted out. The poet certainly knew the apocalyptic sections of the Bible, but he was also thoroughly familiar with Ovid, and the opening of *Metamorphoses*, with its fanciful description of a world turned upside down by Deucalion's flood, offers a second, non-biblical, model for Salura's vision of a world where sea has turned to land and land to sea. Men catch fish in the tops of elm-trees, dolphins swim through the woods – and here too the aggressor becomes the harmless fellow of his victim: 'the wolf swims among the sheep' (*Met.* I.304). The author of the *Ysengrimus* relishes the comic absurdity of the 'world-upside-down' as keenly as Ovid. But if the ending of the poem testifies to his sense of comedy, it also testifies to the *grandeur* of his satiric vision. The greed of the monk-bishop affects not only the members of his diocese; it is a local manifestation of a disaster enacted on a cosmic scale. Historically speaking, the greed of the monk-bishops is not, perhaps, an important subject, but in the satiric vision of the *Ysengrimus* it takes on cosmic dimensions that fully justify the title of epic.

Notes

1. All quotations and translations of the *Ysengrimus* are taken from Mann (1987). The Introduction contains a fuller and more comprehensively documented version of the arguments advanced in this chapter.
2. The 'rag-wearer from Clairvaux' is St Bernard, who seems to have incurred the poet's dislike through association with his disciple Pope Eugenius III and the failure of the Second Crusade (see below, pp. 5–6).

≈ CHAPTER 2 ≈

RAPE AND ADULTERY:

REFLECTED FACETS OF FEUDAL JUSTICE IN THE ROMAN DE RENART[1]

Jean Subrenat*

Because the *Roman de Renart* aspired to create a looking-glass world that portrayed the high society of the courtly period through the personae of animals, its characters were committed to depicting the tragi-comic ambiguity of erotic love and the traditional theme of tensions between husbands, wives and lovers – all of which provided an ideal opportunity for its authors to display their artistic verve.

What is perhaps more surprising is the fact that the resulting stories extend into the realm of the king's justice: that is, in the context of feudal law, that the accused must be assumed to be guilty, a personification of cunning, hypocrisy and fraudulence. The authors of the *Roman de Renart*, in engaging with a subject that lends itself so well to both the generating of fantasy and objective scrutiny of a fundamental aspect of society, and in manipulating an interplay of nuances of humour, proffer an original and singularly effective picture of the world around them, or one which they reconstruct. Other courtroom episodes that follow later in the evolution of this story over several decades, affirm that the idea was sound and destined to thrive.

Ever since Lucien Foulet[2], there has been general agreement that the two branches known as II and Va together comprise the original base of a group of texts to which Branch I was very soon added by an author who was explicit in regarding it as an essential adjunct.

> Perrot ... forgot about the *lawsuit* brought for *judgement* in the court of Noble the lion concerning the gross fornication perpetrated by Reynard, that master of iniquity, against Lady Hersent the she-wolf (I 5–10).

It is evident that the author of Branch I regards as common knowledge the 'fornication' of Reynard – that is, the whole of the last part of Branch II: the Rape (*le Viol*). In the course of the unfolding of the pre-trial investigation of the case, the author of Branch I recalls more than once the solemn oath that was never made – that is, the subject matter of Branch Va – the interruption of which gives rise to the 'new scrutiny of the matter' that constitutes his own contribution to the adventures of the fox: the Judgement (*le Jugement*).

Briefly, then, the sequence of events shows Reynard deliberately picking quarrels with the cock, the titmouse, the cat and the crow. All reprehensible, of course, but entirely consistent with his animal nature. There follows the amorous encounter with the she-wolf, then the rape, all so vivid that the whole work spills at this point into a register that is, if not quite human, at least anthropomorphic. This is the ending of Branch II, to which Branch Va adds the judicial consequences that immediately follow. The court of King Noble, at which the law is enacted, will from now on be the favoured setting for the action.

In its way, the *Roman de Renart* can be said to conform to the dominant trend in the literature of the period, not least by its preoccupation with the 'great and mighty of this world', the upper echelons of society – just as in the epics about Charlemagne and his royal vassals, and the Breton romances of Arthur and his court.

We are also aware of a degree of intellectual complicity between the authors and a cultured readership conversant with the domain of the law; we recognise too that the convening of a solemn court, trial by ordeal and the swearing of an exculpatory oath are elements that occur in literature rather more often than in life. In their writings, the authors of the first branches of the *Roman de Renart* are to hint at links with other literary works that will undoubtedly enhance the pleasure that their readers will find in them.

I. The Great Trial for Rape

Let us look at the facts. Reynard has succeeded in getting into Isengrin's lair, invited there most enticingly by Hersent. Then, before leaving, he wrecks the place, insults, beats and urinates all over the wolf-cubs (II 1,022–1,155). There are more than enough grounds for complaint by the time the master of the house, Isengrin, returns and finds out about these unfortunate happenings and, even though Hersent has sought to vindicate Reynard, his mind turns at once to *personal vengeance*, to a *private vendetta*:

> ... he said that a good lookout would be kept for Reynard before their *war* might be waged in the open (II 1,212–3).

While reconnoitring, the two wolves come across Reynard and give chase. Isengrin loses his way; Hersent stays close behind Reynard who dashes into his hole; she tries to reach him, but finds herself stuck in the entrance; the fox, emerging from another hole, takes advantage of the situation to rape her. Isengrin, who has by now found his way back, arrives on the scene just as the 'wedding' takes place (*ès noces*). Reynard denies everything, offering to swear a solemn oath to clear his name – thereby intensifying the fury of Isengrin, who had caught him in the act:

> the whole thing's perfectly obvious (II 1,326)

This private war is all the more contentious because Noble had issued a declaration of peace throughout his kingdom, a declaration that Isengrin will remember to make use of when he comes to charge Reynard, before the court, with violating this very peace. But it will all end only in ludicrous defeat for Isengrin and, in effect, the spurious rape of Hersent[3]. Admittedly, Reynard has seriously worsened the case against him by committing a second offence, but he is comfortably ensconced under the protection of his own roof!

The narrative then takes up the solution proposed by Hersent: a formal complaint to be lodged at court, in right and proper legal form:

> It's at Noble the lion's court that *cases are brought and heard regarding mortal battles and disputes* (V 276–8).

Action will now ensue according to the law, to deal with a situation that is, from the outset, extremely complex:

- Reynard, in the presence of the wolf-cubs, had an amorous encounter with a more-than-friendly Hersent; on a second occasion, he raped her. In addition to this, he plundered and ravaged the wolf's dwelling place.
- Isengrin wanted to exact private revenge, believing that his marital misfortune and the pillaging of his home were matters of common law. This brings only further ridicule upon him.
- Hersent wanted to defend herself by swearing an exculpatory oath.
- Reynard himself made the same offer.
- Isengrin is to appeal through the royal system of justice.

A. The grievances

In the midst of a general hush (Va 313), such as customarily occurs when the chief officer of the court is speaking, Isengrin sets out his grievances: his honour has been defiled by Reynard's wicked behaviour towards his wife:

> [for] he has dishonoured me through my wife (Va 326).

This means that the fox will have committed a crime against the king, since he had proclaimed

> a *royal edict* forbidding the wicked breaking or disruption of marriage (Va 319–21).

The reasoning is clever: Reynard's misdemeanour now assumes a political dimension. After Hersent has testified to the outrages that she was subjected to (without by any means revealing every detail!), Isengrin expresses his grievances in the following way:

> I *appeal* to you before all your barons, give me *justice* for all the deeds of which he stands *accused*! To start with, I *accuse*... (Va 360–4).

After listing the different offences – the insults, the vile treatment of the wolf-cubs, the rape of Hersent – the wolf ends by saying:

> So give *judgement* for this in my favour and obtain prompt *compensation* for this misdeed and dispute, so that no other idiot goes and imitates him! (Va 383–5).

His words are couched in a tone of impeccable formality, and Isengrin even goes so far as to remind the king, who is feeling inclined to settle the business amicably and to defuse the emotionally-charged situation, of his duty:

> 'Sire', he said, 'you should not, if you please, *defend* either me or him but, whatever anyone says, hear out the case for both *the prosecution and the defence...*' (Va 414–17).

As a result, the king decides that the grievance shall be officially investigated:

> 'Proceed, then, with due *reason and justice*"(Va 442–3).

Isengrin has every reason to be satisfied: he has overcome the reluctance of Noble, who was inclined to show clemency towards what he regarded as mere romantic folly. The wolf had argued the case on the basis of having caught Reynard red-handed:

> 'I *surprised* them in the act and blamed him for his behaviour' (Va 378–9).

He adds, with honesty but perhaps without thinking carefully enough:

> 'Then he offered to *answer to me for it* and *defended himself on oath* wherever I wished' (Va 380–82).

Isengrin calls for a judgement: Reynard had proposed swearing an oath; some would remember this.

This analysis of Isengrin's complaint shows too that literature does not lose sight of its own terrain: there is a certain subtlety, but also a certain naïvety in the figure of the husband who himself exposes to public gaze his own marital infelicity: the injured modesty of a wife who is widely known to have welcomed her lover very enthusiastically. All of this can only make us smile, and demonstrates that the author never loses sight of his sense of humour. At times, his collusion with the character he is writing about constrains him to propose a judgement that conforms to reality. He is fully aware of the amusing effects generated by the application of scrupulous procedures to a case that is, to put it mildly, rather odd: a situation involving customs and emotions among animals that savagely parody stock situations in courtly literature. As a result, the law is always to be rigidly upheld, which is why the king must submit the case to deliberation.

B. The deliberations of the court

The vassals take their leave of the royal tent:

> to *pass judgement* on the case (Va 507)

The focus of their discussion must from now on be consideration of the complaint lodged by the wolf.

Firstly, on the factual level, Plateau the deer, ignoring the rape, concentrates on the most easily-proved aspects of the case, the material damage done by Reynard: the stealing of food, the attacking and injuring of the wolf-cubs (Va 575 ff.). His arguments are entirely convincing and Brun, who approves of it, is not wrong. A severe punishment 'that calls for a heavy fine' (Va 585) will be the right and proper outcome. But Plateau is supported by hardly anyone apart from Brun, who is in favour of any compromise that will defeat Reynard. Everyone else is well aware that the real problem is Reynard's 'fornication'.

Next, on the procedural level, Brichemer wants to see total respect for the rights of the accused. The only testimony before them is that of the victim, a scared wife, dominated by her husband. He reminds the court of the need for objective witnesses (Va 525 ff.).

> Baucent the boar is in full agreement
> [he] *would not disregard the law* in the slightest way (Va 515–16).

He goes on to point out the risks of creating a dangerous judicial precedent, implicit in settling for the testimony of Hersent alone (Va 552–74). Brun intervenes here, willing to resort to whatever means will reinforce his point

> he declared that he would like to bring Reynard to grief (Va 513).

His argument is spectacularly specious; its content, which is satirical and far from unprejudiced, can be crudely summarised as follows: 'Given that Isengrin is a very high-ranking lord, firstly, what he says must be true and, secondly, his wife's evidence is perfectly admissible' (Va 539–51, cf.809–20).

Ultimately, the humour lies in the fact that although Isengrin had told the truth, any fair judge had no option but, like Baucent, to reject Brun's hypocritical line of argument.

At this point in the debate, it becomes necessary to concede the impossibility of adhering to the charge of *flagrante delicto*, since there is no objective witness to corroborate it. Such testimony was vital, because being caught in the act would ensure the instant condemnation of the offender. Therefore, in the absence of testimonial proof, Baucent, who is preoccupied at all times with preserving legal propriety, comes up with another procedure: judgement following *a debate for and against the accused*, to enable Reynard to speak in his own defence:

> 'I don't know what we could say until *we hear them together*. Once Reynard has come to court we can examine *the charge laid here by Isengrin*' (Va 785–9).

The boar's principal concern is to avoid an escalation of violence, whereas Brun the bear is constrained by no sense of moderation. And so, with the idea of *debate for and against the accused* as a point of departure, and with a view to reaching amicable agreement (Va 843–52), the situation shifts towards collaborative endeavour. Brichemer (the seneschal), who had opened the debate and then left his colleagues free to express themselves as they wished, seizes skilfully on what Baucent had said to arrive at the perfect solution. Baucent has just spoken of amicable agreement (*aucune acorde*); Brichemer goes further in speaking of reconciliation (*acordement*):

> 'My lords', he says, 'let us now *fix a day for agreement*. Have Reynard take *the oath* and *pay compensation* according to the terms *he has promised Isengrin*' (Va 858–62).

Beyond the flawless diplomacy of the suggestion, this recourse to the swearing of an oath is not merely a possibility, it imposes positive constraints, since Reynard had proposed

> 'Never have I wronged your wife in any way. And *in my defence and hers too, I'll swear you an oath wherever, on the advice of your best friends, you wish to accept it* (II 1,316–19).

It was sufficient to take him at his word, which was without doubt why Brichemer had so assiduously specified that the proposal should come from Reynard himself. And it is Isengrin who, as has been said, had personally (unfortunately for him) given evidence before the court. From the very moment that one of the protagonists calls on God, human justice finds itself displaced – Hersent is to exploit this procedure with ingenuity, as we shall see.

The debate comes to a halt; nobody adds anything, not even Brun. All that is left before making their summary account to the king is to set in train the procedure for the taking of the oath. The ceremony is to be presided over by someone generally considered to be of unblemished reputation: Roenel the dog, who is independent of the court because he is a farmyard dog. It will take place, as we learn in due course from Brichemer, on a Sunday morning – that is to say, a day of serious piety when the public will be there in large numbers to observe how the law functions (Va 923).

The report made to the king by the seneschal is a scrupulous record of the purport, the spirit and the conclusions arrived at in debate:

(i) Isengrin must be granted 'all his rights' (*tote sa droiture*, Va 905);
(ii) the testimony of Hersent is not admissible: there ought to have been two witnesses (Va 907–14);
(iii) the procedure of swearing an oath is the one they settle on;
(iv) to conclude, it is right and proper that Reynard should conduct himself so as to make 'his peace in God's name' (*sa pes de par Dé*, Va 927).

The case has been argued and weighted evenly, in order to find the just path between a plaintiff in pursuit of the most serious possible condemnation and a king ready to pardon, but ultimately more than happy to see this whole embarrassing case taken out of his hands and handed over – to God (Va 929–35). Furthermore, it is evident that the characters in the narrative – and the author – are insistent on:

- scrupulous respect for the law;
- careful avoidance of judicial error;
- enduring determination to maintain the peace:

> '... the verdict regarding a crime in deed or words that is neither clear nor admitted should not be to execute or ruin a person: instead, *a settlement should be reached*. Above all, let us take care through our moderation to avoid any judicial error...' (Va 864–70).

Such is the conviction of people who are serious and meticulous about fulfilling their responsibilities, and who must resist any enticement to unjust violence advocated by others – in this instance, as it happens, by Brun.

C. The camel's speech

Strange as it seems at first, an episode that markedly provokes laughter is in fact an affirmation of its seriousness. This is the speech of the pontifical legate[4,] Musart the camel, who does not belong to the court, nor does he take part in the deliberations of Reynard's peers, but is there instead as a man of sound judgement and a friend of the king, by whom he has been invited to put forward an opinion – in a sort of advisory capacity, you might say. Because we cannot resist laughing at the blunders of this foreigner, whose command of French is very poor, we lose track of what he is trying to say. The author, though, at no point hints that his speech should be regarded as ridiculous; on the contrary, he describes this character as 'extremely wise' (*molt sages*) and a 'fine jurist' (*bon legistres*) (Va 451) who stays close to Canon Law, Gratian's *Decretum*, (Va 458) in condemning adultery with the utmost severity. If Reynard is not able to exonerate himself, he will have to be punished by confiscation of everything he owns, or by death. The legate adds that it is the responsibility of the worthy king to enforce justice and to protect his nobles. He speaks as a strict moralist and with the authority of the Church, in words firmly founded in infallible texts; he does so before a lay prince whom he seems to consider too lenient. We are shown, too, the reaction of the court:

some of them were jubilant (Va 496)

(probably referring to Isengrin and the enemies of Reynard)

others enraged (Va 497)

(among them, doubtless, the king himself, who could not avoid being involved and was caught on the wrong foot: for him, an amorous misdemeanour is not a crime; for the legate, on the contrary, the deference due to marriage is not to be taken lightly).

As soon as he has heard all this, Noble asks his barons – though not, it must be said, without a degree of hypocrisy – to 'pass judgement on the case' (*jugier de ceste clamor*) by changing the form of the complaint.

The legate has to be satisfied with the agreed procedure. Moreover, he is to be present at the ceremony (Va 1,042), since the oath, which is a religious procedure as well as a judicial one, will, if conducted properly and without omissions, either vindicate or condemn Reynard.

D. Reynard's solemn oath

To understand well the unfolding of the scene so solemnly set up by the court of Noble, it is essential to bear in mind the importance of the spoken word in a society based on oral law. In this society, everything of importance that took place in life was made symbolically concrete by means of an act carried out in the presence of witnesses who would subsequently affirm that it happened and, therefore, its veracity. More than this, the swearing of an oath of exculpation only makes sense in a society where the prevailing faith will tolerate no compromise dictated by personal considerations. In other words: *Jurare est aliquid affirmare vel negare, Deo adhibito inspectore,* and *jurare est testem Deum invocare* (To swear an oath is to affirm or negate, with God as overseer ... to swear an oath is to call upon God as witness.) This is how the oath is always defined; it is to this that whoever swears it submits; this which, if he is lying, incurs divine punishment. Indeed, it could be said that God, who is 'the way, the truth and the life', would not grant bail to someone who commits perjury, and so the truth blazes forth, bright and clear.

What possible developments were there, then, for the author of this branch, clearly committed as he was to accurate portrayal of both laws and customs?

(i) Either Reynard could have sworn a profane oath and, in one way or another, divine power would show itself and Reynard would die – something unthinkable in literary terms;
(ii) or he would have to avoid the formal ritual necessitated by an oath, in which case his words would be no more than a banal lie – reprehensible, certainly, but not perjury. If this were to happen, the witnesses to the oath would be bound to notice it and would insist that Reynard observe the proper forms. We are reminded of the Brichemer's meticulous rigour and that of several others;
(iii) or he would somehow manage to fulfil all the conditions but would nevertheless utter an oath that is ambiguous – just as Queen Isolda did, in somewhat different circumstances, and as Hersent was soon to do (we will come back to this) – or to make a mental reservation. This last hypothesis would make it difficult to arrive at a denouement that is viable as literary narrative, because nobody but the reader would have spotted the trickery while, for the characters within the story, it would be perceived as

irrefutable proof of Reynard's innocence. Anyway, it was inconceivable that a judicial error would have been endorsed by God.

In fact, at this point the author chooses another kind of denouement to bring his branch to an effective end. The oath does not take place because of Isengrin, who is so eagerly bent on blind vengeance that he provides Reynard with an undreamed-of chance of saving himself and even, to some extent, emerging in the best possible light. The ceremony observes all the necessary formalities:

(i) Reynard is asked to attend (Va 952–632);
(ii) each faction gathers its supporters together, as a guarantee in case any points of law should arise (Va 1,030–37, 1,049–90 ff.);
(iii) the great dignitaries of the court, such as the camel, are introduced ex officio, some even at the express wish of the king (Va1,038–48);
(iv) Brichemer presides over the proceedings with due solemnity and asks Reynard to swear the necessary oath (Va 1,113–30).

We remember, however, that Roenel had been appointed to handle this; but, in the event, a piece of skullduggery on the part of Isengrin prevents him from doing so. The wolf had sought him out in order to bribe him and the dog proved to be treacherous, proposing that he should pretend to be dead and transform himself into – a sacred relic:

Saint Roenel the scowler (Va 1,127).

This way, he could get Reynard between his jaws without having to go to the trouble of first setting up an ambush:

well over forty of the most fierce, savage mastiffs (Va 1,024–5).

When Reynard, already naturally inclined to be on his guard and on the lookout for an escape route, sees through the trick being played on him, he has good reason to avoid swearing a stipulated oath that would be invalidated by the circumstances, and to take flight. Chased by the dogs who lay in wait for him, he is injured, but saves himself. Moreover, he is in a position to plead good faith and to level the charge of treachery against his accuser.

This, then, is the first court action against Reynard. It was not completed, so the story can carry on to an inevitable second stage, but the thwarting of the solemn oath ceremony calls for some comments: the solution arrived at seemed to satisfy everyone – except Isengrin, who had perverted the course of justice. The court sought a proper procedure, which would restore peace and reconcile the two adversaries. Nobody seemed able to envisage any outcome other than one that would exculpate Reynard. There is an implicit certainty that the fox is innocent – perhaps because the king was predisposed to regard transgression prompted by love as deserving leniency?

When the 'Saint Roenel trick' is not spotted as such by anyone during the panic that follows the fox's escape, Isengrin is able to be optimistic about the prospect of successfully launching another ploy. This was the understanding of the author of Branch I, when he maintained that Pierre de Saint-Cloud 'forgot about the lawsuit and the judgement' of Reynard for his gross act of 'fornication'.

2. The Second Complaint Made by Isengrin and the Oath Taken by Hersent

In the presence of a new assembly of the court, similar to the previous one, the wolf

> *makes his complaint* before all the others (I 28).

At first, his grievance remains unchanged:

> '... *grant me justice* in the matter of Reynard's adultery with my spouse, Lady Hersent, once he had her shut up in his lair at Maupertuis for the purpose of violating her. What's more, he urinated over all my cubs...' (I 30–5).

Such is the opening part of the charge. Is he covered with shame? Is he deeply moved? Isengrin makes no mention of the consenting adultery of Hersent – which he knows all about from the account given by the children. Moreover, he telescopes in a strange way the rape at Maupertuis and the defiling of the wolf-cubs with urine.

But, following the failure to comply with the law recorded in Branch Va, the gravity of the charge was further intensified by a second factor: the refusal to swear an oath. On this particular point, Isengrin's way of presenting the case calls for careful deliberation on our part:

> 'Reynard had the date fixed for his *defence* against the charge of adultery. Then when the holy relics were brought, I don't know who counselled him, but he promptly withdrew and dashed off into his den' (I 37–42).

He is rather wary of saying that he does not approve of the procedure for swearing an oath, that he had behaved in a wilfully profane manner, and that the relics were not genuine. Implicit in his apparent acceptance of the exculpation procedure as having been properly conducted is the suggestion that Reynard's disappearance is an admission of guilt, because it is a feature of legal practice at this time that any shirking of an obligation to submit to trial by ordeal is interpreted as proof of guilt, demonstrating that the accused, fully aware that he has committed a crime, knows – or thinks he knows – the drastic inevitability of the outcome. Isengrin thus contrives to project himself in the most favourable possible light, even though, as we have seen, he is just as bad as his adversary.

Furthermore, to project the matter in this way is to accuse Reynard of thumbing his nose at the authority of Noble, a suspicion made all the more plausible at the very moment when the fox has failed to respond to the royal proclamation calling upon the court to convene right away. This means that Isengrin's second charge is addressed to an assembly far more receptive than it had been the first time, and that the proposal for a judgement given after due hearing of the parties put forward by Brun the bear now seems to be reasonable:

> 'If Isengrin's *bringing a charge* against Reynard, then *pronounce judgement* in the matter: that's the best course in my eyes. If one of them's in the other's debt, let him settle up and pay you a fine for his wrongdoing. *Send* to Maupertuis for Reynard...' (I 70–5).

It is evident too that even Bruyant regards this approach as one that will expedite the whole business, since no purpose would be served by a verdict based on

> a case about something so widely known and obvious for all to see (I 89–90).

It is going to take all the patience and tact of Grimbert to calm things down and to steer the charge towards moderation. With consummate skill, the badger puts forward the opinion which is that of the king himself: this is a simple case of romantic love – as Noble himself had said in Branch Va. Hersent would have preferred to keep the whole matter secret; it is Isengrin who 'has taken it too much to heart' (*l'a trop pris en gref*) and has been guilty of a grave discourtesy towards his wife. (I 103–33).

This speech, very much more emotive than legalistic, achieves what it set out to do: it seriously undermines the charge as well as weakening Isengrin's position. As a result, the she-wolf is able to take the stand, all the while sighing deeply, evoking as evidence her marriage and the obsessive jealousy of her husband. We seem to be in the realm of a romantic novel, but in fact it is all highly contrived, enabling Hersent to reiterate her claim that she would like to defend herself by undergoing a trial by ordeal:

> He [Reynard] certainly never had anything of that sort from me in that way. So I'd be quite prepared to undergo *an ordeal by scalding water or burning fire*. But alas, poor wretch that I am! it's no use my *denying* it, when they'd never take my word in the matter (I 140–6).

The idea had been in her mind for quite a while; it was already there when Isengrin returned to his lair and, discovering the destruction wrought by Reynard, had heaped insults on her, to which she had replied:

> '… if you allowed me *to defend myself by taking an oath, or undergoing a trial by ordeal*, I'd do it on the understanding that I'd be burned or hanged unless I could *prove myself innocent* in this affair' (II 1,196–2,000).

Clearly, Isengrin had not followed up this suggestion. And now, before the entire court, without waiting for the outcome of a trial by ordeal, she asserts that nobody would believe her – she is obviously referring indirectly to her husband here – and moves on, allowing no time whatsoever for anyone to react by interrupting her:

> '*By all the saints we worship, though, so help me God,* Reynard never did anything to me he wouldn't have done to his mother' (I 147–50).

She concludes her statement with these words:

> '… never, *by my faith in Holy Mary*, have I personally indulged in any more lechery, wickedness, or wantonness than a nun might commit' (I 175–8).

That is, without any preamble, without even excusing herself on the grounds that it would be pointless to attempt any self-justification that no-one would listen to, Hersent startles everyone by swearing an oath, using the correct terms to formulate it: 'may God and all his saints help me...' (*si m'aït Dex et tuit li saint*). The outcome is total legal exoneration beyond question, as the author himself emphasises:

> When Hersent had had her say and *made her denials*. ... (I 178–80).

But just what is the substance of this oath? Two affirmations:

(i) Reynard had never behaved badly with her;
(ii) she herself is a virtuous wife

(we will come back to the ambiguity inherent in these formulations).

The conclusion, in a juridical context, is that there is no point in insisting that the fox should justify himself in person. Hersent has done it for him. This is just how the situation was understood by the king, who was by now strongly inclined to be amazed that anyone could still want to subject the fox to litigation:

> 'You are wrong to *prejudge* Reynart' (I 228–9).

He was in favour of advising Isengrin to drop the matter (I 237–40). When it came to it, he could hardly say anything else. By her oath, Hersent had placed her case openly before the tribunal of God himself, who had cleared her of all guilt.

But had she not taken a great risk in offering to submit to the test of ordeal by water or fire? Close scrutiny of her words will make it possible to judge them and – to come to the conclusion that she was taking no risk at all. After all, just what had she sworn with such solemnity?

(i) That Reynard had done nothing to her that he would not have done to his mother! A somewhat ambiguous formulation, since Reynard would have been perfectly capable of incest? Hersent's words imply that she believes this to be so; therefore, she is telling the truth. The noble persons hearing her would not for a moment have thought of incest; they would conclude that Reynard had treated Hersent with utmost decency;

(ii) that Hersent herself had behaved as decorously as a nun? Here again, her oath can be interpreted in two diametrically opposed ways, according to whether one believes that life in religious orders was morally impeccable or, in line with traditional anticlericalism, that some members of these orders allowed themselves considerable leeway in relation to the vows that they had taken. In her own mind, of course, Hersent leans towards the sense that suits her best: the one that allows her to walk away without having to undergo trial by ordeal.

If the letter of the law is respected, the spirit of both justice and the faith is clearly distorted. To be fully grasped, this attitude should perhaps be seen alongside the entirely parallel behaviour of Queen Isolda, in Béroul's *Tristan*[5.] We are reminded of the intelligence and skill that she mustered in arguing her innocence by means of a calculatedly ambiguous affirmation relating to Blanche Lande, proffering unequivocal insistence in the face of uncertainty and proposing an immediate trial by ordeal challenged by the assembled court. If we keep in the backs of our minds a glimpse of this famous love story, we are better able to grasp the significance of the events that unfold. When the king proposes a trial by ordeal, he is merely activating an ordinary procedure; but he is not fooled for a moment, for he knows very well what Hersent is up to. Isengrin, on the other hand, holds on to a naïve, crude and short-sighted view of the whole business. He has seen for himself, and he knows that a trial by ordeal will result in the condemnation of his wife. More than this, he is a victim of his own logic when he opposes her undergoing a test that would confirm her guilt and, in his view, expose him to disgrace as a husband. He is naïve enough to admit:

> 'If Hersent undergoes the ordeal and is burned to a frazzle, then anyone who doesn't know the truth will learn it (I 250–3).

He asserts once more that he could seek redress through a private war (I 250–3). In other words, he comes back to where he started from, even though his first foray in the direction of personal vengeance had made him look ridiculous because it had brought about the rape of Hersent before his very eyes. There is no longer any doubt when Noble, in the interests of peace, declares that the affair is over and the utter impotence of the wolf becomes clear as he sits there on the ground with his tail between his legs (I 267–72). He does not know which way to turn and there is nothing left for him to do. However, the king has not committed any abuse of power, because Hersent's word has left Reynard free of guilt.

This analysis confirms the complex nature of the proceedings. Starting, as it did, as a legal matter that Isengrin wanted to settle privately, it came to involve the State, partly because of the foolish tenacity of the wolf, but also because the author of Branch I, remembering that Hersent's panic had driven her to play for time by proposing a justificatory oath, wanted to create a literary parody of the *Roman de Tristan*.

If we put to one side the playful mockery of the judicial system, important though that is to the fictional narrative, where do the authors stand on the issues arising from the amorous relationships between the characters? To start with, they defer to the strict moral standpoint of the papal legate, conforming to the criteria of conscience, making no exceptions for anyone. This was certainly the approach prevailing in the period of King Philippe-Auguste (reigned 1180–1223), and indeed at all other times. In another context, it was also the stance of the hermit Ogrin (in the *Roman de Tristan*) in respect of the Cornish lovers during their first visit. We see, too, a satirising of certain types in high society: the husbands who are stupid and overflowing with self-importance and who, on the pretext of defending their reputation, succeed only in making themselves more and more ridiculous and abased and increasing the humiliation of their wives. Between the two aspects, the distinctly uncomfortable position of the court and of the king merit and hold the attention.

In Branch Va, Brichemer conducts himself with tact and diplomacy, first allowing his peers to express their feelings, whether sincere or hypocritical, before uniting them around a decision calculated to restore tranquility. It is as if he were convinced that Reynard's oath would calm down a situation exaggerated out of all proportion by Isengrin. In other words, nobody takes Isengrin seriously. Those who are inclined to support him, are not prompted by conviction but only by the universal loathing of Reynard.

In Branch I, the court does not even have time to express its views, because Hersent imposes the test of her innocence – this test is a parody, of course, but we find ourselves swept along by the spirit of the game the author is playing. In spite of this, we should not ignore the words of Grimbert, when he speaks in favour of the most lenient interpretation of the facts: this is not about a crime, nor about any threat to the Establishment – it was Isengrin who alleged that the king's authority had been flouted – it is about an emotional predicament that had not led to the committing of any violence:

> 'And as there was no violence or breach of the peace, and if Reynard did it to her out of love, there's no case for anger or complaint. He'd been fond of her for some time' (I 109–13).

He is implicitly challenging the charge of rape between long-standing lovers. If Hersent feels ashamed, it is because of her husband's wild accusations. That is where the blame should fall.

It is particularly interesting that Grimbert does no more here than return to the idea expressed by Noble in Branch Va: the king had at first emphasised the contradiction in Hersent's confused statement – heard by her husband – in which she claimed to have been raped by a 'man' with whom she had willingly agreed to be alone (Va 394–401). Then, when he had been obliged to open the legal proceedings – particularly after the papal legate's speech – he had gone ahead on these terms:

> 'Proceed now', he says, 'you most worthy and distinguished beasts here present, to pass judgement on this case as to whether he who is smitten by love should be found guilty of the act which has brought contempt on his companion' (Va 499–504).

It becomes perfectly clear to anyone with even the slightest liberality of outlook, that the problem is one of a relationship between lovers – which sends us back to the courtly context, where Hersent's parodic statement is entirely in keeping. Furthermore, divine justice bestows its seal of approval on Hersent's word, just as it decreed that Isolda was in the right.

Noble is a king who is aware of his responsibilities. He is to adopt a far more severe attitude to Reynard when the issue of murder arises. But for him, justice is not an end in itself, it is an instrument that serves the harmony of the kingdom – another reason for not debasing it by putting his trust in the utterances of a jealous husband, that character so despised in courtly literature.

We should not take more seriously than it deserves the founding episode of the *Roman de Renart*, for the intention of the authors is above all comic and satirical and we must admit that, in this specific instance, the behaviour of the fox is without either elegance or refinement. Nevertheless, as far as the Hersent and Reynard adventure goes, beyond the satire there lies a serious question about civilisation and, particularly, about the literature of its time that it brings to mind. The literary parody must have been a great delight to its readers.

Notes

1. This article is a development of an aspect of the argument in Subrenat (1991: 239–92). The text is quoted in the translation by Owen (1994). The French text is from the edition of Martin (1882–5) which has since undergone frequent revisions.
2. Foulet (1914, repr. 1968: 165–237). The discussion found there has subsequently been summarised and extended by Varty (1985: 44–72).
3. On the question of this rape, see Varty (1984: 411–18).
4. On this passage, see Deroy (1981: 102–110).
5. *Le Roman de Tristan*, ed. Muret-Dufourques (Paris, Champion), lines 4,199–4,211.

CHAPTER 3

MORALS, JUSTICE AND GEOPOLITICS IN THE *REINHART FUCHS* OF THE ALSATIAN HEINRICH DER GLICHEZAERE

Jean-Marc Pastré

In the second half of the twelfth century, an Alsatian poet, Heinrich, was inspired to use a good dozen of the Branches of the French *Roman de Renart* in order to depict, by hints, a satire of the morals and politics of the Holy Roman Empire. Under the nickname of *der Glichezaere* (= the hypocrite, the trickster) our poet uses the protective cloak of animal fable in order to smooth the way for his message about morals and geopolitics. He guides his reader from German-speaking Alsace to Italy via Bohemia and thus outlines the vast political realm that was at that time the German Empire, and conjures up events which, local or European, are deeply rooted in the imagination and collective memory of the Middle Ages.

The dating of the work is still the subject of controversy. Some date the written version as shortly after 1162, others, however (and they are now more numerous) place it in the last years of the twelfth century. But all agree that Heinrich was the first to compose a clearly constructed work based on branches of the *Roman de Renart* with an introduction, clearly defined parts and a conclusion, all subject to a development which takes us from the fox's brush with the little animals to his confrontation with the wolf Ysengrin, and from there to the trial at which the assembled animals witness Reinhart's triumph over his peers and over the lion-king Vrevel (Göttert 1976; Düwel 1984; Buschinger and Pastré 1984).

Punctuated by proper names which go back to the times of Heinrich and to the vast space that the Hohenstaufen claimed as their Western Empire, *Reinhart Fuchs* only gains its full meaning if one places the work into the political and historical context of the years 1160–1200, the years of the Holy Roman Empire under Frederick Barbarossa and his son Henry VI (1165–97). Critics have, in fact, discovered allusions to history in a number of important motifs in the work: the destruction of the ant-hill (lines 1250–66); the allusion to Walther von Horburg (lines 1024–29); the illness, the healing and the poisoning of the king (1,999–2,076 and 2,165–248); the injustice of the king who has the wolf, the bear and the cat flayed (1905–70), the camel of Tuschalan and the Convent of Erstein (2,117–56); the elephant from Bohemia (2,097–2,116); the leopard with the plumed helmet (2,003–08) and, finally, the rise of Reinhart and of the fox in general in the French Renardian tradition.

The Destruction of the Ant-hill

The tale of the ants, which is at the beginning of the story of the lion's illness and the trial of Reinhart, relates how king Vrevel destroys down to its very foundations an ant-hill that resisted his claim of sovereignty. Critics have seen in this story of destruction either the destruction of the Alsatian fortress of Girbaden or the destruction of the town of Milan. Both were destroyed in 1162 by Barbarossa's troops (Heer 1952: 160 and 230; Schwab 1967: 58 and 224–5; Spiewok 1964: 281–88).

Literary historians have thought that they could identify the ant-hill as the fortress of Girbaden because Heinrich quotes in line 1024 a certain Sir Walther von Horburg, whose favourite saying was that any misfortune that happened to him could always have an advantageous consequence. The fortress of Horburg, which lies very close to Colmar, was destroyed at the time of Walther in 1162 by his rival Hugo von Dagsburg with the help of Bishop Stephen of Metz and Duke Berthold of Zähringen. After what was so far only an episode in an armed quarrel between two Alsatian feudal lords, the people of the garrison of Horburg were taken to the fortress of Girbaden and kept prisoners there. At this point Barbarossa intervened. In order to keep the balance of power he put a stop to the war between his two vassals, freed the prisoners and destroyed the fortress of Girbaden, thus curbing the power of the Dagsburg (which had grown too much), in favour of the lords of Horburg.

The case for Milan is based partly on a detail in Heinrich's text, partly on the politics of the Hohenstaufen in Italy. The term *burc*, by which Heinrich describes the ant-hill, can mean in Middle High German a town as well as a fortress. The world of the ants is here a world of its own: it does not appear in the first part of the work although that part deals with small animals. It differs from them by the minute size of these insects. This world, which is not directly subject to the lion, does not appear on the list of the animals who come to court in order to complain (lines 1,331–60). It only finds its place in the third part of the work, which deals with the external politics of the emperors, whilst the first and second parts deal with internal conflicts which oppose the fox to his peers and then to the grand feudal lords represented by Ysengrin and his family.

The lord of the ants speaks of his race (*chunne*, line 1,269) and of his poeple (*diet*, line 1,297) for whom he seeks revenge. The lion kills his enemies the ants by the million, a symbol of the masses which also serves as a symbol of what at that time was the biggest of the North Italian towns. The ants are also, in biblical tradition, a symbol of courage and wealth, capable of working incessantly without needing a prince who forces them to do so, which is perfectly fitting for the hard-working and powerful Lombardian towns in general and Milan in particular. Free of the feudal system, having created their own free institutions and their autonomous legal system, the Italian communes were indeed, in the Emperor's eyes, worlds of their own. And the Italian campaigns were, in the eyes of Frederick's contemporaries, battles against another world, against elements outside the Imperial realm which had a different way of seeing, feeling and reacting. The terms used in Heinrich's episode echo in a strange way the terms used in 1150 in the *Chronicle of the Emperors* for the destruction of Milan by Otto I towards the middle of the tenth century (Pastré 1993a).

The ants learn with amazement (*vremde mere*, line 1,254) that the lion demands their submission, and they refuse. Furious at meeting this resistance, Vrevel considers himself authorised to crush these feeble creatures (line 1,260). We have here a perfect example of the mutual misunderstanding of historic rights in both camps. The master of the ants believes that he has every right to defend his sovereignty (lines 1,289 and 2,054), to resist Vrevel and to try to save his race, just as the

Italian towns had become, little by little, completely independent of the Empire of which they were only subjects by name since they had either bought or otherwise acquired the greater part of their sovereign rights. Frederick I claimed back rights that were at that time nothing more than a historical memory, as the rights of royal sovereignty had long since been taken over by the communes, be it by good will or by force. But the King of Germany had first and foremost to govern Italy if he wanted to be the successor of the Roman Emperors. Resolving political problems in Italy was therefore all-important for the restoration of the Roman Empire, an idea very dear to the Hohenstaufen. Whilst his predecessors Lothar and Conrad II had intervened only a little in Italian affairs, and that without success, Frederick I planned to restore the old Roman Empire to its full sovereign glory, and therefore did battle with all the territorial powers that had come into being in Italy. The Lombardian Republics refused to submit to Imperial domination.

Refusal to obey by the Italian communes amounted, in Imperial eyes, to a rebellion, a crime of lese-majesty against the Emperor which forced the Emperor of the West, King of Kings, to indulge in bloody repression; and never did Frederick I or Henry VI act in Germany with such cruelty as they did in Italy. The inhabitants of Italian towns got to know the devastating effects of the *furor teutonicus* (tutonic fury) just as the ants had to endure Vrevel's rightful wrath. Frederick had to cross the Alps five times at the head of the Imperial army, and he destroyed Chieri, Asti, Tortone, Spoleto, Cremona and, above all, Milan. In 1159 the consuls of the town chased out three Imperial emissaries who had come to establish an Imperial town-government, just as the ants already knew the lion's demands but did not want to recognise them (lines 1,282–83), hence the destruction of the ant-hill and the town of Milan in 1162, a symbol of the resistance and the destruction of so many Italian towns.

The Lion's Illness.

The fable of the ants only gains its full meaning if it is seen as the cause of the lion's illness. He is ill because he is tormented by the ant that got into his brain, (lines 1,307–08): the king pays a high price for his policy of territorial expansion. Historians agree that Italy under Frederick I, and even more so under Henry VI, was the centre and the climax of the Imperial idea. Under those two Emperors German forces were predominantly used to force Italy into submission. The Italian policy of the Hohenstaufen was the foundation of their idea to restore the Roman Empire, and it was also the reason for the failure of this idea. The Holy Empire was enfeebled by its Italian policy. The lesson of the fable about the lion and the ants seems to point to the fact that the Emperor, and by analogy the Empire, is ill because of his desire to dominate Italy.

Some comparisons can throw still more light on this aspect of Heinrich's work. We know that the Lombardian League, founded by the reconstructed Milan, defeated Barbarossa on 29 May 1176 at the battle of Legnano: the Imperial troops had been decimated by an epidemic of malaria. Frederick's partisans were horror-stricken and believed they were slain by the sword of the Angel of Death. This defeat was a severe blow to Imperial politics, and its ambitious pretensions were broken. The Emperor had to grant a pardon and privileges to the Lombardian cities. Barbarossa had to reconcile himself with Milan at the Peace of Constance in 1183. Perhaps we can hear the echo of this event in the liberation of the master of the ants by the help of Reinhart (lines 2,075–80); once the Italian problem was solved, the illness that gnawed at the Empire came provisionally to an end, and Vrevel regained his health (line 2,064).

The Lion's Death

But the lion had to die by poison as did (at least so it has been believed for centuries) Henry VI at Messina, victim of the second stage of the domination of Italy. Frederick I had turned his attention mainly to the north of Italy. In order to be master of Italy and of the Pope he had, however, also to make sure that he dominated the south and Sicily which was then in the hands of the Normans on whom the Pope could rely as allies against the Emperor. His son Henry had a legitimate claim to the crown of Naples and Sicily as his wife Constance was the heir of Roger I. Henry VI led a campaign in Southern Italy in 1191 and then again in 1194, and succeeded in assuming a power which manifested itself in a particularly cruel way after a failed conspiracy that had been stirred up in the immediate entourage of Constance and supported by the Pope and the Lombardians. The fever of which he had been cured attacked him again in 1197 and killed him on 28 September of the same year.

Henry VI died in Messina, poisoned, so it was believed, by his own entourage because of his Italian policy. This event is reflected in the death of the lion Vrevel, assassinated by his vassal, and carried off by a potion that Reinhart brings back from Salerno, a town, so the fox remarks ironically, in which Vrevel has so many good friends (lines 1877–80). Now Salerno was destroyed and looted by Henry VI's troops in 1194 (Toeche 1867: 335 and 470). From Salerno where, at that time, the famous School of Medecine had its seat, comes Death disguised as healing and the poison disguised as a potion. We can see what a long shot Heinrich has fired at the end of his work: the Empire totters through Frederick I's policy regarding Milan, and agonises under Henry VI: the death of the lion following the destruction of the ant-hill.

The Normans rebelled; Constance had the Germans chased from Sicily. This was soon followed by the looting of all Imperial possessions in the whole of Italy; and interregnum and civil war, the young Frederick, the future Frederick II, being only three years old. An atmosphere of decay surrounds the Imperial defeat of 1197, the spectre of the *discessio imperii* predicted for the end of time is present in the apocalyptic spectacle of King Vrevel whose head falls into three pieces, his tongue into nine (lines 2,243–44).

This lion's head that splits into three pieces and this tongue that twists itself into nine pleats deserve to be specially considered. This stark image of the decomposition of the lion's court admirably reflects the decomposition of the Empire after 1197, torn apart between three legitimate pretenders for the Imperial crown: Philip of Swabia, the brother of the deceased Emperor, crowned in 1198 by his followers; Otto of Brunswick, his cousin, the son of Henry the Lion, crowned in the same year by his supporters; and the young Frederick, the future Frederick II, the son of the deceased Henry VI, who was only three years old in this fateful year and who had already been appointed as successor while his father was still alive. It is the meaning that Cesar of Heisterbach gave in 1206 to the vision that two clerics had seen on the occasion of a great regal court assembly of Philip of Swabia: the sun had divided itself into three parts like a lily with three flowers: that was the Empire divided between three pretenders (Pastré 1994a, 71–82).

The lion's tongue being folded into nine branches recalls not only the state of affairs in the Empire, but also the Christian interpretation of the multiplication of tongues. For the great clerics of the Carolingian tradition, the universality of the Empire and of Christianity corresponded to the unity of the Latin language which subsequently divided itself into different vernacular languages. The multiplicity of languages points to sin, to Babel, synonymous with Babylon, and reveals itself, just as the multiplicity of tongues in *Reinhart Fuchs* and of the kings of the Apocalypse, as the sign of the end of time. The drama of the Empire is in fact the mirror-image of mankind. The initial unity of the Latin language of the Empire corresponded to the unity of the language of the descendents of Adam. To punish the pride of men who wanted, by erecting the Tower of Babel, to dominate the heavens and become themselves divine, God scrambled the language of men and dispersed them over the face of the earth. At the end of the eighth century the sons of Louis the Pious had even, through the Strasbourg Oaths, consecrated the phenomenon of linguistic division; Frankish as the language of Louis the German who was to rule over the Eastern part of the Realm, and Romance as the language of Charles the Bald who was to rule over the Western part. In this way the drama of the Empire reactivated the drama of Babel, and the nine pleats of the lion's tongue symbolised the numerous languages that were then spoken in the Empire (Pastré 1993b: 71–82).

The Lion, *Rex Iniustus* (the Unjust King)

It is paradoxical to see how Vrevel, sure of his rights, is unable to perceive that the evil that befalls him is the result of his territorial aspirations. He declares that he was punished by God for not having carried out justice (lines 1,319–20). He then proceeds to fulfil his role as a judge very badly, failing twice in his essential mission as sovereign, and one finds a second justification, one that is no longer narrative but ethical, in the lion's illness. Justice was at that time a guarantee of the Empire's and the world's moral good health. Injustice, on the other hand, brings illness to the lion and the Empire. In spite of his ambition to be a just king, Barbarossa failed in that respect. In order to make peace with Pope Alexander III in 1177, he abandoned his faithful bishops. In 1164 he had made his vassals and bishops swear that they would never recognise Alexander III, and that they would stay faithful to the Anti-Pope Pascal who was supported by the Emperor. After his defeats in Lombardy, Barbarossa had to secure for himself the support of the Pope, and eleven years later he had to resign himself to dismissing the bishops who, during the schism, had kept their oath and supported the Anti-Pope. In

Alsace, the bishops of Basel, Strasburg and Metz were dismissed from office. By a strange coincidence, Louis of Basel had as his successor a certain Heinrich von Horburg, a relative of our Walther von Horburg. Rudolf of Strasburg had been Frederick's chaplain, and we know that Heinrich frequently stresses the fact that Brun the bear is the chaplain of King Vrevel whilst the other important figures at court are never defined by any particular function. As to Dipreht the cat, he is also flayed alive, whereas in the French source Renart tries to persuade Tibert to leave his skin behind, but Tibert manages to escape. (X, lines 1,874ff.). The flaying of the three animals, all three thus making the healing of the lion possible, could well reflect the sacking of the three bishops, for Vrevel stresses at the time of his demise how much he regrets having his noble chaplain flayed at Reinhart's instigation (lines 2,236–37) . Christian, Archbishop of Mayence, and Philip, Archbishop of Cologne, got off much more lightly, like Reinhart and the badger Krimel. We know that Philip even eventually became successor to the Arch-Chancellor Rainald von Dassel, and had to be, like Reinhart, summoned three times before he presented himself before the court of Henry VI at Nuremberg because of the conflict that opposed him to the Emperor. This unjust king is perhaps still the same King Henry VI of whom historians report that he often allowed himself to be bribed, violated the law, and was the monarch whose word could not be trusted; who, spending too much time in Italy, did not often enough uphold justice in the Empire.

The Camel of Tuschalan and the Convent of Erstein

At the trial against Reinhart, the Camel of Tuschalan (lines 1,738–40) is the equivalent of the learned camel thought to represent, in the *Roman de Renart*, the papal legate of Pope Alexander III, Peter of Pavia. The word for camel in Middle High German *olbente* is a noun of the feminine gender. This character symbolises once again, by its proximity to the proper noun Tuschalan, the Italian policy of the Hohenstaufen and in particular, as in the previous case, the relations this policy had with the Roman policy, showing to what extent, in this era, the spiritual power of the *sacerdotium,* (Church), was in open conflict with the secular power of the *imperium,* (State).

Tuschalan, which is in fact Tusculum, an abreviation of Tusculanum (nowadays Frascati) is a symbol for the perpetual struggle by the Imperial party to keep the upper hand over the papacy, partly in the matter of electing the Pope, partly over papal temporal power and the danger with which it threatened in Italy the policy of the Imperial Hegemony. Thus, after the death of Adrian VI, the Imperial party, which was in a minority amongst the cardinals, elected, at the instigation of Frederick's Chancellor Rainald von Dassel, the Anti-Pope Octavian of the House of the Counts of Tusculum.

It is Tusculum, situated near Rome, that, in 1167, became the battleground between Imperial and Pontifical forces. Here Rainald von Dassel was besieged by Roman troops who wanted to thwart Barbarossa's campaign to get Alexander III out of Rome. Rainald von Dassel made a sortie with his troops on 29 May and routed the Roman army, although its troops were far more numerous. This was seen as a great victory and as the greatest military success of the Imperialists in Italy. It was a serious defeat for Rome, which was taken only two months later. However, fate soon undid Barbarossa's and Rainald's triumph: in the same year a plague epidemic decimated the German army and Rainald himself died of the plague.

Tusculum achieved sad fame under Henry VI. In order to overcome Pope Celestin III's hesitation to crown him Emperor, Henry, the young son of Barbarossa, did not hesitate to hand over to the Pope the town of Tusculum, although it had always been loyal to the Emperor. The Pope handed the town over to his troops who indulged in bloody carnage and utterly destroyed the town. Tuschalan does not only symbolise imperial aspirations to overcome the spiritual and secular power of the Pope, but also the perfidy of Henry VI who, like his father Barbarossa, abandoned his most faithful defenders and sacrificed them to the interests of the Empire in order to gain the support of the Pope.

On the eve of this treacherous handing over, 17 April 1191, Henry gave the Abbey of Erstein to Conrad von Huneburg, Bishop of Strasburg, as a gift of gratitude for the Bishop's help in Italy: the deed of gift was drawn up near Tusculum. These two facts appear together in *Reinhart Fuchs*: the fox proposes to Vrevel to give Erstein to the camel as a gift of thanks because the camel stayed on his side at the time of the siege. (lines 2,120–23), just as we assume that Philip von Heinsberg, the Archbishop of Cologne and Chancellor of the Empire, advised Henry VI to give Erstein to the Bishop of Strasburg. Erstein was a convent founded in 850 by Irmgart, wife of Lothar: it is situated south of Strasbourg on the River Ill. Empresses and ladies of the highest nobility stayed in this convent. Its special mission was to pray continously for the Emperor and the Empire. Heinrich knew that was so, for he has the fox say that this gift will bring about the saving of Vrevel's soul because very many prayers are said there (lines 2,124–25).

This gift was, just like the handing over of Tusculum, another act of treachery. By this same act Henry VI neither respected the election of the abbess by her sister nuns, nor the canonic investiture which only the Pope could confer. Its only aim was to enrich the bishop who supported the Empire just as the camel in our text is interested only in the wealth and benefices which are attached to the control of the abbey (lines 2,129–30 and 2,134–5). This is how Henry VI thanked the ladies of a convent entirely devoted to his cause. This act was annulled eleven months later, 4 March 1192, as illegal. Probably giving way to pressure from the convent, the Emperor took Erstein back from the Bishop of Strasburg. Again this is reflected in Heinrich's text: these ladies, skilful with their pens and in getting their grievances and humble petitons granted, slashed the camel's hide and pushed it as far as the banks of the Rhine (lines 2147–53).

The Elephant of Bohemia

The elephant is absent from those branches of the *Roman de Renart* which were Heinrich's direct source. It doubles the motif of the camel. Just as exotic as the camel, it is a stranger at the court, as in Branch XI, attributed by some scholars to the end of the twelfth century. Here the elephant belongs to the Saracen army led by the camel (lines 1,765–75) in the war against King Noble. To have done what was strictly right, as the camel said, and at the same time to have been of service to the fox, the elephant finds itself rewarded by Reinhart: he proposes to the king, that the elephant should be given a fief. Vrevel forces the elephant to accept Bohemia (lines 2,097–2,102), but when there, the elephant gets beaten up and is chased away by the inhabitants. Only its thick skin saves it from wounds and death (lines 2,109–16).

Here we have an ironical allusion to the numerous interventions of the Emperors in Bohemia at the frequent crises of succession that occurred in that country during the second half of the twelfth century. Although it is difficult to assert that we have to do here with Wladislaw II, Sobieslaw II, or Frederick of Bohemia, since the history of that country does not offer an episode that corresponds exactly to Heinrich's text, we are nevertheless inclined to see here an allusion to Sobieslaw II. Barbarossa had indeed put pressure on the latter to accept the ducal crown against Frederick, son of King Wladislaw. By order of Barbarossa, Sobieslaw had been freed from the prison of Pfraumberg in which he had spent thirteen years. This is probably reflected in line 2,207: he had arrived poor at court and now he has become a sovereign. A genial prince, he was chased from Bohemia in 1179 by a revolt of the high-ranking lords of the kingdom, and he died in January 1180.

Events like this fit well into the Italian policy of the Hohenstaufen. In fact, in exchange for his promotion, Sobieslaw and his younger brother had to promise Barbarossa to accompany him with an army into Lombardy. Tuschalan, Erstein, Bohemia, bishops chased away like thieves, all this recalls the foreign policy of the Hohenstaufen. By fitting the motif of the trial, an interior-policy motif, into the plot furnished by the destruction of the ant-hill and the liberation of the ants, an external-policy motif which forms both the beginning and the end of this part of the work, Heinrich skilfully underlines how closely politics within Germany were linked to politics in Italy, and how much German policy had to suffer on account of Italian policy.

The Leopard with the Plumed Helmet

Amongst the animals who, summoned by the lion Vrevel, come running to the royal tribunal, is the leopard who immediately attracts attention by the plumed helmet that he wears (line 1,338). In order to heal the sick king, Reinhart gets the idea of having a bath prepared for him. Vrevel gives the necessary order and the leopard has to resign himself to the job of fetching the bath-water without delay (lines 2,003–08). Rare at this time, the motif of the plumed helmet has always been associated with Richard the Lion Heart because of his second seal, created in 1195, which shows, in addition to the three leopards painted in gold on the shield, a helmet with plumes. In the same way in which this emblem identified Richard I, the leopard with the plumed helmet in *Reinhart Fuchs* seems to have been invented by Heinrich to make the King of England recognisable behind the animal that he had chosen as his emblem.

This leopard, choked with anger at being given the role of water-carrier, forced to bring the healing bath-water for the king, reminds us of Richard the Lion Heart who was forced to provide Henry VI with a huge ransom which Henry then used to conquer Apulia and Sicily. After Richard had left the Holy Land, he had been shipwrecked in the Adriatic and made prisoner in 1192 by men belonging to Leopold of Austria. On 23 March 1193 he was handed over to Henry VI who demanded a ransom of 100,000 marks for Richard's release. News of this infamy got quickly known in Europe and contributed to ruin the reputation of the Emperor. Under the pretext that the Emperor would not demand Richard's participation in the next expedition into Italy, another sum amounting to half the original sum was added to it, as well as the cost of fifty ships that Richard had to contribute to this same expedition. As early as November 1193 the whole ransom was amassed at Saint-Paul, and Imperial agents went there to see that all was fulfilled before taking it to Germany for the political well-being of Henry VI, just as the water brought by the leopard contributed to the healing of the lion Vrevel. The heavy and debasing service at court imposed on the leopard recalls Richard's captivity, thus completing the denunciation of Hohenstaufen policy, which is the very aim of Heinrich's work (Pastré 1994b).

Reinhart's Rise

After the fox's failure in his country of origin, the humbler nobles like the cock, the tit, the crow and the cat, know only too well the treacherous nature of their evil cousin. Reinhart then tried, in vain, to satisfy his ambition in the company of the high-ranking nobles of the kingdom. He made a pact with the wolf in which he proposed to add cunning to strength, a pact of mutual support (line 397). This motif was borrowed from a similar motif involving the cat Tibert in the *Roman de Renart*. Following this pact the fox immediately takes the initiative by saying that, with the help of Isengrin's strength, he could destroy a castle (line 401). This is the first time that the anthropomorphic theme of Reinhart's territorial ambition appears explicitly. This motif is an addition made by Heinrich.

Cheated by the wolves who devour the ham without him, Reinhart, the loser in this clash of interests between two feudal lords, will not rest until he has revenged himself for this insult, so he pursues the wolf and his wife with tenacious hostility. Isengrin, the unsuspecting lord, has indeed made the mistake of underrating the strength of one who is smaller (lines 1,304–05), and imprudently trusts him with his wife (1,417–18) thinking that there was no risk in his seizing the booty entirely for himself. The great feudal lord hoped in this way to profit without cost to himself from the services of the lesser noble of whom he quickly forgets both role and merits. This blindness of the high and mighty leads to their loss and to Reinhart's success. In the second part of the work, Reinhart has at best succeeded in winning for himself for a limited time the favours of a lady, the she-wolf; something which Heinrich saw as the courtly fashion of the time (lines 841–44). We can see here the symbol and at the same time the satire of the fulfilment of one of the two great ambitions of this German aristocracy, of these knights of the years around 1200, whose ideal was at the same time power and love, feudal benefices and a lady-love.

It is only at the time of the confrontation of the most powerful ones, of King Vrevel and the Master of the Ants that, in the third part of the work, Reinhart manages to satisfy his thirst for power. He transforms his part as the accused who has to appear before the court into a position of strength; he manages to isolate the monarch and at the same time to take his revenge on the little animals that he had not been able to deceive and who had accused him; and he manages to get rid of the big animals, those that he had ill-treated like the wolf, the bear and the cat; others, like the camel and the elephant, under the cover of a show of treacherous gratitude. Better still, he receives from the Master of the Ants countless castles as ransom (lines 2,060–84), symbols of feudal power. In this way he finally reached his goal, having become as powerful a lord as the great feudal lords whom he had just driven from court, – wrongful gain, since he acquires it by high treason, unknown to the king, by forming an alliance (lines 2,063–4) with the rebellious Master of the Ants. Reinhart can only hold on to his new possessions if the one who forced the ants under his dominion disappears, for his new power was given to him by the Master of the Ants. Thus Reinhart, who has isolated the king, as the frightened animals have fled from the court in wild haste, will be able to proceed towards the climax of his perfidy and make an attempt on his sovereign's life.

For that is the outcome of Heinrich's work, the death of an unjust king who has made an alliance with treachery and thus brought about the misery of his kingdom. In order to understand the significance of this outcome, we must remember that Branch X of the *Roman de Renart* (*Renart Médecin*) offers a similar outcome and yet, at the same time, a very different one. King Noble himself offers Renart land as a reward as well as two good castles (lines 1,669–76), and promises him help in case Renart's enemies attack him in his castle. Renart, however, remains in his den below ground for a long time in fear of retaliation from the animals that he had flayed alive (lines 1,701–04), just as Reinhart, his evil deed done, disappears in his den (line 2,218) whilst the animals pour out the direst threats against their King's assassin (lines 2,247–8). Apart from these points in common, the difference is considerable, for Heinrich substitutes for the alliance with the lion the murder of the lion and the alliance with his enemy, the Master of the Ants.

Is it paradoxical to see in Reinhart a feudal German lord who holds his fiefs in Italy? Beyond the chronological syncretism which lets us see in the lion Vrevel, both Barbarossa and his son Henry VI, we find the same polysemy for the persons who played a decisive role in the events at the side of the emperors. Still more than the Archbishop Rainald von Dassel, it seems that it is Philip of Cologne, his successor under Barbarossa and Henry VI, whom we may identify with the fox Reinhart. As we have seen, it was he who profited from the eviction of the schismatic bishops, who advised Henry VI in the matter of Erstein and of Tusculum, who was three times reprimanded, and had to make a solemn oath. Frederick I even had to intervene personally to stop him forming alliances with foreign powers. And, once more like the fox, this same Philip became the leader of the opposition and Frederick's enemy once Frederick had made him rich and powerful for the services he had rendered him.

The ambitions and the greed for riches of these two archchancellors, both having served their Emperors chiefly in Italy, were satisfied as well in Italy. For example, Rainald von Dassel received for his faithful services in Lombardy, a fief on the shores of the Ticino, Raga and Trunkiano. In 1190 Philip of Cologne received from Henry VI 900 marks in silver for having gone with him to Apulia. Or there was also Markward von Anweiler, a former *ministérial* (= a non-noble knight), friend and leader of the army of Henry VI, who became Margrave of Ancona, Duke of Romagnole and Ravenna, Count of the Abruzzi, while Philip Augustus of France offered him a fief in France. This is the oldest example of a fief given to a German by a foreign sovereign. Even the physician of Henry VI, Berard, was richly rewarded with land because he had saved the

Emperor's life before Naples. Henry VI even went so far as to give counties in Apulia to the assassins of the Archbishop of Liège. We see that it was quite common to satisfy the ambitions of the Imperials in Italy in this way. It was in Italy that the lesser nobility and the non-noble knights occupied the highest positions in the administration and not without extracting, once in office, countless favours. So one may imagine (although this remains a hypothesis) that Reinhart, cursed at court for the murder of the king, makes his fortune in foreign lands and makes it by treachery. Thus he would become the symbol for all those who profited from the great disorder caused by the Italian policy of the Hohenstaufen to enrich themselves and secure their positions of power. It remains a paradox that the king's death, made necessary for this kind of extortion and by historical expediency, was at the same time approved by Heinrich who blames Vrevel for having his faithful servants flayed and executed by the traitor Reinhart. Thus the fox becomes an instrument of divine punishment, and it is through the mockery of the punishment carried out by the rascal Reinhart that, at the end of his epic poem, Heinrich calls the lion's assassin 'the good Reinhart' (line 2,248).

The outcome of *Reinhart Fuchs* (Reinhart becomes powerful by an assassination that puts the seal on his alliance with a foreign power) reflects in its way the tendency to dramatise, which becomes noticeable in the *Roman de Renart* at the end of the twelfth century. In Branch Ia, probably composed in the 1190s, the antagonism between the fox and the lion, the vassal and the overlord, is already replaced by the antagonism between two vassals, the fox and the wolf. Renart, who is besieged in his castle-den Maupertuis, commits a capital crime by throwing a big stone on the lion's head and severely wounding him. The fox, who was the loser in the first branches, is now the winner, and feared by all the animals. The lion, decidedly the big loser in this branch, loses all moral stature by considering only his own interest, whereas the end raises Renart to the level of a myth, to the level of a 'superman', albeit of a diabolical nature. This branch, in which the attempt on the king's life terrifies the courtier-animals who dare not even pursue the fox, already indicates the logical outcome of a development towards a more and more powerful and treacherous fox.

In the same way, Branch XI (*Renart empereur*), composed according to Foulet between 1196 and 1200 (much the same time that *Reinhart Fuchs* was probably composed), marks a decisive stage in the growing tendency of the Reynardian storytellers to distance themselves more and more from telling just animal stories. Renart, a feudal baron, a great lord, bold and ambitious, brutal and without scruples, here becomes a conspirator of the kind typified by John Lackland who aspired to the throne of Richard the Lion Heart, at that time a prisoner of Henry VI in Germany: John Lackland trying to usurp the throne of his monarch in the war against their enemies, the Saracens.

In the second half of the thirteenth century, in the *Couronnement de Renart,* the fox will be proclaimed king with the approval of the dying king, Noble, carried off by Pride, Envy and *Renardie* (= cunning), a symbolic fable like Branch XI and *Reinhart Fuchs* because it depicts what could happen at the court of Flanders if law and order were not restored; a fable that castigates a world where the old virtues are dead, where egoistic ambition, treachery and hypocrisy triumph, and where the author, a moralist like Heinrich stands up in accordance with a well-established tradition against the vices of his century. And at the end of this same century, in *Renart le Nouvel*, Renart dreams of killing the king in order to mount his throne (lines 2,278–87), and Noble separates himself from God by forming an alliance with Renart; and then leaves his place to Renart who is crowned by Fortuna. *Renart le* Nouvel is a fable in which Jacquemart Giélee shows how the fox succeeds by his cunning in dominating the world: it is a cry of alarm, as was *Reinhart Fuchs,* to rouse the world to beware of the evil that corrupts the times.

It is the literary and satirical outlook of the moralist which governs the adventurous career of Reinhart, a cynical little lord, ambitious and unscrupulous who, at the risk of losing his life tries, at first in vain, then with success, to quench an inextinguishable thirst for power, exploiting one after the other family ties, courtliness, religion, medicine, until he reaches his goal. As a courtier, Reinhart could well represent that social group which, in Germany, supplanted the old aristocracy of Germanic conquerors, a caricature of those errant knights in search of goodness and honour, and whose new culture was courtliness. Reinhart would be the satirical mirror-image of a certain German aristocracy whose rise corresponds to the cultural flourishing of the years 1180 to 1200.

As one who became powerful by high treason and capital crime, who was present at the destruction of the ant-hill and then cunningly knew how to exploit the situation, Reinhart certainly incarnates those who unscrupulously took advantage of the great upheaval caused by the grand Italian dream of the Hohenstaufen. *Reinhart Fuchs* provides us with a historical dimension which this work, short as it is, does not lead us to imagine at first glance.

This work is characterised by what one might call historical syncretism which makes out of an ant-hill at one and the same time the fortress of Girbaden and the great town of Milan; of King Vrevel, Barbarossa and Henry VI; of the fox, Rainald von Dassel and Philip von Cologne. Heinrich used a method that is always functional to represent something other than what the historian aims at; he aims rather, behind the mask of animal fables and stories, to convey the views of an Alsatian moralist determined to anchor a story which he borowed from France on to the Empire and into his own time.

CHAPTER 4

MEDIEVAL FRENCH AND DUTCH RENARDIAN EPICS: BETWEEN LITERATURE AND SOCIETY

Paul Wackers

Nowadays among scholars the opinion is generally accepted that medieval literary texts can be read as witnesses for the social conditions in which they were written.[1] This then should also be the case for the Beast Epic, but trying to read texts from this corpus in this way raises difficulties. Firstly, for most Beast Epics we only know approximately where and when they came into being, therefore we do not know for whom they were originally intended. Secondly, the Beast Epic mirrors its social context only indirectly. The protagonists are not humans, but animals who behave like humans. I shall try to demonstrate that it is nevertheless possible to analyse the Beast Epic as testimony of certain mental attitudes and qualities, but that this must be done in an indirect way: by analysing the intertextual relationships of the chosen texts first, and by using the results of that analysis as arguments in a sketch of the social context afterwards. As examples I shall use some branches of the *Roman de Renart* and the Middle Dutch Beast Epics *Van den Vos Reynaerde* and *Reynaerts Historie*.

The *Roman de Renart* consists of a number of short to middle-length stories which tell of the fox Renart and his adventures with individual animals, but mainly about his quarrels with the court of the king, the lion Noble.[2] We know these stories from fourteen manuscripts and about ten fragments, each of which contains its own selection from the whole body of stories (Varty 1988: 1–7).

Probably the oldest branch is Branch II.[3] This is a kind of a little anthology of Renart stories. The first part of the branch tells about encounters between the fox and (i) Chantecler the cockerel, (ii) an anonymous titmouse, (iii) Tibert the tomcat and (iv) Tiecelin the crow. These four adventures probably existed first as single stories, probably orally told, and they were joined by parallel structures and through internal cross-references, etc.

Let us first consider the last two adventures (lines 654–842 and 843–1,026).[4] When Renart meets Tibert he is in a very grumbly mood, for he has not eaten all day. But he does not dare to challenge the cat because Tibert is strong and well armed with teeth and claws. He asks Tibert to assist him in his fight with Isengrin the wolf. Tibert swears to serve Renart faithfully, as a vassal should. But Renart has not abandoned his evil intentions. He has seen a trap just before meeting Tibert. Now he suggests a race to pass the time. Tibert agrees. Renart invites Tibert to run as fast as possible in the direction of the trap. Tibert senses the danger and swerves at the last minute. Renart tries a second time, but now Tibert jumps over the trap. Then two hunting dogs arrive and drive both animals again in the direction of the trap. When the fox wants to avoid it, the cat pushes him and throws him into the trap where Renart is eventually mauled by the dogs and attacked by their master, but finally escapes.

The author makes this a comical story by exploiting the chivalrous concept of comradeship between knights. In the French war epics (*Chansons de geste*) knights often swear to each other faithful assistance. The phrases which the author uses to describe the alliance between Renart and Tibert are very similar to the ones used in the *Chansons de geste*. But the basis of this alliance is totally different from the one between knights. In the *Chansons de geste* brothers-in-arms are absolutely faithful to each other. Here both have bad intentions. Renart uses the promise of faithful assistance in order to placate a potentially dangerous enemy, but he nevertheless tries as hard as he can to harm him. Tibert never trusts Renart and tricks him when he has a chance.

The relationship between Branch II and the *Chansons de geste* is emphasised by the use of metaphorical language. The race between the two animals is described like a horse-race.

There are moments when one cannot tell whether the narrative is about a racing animal or a knight on horseback. In the description of this race the author uses again vocabulary from the *Chansons de geste*.

So we have here a parody of certain elements found in serious literature. There are two possible causes for this. Either the author of Branch II wants to criticise a particular aspect of chivalry, or he wants to make fun of the concept of the bond between knights in literature as a whole. Scholars do not agree as to which of these two possibilities is the more likely one.

The fourth adventure, Renart and Tiecelin, is a variant of the well-known fable of the Fox and the Crow. It opens with a description of Tiecelin's taking of a cheese from an old woman. This description resembles that of a knight going into battle and making a prisoner – another allusion to the literature of chivalry. The crow holds the cheese between a branch of a tree and one of his claws and feeds from it. Small pieces of cheese fall onto Renart who is lying under the tree. Renart flatters Tiecelin and begs him to sing. He urges him on to exert himself until the crow drops the cheese. But now, different from the fable, the story continues. Renart does not take the cheese. He even complains that its bad smell is making him feel ill. He has a bad wound (from the Tibert adventure), and as everybody knows, a strong smell is bad for wounds. 'Please Tiecelin, take it away. I would do it myself if I were not so weak.' Tiecelin believes the flatterer and flies down from the tree. Renart jumps at him but gets only four feathers, and Tiecelin escapes. Renart keeps only the cheese.

Besides the links with the literature of chivalry, this 'fable' mainly alludes to other animal stories. As already mentioned, it is a variant of (even in the Middle Ages) a very well-known fable. The audience is expecting the usual ending: the fox gets the cheese. It looks as if this expectation is not to be fulfilled, but then, at the end, it is. Furthermore, this story is a variant of the first story in Branch II, the meeting between Chantecler and Renart (lines 23–463). Chantecler is also tricked through flattery. Here Renart manages to seize him, but during the fox's return home Chantecler uses a similar trick against Renart, and the cock escapes. Renart has troubled himself for nothing. Here Tiecelin escapes as well, but Renart at least keeps the cheese. In this way we are offered variations on the theme of trickery. One could even say that all four stories of the first part are variations on this theme, but to demonstrate that would lead too far from my main argument.

These variations on and allusions to other literature show that Branch II is meant to be compared with other texts. In fact we find allusions to other literary genres and topics right at its beginning. In the prologue we read:

> My lords, you have heard many a tale from many a story-teller: how Paris carried off Helen to his great trouble and woe, La Chèvre's splendid story of Tristan, various fabliaux and chansons de geste; and many another goes around the country telling the romance of Yvain and his beast. But you have never heard of the great, grim war between Reynard and Isengrin that they waged so long and bitterly. The fact is that there was never any love lost between these two lords; but to tell you the truth, they often engaged in fights and brawls... (lines 1–17; Owen 1994: 53)

This prologue is difficult to interpret. For instance, we do not know whether 'La Chèvre' is the name of an author or whether it is saying something about Tristan himself (Lodge 1983). But whatever the problems of interpretation, what matters for my argument is the fact that this prologue places the following Renart adventures in relation to other literary texts; to the Matter of Troy (Paris and Helen), to the Tristan legends, to the *Fabliaux*, and the *Chansons de geste*. Right from the beginning, this text is seen to be a reaction to other texts, or their mirror-image. It is important to keep this in mind.

Another reason to quote this prologue is the fact that it points to the chief topic of the *Roman de Renart*: the hostility between fox and wolf. The reason for this hostility is the adultery between the fox and the she-wolf. This topic is introduced in the second part of Branch II (lines 1,025–1,396; Owen 1994: 67–72). Here we find two scenes centred on the fox and the she-wolf. In the first scene the fox gets inadvertently into the wolf's den. He is afraid of the she-wolf who makes fun of him and asks why he had not visited her sooner. He answers that he did not dare to because the wolf was telling all and sundry that he, the fox, had an eye on his wife and that he intended to beat him up for it. The she-wolf gets angry. If she is being accused, they might as well take advantage of the situation, so she invites the fox for a romp. This is without doubt adultery. A few days later the she-wolf and the wolf meet the fox, and chase him. The she-wolf is faster than the wolf. The fox dashes into his den. The she-wolf tries to follow, but is too big for the entrance, and gets stuck. The fox emerges from his den by another exit and rapes the she-wolf before the very eyes of the wolf just as he arrives on the scene.

Again and again these two scenes are alluded to in subsequent branches. The problem is that the wolf can rightly make the accusation that his wife has been raped; but he remains a cuckold. This part-serious, part-comic matter is again and again treated, most often in the form of a trial (Varty 1984; Varty 1986).

Two of these trials are important in my argument: the one in Branch Va which is thought to have originally belonged to Branch II, and the one in Branch I, the most famous and the most popular branch. In both trials the action follows fairly accurately the procedure of trials in France at that time. But we also find mockery and ironic treatment of legal procedures, especially in Branch Va where a papal legate arrives, a camel from Lombardy. This camel speaks a strange linguistic mixture:

> Wherefore, sire give me audition! By us is found in the Decretal scribed under the rubric published anent violation of marriage, that, primo, by you shall be examined the accused, who, if incapable of exculpation, may suffer punition by you ad libitum, inasmuch as his act was gravely peccable. My verdict is quod sequitur: if he lack volition to render quid pro quo whereby his wherwithal shall in totality suffer public sequestration, then let the said diabolical Reynard undergo lapidation or incineration in persona! Exhibit then your regality nulli secundus: should some party infract or bring into disrepute the law, then let him yield repuration in extremo (lines 457–74, Owen 1994: 95).

The main topic in these two branches lies not in the domain of legal matters, but in the theme of love. In Branch Va the trial resembles that of a *cour d'amour* and one finds casuistry much as in questions about courtly love. For instance, the king answers the question of what exactly has to be judged in the following way: 'whether he who is smitten by love should be found guilty of the act which has brought contempt on his companion' (lines 501–04; Owen 1994: 95). And he says to the wolf: 'that Reynard loved her [= the she-wolf] mitigates his sin to some extent, since he deceived out of love. He is certainly a noble, distinguished person' (lines 436–9; Owen 1994: 94).

In Branch I we find a parallel to the trial in the Tristan story. Isolda has to submit to divine judgement, because she has been accused of adultery with Tristan, the nephew of her husband, King Mark. The accusation is well founded. In order to reach the place of judgement, Isolda must cross a small stream. Tristan, disguised as a beggar, is waiting there. She asks him to carry her across so that she does not get wet. He does this, but intentionally stumbles when he reaches the other shore, and falls on top of Isolda. Everybody witnesses this small accident. When Isolda makes her oath of innocence she says that she has never lain in the arms of another man but her husband's and the beggar's. The divine judgement speaks for her and everyone believes in her innocence.

At the centre of this story is the wording of the oath. By means of the trick of Tristan's disguise as a beggar, Isolda can swear something that is true and yet does not contradict the rightful accusation, although it seems to do so. But only two people know this, the two lovers. In Branch I there is also a play with the wording of the oath. When Hersent the she-wolf defends herself, she uses the following phrases: 'Reynard never did anything to me he wouldn't have done to his mother' (lines 149–50; Owen 1994: 7). And: 'never have I personally indulged in any more lechery, wickedness, or wantonness than a nun might commit' (lines 176–9; Owen 1994: 7). Here also the words are ambiguous. They are meant to underline Hersent's innocence but because there is no guarantee at all that Renart has treated his mother only honourably and because every nun is able to be lecherous, wanton or wicked (although she should not be), their effect on the public is contrary. In fact they emphasise Hersent's adultery.

I have shown that in these two trials the *Roman de Renart* hints at other literature, and only indirectly at the social conditions of the time in which it was composed. It is important to state that this kind of literature can only function when the audience is sufficiently knowledgeable about other literary texts to pick up and decode the given signals.

Let us now look at the Beast Epic in the Dutch tradition. In Middle Dutch we have two Reynaert stories. The first, *Van den Vos Reynaerde*, was written in the middle of the thirteenth century and is a reworking of Branch I with a new ending.[5] The second, *Reynaerts Historie*, was written about 1400.[6] This later version follows *Van den Vos Reynaerde* very closely but changes the end in order to tell about another confrontation between Reynaert and Nobel's court. *Reynaerts Historie* is the basis for the later European Reynard tradition (Menke 1992). If you know Goethe's *Reineke Fuchs*, the Low German *Reynke de Vos* or Caxton's *Reynard the Fox*, then you know the story of *Reynaerts Historie*.

Let us start with the older text, *Van den Vos Reynaerde*. There we find, as in the *Roman de Renart*, allusions to other literary texts. For instance the big court day at the beginning mirrors the traditional beginning of many Arthurian stories (Van Daele 1994: 281-3). Also, the scene in which the bear Bruun is ill-treated by the villagers contains allusions to battle-scenes in chivalrous romances (Knapp 1982). These allusions, however, are more global than in the *Roman de Renart*. They do not point to one concrete text but to genres in general. This means the audience does not need such a large and precise literary knowledge to appreciate the fun (Bouwman 1991b; Van Daele 1994).

In addition to that, the author of *Van den Vos Reynaerde* tries his best to tell a story that can stand up entirely on its own. It has a much stronger inner coherence than the different branches of the *Roman de Renart*. This becomes very obvious when one compares *Van den Vos Reynaerde* with Branch I, of which it is a reworking. Both stories begin with a big assembly at the royal court. Complaints about Renart/Reynaert are laid before the court. These are contradicted, but the dead body of Reynaert's last victim is abundant proof of his wickedness. Three times Renart/Reynaert is summoned to court. He obeys the third summons to face the complaints made against him, and is sentenced to death.

Branch I then tells how Renart was surrounded by the other animals and mistreated. Following an emotional supplication by Grimbert the badger, the king suddenly changes his mind and sends Renart on a pilgrimage (or crusade, the text is ambiguous here) to the Holy Land. No reason is given for this decision. It comes unexpectedly and gives a new direction to the narrative.

In *Van den Vos Reynaerde* the story runs quite differently after the death sentence. Reynaert begs to be allowed to make a public confession before his execution. In this confession he mentions a treasure and states that the treasure was to be used to finance a conspiracy against the king. He (Reynaert), so he says, has spoiled the plot by stealing the treasure. The conspirators were partly his relatives, partly his enemies: the bear, the wolf and the tom-cat. The king wants to have the treasure, so he pardons Reynaert. And because of the accusations the king also has Reynaert's enemies arrested and ill-treated. All phases of the story are clearly linked, and one builds upon the other. In this way *Van den Vos Reynaerde* has much more in common with modern stories than with the branches of the *Roman de Renart*. Explaining this difference in literary structure, and the aesthetic concept that goes with it, is difficult. Important for my present argument is the fact that the audience did not need any prior literary knowledge to follow the whole story and to appreciate it.

This is also obvious in the fable of the frogs who want to have a king (vv. 2,299–2,322). As mentioned above, the fourth story of Branch II was a variant of the fable of the fox, the crow and the cheese. This variant is not explicitly pointed out; the prior knowledge of the audience is assumed and played upon. In *Van den Vos Reynaerde* the fable of the frogs resembles the same fable in the *Esopet*, the first collection of fables in medieval Dutch literature.[7] The audience is informed why this fable is being told. Reynaert needs it in his confession to explain why he does not want Bruun the bear to become king instead of Nobel, which is what the conspirators want. Reynaert compares Bruun with the stork, who is the frog's king and who gobbles them up. Who wants such a king? The audience clearly needs no prior knowledge to understand this fable and its application.

These examples make clear that the author of *Van den Vos Reynaerde* does not expect any prior knowledge in his audience, and refers to other literature much less than the authors of the branches of the *Roman de Renart*.[8] However, this does not mean that he expected no foreknowledge at all. In legal matters, for instance, *Van den Vos Reynaerde* goes further than its source (Bouwman 1991b: 397–402). We have mentioned already that the legal procedures in Branches Va and I are similar to a *cour d'amour*. These similarities have been omitted in *Van den Vos Reynaerde*. On the other hand, some details, reflecting the actual legal practice of the thirteenth century, have been added. These additions are mainly in the first part of the narrative. The effect is that the complaints against the fox are treated more fully than in the French source, in particular the hearing of witnesses; hearing that inevitably leads to legal proceedings against the fox. A second effect of this alteration is that the relation between the king and his barons (i.e., his advisers) is much more important. At every legal step the king asks for the advice of his barons and follows it. In Branch I the king decides that Renart be summoned to court and he chooses the three messagers to carry the summons. In *Van den Vos Reynaerde* all this happens following the advice of the barons. The feudal bond between a lord and his vassals is emphasised. This feudal harmony, however, gets threatened in the course of the narrative. When Reynaert talks about the treasure, the narrator says: 'The king and the queen, both hoping for gain, took Reynaert apart for consultation' (lines

2,491–93). This is the first time that the king does not act publicly but separately from his court. It is also the first time that he does not allow himself to be advised but acts independently. The author uses here the expression *te rade* (in consultation) to describe the discussion between king, queen and Reynaert. Previously, the author used this expression only when the king was holding counsel with his barons. From this point onwards the king isolates himself more and more until nothing is left of the harmony between feudal lord and vassal. The two most important ones, bear and wolf, will be arrested and mutilated at the king's command, urged on by Reynaert.

This shows that the alterations made in the domain of the law were intentional. They strengthen the importance of the feudal bond between lord and vassal in the narrative. Here *Van den Vos Reynaerde* deviates noticeably from its source. Signals given to the audience in legal matters are always minor details, short informative phrases, the use of fixed formulae, etc. This implies that the audience was well acquainted with legal procedures, otherwise these signals would not have worked.

The *Roman de Renart* and *Van den Vos Reynaerde* differ in the number and kind of literary allusions. How about the other Middle Dutch Reynardian epic? Here the situation is different yet again. Compared with *Van den Vos Reynaerde*, *Reynaerts Historie* points frequently to other literary texts. In this way it resembles the *Roman de Renart*. But In the *Roman de Renart* many of these allusions are implied; the audience must work out the link for itself. In *Reynaerts Historie*, allusions to another text are always fully explained. Thus we find references to important authors or texts, for instance: 'Seneca speaks to us: "a lord must everywhere do full justice"' (lines 4,757–58), or 'Mark what is written in the Gospel: *estote misericordes*, i.e. be merciful. And it also says: *nolite iudicare et non iudicabimini*, i.e. Judge not, lest ye be judged' (lines 4,777–84). We find here an accurate quotation from Luke 6: 36–37, in Latin and in the vernacular. It is used to refer to the highest possible authority. In cases like this the audience is to recognise the authority as such, but that is all. The text itself explains the meaning of the quoted authority.

The same pattern exists when not just a quotation but a sizeable part of another text is referred to (Wackers 1986: 100–120). Very often in such cases a short summary is given. In this way the story of the adulterous woman is briefly told (John 8: 1–11; lines 4,785–93), also the judgement of Paris with information of prior events and consequences (lines

5,499–5,563); and, finally, a part of Adenet li Roi's *Cleomades* (lines 5,591–5,627). The material used is very varied: Bible, classical and courtly literature. The fact that all allusions are explained suggests that no prior knowledge was expected from the audience.

This does not mean that the audience could accept the narrated stories uncritically. The quoting of authorities and the summarising of other texts is not done by the author but by protagonists in the narrative. They quote with ulterior motives. The authorities that I mentioned and the story of the adulterous woman are used by the she-ape Rukenau, an aunt of Reynaert, when she defends him before the king. She uses several arguments, one of them being that no one is without sin, and that this should be the reason for negating the mistakes made by others (i.e. Reynaert), or for forgiving them. Morally this is a praiseworthy attitude in private life, but as a part of a legal investigation, as it is here, it is of questionable validity. Whoever adopts this attitude wholeheartedly must abolish all penal jurisdiction. That is not Rukenau's intention. All she wants to achieve is lenient treatment for her nephew, if not an acquittal. Reynaert himself tells the story of the judgement of Paris and the adventure of the flying horse from *Cleomades*. The context is as follows: the king accuses him of having sent him a bag containing the head of Kuwaert the hare. The king assumes (and rightly so) that Reynaert has killed Kuwaert. Reynaert says, however, that he did indeed send a bag to the king, but that it contained three jewels: a ring, a comb and a mirror. That is a lie. To make it convincing he describes the jewels in minute detail. Surely only someone who has owned these things could describe them in such detail. Reynaert says that the judgement of Paris was depicted as decoration on the comb. The wood of the mirror frame, so says Reynaert, was similar to the wood of which the flying horse was made on which Cleomades rode during some of his adventures. Reynaert then gives a short version of these adventures. He uses these stories to impress the animals at court. The audience of *Reynaerts Historie* was expected to detect Reynaert's intention.

The situation here is completely different from the one in the *Roman de Renart*. There, the author alluded either directly in his narrative, or via speeches of the animals, to other literary texts. The audience is to recognise the allusion and to interpret it. The author's intention is to achieve a comical and ironical effect. In *Reynaerts Historie* allusions to other texts are always explained.

They are given by the animals in the story, and are always accompanied by a moral. This becomes most obvious when Reynaert describes the decoration of the mirror (lines 5,633–5,881). This consists of four illustrated fable situations. Reynaert relates all four and always adds a moral. All four morals aim at actual situations at court. What the audience of *Reynaerts Historie* must see is that the protagonists misunderstand the offered morals in the way the narrator intended them to. The author's intention is not to allude to other texts but to give meaning to his own story (Wackers 1986: 216–27).

I have shown how, in three different Beast Epics, allusions to other (mostly literary) texts are employed in three different ways. Hence it is clear that Reynaert has to do with literature. But how about his link with society? This becomes relevant when one tries to explain the differences.

Most *Roman de Renart* research published in the last ten years deals with the intertextuality of one or several stories, or with traces of an oral tradition, or with the way it was presented. Research into the nature of the audience for these texts, or about the social context of the extant manuscripts has hardly been undertaken. What now follows is based on my own observations and hypotheses, using the scanty material available.

In the most recent investigations about the likely audience for the *Roman de Renart*, the consensus is that the audience was aristocratic.[9] This argument is based mostly on the nature of the texts. References like the one to the Tristan story in Branches II and Va can only be meaningful to an audience that is well acquainted with these stories (Regalado 1976). It is generally assumed that the Tristan story was meant for an aristocratic audience. Therefore the same must be the case for the Renart stories. This makes sense to me. I believe an examination of the manuscripts, even if they do not represent the oldest form of the story of the *Roman de Renart*, would provide additional arguments for this hypothesis. Several manuscripts have numerous miniatures and many of them are valuable and of high quality. But, as I have already pointed out, there is as yet no published research about this aspect of the manuscripts.

The aristocratic courtly culture is essentially a play-acting culture with which an élite aimed to distinguish itself from the ordinary society by way of a consciously stylised lifestyle. (Van Oostrom 1992: esp. ch. 3). This stylisation of life can take various forms, but all of them are the result of a mentality that aims to impose beauty, luxury and pleasure on to the ordinary reality of life. Courtly literature is a part of this courtly lifestyle (country bumpkins cannot appreciate it). It is the mirror of courtly life (its heroes give good examples; they represent the ideal of the world of chivalry). And sometimes it even questions the courtly ideal. This questioning can take different forms. One can think of texts which mock, but there is no need to go so far. In the vast corpus of the prose *Lancelot* texts, it is remarkable that even the greatest heroes offend sometimes (slightly) against courtly etiquette. That does not make their behaviour at large less exemplary; it only makes them more human.

I think we must see the texts of the *Roman de Renart* in this perspective. They relate to classical courtly texts and they play with them. Traditional formulas, scenes and events of courtly literature are now represented by animals. These scenes and events are thus rendered ironically. That is not to say that the *Roman de Renart* is void of serious intentions. If extra-marital courtly love is represented as animal-lust, if the bond between knights is depicted as a means to betray a brother-in-arms, or if knightly bravery is depicted as a means to pursue egotistical aims, then this points to criticism of some aspects of the courtly life. And it was, of course, unavoidable that real life in the France of the twelfth and thirteenth centuries would seem to be wanting when compared with the courtly ideal. The texts of the *Roman de Renart* show an awareness of this, and in that sense they are perfectly serious. But this serious attention is surrounded by an astonishing amount of playful elements. The frequency of allusions to literary sources is much greater than the frequency with which their moral or social content is questioned (Scheidegger 1989). If we look at the *Roman de Renart* as a whole, we are surprised by the nature and quality of the in-breeding in the later branches. These are hardly more than variants of earlier themes, and their character as variants nearly always dominates all possible moral criticism. To sum up, we can say that the playful elements are very much in the foreground. In this way the *Roman de Renart* resembles numerous other literary texts in the same social context.

There is little certainty as to the social context of *Van den Vos Reynaerde*.[10] A considerable amount of research has been dedicated to questions of origin and reception, but reliable evidence is lacking. All researchers agree that the text was composed in Flanders, and of late most researchers date it in the middle of the thirteenth century. At this time, and moreover during the whole of the thirteenth century, the court of the Flemish counts played an important role as a centre for French literature. For example: Chrétien de Troyes begins his *Perceval* following a commission from Philip of Alsace; Gwide of Dampierre employs Adenet li Roi (mentioned above); and the *Couronnement de Renart*, a later French Renart text, was written in memory of William of Dampierre. There is a lot of evidence that the high Flemish aristocracy used French as a common language. For whom then were all the texts written in Flemish? *Van den Vos Reynaerde* was by no means the only Flemish text from this century (Besamusca 1991; Janssens 1992; Janssens 1994).

Most often it is assumed that the audience for these texts was composed of the patricians who lived in Flemish towns which, in the thirteenth century, were (because of an economic boom) already a considerable political power. The patricians used French in commerce and dealings with the court of the Flemish counts, but in daily life, amongst themselves, they spoke Flemish. If this hypothesis is correct we have here a very cultured audience, but one that took considerably less part in the life at court than did the audience of the *Roman de Renart*. The observations I made in connection with *Van den Vos Reynaerde* fit well into this hypothesis. The text presupposes much less literary knowledge than the *Roman de Renart*, and is much less playful. (This does not mean that the text is not funny; in fact it is often very funny, but the comical elements do not need comparisons with other literary texts.) On the other hand, the text has more educational and moralising tendencies. In this regard there is a link between *Van den Vos Reynaerde* and *Lantsloot vander Haghedochte* (Van Oostrom 1981; Janssens 1994). The latter is a Flemish adaptation of the French prose *Lancelot*. Surprisingly, this Flemish text is in verse, so it does not follow the innovatory prose form of its source. It is also noticeable that in the Flemish version the courtly character of the action is very much emphasised. What is implicit in the source becomes explicit in the reworking; small deviations from the norm are systematically retouched. This is explained by pointing out that the audience of the *Lancelot* was so well acquainted with the rules of courtly life that the author was free to let his characters behave naturally, whereas the audience of the *Lansloot* was much less knowledgeable about the rules of courtly life and needed more precise examples and explanations about courtly rules and ideals. In *Van den Vos Reynaerde* we find a similar phenomenon. The text is not so much concerned with a greater idealisation but with the wish to explain, clarify, and develop the conflict found in its source.

So far the model I have presented seems convincing, but it is not without problems. How did the patricians come by their French sources? Did they have to borrow them from their aristocratic acquaintances? Or did they fetch them from France and if so, from whom? And why did they commission the creation of Flemish adaptations if they understood French? An imitation of the way of life at court could have been done as well while using French.

And there are some indications that there might have been some interest in Flemish texts in the circles around the count after all. We know that some scribes at court wrote in French but also in Flemish. Some of these latter manuscripts have been preserved. There are also more specific literary indications. The so-called Yale manuscript of the prose *Lancelot* was probably in the possession of one of the sons of Gwide of Dampierre. In this manuscript there is a marginal drawing (on fol. 133v; see figure 4.1) depicting a fox which is holding a hare between its forepaws (Bouwman 1991a: 52–53). The hare has a book in its hand. This picture refers most probably to a scene from *Van den Vos Reynaerde* in which the fox wants to teach the hare to read the Credo, and in which this particular posture is described. This scene does not exist in any French Renart text. The same picture is also in two Latin Psalters of which one probably belonged to Gwide of Dampierre himself (see figure 4.2). This suggests that the court of the Counts of Flanders probably knew the Flemish Reynaert story.

Also the emphasis on the topic of feudalism in *Van den Vos Reynaerde* as compared with its source could point in the same direction. During the thirteenth century the relation between the French king and his vassals deteriorated continually. The way the relation between Nobel and his vassals is treated in *Van den Vos Reynaerde* could reflect this state of affairs. The very ambiguous reconciliation between Nobel and his vassals at the end of the story seems to me to be especially meaningful in this connection. This scene has never been satisfactorily interpreted (Van Daele 1996).

Generally speaking, the encouragement of literature in the vernacular could have been a way of stimulating national feeling. The dukes of Brabant certainly worked consciously towards that end during the fourteenth century. Much more research is needed about the relation between French and Dutch literature in Flanders in the thirteenth century if one

Figure 4.1 *Reynaert teaching Kuwaert the hare the Creed. Marginal illustration in a* Lancelot *manuscript. Yale 229, f. 133v. (Randall 1966, fig. 195)*

Figure 4.2 *Reynaert teaching Kuwaert the hare the Creed. Marginal illustration in a Latin psalter, probably owned by Gwide of Dampierre, Brussels, Royal Library, 10607, f. 86r. (Randall, 1966, fig. 194).*

wants to have precise ideas about the link between the contents of *Van den Vos Reynaerde* and the political problems of the counts. More research is also necessary on the possible role of the counts as patrons of Flemish literature. These thoughts are therefore only suggestions. But they show, in any event, that the social context of *Van den Vos Reynaerde* is different from that of the *Roman de Renart*.

With *Reynaerts Historie* the situation is again quite different. There are hardly any points at which one could link the text to a specific social context. For the time being any dating other than about 1400 is impossible and, although there is an acrostic in the text referring to the Flemish town Diksmuide, the meaning of this reference is as yet unclear (Berteloot 1988; Berteloot 1993). Paradoxically, the social conditions reflected in the text can be quite clearly described. We see in the whole of Europe in the thirteenth and fourteenth centuries that the structure of feudalism is being replaced by the gradual forming of nations and that this development is accompanied by the increasingly powerful and ever-growing class of administrators (Murray 1978). These administrators were recruited from intellectual circles, men who had either studied law or the arts. At the same time a money market develops: a considerable part of this money is handled at some time or another by these administrators. This development was not gladly received by everybody. There were numerous complaints about bad advisers of princes who did not work for the honour of their master but rather for their own advantage. *Reynaerts Historie* fits exactly into this context (Wackers 1986: 73–86).

We have already shown that the protagonists in *Reynaerts Historie* misuse their erudition. They use their knowledge for their own advantage. The text as a whole shows this even better. Furthermore, the author himself puts this into words in the epilogue as part of the message of his text. This makes it evident that there is a connection between the social development that is taking place all over Europe and the contents of *Reynaerts Historie*.

This does not help us to arrive at a clear view of the original audience of *Reynaerts Historie*. This view is further obscured because we do not know what the author expects from his audience. I have already mentioned that the audience had to discover for themselves the misuse of knowledge by the story's protagonists. The question whether this knowledge itself was expected from the audience remains open. It is not necessarily so. The audience can follow the story and understand the message in the epilogue without having the same information that the protagonists have. But the protagonist's knowledge has noteworthy peculiarities. When Reynaert speaks about the judgement of Paris he describes it as an unusually positive event. This is particularly remarkable because all other medieval descriptions of this judgement known to me are decidedly negative. Either it is described as the starting point of the Trojan war which led to the destruction of the first city ever known, or it is pointed out that Paris opted for a life of lasciviousness instead of reason and contemplation. Hence there is something suspicious about Reynaert's knowledge, just as there is about the use he makes of it (Wackers 1986: 199–202). I believe this suggests that the audience understood this and was therefore sufficiently learned to do so. This means the text functioned within the élite, that it was intended for people who experienced in reality the problems described in the text's fictional world. However, we do not have to exclude a much less knowledgeable audience. In this case one would think of people who had to do with government and administration. For them the story would contain the criticism of an outsider of the goings-on in the centres of power.

I have tried to show with three examples that it is possible to reconstruct at least approximately the *social* context of animal stories by means of studying their *literary* context. In the cases of the *Roman de Renart* and *Reynaerts Historie* this was obvious; in *Van den Vos Reynaerde* perhaps less so. But there most of my comments are based on comparisons of *Van den Vos Reynaerde* and its source, Branch I of the *Roman de Renart*, so in this case too Reynaert stands halfway between literature and society. I realise that all this contains many uncertainties and hypotheses, but I hope to have demonstrated that the old Dutch proverb 'Two see more than one' has to be altered for a medievalist into 'In two (texts) one sees more than in one' (Van Oostrom 1984a: 30).

Notes

1. This chapter is a slightly adapted translation of an article originally published in German: P. Wackers, 'Reynaert-Erzählungen zwischen Literatur und Gesellschaft', *Zentrum für Niederlande-Studien, Jahrbuch* 4 (1993): 145–63.
2. See as an introduction to the *Roman de Renart* Flinn (1963). A useful edition is Dufournet and Méline (1985). Translations of the most famous

branches are Terry (1992) and Owen (1994). An indispensable guide to the research on the *Roman de Renart* and its tradition is Varty (1998).
3. The numbering of the branches is not based on their chronology, but on their order in the first scholarly edition: Martin (1882–87). Martin based his numbers mainly on the order of branches in his primary manuscript. Cf. Flinn (1963: 10–19) and especially Varty (1998: 1–7). For Branch II see Owen (1994: 53–72) and Dufournet and Méline (1985: vol. I, 208–79). My remarks on this branch are based on Varty (1985) and on Lodge and Varty (1989).
4. Line references in my text are to Dufournet and Méline (1985); quotations are taken from Owen (1994).
5. The standard edition is Hellinga (1952). The best study edition is Lulofs (1983), line references are to this edition. An English translation can be found in Colledge (1967). The most recent books on the text are Bouwman (1991b) and Van Daele (1994). On the relations between Branch I and *Van den Vos Reynaerde* see Bouwman (1990) and on the relations between these two texts and *Reynaerts Historie* see Wackers (1998).
6. The text has been edited in Hellinga (1952) as Ms B (line references are to this edition). See also Goossens (1983b). The most recent book on this text is Wackers (1986). Cf. also the first two sections of chapter five in this book.
7. For the *Esopet* see Stuiveling (1965): esp. I, 31. Cf. Wackers (1981: 463–5) and Bouwman (1991b: 256–61).
8. For a different point of view see Besamusca (1996).
9. See Scheidegger (1989: 293–304 and 361–87) and the literature mentioned in the notes on those pages.
10. The whole discussion of the social context of *Van den Vos Reynaerde* is based on Bouwman (1991a).

CHAPTER 5

THE PRINTED DUTCH REYNAERT TRADITION:

FROM THE FIFTEENTH TO THE NINETEENTH CENTURY

Paul Wackers

Introduction

The Middle Dutch Reynaert tradition consists of two texts: *Van den Vos Reynaerde* and *Reynaerts Historie*.[1] The first text is an adaptation of Branch I of the *Roman de Renart* and was probably written around the middle of the thirteenth century. The second text is an adaptation and continuation of *Van den Vos Reynaerde*. It dates from the end of the fourteenth or the first half of the fifteenth century. The printed Reynaert tradition in Dutch starts in the second half of the fifteenth century. It is solely based on *Reynaerts Historie*. This printed tradition is fairly stable until the beginning of the nineteenth century. Then *Van den Vos Reynaerde* is rediscovered and takes its place next to (and later above) *Reynaerts Historie*, and new developments in scholarship and cultural ideas lead to a variety of Reynaert versions. In this chapter the printed Reynaert tradition in the Low Countries is studied from its beginnings until the moment it stops being a unity. Many approaches are possible. Here attention is paid only to those aspects which can be used as pointers to the kind of public that read the story and the ways in which it was used and interpreted. These are book production and, more specifically, typographical aspects; the ways in which the story has been presented to the public; the ways in which the contents have been adapted during the centuries; and lastly the ways in which the meaning has been presented.

By way of introduction, however, we start with a few remarks on *Reynaerts Historie* itself and on its printed tradition as a whole.

Reynaerts Historie

It is not certain when *Reynaerts Historie* was written. The text contains elements referring to the second half of the fourteenth century, so it cannot have been written earlier. On the other hand, it must have been written before c.1470 because one of the remaining manuscripts dates from that time (Berteloot 1988). The dialect of the text probably indicates that it was originally written in West Flanders. The end contains an acrostic: DISMWDE, referring to Diksmuide, a small but fairly important city in that region (Berteloot 1993). It is as yet unclear whether this points to the author or the patron. Like almost all Middle Dutch epic stories, *Reynaerts Historie* is in verse. We know the story from just one complete manuscript (parchment, probably from Utrecht, c.1470) and one fragment (paper, Holland, 1477).[2]

It is a bipartite story. The first half tells the reader that Nobel, the lion, king of the animals, has called together all the members of his court. Everyone has come except Reynaert. He is accused by various animals and defended by his nephew Grimbeert, the badger. The arrival of the funeral procession of Coppe the hen, Reynaert's last victim, however, proves his guilt. Reynaert is summoned three times. The first two summoners, Bruun the bear and Tibeert the cat, he brings to ruin. With the third, his nephew Grimbeert, he comes to court. He is accused again and sentenced to be hanged. But when he gets permission to make a general confession, he weaves into it a reference to a (non-existing) enormous treasure. The king is greedy, takes Reynaert aside and promises to forgive him everything in exchange for the treasure. Reynaert accepts this deal. When the king wants him to lead him to the place where this treasure lies hidden, Reynaert says he is excommunicated and must go to Rome to ask the pope to lift this ban. Afterwards he will travel as pilgrim to the Holy Land. With help of the queen he obtains shoes and a bag for this pilgrimage. The shoes are removed from the paws of Ysegrim the wolf and from Eerswijnde, his wife; the bag is made from Bruun's skin. Reynaert leaves the court in the company of Kuwaert the hare and Bellijn the ram. He takes Kuwaert with him into his den, decapitates him and gives him as food to his wife and children. Kuwaert's head, however, he sends back in his pilgrim's bag with Bellijn. Thus the king discovers that he has been deceived. He lets himself be reconciled with the bear and the wolves, and prolongs the meeting of his court to do them honour.

Then the second part of the story starts. Again Reynaert is accused of misdeeds, this time by Lapeel the hare and Corbout the crow. The king decides to make war on Reynaert. Grimbeert warns his uncle about the king's intentions and again Reynaert comes to court. He refutes Lapeel's and Corbout's accusations and explains why he can be at court, although he was supposed to go to Rome, by describing a (fictional) meeting with his uncle Mertijn the ape who goes to Rome on his behalf. The king is not impressed and says he will hang him. Mertijn's wife, Rukenau, defends Reynaert. Thereafter Reynaert speaks again. He says that he put three jewels in his pilgrim's bag, meant as gifts for king and queen. Again the king forgets reason out of greed. But Ysegrim the wolf is unconvinced and after losing a debate with Reynaert he challenges him to a duel. Reynaert is victorious and becomes the highest official in the realm under the king.

The printed tradition

Reynaerts Historie's printed tradition starts with two editions by Gheraert Leeu, one of the most important printers in the Low Countries during the fifteenth century.[3] He printed *Reynaerts Historie* in prose in 1479 in Gouda. This book is usually called the *prose incunabulum*. A reprint was made by Jacob Jacobszoon van der Meer (in Delft, 1485). Leeu printed *Reynaerts Historie* again after the transfer of his firm to Antwerp (somewhere between 1487 and 1490), this time respecting the original form. Of this *rhyme incunabulum* only a fragment is left. There are arguments for assuming that the prose version from 1479 is not the first edition (Witton 1980). So there must have been at least four editions of *Reynaerts Historie* in the fifteenth century.

The first sixteenth-century extant Dutch Reynaert edition dates from 1564 and was printed by Christoffel Plantijn for the bookseller Peter van Keerberghen. In 1556 Plantijn published another Reynaert book, this time under his own imprint.

After Plantijn we find a division in the Reynaert tradition. In the northern parts of the Low Countries a version of the tale circulates which resembles the story in both Plantijn editions. The oldest extant edition in this northern tradition stems from 1589 and we know of twenty-one different editions before the nineteenth century; the most recent one is from c.1780. In the southern parts of the Low Countries the Reynaert story was placed on the *Index librorum prohibitorum* in 1570. Only after a drastic revision did it become acceptable again. The oldest extant copy from this southern tradition stems from the end of the seventeenth century. We know, however, that there must have been earlier editions. We have proof or indications for at least thirty editions before the twentieth century. There were other lost and unusual editions (Menke 1992), but in this study, we confine ourselves to the mainstream tradition and to extant editions. This implies that the changes we shall consider cannot be described as a continuous process. Attention will be given mainly to changes in the incunabular phase, to changes in the phase between the incunabula and the sixteenth-century editions, and lastly to specific changes in southern chapbooks. In this way the relation between changes in book and story can be related most clearly to more general sociocultural changes.

We shall make generalisations about Plantijn editions, northern and southern chapbooks, but when quotations are needed, most will come from the Plantijn 1566 edition, from Schinckel 1589 as representative of the northern chapbook tradition, and from Verdussen c. 1700 as representative of the southern chapbook tradition.[4]

A final introductory remark: there is a very important difference between manuscript production and the production of printed books. A manuscript is always an *unicum* even if it represents a very popular type like the Book of Hours. Mostly the copyist knows for whom he is working, and even if this is not the case, a buyer can ask for specific changes before he purchases a book. Printed books are for anonymous buyers. Moreover, they must be produced in large numbers, otherwise the production process is too expensive. So the producer of printed books must make sure an anonymous public can decide what kind of book he has to offer and whether it wants exactly that and nothing else. After all, he hopes it will also buy his next book. This difference between manuscript production and the printing of books leads to a number of differences which will be treated below.

Book Production and Typography

The one complete manuscript of *Reynaerts Historie* starts with a prologue. It has no title and no specific indication of the content. The owner knew, after all, what it contained. It ends with an acrostic in which the copyist gives his name: Claes van Aken. The extant fragment of *Reynaerts Historie* contains only a bit more than the last one thousand lines of the story, so we cannot determine how that manuscript started. It ends with a formula stating the date on which it was completed. So, as far as we can see, both manuscripts lack any explicit typographical signal about their content. They give only some information about their production process, both at the end.

The prose incunabulum starts with a Table of Contents. Its headline can be seen as an indication of the story to be told: 'This is the table of contents of this book which is called the history of Reynaert the fox' (fol. a1r). Anyone looking at the first page of this book sees immediately that its main character is Reynaert the fox and, by reading the chapter headings, he gets an idea of the story. The indication *hystorie ... van reynaert die Vos* is repeated at the beginning of the prologue which follows this Table of Contents (Figure 5.1). The last page ends with a formula stating that the book was printed by Gheraert Leeu in Gouda and was completed on 17 August 1479 (Figure 5.2). Regarding typography there are thus almost no differences between this printed book and the manuscripts. We have neither the beginning nor the end of the rhyme incunabulum, so nothing can be said about them.

Both the prose and the rhyme incunabulum have another link with manuscript production: where they needed initials, these were not printed (Figures 5.1 and 5.3). Space was left to fill them in manually with red or blue ink, just as was done in manuscript production.

From the Plantijn editions onwards we find title pages like the ones we know today. As an example, the text of the 1564 edition's title-page is:

> Reynaert the fox, a very pleasant and amusing story with its morals and short explanations.
> It can be bought in Antwerp from Peeter van Keerberghen, living at the cemetery of Our Lady in the Golden Cross.

The first page of this book is now completely devoted to information *about* the story. Attention is focused on the main char-

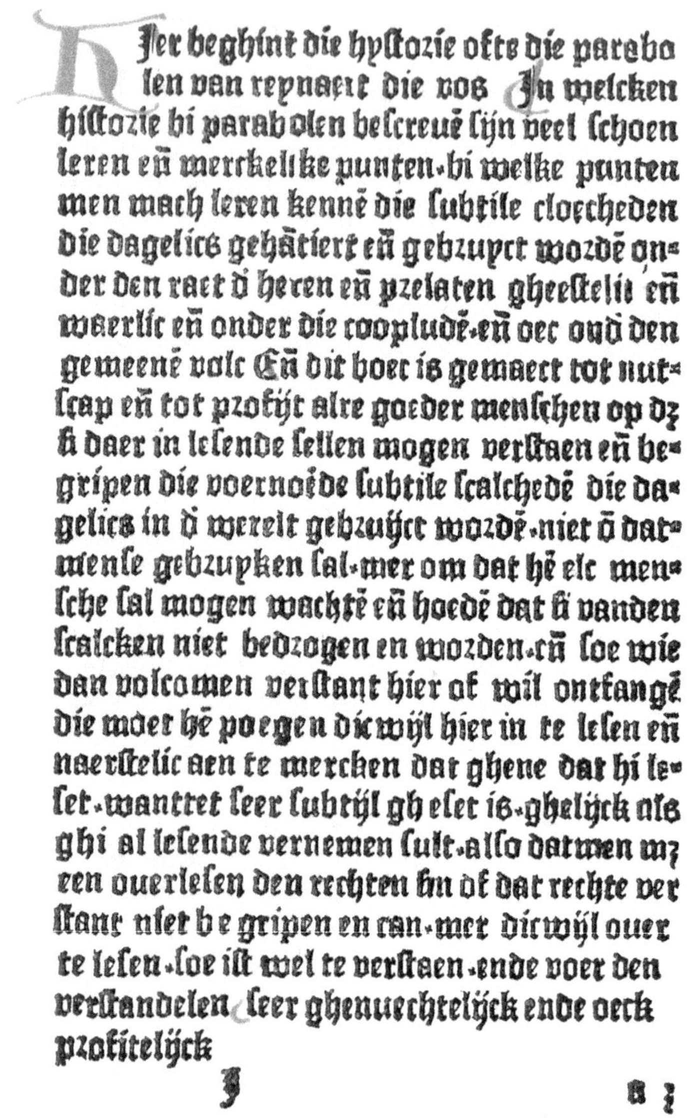

> Hier beghint die hystorie ofte die parabo
> len van reynaert die vos In welcken
> hystorie bi parabolen bescreuē sijn veel schoen
> leren eñ merckelike punten.bi welke punten
> men mach leren kennē die subtile cloesheden
> die dagelics gehātiert eñ gebruyct wordē on-
> der den raet d' heren eñ prelaten gheestelic eñ
> waerlic eñ onder die cooplude.eñ oec oud den
> gemeenē volc Eñ dit boec is gemaect tot nut-
> scap eñ tot profijt alre goeder menschen op dz
> si daer in lesende sellen mogen verstaen eñ be-
> gripen die voernoēde subtile scalchedē die da-
> gelics in d' werelt gebruijct wordē.niet o dat-
> mense gebrupken sal.mer om dat hē elc men-
> sche sal mogen wachtē eñ hoedē dat si vanden
> scalcken niet bedrogen en worden.eñ soe wie
> dan volcomen verstant hier of wil ontfangē
> die moet hē poegen dicwijl hier in te lesen eñ
> naerstelic aen te mercken dat ghene dat hi le-
> set.wanttet seer subtijl gh eset is.ghelijck als
> ghi al lesende vernemen sult.also datmen mz
> ten ouerlesen den rechten sin of dat rechte ver
> stant niet b e gripen en can.mer dicwijl ouer
> te lesen.soe ist wel te verstaen.ende voer den
> verstandelen seer ghenuechtelijck ende oeck
> profitelijck

Figure 5.1 *Prose incunabulum: Prologue. The Hague, Royal Library, 169 G 98, f. 3r.*

acter because it is the first to be named, and his name is printed in a different and larger font. The story is praised because it is amusing but also instructive. And lastly the place where it can be bought is stressed. This information no longer comes at the end. It must be at the beginning because it is vital. Everyone who wishes to obtain a copy of this book must

boertelīken.hi vint daer vele wīſe leren ende
goede ſinnen pn dat hem licht hier na doghet
ende ere in brengen mochṫ Daer en is nyemāt
goeders pnne beloghen Yet is īnt ghewepne
voert ghebrocht Eīck die trecker s hem aen dz
hem toe behoert Soe wie dattet verbeteren
kan die maket bet Wie dat ſijn beſte doet die
en is niet te witen Oer die alle dinck bereḃ-
ten wil die en is gheen dinck te wille te wa=
ken En ſoe wie dit verſcrijſt die wil dit doch
laten alſoe hijt vijnt

Hier epndet die hyſtozie van repnaert
die vos.ende is ghepzent ter goude in hollant
by mi gheraert leeu den ſeuentienden dach in
auguſto Int iaer m̄. CCCC. eñ lrrix
Deo gracias

Figure 5.2 *Prose incunabulum: Impressum. The Hague, Royal Library, 169 G 98, f. 113r.*

be able to find this information immediately. This is now an economic necessity. The title pages of all books from the later Reynaert tradition contain the same type of information. They also contain a woodcut, which is on the one hand meant as decoration, but which functions also as a pointer to the story because it shows the central situation of the story: King Nobel

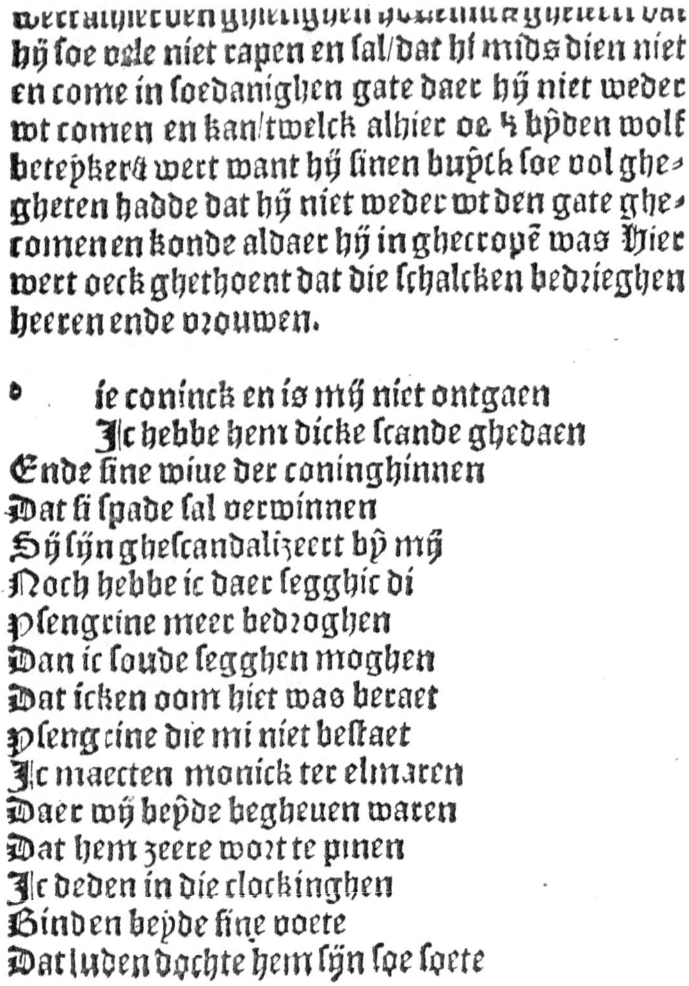

weer alijnet uen gjjieligyen justemieegyeielit uat
hij foe vale niet capen en fal/dat hi mids dien niet
en come in foedanighen gate daer hij niet weder
wt comen en kan/twelck alhier oe ḣ hpden wolf
betepkert wert want hij finen bupck foe vol ghe-
gheten hadde dat hij niet weder wt den gate ghe-
comen en konde aldaer hij in ghecropē was Hier
wert oeck ghethoent dat die fchalcken bedzieghen
heeren ende vzouwen.

    ie coninck en is mij niet ontgaen
    Ic hebbe hem dicke fcande ghedaen
Ende fine wiue der coninghinnen
Dat fi fpade fal verwinnen
Sij fijn ghefcandalizeert bij mij
Noch hebbe ic daer fegghic di
Pfengrine meer bedzoghen
Dan ic foude fegghen moghen
Dat icken oom hier was beraet
Pfengrine die mi niet beftaet
Ic maecten monick ter elmaren
Daer wij bepde begheuen waren
Dat hem zeere wort te pinen
Ic deden in die clockinghen
Binden bepde fine voete
Dat luden dochte hem fijn foe foete

Figure 5.3 *Rhyme incunabulum: first leaf of fragment (f. h2r). Copied from Breul 1927, 2.*

holding court. See for an example Figure 5.4. Only after this external introduction by the title page does the book really start. As already stated, modern buyers of books consider this completely obvious, but in fact we see here the end of a development from production for specific customers to production for an anonymous mass. This development is, of course, a general phenomenon. We find it in all books, but the Reynaert tradition illustrates it very clearly.

REYNAERT DE VOS.

Een seer ghenouchlicke ende vermakelicke historie: in Franchoyse ende neder Duytsch.

REYNIER LE
RENARD.

Histoire tresioyeuse & recreatiue, en François & bas Alleman.

T'ANTVVERPEN,
By Christoffel Plantijn, inde gulden Passer.
Intiaer M. D. LXVI.
MET PRIVILEGIE.

Figure 5.4 Reynaert de vos ... Plantijn, Antwerp, 1556. Title page.

Typographically, the prose incunabulum is fairly simple. The text is printed in one column, divided into parts by chapter headings and by initials. There are no illustrations nor any decoration of the text. It is a simple but well produced book. It is, however, one of the first epic (or literary in the modern sense of the word) texts in Middle Dutch which were printed, so the printer took a certain risk. Would there be a large enough public for such a book? One should also realise that in this first stage of printing even simple books were not cheap. Hence it is understandable that Gheraert Leeu decided to produce a carefully done but relatively modest book (Pleij 1987).

The experiment was probably successful: the rhyme incunabulum is a far more luxurious book. This is mainly because of the illustrations. At least forty were ordered and they were done by an unknown, major artist (called 'The Haarlem Master' by modern scholars).[5] It is difficult to say more about this book because only a few leaves of it remain. It can be safely concluded, however, that both books by Gheraert Leeu were meant for a public as large as possible, but in fact restricted to people with money to spare.

The Plantijn editions are also carefully produced books. The 1564 edition looks remarkable to modern readers because of the font used for the greater part. This is called 'civilité font' (Figure 5.5). It was developed in the sixteenth century for people who could read and write but who were not used to the roman fonts then normally in use for the production of printed books. It closely resembles the writing style of the time. The 'civilité font' was often used for school books and it is possible that this Reynaert edition was also used in schools.

It is certain that the 1566 edition was used in schools: it is designed as a book for pupils learning French. It gives the story twice, in two columns (Figure 5.6). One column contains the Dutch text, the other one the French translation. By comparing them the student gets acquainted with French syntax and vocabulary. The French translation was made by Johannes Florianus, schoolmaster at one of the better Latin schools in Antwerp. This book contains forty woodcuts, ordered in Paris, designed by G. Ballain and produced by J. de Gourmont, famous artists and craftsmen at that time (Figures 5.4 and 5.6). The decorative aspect of the illustrations is further enhanced by borders in renaissance style. It is clear that Plantijn wanted to present a modern and very well-produced book. It was meant for higher social circles, or at least for their children, and it was expensive.

All the books discussed until now were not meant for the masses, but both the northern and the southern chapbooks were. One glance suffices to prove that the northern chapbooks are far cheaper books (Figure 5.7). They contain illustrations, but fairly crude ones; the paper is of mediocre quality, and they were produced as fast as possible. It is remarkable that the quality slowly deteriorates: woodcuts stay in use even if their results become ugly. When new blocks are really

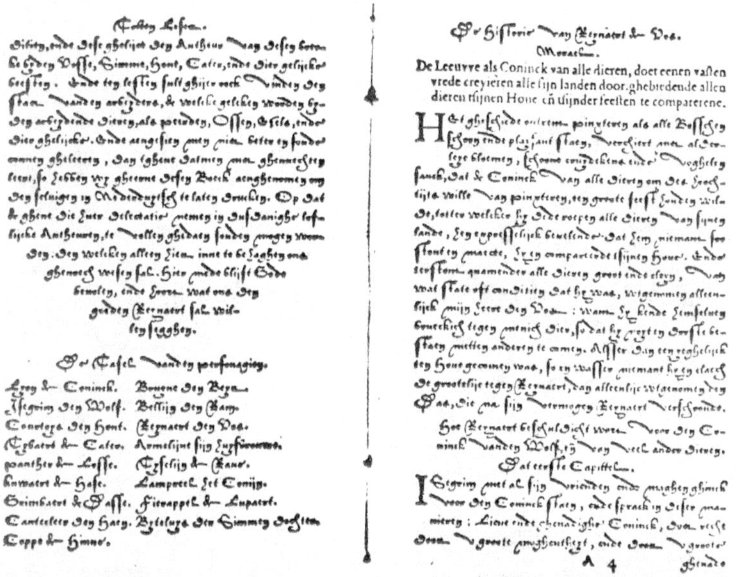

Figure 5.5 Reynaert de vos ... Plantijn for Peter van Keerbergen, Antwerp, 1564. Freiburg, University Library, E 7963 (Rara), f. A3v–A4r.

Figure 5.6 Reynaert de vos ... Plantijn, Antwerp, 1566, f. B1v–B2r.

Figure 5.7 Van Reynaert die Vos ... Schinckel, Delft, 1589, f. A2v–A3r.

Figure 5.8 Reynaert den vos ... Verdussen, Antwerp, c. 1700, pp. 8–9.

needed they are produced as fast and cheaply as possible. Correction of the text is seldom done. It seems as if the text becomes slowly the property of poorer and poorer people. Or is the explanation that the text was so popular that the books were sold even if their quality was almost unacceptable?

The southern chapbooks show a similar pattern. The late seventeenth-century copies which have survived are simple but well-produced books (Figure 5.8). They contain reasonable types and nice, well-executed illustrations. In the eighteenth century, however, the quality deteriorates rapidly, especially that of the woodcuts, but in the nineteenth century the firm Snoeck-Ducaju en Zoon again produced a number of reprints of very reasonable quality. This seems to indicate that the story remained popular in the same circles and that it depends on the 'greediness' or the taste of the publishers as to how the books look.

Presentation of the Story

We now discuss which external elements are added to the story as a help to the public and how these elements influence the understanding and interpretation of it (Schlusemann 1991: 74–82).

In the manuscript period the only 'external' elements in Middle Dutch Reynaert texts are a prologue and an epilogue. Both *Van den Vos Reynaerde* and *Reynaerts Historie* start with a prologue. This informs the audience that the author wanted to tell the story of Reynaert the fox in Dutch, that he did it for educated and sympathetic listeners, not for ignorant boors, and that he did it at the request of a lady. In *Reynaerts Historie* the last sentence adds that the story contains much wisdom. *Van den Vos Reynaerde* ends without adding any external material; *Reynaerts Historie* ends with a lengthy epilogue in which the meaning of the story is given explicitly, that is, it shows the situation in the courts of the world. Everyone there desires gain, or more specifically money; those who behave like Reynaert get it. Right and justice are neglected, selfishness reigns. Further, the author stresses that, though this is fiction, it nevertheless tells the truth.

The prose incunabulum starts with a 'Table of Contents' in the form of a list of chapter headings. These headings outline the action in the story. Taken together, they can be read as a summary of it. This is a new phenomenon in the Dutch Reynaert tradition. Chapter headings and tables of content themselves are no new phenomena. They can be found in manuscripts from the second half of the twelfth century onwards and are used to make it easier to find specific data in large amounts of complicated or heterogeneous material. This function is not absent here (it is now possible to find a specific scene more easily) but the main reason is probably to give an outline of the story at the beginning as a help for a potential customer whether to buy or not. The strongest argument for this opinion is that the chapter headings concentrate on the action and not on the importance of textual elements. The duel between Reynaert and Ysegrim (459 lines), for instance, gets three headings. Reynaert's big speech about the jewels he was supposed to have sent to the royal couple (833 lines), however, only gets one although it is of paramount importance for the development of the story, and its structure is far more complex than that of the account of the duel (Schlusemann 1991: 79). An old technique gets a new use here.

After this Table of Contents a prologue follows (Figure 5.1) which also makes use of a long-approved scheme, that of the 'philosophical *accessus*' (Schlusemann 1991: 82–86). An *accessus* is a formalised introduction to a text. *Accessus* are found abundantly in the medieval Latin tradition. This specific type discusses four elements: the *materia* or subject matter, the *intentio* or meaning, the *utilitas* or usefulness, and lastly the *pars philosophiae* or type of intellectual question which is discussed. The *materia* is described as the history or parable of Reynaert the fox. Main character and fictional aspects are also stressed. The *intentio* is to demonstrate some types of cunning and insidious misdemeanour which can be found in courts, in merchants' circles and among ordinary people. The meaning is generalised: it is no longer a story about courts, it is a story about society as a whole. The *utilitas* is not to teach the public how to practise these misdeeds, but how to beware of them. The *pars philosophiae* is not discussed explicitly but several times it is stressed that the story contains instruction, and from the wording it is clear that this instruction pertains to ethics, one of the traditional fields within philosophy. The prologue is concluded by an exhortation to all readers to read the book several times. The subject is complex, and it is possible that one does not understand everything immediately. By re-reading, everything will become clear and then the book will prove to be amusing and useful. It has been argued that this emphasis on reading and re-reading is a sign for a change in reception: as the story in manuscript form was meant to be listened to in a group, this printed form is meant to be read privately. This is possible but not necessarily true. But it is surely correct to say that this prologue aims to give an anonymous public a clear indication of the book's contents, that it stresses its general applicability and that it tries to prevent disappointment. In other words, it is characteristic of a printer's needs in the fifteenth century. At the end of the prose incunabulum the fictional aspect of the story is again stressed. It is stated that the story was told with good intentions and the real end is the *impressum* (Figure 5.2).

In the Plantijn editions and in the chapbook tradition the books begin with a title page (see above, Figure 5.4).[6] Then follow a Table of Contents and a prologue, just as in the prose incunabulum. Both contain roughly the same information as those in the prose incunabulum. An addition is that the chapter headings now contain a number (see also below). Another, final addition is a list of characters (Figure 5.5). It contains entries like: 'Lion the king, Reynaert the Fox, Armelijne, his wife'. This is remarkable, because in the manuscript tradition the public is clearly supposed to know about the characters when it starts listening or reading. For the prose incunabulum the same seems to be the case. Here, however, the presentation reckons with a public with no foreknowledge. Does this indicate a wider public than before, or is it just another measure to make the potential public as large as possible?

In the manuscript traditition the Reynaert story is always presented as a whole. The story contains initials and paragraph signs. These indicate transitions in the story but are not meant to divide the plot into coherent wholes. They also mark, for instance, the start of a speech or a change of speaker. The way the manuscripts are written suggests that the public is supposed to see the story as a whole. If someone wants to highlight a specific moment, he must do this for himself.

The prose incunabulum divides into chapters. This has a double effect. The table of contents, which is a result of this process, serves as a summary of the story (see above) and the insertion of the chapter headings makes it easier to retrace a specific moment. That these chapter headings are seen as something 'extra' is suggested by the fact that every chapter also begins with an initial which, strictly speaking, would have been unnecessary. On the other hand, the chapter structure is based on the initials in the manuscript tradition: the places where we find both correspond closely (Schlusemann 1991: 214–26).

The rhyme incunabulum is also divided into chapters, which are numbered. The chapter numbers in the Plantijn editions and in the chapbook tradition may probably be traced back to this book. The rhyme incunabulum contains two other innovations: chapters contain in principle an explicit moralisation – in prose! – (between heading and actual text, see Figure 5.3) and an illustration.[7] This moralisation seems to be based on the action in the chapter itself. This implies a change compared to the manuscript tradition. There the story was presented as a whole, and the explicit meaning given in the epilogue was also based on that whole. There is enough material in *Reynaerts Historie* which could have been used for separate, specific moralisation (for instance the numerous gnomic utterances and the inserted stories [Wackers 1986]) but this material is not highlighted nor interpreted separately. This structure (heading, explicit moral, illustration, story) links the typography of the rhyme incunabulum with that of printed fable books from the fifteenth century. It is tempting to explain the specific handling of the Reynaert story we find in this book as the result of the influence of that fable tradition, but it is impossible to prove this. We do not know enough about the rhyme incunabulum as a whole, and although we do know that the distinction between animal epic and fable was unimportant in the Middle Ages, there is no specific evidence to support the hypothesis that this really is the explanation for the format of the rhyme incunabulum. In fact, the later tradition seems to suggest that the division into chapters and the adding of morals to specific moments in the story are separate developments.

In the Plantijn edition of 1564 we find the following headings (Figure 5.5) directly after the list of characters:

The History of Reynaert the Fox.
Moral.
The Lion, king of the animals, orders the announcement of a secure peace throughout his realm, and orders all animals to come to his court and festival. (fol. A4r)

Then follows a short sketch of the situation at the story's opening, and then the first chapter begins, entitled:

How Reynaert is accused before the king by the wolf and by many other animals.
The first chapter. (fol. A4r)

Within that first chapter the complaints of Courtois the dog and Tibeert the cat are preceded by 'sub-headings' (Figure 5.7). After the complaint of Courtois we find a Moral, but at the end of the chapter a moral is missing. The second chapter has two morals, one somewhere in the middle (with no discernible reason) and one at the end (Figure 5.6). The third chapter has no moral, the fourth no heading with an indication of the content nor a moral, the fifth has no content-specifying heading but it has a moral. From the sixth chapter onwards we always find the same type of heading and always a moral at the end.

The 1566 Plantijn edition and the oldest northern chapbook (Schinckel 1589) have the same structure. They lack only the headings *De Historie van Reynaert de Vos* and *Moral* directly after the list of characters. In the southern chapbooks the story opens with the heading of the first chapter and the only irregularity is that some chapters have no moral at the end. This situation could be explained by assuming that the rhyme incunabulum had a regular structure, that some version between the rhyme incunabulum and the later tradition mangled this structure and that we find traces of it in the Plantijn editions and in the northern chapbooks. It is as least as probable, however, that we find in the later tradition indications of the structure of the rhyme incunabulum. And if that is the case the adding of headings with regard to content and the adding of morals to specific moments of the story are independent developments in the rhyme incunabulum. But, whatever the explanation, the change from a story presented as a whole and with one coherent meaning to a story divided into parts which can be interpreted and moralised individually, is a major development in the history of the Reynaert story in Dutch.

A last aspect of presentation that needs some attention is the form of the story. In the manuscript tradition the story is in verse. In this respect the Reynaert story corresponds to the bulk of the Middle Dutch epic tradition. In France, for instance, much epic material coexists in verse and in prose. In the Low Countries, however, epic material is mostly in verse during the manuscript period. Prose only becomes dominant in printed books. And in the first stage of printed books we find many experiments with combinations of verse and prose. This subject leads too far away from the Reynaert tradition, but this long preference for the combination verse – epic material in the Low Countries could be the explanation for the strange phenomenon that Leeu produced first a prose adaptation of a verse text and afterwards a reasonably faithful version of this verse text, with changes only to the presentation.[8] In the prose incunabulum the prose text follows the verses closely. Often the rhyming words are still discernible. In the later tradition the prose rendering is more free. This phenomenon is undoubtedly related to the other changes in story and moral which we find there.

Adaptation of Story and Structure

All the printed versions of *Reynaerts Historie* contain the same story. It is told differently, however, in the various stages of the tradition and some aspects have been adapted. In the previous section we have discussed external structure, in this section we analyse style, literary techniques and the way the story is structured. The rhyme incunabulum will be neglected again because its surviving fragment is too short to reach valid conclusions on these points.

The stories of the manuscripts of *Reynaerts Historie* and that of the prose incunabulum are very similar. As already stated, one can often still discern the rhyming pattern in the prose wording. But closer attention shows that there are many minor differences between the manuscript texts and that of the prose incunabulum. Moreover, these differences show patterns. They are meant to help the public to follow the story and to interpret its meaning unambiguously. We see, for instance, that pronouns are replaced by specific references (*hi* (he) by *heer reinaert* (sir reinaert)) and that generic names are added to proper names (*Cantecleer* becomes *Cantekleer die haen* (C. the cock)). Sometimes a term is explained by adding a synonym. Often peculiarities are added (*si riepen* (they called) becomes *si riepen beyde rouweliken* (they both called very sadly)) or actions are explained (when is said that Reynaert's father wipes out his trail, the prose incunabulum adds that he does this to prevent anybody following him). Irony is normally replaced by an unambiguous statement. This type of change clarifies the story. Leeu seems not to expect his potential readers to have problems understanding the social situation in which the story is placed, but he does his best to guarantee that they will understand the internal logic of the story. Comparable techniques (examined in the next section) are used to change the meaning. The differences between *Reynaerts Historie* and the later tradition are bigger. The same story is still told, but it is now shorter, simpler, and specific elements have been changed, partly because they were no longer understood, partly because of bowdlerisation.

Reynaerts Historie is a complex story, especially in its second part which contains many inserted tales, told by one of the characters to illustrate a specific point, but which have no direct relation to the main plot. It would be easy to shorten the story by eliminating a number of these inserted tales. This, however, does not happen. Almost every element in *Reynaerts Historie* is kept, but reduced to an absolute minimum. The description of the comb may be used to illustrate this process. In his second 'treasure tale' Reynaert says that he has sent three jewels to court, a ring, a comb and a mirror. The comb's description in *Reynaerts Historie* needs 113 lines (5,450–5,513). Reynaert tells that it was made of the shoulder-bone of a panther. He tells where this animal lives. He describes the panther's properties and then concentrates on the bone. When one removes it from a panther's body while the animal is still alive, the bone is unbreakable, cannot rot, and smells deliciously. Whoever owns this bone has no need of food or drink and is completely healthy. Reynaert goes on to describe how the comb was made out of such a bone. It has been polished, teeth have been carved and it has been decorated with enamel work. The decoration depicts the story of Paris's judgement. Reynaert recounts how it came to pass, he relates the promises the three goddesses made to Paris (that of Venus is even given in direct speech), and he briefly tells the story of Paris and Helen. In the oldest southern chapbook (Verdussen c.1700), here representative of the whole later tradition, the comb's description takes up only half a column. The following quotation gives an idea of its style:

> It [the comb] had such beautiful and pleasant colours that nothing on earth was its equal. It smelled so sweetly that it healed all illnesses; …And firstly it contained the story of Paris, who judged which of the three goddesses, that is Venus, Pallas and Juno, was the most beautiful. It contained also the story how this said Paris abducted Helen… (pp. 48–49)

This quotation not only shows how long elements are reduced to a bare minimum, but also that in the later tradition explanations are added, just as in the prose incunabulum: the public of *Reynaerts Historie* is supposed to know that Venus, Pallas and Juno are goddesses. In the chapbook this is told explicitly. The inserted stories and the longer digressions are almost all part of the second half of *Reynaerts Historie*. This implies that this second half is more shortened than the first half. In the northern chapbooks the first half (*c*.3,500 lines) is told in thirty-nine chapters. For these chapters, fifty-two pages were needed. The second half (*c*.4,300 lines) is retold in thirty chapters and needs thirty-eight pages. In the southern chapbooks the first part is retold in nineteen chapters (thirty-five pages) and the second part in twelve chapters (twenty-nine pages). This shows that in the seventeenth century short chapters are less necessary than in the earlier period.

We find different types of simplification in the later tradition. A first one is syntactical. We have mentioned that in the prose incunabulum words or phrases were added to make the text more explicit. The same phenomenon can be found in the Plantijn editions and the northern chapbooks. Interestingly, we find the contrary process in the southern chapbooks. Long and complex sentences are reduced to a kernel of information. Compare, for instance:

> ... And next to that being summoned to prove his innocence and to explain his conduct, seeing that his falseness would become clear to everyone, he never wanted to reach an agreement ... (Plantijn 1566: A7r)

> Moreover, being summoned to come to explain his conduct, he did not want to reach an agreement. (Verdussen *c*.1700: p. 3)

This phenomenon may be explained in two ways. The long-winded and explicit style of the prose incunabulum might have been a help for inexperienced readers. By the end of the seventeenth century most people would probably no longer have had a problem with reading, so this type of extra help was no longer necessary and hence was removed. Alternatively: the public of Verdussen's book was (still) less schooled than that of the Plantijn editions or that of the northern chapbooks, so it needed simple sentences and the removal of difficult or unusual words. Both explanations are plausible. Choosing between them is impossible armed with only the information from the Reynaert tradition. To make a choice, we would need to know more about reading habits in general in the sixteenth and seventeenth centuries.

Another way of simplifying the story is the removal of characters or scenes which can be safely omitted. When, for instance, Rukenau the ape, Reynaert's aunt, defends her nephew, one of her arguments is that many animals at court are willing to support him. As examples she mentions her three children and describes their appearances and habits in seventy-one lines (5,102–73). Next she calls for general support and many animals – first of all her children – answer her call. In the Plantijn editions and the chapbooks she does not mention her children but just asks for general support, which she gets. (So we have here also another example of the tendency to keep all elements, but reduced to their bare minimum.) Another example of this technique may be found in Reynaert's first treasure story. In *Reynaerts Historie* he tells that his treasure lies hidden in Kriekepit. When the kings doubts the existence of that place, Reynaert calls Kuwaert the hare as witness and he confirms that it really does exist. In the later tradition Reynaert says only that his treasure lies at a hidden place. The king has no doubts and Kuwaert's testimony can be left out.

Related to this type of change is the removal or the changing of elements in the story which are no longer understood. Mostly this relates to aspects of the administration of justice. For example, in Ysegrim's first complaint he says among other things that Reynaert had promised to swear his innocence on holy relics, but that he refused to do it at the last moment (*Reynaerts Historie*, lines 88–95). In Plantijn 1566 it is said that Reynaert refuses to come to justify his conduct and in Verdussen we find the same information in shorter form (see above). In *Reynaerts Historie* we find another oath on relics at the beginning of the duel between wolf and fox: both swear that they fight for an honest cause (lines 6,908–18). In Plantijn 1566 it is only said at the corresponding moment that both swear an oath. In Verdussen this part of the preparation for the duel is left out completely. Comparable to these examples is the handling of Reynaert's pardon by the king. In *Reynaerts Historie* the king takes a straw from the ground and gives it to Reynaert (lines 2,567–70). This is a medieval ritual, called *festucatio*, which was indeed part of the administration of justice. The straw was a symbol for what the accusations or the misdeeds had become: a nothing. This detail may still be found in Plantijn 1566 (E6v), but in Verdussen all that is said is that the king forgave Reynaert all his misdeeds. A detail which has become incomprehensible through changes in juridical tradition is removed, but the story-line remains the same. In all these examples the technique is basically the same: the story is told in a more general or abstract way. Details referring to specific procedures or customs are removed; the essence is kept and described in general terms. The background of these changes is probably also always the same: because of social changes a detail was no longer understood. To prevent misunderstandings the detail was removed or reduced to its abstract essence.

A third way of simplifying the story is by restructuring elements. The narrative technique of *Reynaerts Historie* is at times very complex. The Plantijn editions and the chapbooks strive at greater simplicity. A good example of this tendency is in the handling of Reynaert's meeting with his uncle Mertijn the ape (lines 4,406–4,613; see Goossens 1980). When Reynaert comes a second time to court in *Reynaerts Historie*, he immediately begins to speak to the king. He says that he was desperate when Grimbeert told him that the king was preparing an attack on his home after Lapeel's and Corbout's complaints. In his distress he wandered on the heath and there met his uncle Mertijn, who asked him why he was desperate, and Reynaert replied that he was excommunicated and thus had to go to Rome, but that he also needed to go to Nobel's court to refute the (according to Reynaert) false complaints against him. Now he does not know what to do. Mertijn offers his help. He will go to Rome instead of Reynaert and he will lift the excommunication with the help of some highly placed friends and some bribery. Reynaert can therefore go to Nobel to defend himself. This speech of Reynaert's seems to be just an account of his meeting with his uncle. In fact, however, it is at the same time a refutation of the most recent complaints against him (because Reynaert tells his uncle his version of what happened between him and the hare and the crow), and an explanation why he can be at court while he should be on the way to Rome. Because it is not presented as refutation or explanation its reasoning is more difficult to attack. Besides, Reynaert complicates matters still more by giving long parts of his account in direct speech. He 'replays' for the king his conversation with Mertijn and he does the same for Mertijn with his conversations with Lapeel and Corbout. So Reynaert impersonates for the king not only himself but also three other characters. In film terms we have here a flash-back-in-a-flash-back, because the past of the past is presented as the present. This combination of literary techniques makes considerable demands on the listener or reader. In the later tradition this part of the story is simplified. First Reynaert refutes the complaints of Corbout and Lapeel. Only after he has finished this, does he start speaking about his meeting with Mertijn (now called Marten) and his need to go at the same time to Rome and to Nobel's court. He no longer uses direct speech, so that it is always clear that his words relate to the past. It is far easier to follow this part of the story in the new form. In the southern chapbook this speech is changed still more compared with the Plantijn editions and the northern chapbooks because the excommunication is not mentioned, and Marten has been changed into the imperial eagle. These changes can be explained as elements of bowdlerisation, a phenomenon to which we will now turn.

Bowdlerisation affects two aspects of the story: on the one hand sexual scenes, which often also contain scatological elements and brute force and, on the other hand, criticism of religious matters or persons and, to a lesser degree, of the worldly government (on the first of these, see Goossens 1988). First, some examples of the censure of sexual matters. In *Reynaerts Historie* Reynaert is twice accused of raping the she-wolf. Both accusations are still in the prose incunabulum but are removed in the later tradition. Linked with the first complaint is the accusation that Reynaert has urinated on the wolf-cubs and so has blinded them. This can still be found in the Plantijn editions and in the northern chapbooks, but in the southern chapbooks only a request remains to punish the fox for all he did to the wolf and his family. When Tibeert is sent to bring Reynaert to court, the fox leads him to a barn where the cat expects to find mice. He gets caught, however, in a snare. The owner of the house, a priest, attacks him and Tibeert defends himself by biting off one of the priest's testicles (lines 1,275–1,880). In the Plantijn editions and in the chapbooks Tibeert bites off the nose of the owner of the house, now depicted as (an unspecified) man. During the duel between fox and wolf Reynaert squeezes Ysegrim's private parts so hard that the latter throws up blood, empties his bladder involuntarily, and faints (lines 7,335–54). In Plantijn 1566 this is told in the following way:

> Skilfully Reynaert put his hand behind Isengrin and grabbed hold of his cock and pulled at it so awfully that he made him piss and vomit blood because of the pain. (K4v)

In Verdussen we read:

> Reynaert skilfully put his paw under Isegrim's belly and grabbed hold of him there and squeezed him so much that he made him vomit blood because of the pain. (p. 61)

Here it looks as if the taboo on sex is stronger than on violence. The rape is avoided everywhere, but the sexual violence against the wolf is kept, although in Verdussen it is only suggested. This also suggests that the scatological taboo is stronger than that on violence: in Plantijn we still find 'piss', in Verdussen it has been removed. This last idea is strengthened by the end of Tybeert's mistreatment and his revenge. After Tybeert's attack Reynaert 'comforts' the man's wife. In *Reynaerts Historie* he says that the priest has lost only one ball and that he still will be able to perform with the other. In Schinckel 1589 (the oldest extant northern chapbook), B5v, Reynaert says to the wife that the loss of her man's nose implies that he will no longer smell her farts. In Plantijn 1566, D1r, Reynaert says that without his nose the man will no longer be bothered by unpleasant smells or by stench. Verdussen has removed the scene completely. This example is interesting because here all the distinct parts of the tradition show a different sensibility. This is very unusual.

This growing reluctance to speak openly about sexual acts and bodily functions can be explained elegantly with help of Norbert Elias's civilisation theory (see Goossens 1988: 114–23). Briefly, Elias states that at the end of the Middle Ages a process of individualisation and privatisation started as part of the wish of the higher classes to distinguish themselves from the mass by showing more civilised behaviour. This showed, for instance, in speaking carefully and not showing emotions openly. But slowly it began also to imply a certain shame in openly showing some types of bodily behaviour (such as sex, urinating, defecating). These things are now done alone, in private. And later still the shame felt at performing these acts openly leads to reluctance to speak about them in explicit terms. Over time this 'restricted' behaviour affects more and more sections of society. The 'widening' of this type of behaviour is reflected in the fact that we find more bowdlerisation of this kind in southern chapbooks than in other parts of the tradition.

Most of the changes in southern chapbooks, however, concern not sexual nor scatological elements but religious ones. The reason for this is evident. The book had been placed on the *Index*. There was a war going on between the northern and the southern parts of the Low Countries and its main motive was religion. The only chance of getting permission from a clerical censor to republish the book was to remove everything that could be objectionable, especially regarding religious matters. And so confessions, prayers, curses, oaths on relics, and so on, are all removed. All the priests in the story are also removed. By describing the way this was done we get a good idea of the changes made in the handling of religious aspects in the Reynaert tradition.

In *Reynaerts Historie* three priests are given roles in the story: the parson in the village where Bruun and Tybeert are maltreated; Bellijn the ram, the court's chaplain, and Mertijn the ape, the bishop of Cambrai's advocate. Already in the Plantijn editions and in the northern chapbooks the human parson has been changed into an anonymous man. But in those parts of the tradition Bellijn and Mertijn still have their roles as priests.

Reynaert's speech about his meeting with Mertijn shows some of the most biting criticism in the whole of *Reynaerts Historie*. Mertijn is abolutely not interested in the spiritual aspects of religion. For him everything is politics. That Reynaert could have sinned and, as a result, be excommunicated is not even thought of. Excommunication is a clerical decision which can be changed by influencing high-placed friends, by bribery. And if Nobel is not willing to give Reynaert his due, his whole land will be laid under an interdict until he bends. How is this possible? Mertijn says that in Rome nobody pays attention to the pope any more. All the power is in the hands of cardinal 'Money' and his girl-friend is Mertijn's niece. Whatever he asks, she can grant. The aim of this clergyman is not spiritual care but political power. And by the way this is presented, the public becomes convinced that the whole higher clergy thinks and acts like Mertijn.

In Plantijn 1566 the kernel of this is still discernible. Marten still aims at bribery, but he wants to do this *inden Hove* (at court), which suggests that he means King Lion's court. But he also says that he will go to Rome on behalf of Reynaert and will bring him from the pope forgiveness for his sins and a lifting of the ban. He no longer explains how he expects to achieve this. Thus the criticism is weakened and changed. In *Reynaerts Historie* attention is paid mostly to the situation at the papal court. In Plantijn it is shown that a clergyman is able to bribe and is unsuitably unimpressed by religious punishments. In southern chapbooks we find an imperial eagle[9] instead of Marten the ape and the eagle only says that it will ask the emperor to write King Lion a letter with a request to judge Reynaert fairly. In this form there is no longer any implicit or explicit criticism, neither of the clergy nor of secular government.

Bellijn plays his role as court chaplain mainly when Reynaert wants to leave the court again after the king has pardoned him in return for the (non-existing) treasure (lines 2,919–82). The king wants Reynaert to lead him to the place where the treasure is hidden. To prevent this Reynaert says he has been excommunicated and that it would be disgraceful for the king to travel with him. He says he wants to go to Rome to have his excommunication lifted. From Rome he will travel on as pilgrim to the Holy Land. For his pilgrimage he asks for (and gets) shoes from Isegrim and his wife and a bag from a piece of Bruun's skin. When Reynaert takes his leave, the king asks Bellijn to hold a short service for him. Bellijn refuses because Reynaert has been excommunicated, but when the king becomes angry, he yields. At the end of the first part of the story Reynaert puts Kuwaert's head in the pilgrim's bag. In Plantijn 1566 Reynaert says nothing about excommunication but only that he wants to make a pilgrimage. He asks for shoes and a cowl to clothe him as pilgrim. When he takes his leave from the king we read:

> The king sent for Bellijn and ordered him to give Reynaert a staff, a bag and also his benediction. Bellijn answered the king that he did not dare to do so because Reynaert had been excommunicated. (F2r; see Schinckel 1589: C8v)

The rest of the story is very similar: the king becomes angry, Bellijn yields, the hare's head is put into the bag. But in the king's request to Bellijn we find the bag, for which Reynaert had not asked, and in Bellijn's answer we find the excommunication, about which Reynaert had not spoken. In the southern Dutch chapbooks Reynaert says he wants to make a long journey. He asks (and gets) shoes and a hood for that journey. The conflict between the king and Bellijn has been completely removed, so Reynaert gets no bag. But when Bellijn comes back to court after having accompanied Reynaert (and the hare) to Malpertuus, we read in Verdussen that the king *seer verwondert was, dat Bellijn den Ram met de male wederom quam* (was very surprised that Bellijn the ram came back with the bag; p. 33). The 'mistake' of the previously unmentioned excommunication has been corrected, but as a consequence we now have a previously unmentioned bag.

This material centred on Bellijn shows two things. The first is that bowdlerisation in southern Dutch chapbooks is very severe when it concerns religious matters. Even tiny details are reworked. The second is that the reworking of content is done in the whole tradition on the level of individual scenes. An adaptor changes and removes what is incomprehensible or unacceptable there. He does not take time to think through all the consequences of his adaptations and he does not check whether they raise problems in other parts of the story. This leads to a number of minor 'errors'. On the whole, however, the adaptations are done competently and work out well.

Adaptation of Meaning and Moral

In *Reynaerts Historie* the meaning of the story is only given explicitly at the end. During the story the public must draw its own conclusions. This is sometimes difficult because all the characters have bad traits, and it is difficult to identify with anyone of them. Moreover, the text largely consists of very complicated lies. This is done to show the force of these lies. It implies, however, that the public has 'to work hard' to see what the author really means. Clearly the story discusses the situation at courts, but it can be read in a more general way because courtiers are, after all, also people; but attention concentrates on situations found only at court. Courtly misbehaviour is also the main theme in the epilogue. In the prose incunabulum the meaning is given at the beginning, and during the story the badness of Reynaert is regularly stressed while the negative aspects of his opponents are reduced or even removed. This implies that the meaning of *Reynaerts Historie* itself is more pessimistic: everyone is bad, Reynaert is only exceptional because he performs his misdeeds more intelligently. In the prose incunabulum there is another focus: Reynaert behaves badly, you must not act like him. This type of adaptation is consistent with the prologue (see above). This states that the story not only shows situations which can be found everywhere in human society, but also stresses that the story is not told to encourage the following of its negative examples, but to beware of them. This message is easier to accept when wrong examples are concentrated in one character.[10] Another notable aspect of the prose incunabulum is that the meaning of the text is presented as generally applicable. Although the story has been changed only slightly, it is not presented as if it concerned only courts but society as a whole. This is done, of course, to reach as large as possible a public. From the rhyme incunabulum onwards the meaning of the story becomes fragmented. In the Plantijn editions and in the chapbooks we find prologues which give roughly the same introduction to (the meaning of) the text as that in the prose incunabulum, but next to that we find in the rhyme incunabulum and in the later tradition an interpretation by chapter. This large number of explicit interpretations makes the meaning more fragmented. There is no longer a clear focus on the story as a whole. All kinds of details can lead to moralisation. And the range of the moralisations is fairly wide. This makes the story still more general and generally applicable than the prose incunabulum wanted to be. The moralisations are typographically marked. This implies, paradoxically, that they can be more easily neglected. A reader can skip every *Morael* or *Bedietsel* and just follow the story without once having to think. Of course it is also possible to read *Reynaerts Historie* just for fun: in that story the moral is only given explicitly in the epilogue. But because the story in that text is much more complex it is less easy not to think about what it means. Someone who wants only the tale and nothing else, is better served by the later tradition.

Conclusion: Public and Reception

We have seen how, over four centuries, the Reynaert tradition changed, typographically, regarding both content and meaning. Let us now by way of conclusion examine the data again globally, but now exclusively from the perspective of the public and the way in which the books were received and used.

Reynaerts Historie itself has been composed within a literary tradition of tales meant for oral delivery before a group. This does not mean that the manuscripts which have survived, were used thus (both the complete manuscript and the fragment look like manuscripts for private use), but it explains the background for the tale's structure and literary technique. In the prose incunabulum this was changed. The story is here presented for an individual reader, and this is true for the whole of the later tradition.

Reynaerts Historie was a text with a fairly specific meaning. It treated the situation at courts. This was also changed. In the prose incunabulum it was done by stating at the outset that it treated the situation in the whole of society, and by setting bad behaviour more clearly apart. This generalising was strengthened from the rhyme incunabulum onwards by the addition of specific morals to the chapters. The story's contents were also generalised. Details and themes which could only be understood from a fourteenth- or fifteenth-century perspective were removed or changed. Difficult passages were restructured, long elaborations were reduced to essentials, possible miscomprehension was countered by a process of abstraction. What came into existence by these reworkings was a tale appropriate for different types of society and for almost every social level. This process took approximately a century. It was finished in the second half of the sixteenth century. From then onwards the tale could stay the same in the north of the Low Countries until the nineteenth century. That it was adapted again in the southern parts was a side-effect of a major political and religious conflict. It was not caused by an inner necessity.

The manuscripts of *Reynaerts Historie* were probably produced for specific individuals. The printed Reynaert books were all made for an anonymous public. This leads to typographical changes, most notably the 'invention' of title pages and tables of content. Because the public became anonymous it is almost impossible to identify the kind of people who read the Reynaert story from the fifteenth until the nineteenth century. It is very probable that the story has been used as a school book. The prologues of both Plantijn editions, for instance, speak about the effect of pleasure on learning: you remember better what you learned pleasurably. This statement may still be found in the prologue of the southern chapbooks, indicating, perhaps, that they also were used in schools.

When we look at the kind of books to which the northern and southern chapbooks belong, it is also probable that they were often used in families. Both were books produced for the masses. One could argue that the fact that the quality of the books generally deteriorates over the centuries points to a process of vulgarisation. Then the Reynaert story would slowly have become the 'property' of the lowest classes, a clear example of *gesunkenes Kulturgut*. I believe, however, the situation is more complex, and that the Reynaert story was also generally known in higher circles. An argument for this opinion may be found in Hendrik van Wijn's *Historische en letterkundige Avondstonden* (Amsterdam 1800), the first book in the Low Countries which discusses medieval literature from a literary historian's point of view. In this book Van Wijn gives the results of his historical and literary historical work in the form of a (fictional) conversation between himself (he calls himself Volkhart) and his neighbours, Reinout and Aleide, a cultured couple, eager to learn something about the past of their own country about which they know almost nothing. When Reinout asks whether original literary works were written in this region in the Middle Ages, Volkhart answers that they were, but he hesitates to mention them. Reinout asks why:

> VOLKHART. What would you say if I spoke to you about the Swan Knight? Or about Haymon's children? ... See ... Aleide is already starting to laugh.

ALEIDE. Forgive me. I confess that if we go along this path we will descend to children's school and to, for instance, Reynard the fox. You are right to skip such pranks. (pp. 270-271)

This short quotation is an extra argument to support the view that the Reynaert story was often used in school. It also seems to corroborate the opinion that the Reynaert story had become something for vulgar people. After all, here a cultured lady considers it just a prank and not worthy of serious consideration. But the central point here seems to me that Van Wijn clearly expects his readers to know Reynaert the fox. He explains everything medieval, but this literary character is one he supposes to be known – by educated, cultured people. Hence it seems better to assume that Reynaert was, at the beginning of the nineteenth century, a character comparable to James Bond today. He is not 'fashionable', he is not seen as culturally important, but he is part of everyone's cultural knowledge – not as an element from the past but as something that is just there and has always been there. Because of the work of Van Wijn and later literary historians this slowly changed. The original medieval Reynaert stories were rediscovered and highly praised. And while Reynaert kept his 'archetypical' status he also became the main character in one of the most outstanding literary works of medieval Flemish literature. This historisation of Reynaert slowly changed the whole view of his character in the Low Countries. But that process deserves to be treated in a separate study.

Notes

1. This chapter is heavily indebted to Schlusemann (1991) and, especially in the second half, to Wackers and Verzandvoort (1989). For a survey of the Middle Dutch tradition in European perspective, see Wackers (1998).
2. The standard edition of *Reynaerts Historie* is Hellinga (1952, MS B). Also very useful is Goossens (1983b). The most recent book on the text is Wackers (1986). On the manuscripts see Goossens (1983b: XII); Menke (1992: 109-10).
3. A bibliographical description of the printed tradition as a whole can be found in Menke (1992: ch. IV). On Leeu himself see Goudriaen (1993) and on the Leeu editions also Goossens (1983b: XIII). The text of both Leeu editions can be found in Hellinga (1952, P = prose incunabulum; D = rhyme incunabulum). For the prose incunabulum also a photocopy of The Hague, Royal Library, 169 G 98 was used; for the rhyme incunabulum Breul (1927).
4. The Plantijn editions, the northern tradition and the southern tradition have mostly been treated as an entity by Dutch scholars under the head-

ing 'Reynaert chapbooks'. (See Menke (1992: 116–77) and Verzandvoort (1989) on these books.) This is partly misleading because the Plantijn editions have nothing to do with chapbooks. Here the term 'chapbook' will only be used for the northern and the southern tradition. The three groups are clearly linked, but their precise relationships have yet to be determined. For Plantijn 1564 a microfilm of Freiburg, University Library, E 7963 (Rara) was used; for Plantijn 1566 the facsimile edition from 1989; for Schinckel 1589 a photocopy of a privately owned copy; for Verdussen c.1700 the facsimile edition (Verzandvoort and Wackers 1988). [NB the proper names refer to printers here, not to authors.]
5. See Goossens (1983a) for information about this artist and about the tradition founded on his illustrations.
6. The beginning and the end of the rhyme incunabulum cannot be discussed because the extant fragment contains only a part of the story itself.
7. Remarks on the rhyme incunabulum must be provisional because of its fragmentary state. *Reynke de Vos* shows that irregularities in the use of moralisations and illustrations are possible. Cf. Goossens (1983b). See also below.
8. That the rhyme incunabulum was in verse is perhaps an indication that it was meant for a more conservative public. Moreover, the prose incunabulum was printed in Gouda but the rhyme incunabulum after Leeu moved his company to Antwerp. Perhaps this changing of places is also an indication of a change in public.
9. In the seventeenth century Flanders was part of the Austrian empire.
10. There is no real difference between the morals of the prose incunabulum and of *Reynaerts Historie* itself. But in the latter text these ideas are kept implicit until the epilogue, and even there they are formulated rather than veiled.

≈ CHAPTER 6 ≈

THE FLEMISH *REYNAERT* AS AN IDEOLOGICAL WEAPON

Rik van Daele

The war-theme is dominantly present in medieval Reynard stories. The relation between Reynard the fox and Isengrin the wolf is more than once described as the great war between two of the main antagonists of the *Roman de Renart*. In the prologue of the very first medieval Old French story, Branch II, the author introduces it as a terrible war:

> But you have never heard of the great, grim war between Reynard and Isengrin that they waged so long and so bitterly. The fact is that there was never any love lost between these two lords; but, to tell the truth, they often engaged in fights and brawls. (Branch II, v. 10–17. Owen 1994 : 53)

From the oldest branch onwards, the tone is set. Reynard stories deal, amongst other themes, with war and peace. The achieving of peace (and therefore eliminating the fox) is one of the main aims of King Noble the lion. In the index of motifs for the *Roman the Renart* by Jean Subrenat one can see that almost every branch speaks in these terms. But the theme of war in the *Roman the Renart* has been investigated more than once, a theme which is not restricted to the oldest medieval fox stories. Reynard stories right up to the present day use the same motif over and over again. In this essay I first want to give a short but incomplete survey of some medieval Reynard stories that were linked to the war-and-peace theme. Then I want to concentrate on some twentieth-century Reynard stories that can be related to this theme.

Perhaps the oldest mention of conflict and fighting in combination with Reynardian matter is to be found in Flanders. The nineteenth-century investigator Jan Frans Willems quotes the Flemings after the cease-fire by Henry I, Duke of Brabant, in his struggle with Liège in 1215. His opponents called to him: 'Ha, ha, Reynard is a monk, Reynard has become a hermit.' (Willems 1836 : xx). Another very early example of the (possible) knowledge of the (French?) Reynard stories in Flanders refers to a war in 1201 in West Flanders where the fighting armies were called the Blauwvoeters ('blue feet') and those related to the court were called the Isengrimmers.

Many modern researchers have interpreted the Middle Dutch *Van den Vos Reynaerde* as a *roman-à-clef* in which opposing fighting groups are depicted. Luk Wenseleers detects in the stories the struggle between the Welfen and the Staufen with Henry the Lion of Saxony as Reynard. Leopold Peeters, on the contrary, thinks that the thirteenth-century Flemish *Van den Vos Reynaerde* tells the story of the problems between the families of the Count of Flanders, the Dampierres, and their northern enemies, the Avesnes, in the period around 1260. Reynard the fox is, in Peeters's view, Countess Margaretha of Flanders. Up to now, no satisfying solution has been found. In our view, the Middle Dutch Reynard story is not a *roman-à-clef*: it deals with universal human vices.

In 1260 the Minstrel of Reims wrote an allegorical story about contemporary political problems in the Low Countries. He did indeed write a *roman-à-clef* in which he identifies the main characters thus:

> Jan of Avesnes ... was the wolf and his mother the goat; the Count of Anjou and the Count of Poitiers were Roeniaus and Taburiaus. And Jan of Avesnes would have the grain and leave the straw to his mother, because he would take her territory, to which he had no rights, and he would desinherit her (Peeters 1973 : 244).

On 31 July 1385 the French army of King Charles VI had to fight near Damme in Flanders (near Bruges) against the people of Ghent. The French court poet Eustache Deschamps described the situation in a *chant royal* in a Reynardian setting. Damme is Malpertuis; Frans Ackerman, the leader of the inhabitants of Ghent, is Reynard the Fox:

> The fox sat for days in his hole
> The noble lion besieged him
> From one side; but the fox gave the army
> From behind more than one blow
> The canon shot many stones
> And the crossbow many bolts
> The army failed, in spite of the great number
> For it is not the mass which is decisive.
> (Hugaerts 1984 : 61)

The first preliminary conclusion of this incomplete survey of medieval Reynard stories is that they readily reflected and incorporated contemporary armed conflicts. This is not surprising because they deal essentially with war and peace, with lying and telling the truth, words and deeds, human vices, hypocrisy, greed, gluttony. All these elements are closely linked to tense relations between people and peoples.

We now travel in time into the twentieth century for a fox hunt in Flanders's fields.

To understand what follows, one preliminary remark has to be made. During the nineteenth century, the Middle Dutch *Van den Vos Reynaerde* was rediscovered in a romantic search for Flemish roots. The text's popularity grew spectacularly because of the work of eminent German scholars, of whom Jacob Grimm was undoubtedly the most important one. After Grimm published his *Reinhart Fuchs* in Berlin in 1834, Jan Frans Willems edited the old text of *Van den Vos Reynaerde* (or *Reynaert I*) together with the text of the later *Reynaerts Historie* (*Reynaert II*). Before, in 1834, he had translated the Reynard story and he later made the first modern school edition (1839). From that moment on, the Vlaamse Beweging (Flemish Movement) promoted the medieval Reynard story as a masterpiece of the old Flemish culture. This resulted in a much more positive fox image and in the growing popularity of the text for adults and children. By the end of the nineteenth century, the text which was one century earlier a perfect example of what is called *Gesunkenes Kulturgut* [forgotten culture], was again a highly respected and important central, standard, culturally-present text. The modern Reynard was not only much more positive than its medieval counterpart, but it also had a strong Flemish reflex. Two passages were isolated for that purpose. First, the silly French-speaking dog Courtois, who is ridiculed in the old story; secondly, the introduction of the fox's confession to the badger in which Grimbeert answers Reynard's Latin words ('Confiteor tibi, pater noster'): 'Speak to me in Flemish [Diets], a language that I can comprehend' (v. 1,457–59, Barnouw 1967 : 98).

The evolution from medieval villain to modern hero and freedom-fighter was not only Reynard's destiny, but also Tijl Uilenspiegel's. Both figures, Reynard and Uilenspiegel, have been recycled by many social, political and cultural groups: Flamingants in the first place, but also Belgicists, freemasons, Marxists, socialists, Catholics, etc. Both Reynard and Uilenspiegel have been on all sides. Since the romantic period, Reynardian matter has become dynamic again, evolving and adapting itself, chameleon-like, to different kinds of ideologies and groups.

At the end of the First World War, a penny-print (printed by Dirix-Van Riet in Antwerp) was distributed with a song of Piet Welters with the title: *Reinaart de Vos aan de pinhelmen bij hunne overhaaste vlucht uit België, in November 1918* (Reynard the fox to the spiked helms on the occasion of their over-hasty flight from Belgium ...). In this text Reynard is the defender of his Belgian fatherland.

One year later, the popular Flemish author Felix Timmermans published *Boudewijn* (1919), a political-didactic and satirical allegorical criticism on the situation of the humiliated Flemings (and soldiers) in Belgium. During the war, Flemish soldiers in the IJzer-region warfield (the IJzer is the river around which for almost five years the Great War was fought) had to obey their French-speaking Walloon officers. Some of the Flemings had collaborated with the German occupier. Boudewijn is the donkey, even smarter than the fox. *Boudewijn* was thought of as a satirical description of the Flemish emancipation struggle. Boudewijn is also the slave of Courtois (in *Van den Vos Reynaerde*, the French-speaking dog). The story diverges from the old Dutch text. In his public confession, the fox no longer reveals a treasure near Hulsterlo at Kriekeputte, but says that the donkey can produce gold (cf. the fairy tale of the gold-shitting donkey). Boudewijn, the captured slave, is liberated after revealing where the secret for producing gold can be found: near Wittemberg grows the Lanci-Christikruid that has to be conjured up by a dog's tail. To go to that place (where Faust sold his soul to the devil) one needs the hair of a dog and a letter of safe conduct. Tom-cat, bear and wolf accompany Boudewijn. Tybaert the tom-cat gets killed, Bruin the bear escapes with the tail, and Isengrijn the wolf returns to the court. Nobel is furious and returns with Courtois to Paris. Then the donkey can start a new life. *Boudewijn* is a curious testimony of the movement known as activism in Flanders. The text was first published in *De Nieuwe Gids* between November 1917 and October 1918 and later, in 1919, as a book by Van Kampen in Amsterdam.

A parallel Flemish reflex was found in a Reynard play by Paul de Mont from 1925. In this text, there are a few reminiscences of Mussolini, the new rich, soap barons, patriots and Jews.

During the period between the two world wars, several Reynard stories and studies were published in which the medieval text was interpreted in several ideological ways. In 1937 the Antwerp socialist, and later Belgian prime minister, Camille Huysmans, wrote a booklet entitled *Quatres types* in which he confronted Reynard, Uilenspiegel and Satan (demon and devil). Reynard is the prototype of superiority of cleverness over power. Reynard is amoral, a Machiavellist, for whom the end justifies the means. Still, Reynard is a good father and a loving husband. Reynard is a Bolshevik-fascist, one who fights injustice with injustice, violence with violence. Reynard is a defender of the class struggle and an apostle of freedom, a freedom-fighter who fights against social injustice and modern feudalism. In Huysmans's view Reynard is a Belgicist, the hero of a Flemish work with French roots (the *Roman de Renart*).

In 1941, Gerard Walschap, one of the leading Flemish writers of that time, reacts against Huysmans's statements in the journal *Dietsche Warande en Belfort* (1941: 506). Reynard is not amoral. He is a good father and a loving husband, but he is also an honest animal: proud, brave, intelligent, strong, confident, witty, tough and merciless. Reynard is the only figure with a conscience, fighting the powerful and corrupt.

While Walschap was writing his essay on Reynard's high moral standards, a fellow countryman, Robert van Genechten, wrote a fascist Reynard story. In 1941, the *Amsterdamse Keurkamer* published Robert van Genechten's *Van den Vos Reynaerde. Ruwaard, Boudewijn en Jodocus*. '*Jodo*'-cus (jodo is an anagram of jood [= jew]) is an anti-Semitic parody (Van Genechten 1941). In this modern version of the Middle Dutch story, the rhinoceros Jodocus is the central figure. He is the personification of the Jew: he comes from the East, a non-European who does not feel at home anywhere. He is a thick-lipped usurer whose race is spread throughout the whole world. Noble has just died. In the chaos following the king's death, a strange animal (Jodocus) takes advantage of the situation to grab power. This intriguant sets the animals against each other and encourages them to hybridise. Through this multiplying, lower animal species come into being. Jodocus installs a weak form of government: democracy. Finally, Reynard (in Dutch: *rein van aard* = pure of nature) tackles the problem of the strange wandering rhinoceros by demanding its extermination. In the end, the cruel rhino is killed thanks to the fox. Some of the rhino's kindred, however, manage to escape and leave the country.

Van Genechten, who had fled from Flanders to Holland after the First World War was, since the German occupation of the Netherlands in the Second World War, Procurator General of the Peace Court, an institution that had to eliminate resistance (Gielen 1998 : 14–15). Van Genechten used the Reynard story to justify the German invasion and to stimulate persecution of the Jews. In 1941, this was a cruel prediction of what would become the concentration camps.

For some national socialists in the Netherlands the Reynard figure was a symbol. This can be illustrated by a second example. In the archives of the Dutch Association for the Promotion of National Socialism [Nederlandse Stichting ter Bevordering van het Nationaal-Socialisme] a letter was found that carries an emblem with the title *Maupertuus*, a design of Reynard's castle underneath, and the following text: 'Maer die casteel van Maupertuus / Dat was die beste van sinen borgen' (But of all these castles, the best was the castle of Maupertuis) printed below it.

In 1942, the Flemish poet Wies Moens published an anthology entitled *Das Flämische Kampfgedicht (The Flemish Battle Poem)*, in Jena by Eugen Diederichs Verlag. The booklet opens with a short Reynard fragment under the title *Spreek Dietsch/Sprecht Flämisch* (Speak Dutch). The quotation is part of the famous confession, a dialogue between the fox and the badger on the way to Noble's court. The *Reynard* fragment is, in the publisher's view, a Kampfgedicht (Battle Poem).

During the Second World War, the fox gets a lot of attention in Flemish newspapers. In *Volk en Staat* of 3/4 and 5 November 1940, an anonymous writer published two articles on the Reynard story, entitled *Zoo dichtte Dietschland (So did Flanders write)*. Lode Monteyne wrote: *De Reinaert-sage in den strijd der ideeën (The Reynard story in the struggle of ideas)* in *De dag* of 9–10 November 1941. In *Nieuw Vlaanderen* of July 1942, professor Jan van Mierlo, SJ published a long series of articles on *Van den Vos Reynaerde* (from 11 July, the Flemish feastday, to 26 September). The article by Monteyne is especially interesting to us. The author confronts the war-Reynards of Timmermans and Van Genechten and an earlier Reynaert story by Father E. Fleerackers, SJ (*Reinke den vos in de Kempen* of 1910). For

Monteyne, Van Genechten's work is a political allegory, sometimes sharp, made by an outstanding prose writer, who adapts the story to modern times. The only point of criticism is that Van Genechten's imitation lacks the humour and the wit of the original. In the text, not a single condemnation of the book's fascist ideology can be found.

The predisposition of some Flemings towards the Reynard figure during the Second World War is one of the reasons why, after the war, Reynard studies slackened off for almost ten years. Two exceptions have to be made: Piet Punt (pseudonym for Renaat Joostens) and his *Reynaert de vos*, published in 1948; and the Reynard fragments published in several journals and newspapers by one of Flanders's greatest authors, Louis Paul Boon. These articles were brought together in *Wapenbroeders* (*Brothers in Arms*) in 1955. Both Reynard stories are a reaction to the ending of the war, but each author is in an opposite camp.

Piet Punt dedicated his book to the Flemish heirs of Reynard and Uilenspiegel. The different chapters were first published in the satirical Flemish weekly *Rommelpot* (= Rumbling Pot) from 1 August 1947 onwards. The text follows the Reynard story, but is full of contemporary comments. You can feel repression on almost every page of the book. Allusions to existing people can easily be found ('Odil Front, rode Wies, Kamiel Knobbel, Huije rechts, Glabberbeek de kleine geus'). Punt leaves his source story after Reynard's condemnation to the gallows, thus repeating the most essential of the traditional Beast Epic narrative matter and asking the question: how did the fox escape this time? The conspiracy against the king and the story of the treasure are replaced by a new conspiracy in which Bruin the bear plays the most important role. The conspiracy is represented by a black elephant, which hints at the words of the Belgian minister, Fernand Demany, who alluded to a conspiracy in Liège by 30,000 collaborators. As in the original story, the fox wins, is released and leaves court. In the final illustration the fox travels into the wide world with, in the background, Flemish symbols such as the bombed IJzer-tower at Diksmuide, the belfry of Ghent, Antwerp cathedral and the Artevelde statue in Kortrijk. The rising sun symbolises Flanders's sunny future.

Louis Paul Boon published his Reynard contributions in the socialist newspaper *Vooruit* (from August 1946 onwards). In 1953 the Reynard fragments were repeated in *De Kapellekensbaan* (translated as *Chapel Road*), one of the most impressive Flemish novels ever, and in 1955, Boon published them in a separate book: *Wapenbroeders*. It is a very free, but one of the very best, modern Reynard adaptations, an attempt by a modern author to transform the whole medieval Beast Epic into a real novel. In his adaptation, Boon demolishes a lot of Catholic and Flemish values. He propagates republican and socialist ideas. His book contains numerous references to contemporary events. The pilgrimage in Branch VIII of the *Roman de Renart* becomes a pilgrimage to Sinterwolfgang. Sanct-Wolfgang in Austria was the place were the Belgian King Leopold III and his second wife Liliane Baels lived during the war. The pilgrimage becomes a journey by politicians about the return of the king to his country.

Boon strongly identifies with the main protagonists of the Beast Epic. Even more than with the fox, he identifies himself with the wolf Isengrin, the anti-hero from Nivard's *Ysengrimus*, the Latin predecessor of some of the branches of the *Roman de Renart*. 'I always wanted to be Reynard, but I've never succeeded. I am of the kind that loses all the time'.

Chapter 7

The Ill-Fated Consequence of the Tom-Cat's Jump, and Its Illustration

Jan Goossens

From the first branch of the *Roman de Renart* right up to the latest telling of the Reynard story we have the scene of a fight between a trapped tom-cat and a man. In the medieval versions of the story this man is a priest. The fight ends in a disastrous way for him because the cat succeeds in tearing off one testicle (with 'claws and teeth'). In the *Roman de Renart* the cat, who himself has lost an eye, comforts himself with the knowledge that henceforth the priest will be able to ring only one bell. In the Netherlandish version, which is the basis for all subsequent European renderings of this scene, the words of the cat are put into the mouth of the fox. He makes an ironic speech of comfort addressed to the priest's wife who had, prior to this, lamented the loss of the priest's potency. The fox must laugh so much during this speech that he lets off an almighty fart. Thus we find in this scene elements from three domains that can evoke taboo-reactions in Western culture. These are the domains of sex, religion and (to a lesser degree) scatology. Since it is a priest to whom the misfortune occurs, the two first domains are closely linked here. In eight hundred years of the history of this text, this scene has been described several hundred times. Therefore we have here an interesting opportunity to investigate the history of attitudes to these taboos, an investigation which I began over ten years ago and which led to my study *De gecastreerde neus* (Goossens 1988).

In this essay I present a short survey of the iconographical treatment of the culminating action of this scene, that is, the half-castration of the priest. This will provide a general impression of the development of attitudes to the taboos mentioned above. A disadvantage in my choice of topic is that I know of no illustration of this scene before 1495, and know of none that is original from the eighteenth century. Versions from the period of the Enlightenment, as far as they are illustrated, use older pictorial material or copy it. This is regrettable, because it is precisely in the eighteenth century that a change of mentality in the treatment of the text is clearly noticeable.

In the medieval Reynard texts this scene is nearly always described with clarity. Late medieval texts even tend to enrich it with piquant details. The early post-medieval iconography in England bears this out. It consists of two misericords from approximately 1520 in Bristol Cathedral (Figures 7.1 and 7.2), and a woodcut in an anonymous English printed version of shortly after 1550 (Figure 7.3) which was later recut and was used in a London printing of 1701 (see Menke 1992: 229). In the first of the two misericords and in the woodcut, the castration itself is directly depicted. On the second misericord the cat has jumped on the back of the priest who has already lost one testicle. The woodcut is part of Wynkyn de Worde's picture

Figure 7.1 *Tibert castrates a village priest. Misericord, Bristol Cathedral, c.1520. Photograph by Elaine C. Block.*

Figure 7.2 *Tibert jumps up castrated priest's back. Misericord, Bristol Cathedral, c.1520. Photograph by Elaine C. Block.*

Figure 7.3 *Tibert castrates a village priest. Woodcut, c.1495 from a copy of* The History of Reynard the Fox, *c.1560–85, owned by W. Grauwels.*

cycle of c.1495, reconstructed by Kenneth Varty (1980) which is based on a Netherlandish cycle that I have reconstructed (Goossens 1983). From this cycle of 1487–1490 there remain a few fragments of the text which contain three woodcuts set above some text. We can assume that in the late Middle Ages this scene was also illustrated in the Netherlands in an uninhibited way. This same uninhibited attitude remained typical in England throughout the sixteenth century.

German sixteenth-century illustrations of this scene are somewhat different. This is the consequence of the German history of the treatment of the text. A Netherlandish version in verse with commentaries in prose accompanying some chapters was translated into Low German and also adapted in Lübeck in 1498. The author did not alter the text of the scene in any significant way but, presumably being a priest, did his best to defend his profession. For instance he declares in the prose commentary that goes with our scene, that the priest must have been a priest of a different religion. In his rendering, the priest is clothed in a loosely-hanging coat during his fight with the cat, yet the injury done to him is the same as in the French, Netherlandish and English traditions up to this time. The Lübeck edition of 1498 is illustrated but does not have an illustration of this particular scene. The first Low German printed version with an illustration of this scene was published in Rostock in 1539 (Figure 7.4). The woodcuts for this printed version are by Erhard Altdorfer, the brother of the well-known painter Albrecht Altdorfer. Our scene is made to coincide exactly with the text. The priest is lightly clothed, but it is obvious what is happening to him. Parallels in the composition with the one in the Wynkyn de Worde version clearly point to the fact that Altdorfer's illustration is also based ultimately on the Netherlandish cycle, of which the greater part is lost. After 1539 we have, in Germany, in the sixteenth century, at least three more cycles with illustrations of the Reynard story: first an anonymous one, which was first printed in Frankfurt in 1550. The illustration of our scene here is a mirror-image of the woodcut by Altdorfer with the important difference that the little coat goes lower down (Figure 7.5). This is not so in the other two versions which were made by two well-known graphic artists, Vergil Solis and Jost Amman, both in High German and in Latin. The cycle by Solis was used well into the seventeenth century in printed, illustrated versions of the Reynard story. The version by Amman even went well into the eighteenth century. In Scandinavian printed versions from

Figure 7.4 *Tibert attacks a village priest. Woodcut from* Reynke Voss de olde, *Rostock, 1539.*

Figure 7.5 *Tibert attacks a village priest. Woodcut from* Van Reyneken Vosse dem Olden, *Frankfurt, 1550.*

the sixteenth to the eighteenth century we find copies of these series, also of the illustration of our scene. (Menke 1992: 385–9). All of the series mentioned up to here are based in the first instance on the Netherlandish cycle by the so-called Haarlem Master.

Quite outside this tradition stands a cycle of etchings by the Dutch painter Allart van Everdingen (1621–75). We do not know for what purpose the artist made these etchings. They appear for the first time, together with a few others, in the translation of the Low German *Reynke de Vos* into High German by Gottsched, 1752. Goethe was able to buy the cycle of etchings by Everdingen in 1783. An edition of Goethe's *Reineke Fuchs* with Everdingen's illustrations was published in Leipzig in 1921 (Goethe, Hofmann edition, 1921). In his illustration of our scene (Figure 7.6) we find an element of the German tradition (the priest wears a loose coat) combined with the Netherlandish tradition (the weapon is a distaff). The weapon of the German text tradition, a hayfork, is lying without any obvious purpose on the floor next to the mournful victim. The

Figure 7.6 *Tibert castrates a village priest. Etching by Allart van Everdingen (1621–75).*

perspective of the illustration has been carefully chosen in a way that does not show the castration, but clearly suggests it. It is hard to say whether we have here a beginning of the development of abashed modesty.

The artistic highlight of the illustration of our scene is in the series of etchings by Wilhelm von Kaulbach (1805–74) for an edition of Goethe's *Reineke Fuchs* in 1846. This picture has both a foreground and a background scene (Figure 7.7). The happenings in the foreground are clearly influenced by Everdingen's composition. The attacked man may be identified as a monk by his clothing in accordance with Goethe's text. A further element of the German tradition is the hayfork which replaces the distaff. On the floor, where the fork was lying in Everdingen's illustration, we now have a sword. The goings-on in the background are probably Kaulbach's invention, but I think they may be influenced by Kaulbach's knowledge of an etching by J.H. Ramberg (Klitzing 1989: 64). There we see the

Figure 7.7 *Tibert castrates a village priest. Etching by Wilhelm von Kaulbach, 1846.*

Figure 7.8 *Tibert castrates a village priest. Etching by J.H. Ramberg, 1826.*

priest among a group of people in the opening of a door (Figure 7.8). In Ramberg's illustration we see just where the cat is biting, namely in the thigh. We have here in the German iconographical tradition an element on which I would now like to elaborate in the Netherlandish tradition.

This tradition shows, since the Renaissance, deviations from the medieval treatment of the story. They are the consequence of the influence of the above-mentioned taboos. The identity of the unfortunate victim can be altered: in the tradition of the Netherlandish chapbooks from 1564 onwards, he is simply a male inhabitant of the house; later (first in the version *Reinaert de vos*, Willems 1834) he is very often the verger. Sometimes he is a farmer. The lost member of the body is, in the chapbooks, very often the nose. Thus begins a persistent tradition which maintained itself right into the second half of the twentieth century. There are other possibilities, of which two are frequent enough to be mentioned here: one leg or legs, (first in *De zinrijke avonturen van den vos Reinaerde*, Slempkes 1929), or a vague suggestion that the cat managed to injure the man without any indication as to where. The taboo is also noticeable in the texts in different ways which reflect various degrees of bashfulness. The strongest effect of the taboo is where the identity of the man is not described and no part of the body is named; the weakest where both are correctly identified. Between those two are variants in which we find the stylistic means of metaphor and metonymy. Here we can differentiate further: there are colourful unveiled metaphors as, for instance, in the medieval versions which talk about ringing with only one bell. This is certainly less bashful than a paraphrase as, for instance, by Gottsched, who speaks of the sexual organ of the wolf as ' the place where he could not stand much injury', and surely also less than a veiled metaphor or metonymy which will mostly be understood only by somebody who has already the right information. The nose has the function of a veiled metaphor, as can be ascertained from erotic dictionaries, collections of proverbs, literary works (Laurence Sterne's *Tristram Shandy!*), psychiatric descriptions and various kinds of pictorial evidence. The description of the man as a verger and the part of the body as legs have the function of a veiled metonymy.

From the end of the nineteenth century onwards we have, in the Netherlands, more and more illustrations in retellings of the Reynardian epic. They are first and foremost in versions for children and young people, but also in versions for adults. Here, on the whole, we do not find links with the older iconographic tradition. The aesthetic quality of these illustrations is in general rather low. Illustrations of our scene can be found since the beginning of the twentieth century. They mostly illustrate the moment immediately before the ill-fated bite, but sometimes also the moment itself or its result. These pictures faithfully depict the verbal renderings of the scene they illustrate. Some show how the nose is bitten off, or what the verger looks like after his nose has been bitten off. As an example I have chosen the illustration in the book for young people by Rie Kooyman, *Reinaart de Vos*, 1968 (Figure 7.9). The authoress has herself illustrated her book. Other books show the cat biting into the leg. A good example of this is the drawing by Willem Backer (Figure 7.10) in the prose rendering of Slempkes's *De zinrijke avonture van den vos Reinaerde*, 1929. Sometimes it is shown which part of the body really gets lost. A particularly drastic example of this is the drawing by Bert Bouman (Figure 7.11) in *Reinaert de Vos* by Ernst Altena, 1979. A more or less veiled example is the drawing by Dolf de Rudder (Figure 7.12) in *Reinaard de Vos* by Bert Decorte, 1985. In this case, the veiled illustration accompanies an explicit text. Nose and legs occur in the illustrations of the first half of the century, the sexual organ only from the 1970s onwards.

All these observations coincide with the history of the text of our scene in the numerous retellings of the Reynard story. This

Figure 7.9 *Tibert attacks a man's nose. Drawing by Rie Kooyman, 1968.*

Figure 7.10 *Tibert attacks a man's upper leg. Drawing by Willem Backer, 1929.*

Figure 7.11 *Tibert leaps to attack a naked man's private parts. Drawing by Bert Bouman, 1979.*

Figure 7.12 *Tibert attacks a naked man. Drawing by Dolf de Rudder, 1985.*

can be summarised (somewhat simplified) in the following way: the medieval authors can on the whole describe the scene unveiled. Towards the end of this time we even find a tendency to become vulgar by adding increasingly coarse details and naming the parts directly instead of playing with colourful metaphors. The first signs of a more sober attitude can be found in the transition from the Middle Ages to modern times in the Low German *Reynke de Vos*, a book which aims to instil godliness. A prudish reserve in depicting our scene becomes even more noticeable in the oldest prints of the Netherlandish chapbook. These texts were for young poeple who were educated under the Counter-Reformation. Here we find topics under a taboo treated with metaphors which veil or hide vulgar reality, or omitted altogether. Distorting prudery has a real breakthrough at the time of Enlightenment. The taboo is now firmly treated with paraphrases which hide. This attitude remains in place all through the nineteenth and up to the middle of the twentieth century. After cautious attempts in the 1920s we can see a clear turning-point after the Second World War. One can speak of a breakthrough of a totally uninhibited attitude from the 1960s onwards, with the exception of children's books. Smug pleasure and a delight in using coarse language is now the hallmark of the description of a scene that stood for so long under a taboo.

Thus the history of the illustrations runs parallel to the history of the text, albeit with gaps. We do not have illustrations which always run parallel with the iconography in all periods. This is true for the Middle Ages, the eighteenth century and partly the nineteenth. In the chapbooks of the eighteenth century the illustrations tend to show more than the texts, simply because they were taken from earlier times. And finally we can say that Kaulbach, who in his paintings allowed himself attacks on the ultramontanism of his time, saw the potential of an attack in an etching (Everdingen!) from before the time of the Enlightenment, and used it for his own illustration in which he transgressed and possibly altered the limits of acceptability in his day.

§ CHAPTER 8 §

CHOIR-STALL CARVINGS OF REYNARD AND OTHER FOXES

Elaine C. Block and Kenneth Varty

In this essay we explore the appearance of scenes from the Beast Epic alongside images from fox lore and other fox motifs in one particular kind of sculpture, namely, the carvings in wood on the underside of the hinged choir-stall seats called misericords. An examination of these carvings in this study is justified by the fact that parts of two of the earliest and best known Reynardian stories, masterpieces of medieval litarary art, are to be seen on quite a few misericords alongside other scenes representing episodes in other kinds of fox lore. Furthermore, the scenes chosen by the wood-carvers or their patrons, and their particular forms, reveal interesting variations as they cross linguistic and cultural boundaries, in spite of the fact that they were all housed within the Church's domain and meant primarily for the eyes of men in holy orders whose lives were dedicated to the Catholic Church.

At the dawn of the Renaissance, tens of thousands of medieval misericord carvings must have existed. Since then only about ten thousand historiated carvings remain. Although Elaine C. Block has seen and photographed over nine thousand of them, our conclusions about their subject-matter and its distribution will have to be tentative. Even so, we have a far bigger corpus available than anybody else, drawn from churches and museums the length and breadth of

Europe (including Russia), and from museums in North America.

In the descriptions which follow below, we describe within parentheses the position of the relevant misericords. Most stalls are on the north (N) or south (S) sides of the choir. When return stalls (stalls projecting inwards at either the west or east end of the choir) are involved, they are clearly indicated in the text. In a few churches there are two rows of stalls on either side of the choir. In this case we distinguish them by referring to the upper or lower row. Most choir-stalls in Britain, as well as a few on the Continent (mostly Barcelona), have three scenes. The main one is in the centre while the other two, smaller (larger in Barcelona) are on either side and are referred to as supporters. The left supporter is to the viewer's left, the right supporter to his right. The numbers read from west to east.

The topics treated may be grouped under just a few headings, the first of which is, given the main aims of this volume, by far the most important.

1. Reynard's Trial

Five misericords in Bristol Cathedral, dated about 1520 (no longer in sequence, as they once probably were), depict scenes from the story told in several Beast Epics about the summoning of Reynard to Noble's court to answer charges levelled against him (chiefly by Chantecler the cock and Ysengrin the wolf), how he caused the royal envoys (Brun the bear and Tibert the cat) to be grievously wounded, and how, to the great joy of his enemies, he was condemned to be hanged. These narrative elements are first contained in the first parts of the *Roman de Renart*, Branch I, then in both the Dutch epics, *Reynaert de Vos* and *Reynaerts Historie*, then (to complete the list of pre-1520 texts), in their immediate successors, Caxton's *History of Reynard the Fox* and the Low German *Reynke de Vos*.

Following the order of the narrative, the first carving to consider (N 1) depicts Bruin the bear trapped in a half-split log (Figure 8.1). He is shown with his head and forepaws fast in the cleft of what appears to be a nearly upright log. He is being beaten by three men while Reynard looks on from a safe distance. If the carver had worked from a text, he could have used any of the pre-1520 ones named above. In all of them the essential details are the same. The bear gets trapped, head

Figure 8.1 *Bruin caught in a half-split log. Misericord, Bristol Cathedral, c.1520. Photograph by D.R. Maxted.*

and forepaws in a half-cleft log; he is soundly beaten; and the fox watches and taunts him from a safe distance. A detailed examination of all the literary variants of this episode leads us to the conclusion that the carver came closest to the Dutch or one of the Dutch-derived accounts. In them the bear's assailants beat him as he stands caught in the log. At the climax of the assault Caxton's text singles out Lanfert the woodcutter and his brother who 'sprang forth... with a staff and smote the bear upon the head'. In simplifying the scene, the carver reduces the crowd to three men all using sticks, one of which is clearly aimed at the bear's head.

It has long been established that the Bristol carvers used prints as models for many of their other misericord scenes, so did they do so for this Reynard sequence? The only comparison we can make for the scene depicting Bruin's plight is to be found in woodcut illustrations made for the Low German text published in 1498 (Figure 8.2) for, although there are woodcuts in other Reynardian Histories printed before 1520, none illustrating this episode has survived. Particularly striking are the positions of the fox in the middle background, of the two peasants to the left and the third to the right of the log, but still

Figure 8.2 *Bruin caught in a half-split log. Woodcut from* Reynke de vos, *Lübeck, 1498.*

more striking is the position of the log itself. In the Bristol carving it seems to be standing, unrealistically, on one end, while in the *Reynke de Vos* woodcut it lies, as it should, on the ground. The angle of the log is, however, not so very different, and one realises that the Bristol carver has merely given it a slightly more vertical angle while failing to show the receding horizontal lines of the ground's surface which the maker of the woodcut has ably shown.

In the second misericord of the Bristol sequence (N 2), we see Tibert the cat in trouble and, even more so, the naked priest (Figure 7.1). His naked son holds the rope which ensnares the cat while his concubine wields her distaff. It is in the French, not the Dutch and Dutch-derived accounts, that the concubine beats the cat with her distaff, though she joined in the assault on Bruin armed with this weapon and it could be that the Bristol carver was remembering the part she played in that battle and getting her roles a bit muddled. Or that the arming of a belligerent woman with a distaff was a commonplace notion and is therefore of no particular significance. In both the French and the other epics, the priest loses only one testicle when Tibert attacks him just before he can land a heavy blow with a stake. In this carving Reynard stands between the feet of son and concubine to watch the cat's discomfiture. Behind the woman one sees the priest's barn and the hole through which Tibert jumped into the snare. A pre-1520 woodcut of this scene has survived only in Wynkyn de Worde's illustrated edition of c.1495 (Figure 7.3). If the Bristol carver had this in mind, he modified it by including the fox, by placing a distaff in the concubine's hands, by depicting only two men (of whom one plays a completely passive role), and by having the priest turn his back on the cat who attacks him from the rear and keeps all four paws firmly on the ground. One is tempted to argue that this Bristol carver was well able to depart from pictorial models, and draw on what he knew of the story (be it from a recollection of his own, or somebody else's reading of it, or from a retelling he had heard) and to depict the event in his own way. However, without the evidence of other pictorial versions of this event (if ever there were any), we must be cautious.

The artistic independence of the Bristol carver seems to be confirmed when we come to the third misericord in this sequence (S 3) (Figure 7.2). It seems that Tibert's attack upon the priest so delighted him that he made another version of it. In this, Tibert is shown jumping up the poor priest's back. His concubine tries to knock the cat down while Reynard watches from the safety of a tree fork. The barn and the priest's son are no longer shown, while the concubine has apparently found time to don an apron and put on her shoes. The priest, now lacking a testicle, is depicted in almost exactly the same pose as in the previous scene. It looks as if he continues to hold the stick in his right hand, but it has been broken off. Evidently the events in this scene are supposed to happen only seconds after those in the previous scene. Nothing like this exists in any illustrated Reynardian book before or after the date of this carving.

The fourth scene in this sequence depicts the moment when Reynard is brought to the gallows (N 3) (Figure 8.3). In all the pre-1520 versions of this story, the fox is persuaded to answer for his crimes. In one of the early French versions (the one in manuscript f. fr. 371 of the Bibliothèque Nationale, Paris), he finds himself, on arrival at Noble's court, face to face with five of his chief enemies and former victims: the wolf, the cat, the

Figure 8.3 *Reynard mounts the gallows ladder. Misericord, Bristol Cathedral, c.1520. Photograph by D.R. Maxted.*

bear, the cock and the dog, four of whom may be seen in the Bristol gallows scene. Although the Dutch and Dutch-derived texts do not mention an immediate confrontation with any of these animals, the cock is the first to cry out against him after the lion has spoken harsh words to his rebellious baron. Only later do first the ram and the ewe, then the bear, the cat, the wolf, the hare and many other animals rise up in a chorus of complaint. Four of the five members of the Bristol hanging party are easily identifiable: the bear (to the left, and muzzled) who assists the fox up the gallows ladder; the cat (on the gallows cross-bar); the cock (who stands to the right of the gallows, head missing through damage); the wolf (just below and before the lion). Then there is the animal below the gallows cross-bar. It has cloven hoofs and a short horn (a second horn having been lost through damage ?). Is this the ram who spoke first after the cock to accuse the fox, or the goat who joined in the chorus of complaints? More likely the ram who, as priest in the animal kingdom, has a certain role to play on an occasion like this, and who was so cruelly tricked by the fox at the beginning of his 'pilgrimage' in the Dutch and Dutch-derived texts.

A gallows scene has survived in two pre-1520 illustrated Reynards. The Bristol carver's work seems slightly nearer the 1498 *Reynke* woodcut (Figure 8.4) than the c.1495 Wynkyn de Worde cut (Figure 8.5), especially in the positioning of the cat on top of the gallows, and in depicting the lion and lioness seated. However, the Bristol carver here begins to assert his independence once more (that is, if he knew these woodcuts) and at the same time to reveal his knowledge of a literary version (written or spoken) of this episode. This is particularly evident in his decision to include Chantecler the cock in his representation of it and to exclude from it that complete foreigner, the unicorn. One notes in passing, that he gives Bruin a muzzle, and that he dispenses with the ladder in an admirably economic use of line and space.

This carver's apparent independence has already been noted in his rendering of the moment when the ensnared cat attacks the priest, and especially in his depiction of the cat scratching the priest's back. This quality is also evident in the fifth and final carving in this sequence (S 10), where he depicts the wolf and the bear (muzzled again) dancing to the rythm of a drum beaten by a monkey (Figure 8.6). Presumably they are rejoicing at the prospect of the fox's imminent execution. Again, there is nothing like this in any of the early illustrated printed Reynards nor, for that matter, in any of the later ones. But there are lines in both the French and the Dutch versions of this story which could have inspired him if he knew them, with the Dutch coming closer than the French when it picks out the bear and the wolf who, at this point in the story 'vied with one another playfully in jumping over many a fence'. Yet again one feels the Bristol carver, influenced to some extent by available woodcuts, was an independent artist whose inspiration stemmed in part from his knowledge and love of the story, most probably in one of its Dutch or Dutch-derived forms, drawing on its spirit as well as on some of its details.

A few lessons are to be learned from this unique sequence of carvings in Bristol Cathedral. If all written versions of the story of Reynard's Trial were lost, the one we would reconstruct from these five scenes would differ greatly from any of the masterpieces which have in fact come down to us. It would seem to tell us that a bear and a cat got trapped and badly hurt, as did a naked man when attacked by a cat. We would guess that this was all probably due to a fox because he is shown witnessing these violent happenings, and is brought to the gallows by

Figure 8.4 *Reynard mounts the gallows ladder. Woodcut from* Reynke de vos, *Lübeck, 1498.*

Figure 8.5 *Reynard mounts the gallows ladder. Woodcut, c.1495 from a copy of* The History of Reynard the Fox, *c.1560-85, owned by W. Grauwels.*

Figure 8.6 *Bruin and Isegrim dance. Misericord, Bristol Cathedral, c.1520. Photograph by Elaine C. Block.*

(among other animals) a bear and a cat. We would deduce that the impending execution of the fox gave particular pleasure to a monkey, a bear and a wolf who are seen rejoicing nearby. And we might think that they too had been harmed by the fox in one way or another. The real reasons for the fox's being brought to the gallows, for the bear's, the cat's and the naked man's sufferings; the roles played by other animals, in particular the badger and the cock; the fact that the fox was not executed, the reasons for his being pardoned; his setting off on a false pilgrimage and its immediate consequences; all these, and much else besides, could not be recovered from this evidence. We would assume the cat played a specially big part in this story given that he is centre-stage in two out of five scenes, and prominent in the gallows scene. And we might think that the back-scratching episode was especially important. On the other hand, knowing this story well from quite a few different versions, we are made aware that visual retellings can be changed, especially in emphasis, by a number of factors such as the existence of a visual model which may be relatively easy or difficult for a carver to copy; by his knowledge of the story and preference for certain episodes in it; and, presumably, by the instructions he is given and the instructor's aim. Here, it looks as if the instructor wanted to turn a highly entertaining episode in a popular story into a moral lesson, for the implication of the story as told in these five misericord carvings is that the perpetrator of such wrong-doing will come to a bad end and get his just deserts. Recovering lost literature from visual evidence of this kind is a hazardous undertaking.

After Reynard's release from the gallows, he is embraced by Noble the lion, raised by him on a high platform, set between himself and Fière the lioness, and publicly declared to be high in royal favour. There is a much mutilated misericord (S 2) in All Saints, Gresford which illustrates this moment of the fox's triumph.

2. Fox with Cock Pursued by Woman with Distaff

The second most relevant group of misericord carvings, also found only in England, is the one which depicts a fox seizing or making off with a cock or goose and being chased by a woman wielding her distaff. This woman is sometimes shown alongside a man wielding a stick, and / or accompanied by a dog. These are the main protagonists in the climactic scene of the story told in the *Roman de Renart*'s Branch II, in later French Renardian literature such as *Renart le Contrefait*, and in Chaucer's *Nun's Priest's Tale*. They also feature in shorter fable and popular song-poem versions. The story-line in both the French and English narrative poems is much the same. The fox breaks into a poultry yard and makes for the cock who, spotting him, retreats to higher ground. Reynard deceives the cock by telling him that his father, Chanteclin, could crow magnificently, especially when he stretched his neck and closed his eyes. He persuades Chantecler to do likewise. When he does, Reynard grabs him by the neck and runs off. Pinte (Pertelote in Chaucer), the cock's wife, sees the disappearing fox and laments her husband's fate. As she does so, the farmer's wife comes from her house just in time to witness the unfolding drama. From this point the French and English narrative poems tell things a little differently. In the French, the farmer's wife calls out for help. Her husband, Constant, together with some men with whom he had been playing a ball game, come to her side. After reprimanding her for her lack of vigilance, he calls his dogs and they all give chase. In the English, the farmer's wife, on hearing the noise made by her hens, runs from her house, calls after the fox and gives immediate chase, wielding her distaff. She is joined by serving men and dogs, and there is tremendous commotion among the cows, calves, pigs, ducks, geese and even bees.

In two popular poems it is a goose and not a cock that becomes the fox's victim, and these poems (and others like them) may have influenced the carvers when they came to depict the victim. The first of these poems goes by the title *The False Fox* and the other poem begins, '"Pax vobis", quod the ffox'. For the text of these poems, see Varty (1967: 34–6). One notes, in passing, that in both the polished, literary (epic-related) narrative poem, and in the shorter, popular lyrics, the fox throws his victim over his back, and that the woman is armed with a distaff.

In Ely Cathedral a fourteenth-century misericord carving (N, upper, 19) seems to depict the Beast Epic rather than the popular lyric tradition, but it predates Chaucer's *Nun's Priest's Tale* by as much as fifty years (Figure 8.7). The victim is clearly a cock which the fox seizes by the body and holds between his jaws. Towering over the fox is the good-wife wielding her distaff. On the right supporter, a mallet or stake over his shoulder, stands a man who may be Constant, a farm-hand or a serving man. To judge by their fierce expressions and open mouths, both man and woman are shouting loudly after the

Figure 8.7 *Centre: fox with cock chased by woman with distaff. Left: cowled fox preaches to hens and a cock; right: man with stick about to join in fox chase. Misericord, Ely Cathedral, 1338. Photograph by Kenneth Varty.*

fox. The distaff is an interesting detail because it is not mentioned in the French epic tradition, but it is in both Chaucer and in the popular lyrics. However, it has to be said that in a miniature illustrating this moment in a fourteenth-century French manuscript of the *Roman de Renart* (University of Oxford, Bodleian Library, Douce 360, f.21), the woman is shown to be armed with a distaff even if it is not mentioned in the text. Although there are no other pre-Chaucer misericord representations of this scene, there are several pre-Chaucer representations: in stone (Wells Cathedral and Oakham parish church); in glass (York Minster); and in drawings (the Ormesby Psalter, the Queen Mary Psalter, the Amesbury Psalter, and the Smithfield Decretals), details of which may be found in Varty (1967).

A lively misericord carving contemporary with Chaucer is to be found in St Botolph's, Boston (S, lower, 17) (Figure 8.8). Here the farmer's wife chases the fox with tremendous determination as he makes off with a bird that could be a cock. The woman's expression is ferocious as she lunges out with an enormous distaff. Something of the commotion in the literary accounts of this episode is conveyed by the scurrying duck in the foreground and by another one which dashed ahead of the fox in complete bewilderment.

Not long after Chaucer's telling of this tale, a number of fifteenth-century misericord carvings seem to depict a variant of its climactic episode. They are characterised by the portrayal

Figure 8.8 *Fox with goose chased by woman with distaff. Misericord, St Botolph, Boston, 1390. Photograph by D.R. Maxted.*

of a seated woman and / or the representation of what seems to be a kitchen interior. This variant may have told how the goodwife (or the widow) fell asleep in her house, into which the fox penetrated and found a goose which had been killed and lay waiting to be plucked. Seizing the goose, the fox makes off with it, but the woman is awoken by the barking of her dog. When she realises what is happening, she grabs her distaff and pursues the intruder. In St Mary and All Saints, Whalley (N 9), we see the woman sitting down, asleep. Her cat cringes behind her, but her dog stands his ground in front of her and barks after the fleeing fox, who has a goose flung over his back. He nears his hole from which peer two foxes. In St Mary's, Minster-in-Thanet (N 10), the seated woman is clearly awake, a cat and a dog beside her. Neither animal shows any inclination to pursue the fox, who makes off with a goose. In Ripon Cathedral (S 10), the woman is still seated but she has, in effect, shouldered arms, and the dog is in hot pursuit. In Norwich Cathedral (S, transverse, 10), the woman has also joined in the pursuit, leaving behind her a kitchen-living room of which the carver shows a fair amount of detail (Figure 8.9). These four misericords are, of course, post-Chaucerian, and

Figure 8.9 *Fox with duck or goose chased by woman with distaff. Misericord, Norwich Cathedral, 1480. Photograph by J.C.D. Smith.*

his influence may be recognised in them. There are other fifteenth-century representations of the fox chased by a distaff-wielding woman of the more usual variety, but not on misericords. They appear elsewhere in the choir-stalls (e.g., in Tuttington parish church) and in stone (e.g., on a roof boss in St Margaret's, Cley-next-the-Sea). Usually the victim is a goose, but at Cley-next-the-Sea it is a handsome cock. Details of these are also given in Varty (1967).

It is not until we come to the sixteenth century that we detect with near-certainty Chaucer's influence on misericord carvings of this particular scene. In Manchester Cathedral a misericord (S 7) dated 1508, shows a woman who could be Dame Malkyn (Maggie in Coghill's modernised text) about to bring down her (now broken-off) distaff on the rump of the fleeing Don Russell. Just behind her we see a house and a little girl, perhaps one of the two daughters mentioned by Chaucer. She stands at the entrance to the house, just inside the doorway, and holds her arms out in evident consternation. Mother and child witness the fox making off with a goose slung over his back. In Beverley Minster (S, upper, 20), the scene, dated 1520, is very similarly depicted (Figure 8.10). It has, however, one more detail which further suggests a Chaucerian influence. Here we see four ducks in the background, and they appear to be quacking loudly in fear:

Figure 8.10 *Fox with goose watched by woman with distaff. Misericord, Beverley Minster, 1520. Photograph by Elaine C. Block.*

... ducks left the water
Quacking and flapping as on the point of slaughter.
(Coghill 1951: 253).

At Beverley the victim could be a duck or a goose, but not a cock.
The author of Branch II of the *Roman de Renart* tells us that the fox took the cock by the neck and then ran for it. Chaucer and the authors of the short lyric poems tell us, as we have noted, that the fox first threw his victim over his back, then ran for it. An examination of all the drawings and carvings we have discovered of this episode shows that, although there is a twelfth-century stone sculpture in Bristol Cathedral's Lady Chapel which shows the fox in the process of throwing a goose over his back, and another from the late twelfth century showing much the same in Wells Cathedral, it is chiefly from the fourteenth century and later that he is shown (and then not always) with his victim thrown over his back a bit like the way a man might carry a sack full of goods. One wonders how realistic this is, how far it is a literary conceit, an artistic cliché. There are people who say they have seen foxes running off with their prey thrown over their back, and there are zoologists who think this is impossible, even allowing for the fact that geese and most kinds of poultry were much smaller in the Middle Ages than they are now, while the fox remains much the same size. Some of the evidence for these opposing views may be read in Varty (1967). There could be, in our medieval poets' and artists' work, a parodic, anthropomorphic element. Some hunters will have carried their quarry slung over their shoulder and back, just as the fox carries a monk in the world-upside-down image carved on the misericord supporter in St Nicholas's, Castle Hedingham (S 3). And there could have been a reflection of the artist's intention (be he literary artist, graphic artist, or sculptor), to reflect elegant, cultured ways of doing things, as Richard Trachsler has convincingly argued in a study which takes as its starting point Chrétien de Troyes' description in his courtly romance, *Yvain* (from around the middle of the last quarter of the twelfth century), of a lion carrying off a stag which he flung over his shoulder (Trachsler 1994).

The isolation of this dramatic chasing of the fox within churches almost certainly means that it could be given a religious moral point. The cunning fox was for centuries one of the most common symbols for the wily Devil. The cock or goose which he captures doubtless represents the vain or silly unwary soul; and the goodwife that soul's guardian who might not always be as vigilant as she should be, a point made especially clear in those variants in which she is seated and looking away from her charge or asleep.

Two other misericords could be related to this scene. While the fox is shown making off with his prey, he is chased only by a dog. They are in Winchester College Chapel (S 1), and Windsor St George's Chapel (N, upper, 19).

And one other misericord carving could just illustrate a quite different moment in this tale. It is from the early fourteenth century, in Winchester Cathedral (S 17), and shows a fox emerging from behind a large stylised leaf which could represent the cabbage under which he tried to hide before approaching the cock. There is, in fact, a cock on either supporter, neither of which seems to be aware of the approaching fox.

3. The Fox Preacher

Linked to some of the scenes of the fox with prey being chased by a woman wielding a distaff are representations of the fox preaching. This is the case of the Ely Cathedral misericord (N, upper, 19) (Figure 8.7) where, on the left supporter, we see an upright fox wearing a gown and thrown-back cowl. With his left hand he holds a crozier, and from the point where his right hand rests on the crozier flows a scarf-like band separating a cock (below) from two hens (above); or are they ducks? This band was almost certainly meant to be inscribed with the first words of the fox's sermon or greeting, perhaps 'Pax vobiscum', the first words of the second of the popular lyrics quoted above. There is, however, no evidence of an erased, painted or an eroded, carved inscription. The cock is the most prominent member of the fox's congregation and, in the central chase-scene, it is the cock which the fox has grabbed. The implication is that these two scenes are part of some moralising tale: a fox (devil) disguises himself as a man in holy orders to get sufficiently close to the members of an unwary congregation to be able to grab one of them and make off with him. The resulting commotion alerts the farmer's wife, the true guardian of the flock who, for some reason or another, let her guard slip, and she gives determined chase. But for those of us familiar with the Beast Epic, the prominence of the cock makes us think of the climactic episode in both the *Roman de Renart* and in Chaucer's *Nun's Priest's Tale*, even if in neither of them does the poet have the fox approach the cock in this way. There are other carvings (e.g., in Glasgow's Burrell Collection) and drawings (e.g., in the Smithfield Decretals; see Varty 1999), which link, within the one frame, the preaching fox and the distaff chase, but there is no other misericord carving which does this. It is possible that behind these linked scenes is both a moralising version of the Beast Epic episode and a well-known and widespread proverb: 'when the fox preaches beware your geese', a detailed illustrated study of which was published by Kerstin Rodin in 1983. Medieval artists of all kinds were, as is well known, adept at conveying simultaneously more than one message to more than one kind of reader / observer, and this proverb will almost certainly have been in the minds of most people, especially unlettered, humble folk, when they observed carvings like the ones on the Ely Cathedral misericord. On the other hand, members of the clergy and the lettered and relatively learned members of the aristocracy of both Church and State may have recalled the named fox of the Beast Epic or fable, for he too played the preacher, as he does even in the Chantecler branch of a fourteenth-century French version of the Epic, *Renart le Contrefait*. Here the fox poses as a religious in the Order of the Repented, and he tells Chantecler that he has become an excellent preacher, so good that he can make nuns and worthy men sleep by his preaching.

The earliest misericord carving we have been able to find of the preaching fox is in Wells Cathedral (S, upper, 13) and dated about 1330 (Figure 8.11). Beautifully carved, it shows

Figure 8.11 *A fox preaches to a group of ducks. Misericord, Wells Cathedral, c.1330. Photograph by D.R. Maxted.*

the fox leaning forward on his staff and addressing a group of four seated ducks, one of which, right underneath him, has fallen asleep. On the opposite side of the stalls (N, lower, 4) a fox runs off with a duck thrown over his back, perhaps the one that had fallen asleep. The Wells Cathedral carving is unusual in that most representations of the preaching fox show him wearing religious habit and, in particular, a cowl thrown back into which one or more of his congregation has been stored. Next in date after Wells is the Ely Cathedral misericord supporter scene over which we have paused, noting that his congregation consists of only a cock and two hens, none of which has yet found its way into his cowl. In St Botolph's, Boston (S, lower, 6) a much-worn, late fourteeenth-century misericord depicts an enthroned fox-bishop wearing a mitre and flowing, ornate robes (Figure 8.12). In his left hand he holds a crozier, in his right the neck of a cock behind which crouches a hen. The fox is served to his left by a grinning ass which wears priestly garmants and holds an open book. The lettered spectator might have thought of Bernard the ass, the animals' archbishop in the French Beast Epic, and at one point Reynard's companion on a pilgrimage to Rome.

On fifteenth- and sixteenth-century misericords we often see the fox preaching from a pulpit. In Ripon Cathedral, for

Figure 8.12 *A seated fox-bishop, attended by an ass-priest, holds a cock by the neck. Misericord, St Botolph, Boston, 1390. Photograph by D.R. Maxted.*

example (c.1490, N 11) he preaches to a magnificent cock and a beautiful duck (or goose). Both birds hang upon his every word as he preaches, it seems, with great earnestness. In All Saints, Gresford (S 2), a much inferior carving shows a similar division, cock with hens on one side, geese on the other. It is as if these carvers were conscious of the two main sources of inspiration, the literary (Beast Epic) one in which the cock plays the chief role, and the folklore one in which the goose is more prominent. In Bristol Cathedral (1520; N 5) the fox preaches from a pulpit to geese, nearly all of which have lost their heads through wear and tear. One which has not is clearly asleep. This carving shows two scenes in one, for, from behind the pulpit we see a fox (possibly an ape) emerging with a staff held in a threatening manner. This is almost certainly meant to show our preacher (or an associate) a few minutes later attacking the sleepy goose. In St Lawrence's, Ludlow, a much-damaged misericord (1435; N 8) depicts a very piggy fox wearing a bishop's mitre and robes (perhaps a satirical comment on the greediness of bishops) preaching from a pulpit to geese and other birds (mostly lost through wear and tear), while a couple of people, probably women, to the left, gossip instead of listening to the sermon. A misericord in St Mary's, Beverley (1445; N 12), depicts the fox preaching from his pulpit to a friar and a nun. A large cowl flows down his back. His wide-open jaws and gesticulating paws give the impression that he preaches with passion. Both the friar and the nun hold lengthy scrolls in their hands, as do two seated foxes (or apes) at each lower corner of the carving. They were probably meant to have inscribed upon them the text around which the fox preached, but no sign of any text remains. The carver was probably aiming a satirical shaft (similar to many in *Renart le Contrefait*) at friars and nuns, in particular those in the Franciscan Order, for the knotted cord dangling from the man's waist shows him to be a Franciscan; and he is probably suggesting that they are subject to the vices so often represented by the villainous hero of fifteenth-century versions of the Beast Epic: hypocrisy, vanity, gluttony, lust and so on. A similar satiric purpose may be behind another misericord carving in the same church (S 3) where a Franciscan friar addresses two foxes, each of which carries a crozier and wears a cowl out of which lolls a dead goose. Hypocrisy is probably the main vice targeted here. An unusual way of depicting the fox's hypocrisy is to be seen in the right supporter of a misericord in Worcester Cathedral (1397; S 20), where he kneels at an altar with his paws laid, as if in blessing, on the amputated head of some small animal placed on the altar just where one would expect the chalice to be at mass. The extent to which some monks were subject to hypocrisy is suggested in another rather unusual way, as we have noted, by the central scene of the misericord in St Nicholas's, Castle Hedingham, where a monk hangs upside-down from a staff slung over the fox's shoulder. Normally Brother Fox is shown to be quite successful in approaching his intended victims, but a rare exception is in St Nicholas's, Etchingham (N 1), where the geese all flee from him as he stands poised to preach. Even so, the fox (wearing a Franciscan's knotted cord-belt) holds his tummy in a gesture usually associated with a feeling of satisfaction and repletion.

Other English misericord carvings relevant to this topic may be seen in St George's Chapel, Windsor (S, upper, 8); Blackburn Cathedral (N 4); and Moyses Hall Museum, Bury St Edmund's. Abroad he is to be found

In *Belgium*, Aarschot (S, upper, 10).

In *Germany*, Cappenburg Castle Chapel (N, lower, 9); Kempen, St Mary (N, upper, 5; at the side of which, on the arm-rest between 5 and 4, is a fox, cowl slipped down his back, holding a book on the back of a goose which is whispering into his ear. Presumably the goose is confessing his sins); Bardowick (S, upper, 7); Strelen (N 6); Steinfeld (N 7).

In *Spain*, Celanova St Sauveur (S, upper, 4); Plasencia Cathedral (west, upper, 8); Talavera de la Reina (stall no. 2).

In *France*, Evreux Municipal Museum (east, 5); St Pol de Leon Cathedral (S, upper, 4); Bletterans (N, lower, 2); Champeaux St Martin (N, upper, 6); Lautenbach (S 9); Château l'Hermitage (N 6).

In *the Netherlands*, Bolsward St Martin (north, 7).

The many and varied appearances of the preacher-fox in the decoration of other parts of churches in England, and in other media, are described in some detail by Varty (1999: 55–86).

The earliest example in England of a fox preaching from a pulpit is to be found on a c.1370 quatrefoil panel in the choir of Lincoln Cathedral; of a fox preaching from a pulpit to a congregation which includes a human being (in this case a fashionably dressed woman) is on a late fourteenth-century bench end in Holy Trinity, St Austell; and of a fox dressed as a bishop who preaches from a pulpit is on the shoulder of an isolated, mid to late fourteenth-century desk-end kept in Haddon Hall, Derbyshire. This last-mentioned carving is of particular interest for it seems that the depiction of preaching foxes as bishops is peculiarly English. In a detailed study (Jones and Tracy 1994) the Haddon Hall fox-bishop is described as standing

> in a pulpit wearing a clearly delineated mitre and cowled vestment and preaching to a congregation of birds (probably intended to be geese) who stand on the ground before him in the shade of a tree... surmounted by a cockerel. A banderole (apparently blank) issues from the cock's beak and another, still legibly inscribed, issues from the mouth of the fox-bishop... the fox-bishop's banderole reads 'Pes be in here In' by way of episcopal greeting, not, importantly, the 'Pax Vobiscum' in liturgical Latin, but 'Peace be herein' in the Middle English vernacular... The fox preaching to birds as bishop would appear to be a peculiarly English iconographical development: of the nine examples known, only one is not English.

Jones and Tracy go on to say that the earliest representation of a fox-bishop is in the Rutland Psalter of about 1200; that all other manuscript depictions belong to the first half of the fourteenth century; and that three woodwork carvings date from about 1400. Two of these are the misericord scenes, the one in Boston, the other in Ludlow, described above.

4. The Fox-Monk and the Fox-Friar

The fox-monks and fox-friars mentioned in passing in the previous section are included in that section because they are shown preaching. There are many more foxes disguised as monks or friars who do not preach, and are linked to the Beast Epic only in spirit, being critical of the hypocritical. It is possible that even this criticism is unjust, that we witness something of the antagonism between parish priest and itinerant friar. It is also possible that they illustrate another common proverb, such as 'the habit does not make the monk'. These misericord carvings may be divided into four groups: (a) the ones that depict the fox-religious alone; (b) the fox-religious alone but reading from, or simply with, a book; (c) the fox-religious in the company of human beings: monks, nuns, friars; and (d) the fox-religious with prey.

(a) alone

England and Wales, Saint David's Cathedral (S 7): a hooded fox's head. Nantwich, St Mary (S 2, right supporter): a fox-friar carries a bow and arrows. Christchurch Priory (N, upper, 17): the fox's head is on a cushion.

France, Orbais Abbey (S, upper, 5): the fox has a ball or pompom at the end of his hood. His head is turned to one side, and his jaws are open. The surrounding misericords are probably portraits of the monks in the Abbey.

(b) with book

England, Beverley, St Mary (N 14): two foxes hold up and seem to read from a book on a lectern. This is in the form of a winged eagle, but the eagle's head has been replaced by a goose's (Figure 8.13).

France, Pocé / Cisse (S 4): the fox kneels at a prie-dieu with an open book on it.

Germany, Cleves, Minoriten Church (N, lower, 7): a cowl down his back, the fox rests his forepaws on an open book. His brush hangs between his legs. Kempen, St Mary (N, lower, 5): a cowl at his back, his brush curled around him, a fox sits at an open book with one forepaw holding down the page.

The Netherlands, Amsterdam, Oude Kerk (N 13): a bareheaded fox, body clothed, lies before an open book, one paw on the page.

Spain, Zamora Cathedral (N 15): an ape and a fox-monk sit before a lectern with open books.

Figure 8.13 *Two cowled foxes on either side of a goose lectern. Misericord, Beverley St Mary, 1445. Photograph by Elaine C. Block.*

(c) in the company of human beings

England, Chester Cathedral (S 19): a hooded, robed fox faces a half-hooded, robed monk (Figure 8.14). The fox's right paw and the monk's left hand reach out to each other and rest on what could be a closed book. If this is so, this also belongs to the previous subsection. Here it surely illustrates, like the Cologne quatrefoil mentioned below, the proverb 'The habit does not make the monk'. Windsor, St George's Chapel (S, lower, 1): a demon wheels three friars and a fox with a goose, all in a wheelbarrow, to a hell-mouth. Above them is a blank scroll.

Germany, Cologne Cathedral (N, upper, 12, quatrefoil): a cowled fox and a hooded, bearded monk stand facing each other. The proverb 'The habit does not make the monk' surely applies here.

Spain, Plasencia Cathedral (N, upper, 1): a fox-masked man is dressed as a Franciscan. He walks towards a seated person (head missing) who may also have had a fox's head. Behind the seated figure another figure holds something as it stands in a doorway.

(d) with prey

England, Castle Hedingham (S 3): a fox carries a monk dangling upside-down from a pole over his shoulder. The monk's

Figure 8.14 *A fox-monk faces a monk. Each places a hand on a book held between them. Misericord, Chester Cathedral, 1390. Photograph by D.R. Maxted.*

outer garment falls down almost to his chin. Might be included in the previous subsection. Nantwich, St Mary (S 2, left supporter): a fox-friar carries his prey on a pole over his shoulder.

Spain, Leon Cathedral, (S, lower, 3): an animal's head peeks from under his robe.

France, Villefranche-de-Rouergue, Notre Dame (S, lower, 5): a fox has a cock in his jaws.

5. The Hunting Fox with Prey, No Pursuit

Many scenes, all fairly realistic, show the fox taking his prey. No humans are involved. Where the prey is a cock or a goose, these scenes could be a prelude to the distaff-chase episode, but they are not linked in their present situations with that episode. They occur in almost every imaginable place in churches, but the following are the only misericord carvings we know of the hunting fox with prey:

Belgium, Louvain, St Pierre (N 7): the fox seizes a goose.

England, Boston, St Botolph (N 2, right supporter): a seated fox eats a goose. Also, N 3, right supporter: a fox eats a bird. Canon Pyon (N, upper, 1): a fox seizes a goose. Carlisle Cathedral (N 19): a fox kills a goose. Also, S 12: a fox seizes a goose. Faversham (S 7): a fox seizes a goose. Gamlingay, Cambridgeshire (S 10): a fox seizes a goose. Hereford Cathedral (S, upper, 4): a fox seizes a goose. Oxford, Magdalen College (N 4): a fox seizes a goose. Peterborough Cathedral (south-west, 2): there is a fox on either supporter; a cock stands on a vine in the centre. Ripon Cathedral (N 12): a fox stands before a dead goose. Also, S 10: a fox steals a goose. A dog on the right supporter prepares to give chase. Wellingborough (N 1): a fox seizes a goose. Wells Cathedral (N, lower, 4): a fox seizes a goose. Winchester College Chapel (S 10): a fox seizes a goose. Windsor, St George's Chapel (S, lower, 8): flowers separate the scene on the right of a fox carrying off a goose from, to the left, a fox emerging from beneath a leaf to catch a rabbit. Also, N, upper, 20, left supporter: a fox seizes a goose. The central scene shows a dog hunting rabbits. Winchester Cathedral (S, upper, 17): a fox comes from below a large leaf, possibly to hunt one of the cocks depicted on the supporters.

France, La Ferté Beauharnais, Collegiate Church St Bartélemy (N 2): only the head of the fox is shown. It holds a chicken in its jaws. St Claude Cathedral (S, upper, 9): a small fox with a large brush stalks three small birds which walk in a row. A large hawk, wings spread, descends upon the birds. St Jean-de-Maurienne (N, upper, 5): a fox holds a dead cock in its jaws.

Germany, Cologne Cathedral (arm rest between S, lower, 6 & 7): a fox has a goose between his jaws; another lies behind him. Emmerich, St Martin (east, upper, 4): a fox (possibly a wolf) with a lamb in his jaws. Also, but destroyed in the Second World War, a fox hunts in water in pursuit of three birds which are depicted flying away.

The Netherlands, Nederweert (N 5): a fox, brush stretched behind him, hunts in water. Ducks swim alongside him, and are probably his intended victims. Utrecht, position not recorded: a badly mutilated carving depicts the fox hunting in water.

Spain, Barcelona Cathedral (south west, 2, right supporter): a fox is about to steal a goat. (The central scene is of a shepherd, and the left supporter depicts two goats). Toledo Cathedral (N 8): a fox, jaws gaping, stands by a cock.

Switzerland, Basel Cathedral (east, upper, 6): a fox with a chicken on a fence. Estavoyer-le-Lac (S, upper, 4): a fox seizes a cock. Moudon (S, upper, 4): a fox seizes a goose.

6. The Hunted Fox

The hunted fox is much less frequently seen than the fox hunting. In the *Roman de Renart*, Reynard is occasionally hunted, both by humans and by fellow-animals, in particular the wolf, but none of the hunted fox scenes we have discovered on misericords or even elsewhere in the choir-stall area, is clearly related to any of the Beast Epics. Curiously, all three misericords we have found in this category are English, and in two of them the ape plays a part. Gloucester Cathedral (N 15): a fox has climbed up a tree and two dogs, on their hind legs, leap up towards him. To the left an archer fits an arrow to his bow ready to shoot the fox. Beverley Minster (S, upper, 19): in the centre a fox, pursued by three dogs, goes to earth while an archer, running up, takes aim at him. On the left supporter an ape rides a fox; on the right, an ape tends a fox lying in bed. Beverley, St Mary's (S 13): a fox, shot through the middle by a large arrow, consults an ape-doctor who holds up and inspects a urinal. To the left one sees a wodehouse-bowman, presumably the archer who shot the fox (Figure 8.15).

Figure 8.15 *A fox, shot through by an arrow, consults an ape-doctor. Misericord, Beverley St Mary, 1445. Photograph by Elaine C. Block.*

7. The Fox's Feigned Death

In one of the most popular moralising texts of the French and English Middle Ages, the *Physiologus* (otherwise known as the Bestiary), a section is devoted to the fox and the way he sometimes feigned death in order to catch carrion birds. A typical entry includes a description like this:

> Physiologus relates of the fox that he is a very crafty animal. When he is hungry and can find no prey, he entices it thus: he seats himself in a warm place where there is chaff, or else casts himself on his back and holds his breath and swells up his body completely, so that he appears dead. The birds believe that he is really dead, and they fly down in order to eat him up; but he springs up and catches them and eats them up. So also is the Devil very crafty in his ways. He who would partake of flesh dies. To this flesh belong adultery, covetousness, lust, murder.

Versions of this Bestiary account of the fox-devil lying in wait to trick and capture the unwary were probably often told in church sermons. It is often told in a variety of forms in all the Beast Epics, as has been shown in separate studies by Varty and by Combarieu du Grès, both in 1991.

We know of two examples of the Bestiary fox coupled with other images which may reveal a knowledge of some parts or variants of the Beast Epic. They are both from the late fourteenth century, both in Cheshire, England. They are, however, dissimilar in detail, and the reasons for seeing in them links with the Beast Epic are different. One is in St Mary's, Nantwich (S 2) (Figure 8.16), the other is in Chester Cathedral (N 14).

8. The Fox's Execution

In the many pre-fifteenth-century stories about him, Reynard is often threatened with execution, usually by hanging, but is never executed. However, in the plastic and graphic arts, especially in England, the fox may be seen hanged, dead, carried in funeral procession, and even buried. More often than not, geese are the executioners. It is only in England that we find misericord carvings of his demise, and only two of these have come down to us. The first is in Beverley Minster (N, upper, 7); the second in Bristol Cathedral (N 9). In each of these churches there is a misericord carving which shows the fox preaching to geese, then attacking one of them. Although these preaching scenes are no longer side by side with the execution scenes,

Figure 8.16 *Centre, a fox feigns death; left and right, foxes dressed as Franciscans, one with prey, the other with a bow and a flask. Misericord, St Mary, Nantwich, 1390. Photograph by Kenneth Varty.*

they were in all probability conceived as dyptichs and placed side by side in the choir-stalls. In Beverley Minster (N 4) we see the fox in a pulpit, robed, a rosary in his right hand (and therefore a Dominican?) addressing a group of seven geese, all but one of which seem to be paying close attention to his sermon. The one which is not, on the back row, seems to be asleep, and is probably the one that gets carried off by the fox over to the left, behind an ape-like accomplice which also has a dead goose dangling from a stake held over its shoulder. Only three seats removed from this scene (N, upper, 7) is the one of the geese hanging the fox (Figure 8.17). The carving of the left supporter is perhaps a reminder of what happened to the sleeping goose, for here we see a fox stealthily approaching two geese having a nap. In the centre, five geese form a hanging party while, to the right of them, two more watch the execution. One carries a cross and the other a mace. It looks as if there is to be a funeral procession after the hanging (and following the removal of the noose, depicted on the right supporter) which will be led by these two. If this is so, the carver may have meant to recall a story rather like that in Branch XVII of the *Roman de Renart* (Reynard's Death and Funeral Procession). In Bristol Cathedral the almost-certainly-related fox-preacher scene (N 5) shows the fox first in his pulpit, then

Figure 8.17 *Centre, geese hang a fox. To the right of the gallows, geese with a crucifix and a mace. Misericord, Beverley Minster, 1520. Photograph by D.R. Maxted.*

descending from the pulpit with a thick stick held in a threatening manner and making for one of the nearer geese. The gallows depicted to the left are no doubt the ones from which, elsewhere, we see him hanged. In the hanging scene (N 9), eight geese are present. To expedite his demise, two pull on the ropes and one on his brush. There was a third English misericord relevant to this section, at Sherborne Abbey, but it is now missing. A drawing shows that five birds shared in the hanging of a fox while two monks looked on, one on either side of the central scene.

In other English carvings (for example, three related bench ends in St Michael's, Brent Knoll; the stone frieze running round the tomb of John Holland in the Tower of London; [Varty 1967 and 1999]), this particular reversal of Fortune is clear to see. There are also examples of it in other media abroad (see Rodin 1983).

9. The Fox and the Ape

The earliest reference to an alliance between the fox and the ape is to be found in Branch Va, one of the earliest branches of the *Roman de Renart* (c.1175), but no story about their mischief-making together occurs until much later in Beast Epic time. The first Beast Epic in which an important relationship develops between the fox and the ape is *Renart le Nouvel*, of 1289, where the ape joins the fox in his struggle for power against the lion-king. In Jean de Condé's late fourteenth-century *Reynard, Master of the King's Household*, the fox has the lion's complete confidence and appoints whom he will to important posts, two of which he gives to members of the ape family. But it is in the Dutch versions of the Beast Epic (*Reynaert de Vos* in the thirteenth century, and *Reynaerts Historie* in the late fourteenth or early fifteenth century) that the ape plays his most active and, at times, important roles on Reynard's side. This was to become well known in England from the time of Caxton's translation, 1481.

Two late fifteenth-century misericord carvings in St George's Chapel, Windsor, could depict the ape Rukenaw preparing Reynard for his duel with the wolf. On the left supporter of one of them (S, upper, 6) we see a seated fox holding a bowl between his hand, a cloth draped around his shoulders (Figure 8.18). An ape stands before him and appears to be shaving or combing him. The right supporter of the other (south-west,

Figure 8.18 *An ape grooms a fox. Misericord, left supporter. St George's Chapel, Windsor Castle, c.1480. Photograph by Elaine C. Block.*

lower, 2) shows an ape pouring liquid down the throat of a fox lying on his back. As Rukenaw stresses to Reynard, the smoothness of his body and the fullness of his bladder will be important factors in his battle strategy.

The medical profession was burlesqued not only in vulpine but also in simian terms. There are numerous examples, beginning from the mid-fourteenth century, of ape-physicians inspecting urinals or applying ointments. In the parish church at Knowle the ape is even depicted as a Professor of Medicine lecturing to four students. Occasionally the ape is shown in consultation with, or attending, to the fox. For example, in St Botolph's, Boston (N, upper, 19) a seated ape, doctor's hood thrown back, inspects a urinal which, presumably, the worried-looking fox facing him has given to him. The fox holds a bucket in which he probably carried the urinal, but it may have been used to bring a specimen of his droppings. Behind the ape is either another fox who, as he leaves the surgery, looks back quite happily at him, or it is the same fox a few minutes later, after receiving advice and treatment. In St Mary's, Beverley (S 13) we see a fox pierced through the middle by an arrow (Figure 8.15). In front of the wounded fox sits an ape who inspects (rather irrelevantly, in these circumstances, one would have thought) a urinal. The fox holds a bag which probably serves the same purpose as the basket in St Botolph's, but it may be a money-bag containing the physician's fee. In Beverley Minster the central scene of a misericord (S, upper, 19) shows a fox hiding in a cavity as a bowman and his hounds descend upon him. To the right, an ape tends a fox lying in bed. Perhaps we are meant to understand that the fox of the central scene escaped from his pursuers but was wounded and, once home, called on his ape-physician. Quite a lot of Reynard's adventures, as told by narrative poets, end with him being badly wounded in his last-minute escapes from trouble, and in need of medical attention and nursing. But this is usually provided by his wife and his immediate family, never by apes.

Also relevant to this section are:

England, Beverley St Mary (N 4): a fox in a pulpit between two monks, each of whom holds a long scroll. Below them are seated two apes with thrown-back cowls, and scrolls stretching from their hands. Chichester Cathedral (S 19): a seated fox plays a harp (feet resting on a goose that gazes upward) while opposite is an ape (mutilated) who seems to be dancing to the fox's music.

Spain, Zamora Cathedral (N 15): an ape and a fox-monk sit before a lectern with open books.

10. Fox Fables

Fox fables, often pre-dating the Beast Epic, then living alongside it, were sometimes drawn into it while others appear to have lived in total independence of it.

(a) The Sick Lion

The part played by the fox in healing the sick lion is one of his most important. Some scholars think it is at the origin of the Epic. The earliest and well known enactment of this role occurs in one of the fables attributed to Aesop, but the form in which we know it derives from Phaedrus, first century A.D. The fox-physician next appears in the work of Paulus Diaconus during the eighth century. In the tenth he re-appears in the *Ecbasis Cuiusdem Captivi* and then, in the mid-twelfth he turns up in the third book of the *Ysengrimus*. But the longest and perhaps most entertaining story about the fox-physician occurs in the tenth branch of the *Roman de Renart*, probably composed around 1185.

There are quite a few drawings in medieval English art which depict the fox in this role (e.g., in the Smithfield Decretals and in the Amesbury Psalter), but there is only one medieval carving, and this is a misericord in Gloucester Cathedral (N 12) (Figure 8.19). Lying on the ground below stylised foliage is a lion, his head raised towards an erect fox who holds up to the light (and away from the lion) a urinal. This is in the fox's left hand. With his right he reaches out to the lion's forehead. The fact that the lion is not crowned suggests that this illustrates a fable rather than the Beast Epic. Curiously, there are even fewer representations of this fable on the Continent, the chief ones being in a late twelfth-century stone frieze in the crypt of Basel Cathedral, and in a few woodcuts in a late fifteenth-century German blockbook.

Christened Reynardine, a son of Reynard's, the fox-physician reappears in English literature in 1684, in the *Shifts of Reynardine*, a continuation of the narrative as imported from the Netherlands by Caxton. Here Reynardine becomes a doctor on the advice of an ape called Zani who urges him to find himself a disguise before he sets up a practice. Reynardine agrees, but is at a loss for a disguise. 'Leave that to me,' quoth the Ape, 'for I have all things necessary for the purpose. It is not long since I, with my Companions, going out upon a Frolick, found a Pedlar asleep, with his Pack lying by him. This Pack we took

Figure 8.19 *A sick lion is attended by a fox-physician holding a urinal. Misericord, Gloucester Cathedral, 1345. Photograph by Kenneth Varty.*

away, and as equally as we could divided all the Wares between us. By this means I am stored with Razors, Lancets, Scissors, Combs etc., by the help of which I doubt not but to make you a complete Disguise...' In the tenth branch of the *Roman de Renart*, the main story about the fox-physician, it is Reynard himself who, on his way to Noble's court, comes upon a sleeping pilgrim from whose pouch he steals a herb which cures fevers. Somewhere between the telling of this *Roman de Renart* story in twelfth-century France and the *Shifts of Reynardine* story in seventeenth-century England, there seems to have been a fusion of the two, and this seems to be reflected in numerous drawings and carvings uniquely in England (Varty 1967 and 1999). Four misericord carvings show a considerable number of apes stealing from a sleeping pedlar. In St George's Chapel, Windsor (south-east, lower, 4) he sleeps on the ground just outside the gatehouse leading into a town as apes pass around things they have lifted from the pack on his back. In Manchester Cathedral (S 8) they do the same, but there is no particular location. Here one of the apes seems to be examining the pedlar's hair (Figure 8.20). In Bristol Cathedral (N 4) the pedlar is shown to be waking up as one of the apes rifles his pack and touches the purse at his belt. Three others threaten to beat him with staves. In Beverley Minster (S, upper, 6) the pedlar is awoken by an ape that pulls at his hair while the others pass round the things they have stolen.

Figure 8.20 *Apes steal equipment from a sleeping pedlar. Misericord, Manchester Cathedral, 1508. Photograph by D.R. Maxted.*

(b) Fox and Sour Grapes

The Aesopian fable of the fox and the sour grapes finds its way into the *Roman de Renart*'s Branch XI, but here the poet changes the grapes into blackberries. We have found only one misericord carving of this fable, and it is in St Mary of Charity's, Faversham, Kent (S 4). It shows a fox approaching a bunch of grapes.

(c) The Fox and the Stork

The fable of the fox and the stork who invite each other to a meal but serve it in such a way that the guest is unable to partake of the food on offer was very widely illustrated in many forms and media over the whole of the European Middle Ages, especially in churches and religious books. Doubtless it was an illustration of Christ's teaching 'whatsoever ye would that men should do to you, do ye even so to them'. However, as with so many of Aesop's fables, it was turned into a proverb: 'The deceiver deceived' and is included in Breugel's panorama of Flemish proverbs, housed in Berlin's National Gallery. Curiously this fable was never drawn into the Beast Epic. Immensely frequent on the Continent, it is rare in England; and misericord carvings, of which we have traced eighteen, appear only on the Continent where they are distributed over seven countries. This fable-proverb is usually very succinctly carved, usually (but not always) in two phases, first at the fox's place, then at the stork's. A set of two misericords, one for each phase, is to be found in Aosta, Kempen, Lund and Oviedo. In the other places where only one scene is to be found, it is probable that there was once the complementing second scene. Here and there the carvers add comic touches. At Kempen the stork tries desperately to get the liquid food from the flat plate. At Oviedo the stork just watches the feasting fox, while several scenes on side panels add to the story: on one, the fox and the stork compromise by both eating from a bowl; on another the frustrated fox tries to stick his nose into the vase. At Ciudad Rodrigo he barks at the vase.

Misericord carvings showing the fox as host are to be found in:

Germany, Kempen, St Mary (N, lower, 4);
Italy, Aosta Abbey Ours (position not recorded);
Portugal, Coimbra, north-west, lower, 1, as well as north-west, upper, 1;

Spain, Oviedo Cathedral (east, 5);
Sweden, Lund Cathedral (position not recorded).

Destroyed in the Second World War was a carving in Emmerich, *Germany*; and in Oirschot, *the Netherlands*.

Carvings showing the stork as host are to be found in:
Belgium, Aarschot (N, lower, 7);
Germany, Kempen, St Mary (N, lower, 3); Steinfeld (S 6);
Italy, Aosta Abbey Ours (position not recorded);
The Netherlands, Nederweert (N 1); Venlo (N 9);
Portugal, Coimbra (S, lower, 11);
Spain, Ciudad Rodrigo Cathedral (S, upper, 15), and on the side panel, P. 3;
Sweden, Lund (position not recorded).

Both hosts are depicted together on one misericord in *Switzerland*, Basel Cathedral, number 6. Here the fox is presented with a vase, the stork with a plate.

(d) The Fox and the Eagle

Though well known from Classical Antiquity to and through the Middle Ages in most of western and central Europe, but never drawn into the Beast Epic, is the fable in which the friendship between the fox and the eagle turned into enmity when the eagle was tempted to take a vixen's cubs while she had left them to go hunting. We know of only one misericord carving of this: Gloucester Cathedral (N 23). Here the eagle pounces on a cringing fox-cub which does not look particularly fox-like, but a comparison with the way an unmistakable fox is depicted on other misericords (e.g., in the fox-physician carving, N 12), confirms that this is indeed a fox-cub.

11. Foxes in the Upside-Down, Topsy-turvy World

A few misericord scenes which may be related to the Beast Epic are those which depict the fox in world-upside-down situations. From time to time, especially in the *Roman de Renart*, the humour stems from a topsyturvy view of things, as when, at the beginning of Branch XVII, Reynard meets Couart the hare carrying behind him, dangling upside-down from a stake over his shoulder, a peasant who had attacked him but lost the ensuing engagement. This brings to mind the misericord in Castle Hed-

Figure 8,21 *Fox with man dangling from a shouldered stake behind him. Misericord, Castle Hedingham, probably late fourteenth century. Photograph by Kenneth Varty.*

ingham (S 3) depicting the fox with a man dangling from a shouldered stake (Figure 8.21). Also relevant is the misericord in Manchester Cathedral (N 9) which shows the fox riding on the back of a hound, a pole slung over his shoulder from which hangs a dead hare. In Westminster Abbey (N, upper, 6, left supporter), a goose rides a saddled and bridled fox. The scenes of geese hanging the fox also belong, of course, to this topsyturvy group of misericord carvings, all of them English.

12. The Fox Musician

In the *Roman de Renart*, the fox plays, in Branch I, the role of a travelling minstrel and entertainer. Although the fox appears on a number of misericords (and in other carvings and drawings) playing a variety of musical instruments, there is no visual representation of him which can be identified with certainty as being that of the Beast Epic entertainer.

In *England*, Castle Hedingham (S 3), he wears a scalloped cape and blows a trumpet. In Chichester Cathedral (S 19), he is seated as he plays a harp. His feet rest on a goose that gazes up at him. Opposite is an ape who seems to be dancing to the fox's harp music.

In *France*, St Amand sur Ozerain (N 4), a cowled fox plays a harp. Both the *Roman de Renart* text and these carvings should all be seen in the context of many a representation of many an animal (especially the harpist-ass), meant to ridicule and condemn popular music which, according to the Church, was sinful or led to sin.

13. Foxes and Fool

In *France*, Montbenoit Abbey (N, lower, 1) there is a misericord carving showing a man with a basket on his back out of which several foxes peer. A fool carrying his marotte follows the man. The significance of this scene escapes us.

14. The Fox, the Lion and the Unicorn

In the series of woodcuts made for Wynkyn de Worde's c.1495 edition of the History of Reynard the Fox, there are two scenes in which a unicorn, who plays no part in the Epic, looks on, alongside the lion and other animals, as justice of a kind is supposed to be dispensed. One of these occasions is when the fox is on the gallows ladder (Figure 8.5) facing execution, and the other is when he fights a judicial duel with the wolf.

In England, Knowle parish church, there is a misericord (exact position not recorded) which shows a crudely-carved lion with, on one side, a unicorn, and on the other, a fox. The unicorn is recognisable only by its horn, the fox by its brush. The unicorn usually symbolised justice and virtue, the fox deceit and vice. Perhaps this carving shows that the powerful (the lion) has a choice to make between good and bad in exercising his authority.

15. Plain Foxes

There are, of course, many drawings and carvings of unadorned, ordinary foxes, sometimes in their natural habitat, but these are relatively rare on misericords:

In *England*, Beverley Minster (S, upper, 20, left supporter): two seated foxes, back to back, turn their heads to face each other. Garstang, St Helen's (N 6): a fox.

In *France*, Nozeroy (S 1): a fox stands. Besse-en-Chandesse (S, lower, 1): two foxes hold each other's front paws.

In *Spain*, Barcelona Cathedral (south-west, 2, right supporter): a fox looks towards the central scene depicting a shepherd.

Conclusions

The fact that all these carvings appear in churches means that most of them, no matter what the subject-matter, will have had a moral, didactic-religious purpose, even those that seem most obviously inspired by 'secular' Beast Epic episodes and related texts. This overriding purpose will have been a major reason for modifying the received subject-matter. Other, not insignificant reasons for modifying it, will have been the medium used (here, mostly wood), the quality of the tools available, the skill of the woodcarver, and the wishes of his patron. Different regions with their cultural differences and histories will also have made their impact. While the texts and the illustrations which were made for them may have influenced both patron and carver, poets and illustrators may well, in their turn, have been influenced by carvings and drawings in the churches they entered. All of them, texts and their illustrations, carvings and drawings, complement each other and reflect the spirit of the different periods and places (often preaching and moralising, sometimes criticising or subverting) in which their authors worked.

◆ CHAPTER 9 ◆

REYNARD IN ENGLAND: FROM CAXTON TO THE PRESENT

Kenneth Varty

Before Caxton's *History of Reynard the Fox*, a translation he made from the Dutch and published in Westminster in 1481, we know of only two narrative poems which feature the fox and which are related, though distantly, to the Continental Beast Epic. They are *The Fox and the Wolf*, (anonymous, 259 lines, c.1260) and *The Nun's Priest's Tale of the Cok and the Fox* (Chaucer, 695 lines, c.1390). The first tells how the fox got trapped in a well and managed to get the wolf to change places with him; the second, how the fox managed to trap the cock by flattery, but then lost him through his own vanity. Both are related, one way or another, and perhaps remotely, to branches of the *Roman de Renart*; the first to Branch IV, Reynard and Ysengrin in the Well (*Renart et Ysengrin dans le puits*); the second to that part of Branch II called Reynard and Chantecler (*Renart et Chantecler*). In the first, the fox tells the wolf that his name is Renuard. The wolf's name is Sigrim. The cock is twice referred to as Chaunticler. All of these are obvious echoes of proper names in Branch IV. In Chaucer's poem, only the cock's name, Chantecler, has a familiar echo. The fox is Russell, the cock's wife is Pertelote (Pinte in Branch II). But there is other evidence, neatly summarised by Kenneth Sisam (1927) in the introduction to his Clarendon Press edition of the *Nun's Priest's Tale* (xliii–xlviii) to show that Chaucer almost certainly had a French model in mind, later than the earliest form of Branch II, but probably a reworking of it.

In 1479, in Gouda, Gheraert Leeu published *Die Hystorie van Reynaert die Vos*, a prose version of the long-established verse *Reynaerts Historie*. The story-line of the version of the Beast Epic, summarised by Paul Wackers at the beginning of Chapter Five, was to be the same in the earliest English and German-language epics and in their derivations for centuries, as well as for later Dutch-language versions.

In England, Caxton's 1481 text remained largely the same for just over a century, during which time it was frequently reprinted. He himself reprinted it in 1481; Wynkyn de Worde in c.1495 and c.1515; Richard Pynson in the late 1490s and the early 1500s; Thomas Gaultier in 1550; William Powell in c.1560; Edward Allde in 1586. All of these editions, and a few others, are described in detail by Menke (1992: 205–213). The text of each of them differed slighty from its predecessor in its orthography, in its vocabulary (e.g., by the replacement of Dutch loan-words, of older phrases by more up-to-date idiomatic expressions, of older words by latinised ones), and in occasional tiny changes in the syntax. There was also a tendency to expand the text just a little here and there, but these minute changes never affected the narrative. The only important modification during this first stage in the history of the English Beast Epic occurred early on, as early as c.1495, with the introduction of a series of forty-three woodcuts, mostly of good, sometimes very good, artistic quality. Measuring approximately 12.5 cm high by 9 cm wide, they occupied the greater part of the pages on which they were printed. They were made, it seems, for Wynkyn de Worde's c.1495 edition, and were soon afterwards used by Pynson. The earliest use of a nearly complete set of these woodcuts to come down to us is in an edition published sometime between 1560 and 1585. As the first and last few pages of this edition are missing, neither its publisher nor place of publication can be identified. A detailed account of the source, content and history of this cycle of woodcuts is given in Varty (1980).

During the seventeenth century, the History of Reynard the Fox underwent quite a few changes as its popularity grew and it entered a period in which good literature was, more than in the preceding century, expected to be morally profitable, as well as entertaining. The first major change, or, rather, addition to the narrative, took place with the 1620 edition by Edward Allde. This took the form of explanations and moralising comments printed down the verso left or the recto right margins in a smaller font than that used for the narrative. The expanded title drew attention to these comments, and to other (minor) changes: *The Most delectable History of REYNARD the Fox. Newly Corrected and purged from all the grosenesses* [sic] *both in Phrase and Matter. As also Augmented and Inlarged with sundry excellent Moralls and Expositions upon every severall Chapter. Never before this time Imprinted.* We offer just one example of the moral expositions taken from the text of the chapter in which the naked village priest loses a testicle in his fight with Tibert the cat (not considered gross, not purged!). It is headed *The Morall* and it reads, in full:

> By the Fox insnaring of the Cat is exprest, how when wise men will trust their enemies, or give credit to reconciled friends, they evermore miscarry in their designes; and therefore every wise man should so temper his Actions, that he grow not fond of any thing in his enemies power, however agreable so ever it bee either with his Nature or his Power. For by the baytes of an enemy are only gilded pilles, which are faire to look on, but most bitter to tast; By the mischiefe which the Priest received, is showed, that they which harme watch harme catch, and that the trappe which men now and then set for others, bring hurt to themselves.

These comments occur fairly frequently (on almost every other page) up to the end of the tenth chapter. They become less frequent and less lengthy in the middle, and are rare in the last few chapters. Though there is some rewording of the story, it remains essentially the same, in spite of the fact that its division into just over forty chapters throughout most of the sixteenth century has been changed and is now reduced to just twenty-five. The Wynkyn de Worde woodcuts are regularly used, now badly worn, sometimes damaged, sometimes repaired or even replaced. The whole cycle was replaced by fairly good copies made for Brewster's 1671 edition which has the same title as Allde's 1620 edition less, of course, the claim that the moral comments are new. Sixteen or seventeen editions of this kind between (and including) 1620 and 1701 are known (Menke 1992: 213–28).

Meanwhile, in 1672, the publisher Edward Brewster, having given new life to the old Wynkyn de Worde picture cycle in 1671, gave new life to the old History of Reynard the Fox by publishing a sequel: *A Continuation, Or Second Part Of The Most Pleasant and Delightful History of Reynard the Fox Containing Much Matter of Pleasure and Content Written For the Delight of Young*

Men, Pleasure of the Aged, and Profit of all. The new story, the *Continuation*, begins with Reynard in his new role as the lion's chief minister. His first move is to form an alliance with the wolf and make him chief prelate. This makes the bear and the cat jealous so he grants favours to them and wins them over. They all enrich themselves (especially Reynard) and plot against the lion. The leopard and the panther inform the lion of the plot against him, and together they attack Reynard and his allies. After suffering heavy losses, Reynard and his surviving friends retreat to his castle where they are besieged. After a long and fierce resistance, they are taken prisoner. Reynard is put on trial, found guilty of treason, and executed. This sequel was republished for certain in 1681 and probably in 1673 and 1699.

Then, in 1684, Brewster marketed a further sequel, this time to the *Continuation*. Since Reynard was dead, the chief role in this new story is given to one of his sons, the one called Reynardine. It is entitled *The Shifts of Reynardine The Son of Reynard the Fox, Or a Pleasant History Of His Life and Death. Full of Variety (etc.). And may fitly be applied to the Late Times. Now Published for the Reformation of Mens Manners*. This story begins by reporting how Reynard, before his execution (at the end of the *Continuation*) gave his vast hidden fortune to his sons Volpus and Reynardine. He instructed them how to hide it safely away for their future use and made them swear to revenge him on his two betrayers, Firapel the leopard and Sly-Look the panther. However, the young foxes were quite soon attacked and robbed of their treasure. In the process Volpus got killed, but Reynardine made good his escape and, in a distant land, began a peripatetic series of adventures. He first entered the Kingdom of Zalep where he made friends with Brocket the badger. Following the badger's advice he went on to the monastery of Manton where he was admitted as a novice, but he soon tired of the monastic life and made his escape. Retaining his novice's gown he was able to return to Zalep and make a good living by granting easy shrift to the wicked and by selling indulgences cheaply. Eventually the loss of his gown put an end to this phase in his life. He returns to Feraria, his native country, meets Zani the ape, teams up with him and, at his suggestion, turns physician. He assumes the title and name of Doctor Pedanto, and quickly gains a large practice among the common people. His reputation is such that, when the old leopard Firapel falls ill, he is summoned to his bedside. True to the promise he had made to his father shortly before his execution, Reynardine takes advantage of the situation and kills the sick old leopard with an overdose of a sleeping potion. Zani quarrels with Reynardine over the division of money they had got out of Firapel. In spite, the ape denounces Doctor Pedanto as an impostor, but Reynardine manages to leave the country before Noble has a chance to seize him. He then comes into conflict with a mountebank who cuts off his ears and brush. Unwillingly disguised in this way, Reynardine returns to the royal court where, calling himself Crabron, he enters the panther's service, only to carry out the oath he had made to his condemned father by poisoning the panther. He feigns grief at Sly-Look's death so successfully that Noble makes him one of his chief purveyors. In this office he ruthlessly eliminates his enemies but is at last unmasked and, under torture, admits his crimes. Condemned to death, he wins a reprieve by telling monstrous lies from the scaffold. Unrepentant, he returns to a life of crime, but is caught again and, after a full confession, is executed.

The *Shifts* were to be reprinted quite often, and in 1694 and 1701 they were included in one volume together with (and after) the traditional (Caxtonian) History and Brewster's 1684 *Continuation*. The 1701 volume is entitled: *The Most Delectable HISTORY OF Reynard the FOX. Newly Corrected and Purged, from all grossness in Phrase and Matter. Augmented and Enlarged with sundry Excellent Morals and Expositions upon every several Chapter. To which may be added a Second Part of the said History: As also the Shifts of Reynardine the Son of Reynard the FOX, Together with his Life and Death.*

As the seventeenth century drew to its close, W. Onley published, in 1697, a new arrangement of this expanded Reynardian matter by cutting out the *Continuation* and having the *Shifts* immediately follow the traditional Anglo-Flemish story. Just into the eighteenth century, in 1702, Onley reprinted this new two-part form of the epic to which he added a third but non-Reynardian book centred on a rook called Cawood, and this is how the epic appeared again and again in the eighteenth century. The 1702 title reads: *The Most Pleasing and Delightful HISTORY OF Reynard the Fox, AND REYNARDINE his Son. In Two Parts. With Morals to each Chapter, explaining what appears Doubtful or Allegorical: and every Chapter illustrated with a curious Device, or Picture representing to the Eye all the material Passages. To which is added, The History of Cawood the Rook: or, The Assembly of Birds; With the several Speeches they made to the Eagle, in hopes to have the Government in his Absence: How the Rook was banish'd; with the Reason why crafty fellows are call'd Rooks. Together with Morals and Expositions on every Chapter.* Further editions of this arrangement have been traced to 1708, c1710 (?), 1723, 1735, 1749, 1758, 1763 and 1787 (Menke 1992: 234–42). The two Reynardian parts of these three-part volumes were all illustrated with varying numbers of pictures which are mostly, and obviously, inspired by their counterparts in the Wynkyn de Worde cycle. It is chiefly the six cuts made for the Reynardine part of Onley's 1708 edition which are quite new, and which were also subsequently occasionally imitated.

As Norman Blake has pointed out, although all the seventeenth- and eighteenth-century English versions of the Beast Epic can be traced back utimately to Caxton's translation, they differ from it because each new version appears to be a reworking of the previous one.

> Thus there was a continous process of modernisation, adaptation, and interpolation at work. But a return to Caxton's original was made in 1844 when W. J. Thoms produced his edition of *Reynard the Fox* based on Caxton's text of 1481... Another edition of Caxton's text was prepared by Edward Arber for the English Scholar's Library. This edition, which appeared in 1878 and again in 1895, attempts to reproduce the original spelling and punctuation... It is hardly surprising that a story which was so popular and which had been translated by Caxton should also have been printed privately in the late nineteenth century when private presses were numerous. Two private printings were made at this time: one for the Bibliotheca Curiosa in 1884 [by Goldsmid] and the other by the Kelmscott Press in 1892' [by Sparling] (Blake 1970: lxiii)

The best of the nineteenth- and twentieth-century scholarly editions of Caxton, in addition to the four just mentioned (of which, full details in the Bibliography), are: Morley (1889), reprinted 1907; Stallybrass (1924); Sands (1960); and, above all, Blake (1970).

A number of serious, competent metrical renderings of Caxton's text have been made. Of these we mention just two. Brewster was not the only late seventeenth-century publisher of the Beast Epic to feel the need to renew it. His contemporary John Shurley (sometimes spelled Shirley) also felt that need and, in 1681, he published his *Most Delightful History of Reynard the Fox in Heroic Verse*. The iambic pentameters rhyming in couplets are divided into twenty-four chapters and run to 4,000 lines and 114 pages. It was never reprinted. Just over two hundred years later, in 1894, F.S. Ellis published a translation in octosyllabic rhyming couplets based on Sparling's 1892

Kelmscott Press text. This was carefully revised and reprinted on good-quality paper and in a fine binding in 1897. Each of the forty-five chapters is headed by a beautifully designed, illustrated 'device' (by the artist Walter Crane) about one inch high and three inches wide. The full title-page title reads: *The History Of Reynard The Fox, His Friends And His Enemies, His Crimes, Hairbreadth Escapes, And Final Triumph. A Metrical Version Of The Old English Translation With Glossorial Notes. In Verse By F. S. Ellis. With Devices By Walter Crane.*

Although the Kelmscott Press edition and Ellis's 1897 verse rendering are beautifully produced and were intended to appeal to collectors of fine books, there is nothing to compare in Britain with the steady production in Belgium, Holland and France of finely printed and bound copies of the 'native' Beast Epic, which serve chiefly as vehicles for illustrations made by artists of the highest calibre. But there might have been. In 1896 a wealthy Glasgow textile manufacturer and art collector, T.G. Arthur, commissioned one of Britain's finest young artists, Joseph Crawhall, to make ten drawings to illustrate Caxton's *Historye of Reynart the Foxe*. Though Crawhall made the drawings in 1896–97, Arthur abandoned the idea of the illustrated Caxton, and sold the drawings to W.A. Coates, who had them reproduced in facsimile and offered to the public in 1906 in a limited edition of two hundred copies. The originals, never used in the way they were meant to be, are kept in Glasgow's Burrell Collection.

Besides the continuations and sequels, the creeping modernization, modification and amplification of Caxton's text throughout the seventeenth and eighteenth centuries, followed by serious attempts in the nineteenth and twentieth centuries to return to his original text, there have been two other major modifications to the History of Reynard the Fox. The first was to make much-abbreviated, cheap, crudely-illustrated pocket-book versions of it, the chapbooks, perhaps in response to its popularity with the less well-off. In these slender volumes, the narrative is considerably abbreviated, often reduced to about twenty-four small pages measuring about 8.5 cm wide by 15.5 cm high. Even if aimed at the less well-off, the authors clearly expected their readers to be relatively well educated, to judge by the kind of language they use ('It was when the woods was [sic] cloathed with green attire, and the meadows adorned with fragrant flowers; when birds chaunted forth their harmonious songs, the Lion made a great feast at his palace of Sanden, and issued a proclamation for all the beasts and herds to come thereto without delay, on pain of his contempt...'). There are two kinds of chapbook: those divided into twelve or thirteen two-page chapters (like the ones published for Conyers in London between 1685 and 1688; by Saint in Newcastle upon Tyne between 1769 and 1788; and by Smart in Woverhampton, 1780, all called *The Most Pleasant History of Reynard the Fox*); and those divided into nine two-to-three page chapters and all called quite simply *The History of Reynard the Fox* (for example, the ones published and sold in Aldermary Church Yard, London, c.1750; in London, c.1775; again in London, but c.1780; and in Penrith by Soulby, c.1800. (Menke 1992: 231–34 and 248–50). One notes that these chapbooks are often marketed outside London. Most of them are illustrated with poor-quality cuts. The twelve-to-thirteen-chapter chapbooks contain only title-page illustrations; but two of the nine-chapter chapbooks have a mini-series of five or six pictures which begin to deviate in their subject-matter, but uninterestingly, from that of the traditional Wynkyn de Worde cycle.

The second major modification to Caxton's text was to make expurgated, shorter versions in simpler English for young people and for children. Although 'young men' are mentioned as part of the intended readership of Brewster's 1672 *Shifts*, one of the earliest versions intended for the really young was Edward Ryland's c.1775 *The pleasant and entertaining History of Reynard the Fox Represented in a MORAL Light; Fabulously shewing various Devices which cunning Men pursue, and exciting the Innocent & Ignorant to guard against them; a Work equally humorous and instructive to the YOUNG and to the MATURE; Embellished with 17 Copper Plates elegantly Engraved*. Some of these plates are indeed elegant, in particular the frontispiece which depicts a man who seems to be both father and teacher with an open book upon his knees. He seems to be telling his three young children about the wicked fox at which he points as it runs off, on the horizon, with a goose flung over its back. While a few of the engravings are of hitherto unillustrated events, as when the fox steals a suckling pig from its mother's teats, this is due to the inclusion of new material in the narrative. Though the title includes the 'mature' among its intended readership, the condescending tone of the introduction and the size of the children in the frontispiece picture suggest that a really young readership was envisaged. 'Attend, ye youths of infant mold, / To what the following sheets unfold!' exclaims the author at the beginning of the prefatory poem. Nevertheless, the language used in the telling of the tale would often be difficult for the really young, and certainly boring. Many years pass before the publication of another young person's version of Caxton's History; but the wait is well worth while. Summerly's 1843 retelling for children is illustrated by one of the finest of Dutch book illustrators: *The Pleasant History of Reynard the Fox Told by the Pictures of Aldert* [sic] *van Everdingen*. Another of the earliest richly illustrated Victorian young-folk's versions is David Vedder's 1852 retelling, *The Story of Reynard the Fox*. But this is not a direct retelling of Caxton even if the story-line is close to Caxton's. Vedder's text is based on the 1706 English verse translation of Hartmann Schopper's 1569 Latin text (discussed by Wilfried Schouwink in Chapter Ten). This, in its turn, is based, via a 1544 High German shortened translation, on that of the 1498 Lübeck Low German, and thence back to the Flemish on which Caxton drew. Vedder's book is splendidly illustrated by the German artist Gustav Canton, but modestly so and in keeping with a text which has been carefully expurgated and made suitable for decent young people. For example, the episode in Caxton which tells how the naked village priest and his concubine fall upon the ensnared cat, who then bites off one of the priest's testicles, is modified to read:

> The servants were all alarmed, and the cry was set up, 'The Fox is taken!' and away they all ran to where poor Malkin [the cat] was caught in the snare, and without finding out their mistake, they beat him unmercifully, and wounded one of his eyes. Mad with pain, the Cat suddenly gnawed the cord, sprung on one of the head servants, and scratched him so severely that he fainted...'

There have been quite a few illustrated children's versions of Caxton's story-line since Summerly's in 1843, but very few have been well written and well illustrated by fine artists whose work truly enhances the book and makes it memorable. Two of the better ones in relatively recent times are Roy Brown's *Reynard the Fox* (1969), illustrated by John Vernon Lord with numerous black-and-white drawings which sometimes bring the animals close to being cartoon-like creatures, but often convey considerable feeling. More recently, in 1990, Selina Hastings's *Reynard the Fox*, abundantly illustrated in muted colours by Graham Percy (indeed, the space taken up by the pictures is greater than that taken by the text), contains many pictures which show considerable independence from the traditional way of depicted significant moments in Reynard's career. Both text and pictures, adjusting to the intended readership, tone down the violence which permeates the original animal epic.

As interest in the much-modified Caxton version of the Beast Epic waned in the eighteenth century, and all but disappeared as far as the general reading public was concerned in the early nineteenth century, there was a revival in Reynard's fortunes in the middle and latter half of the nineteenth century through the growing reputation of, and familiarity with, Goethe's *Reineke Fuchs*. This was first published in 1794 and often reprinted in Germany. In 1846 it was brilliantly illustrated by Wilhelm von Kaulbach. This text, translated into English, and this artist's pictures, played an important role in the renewal of interest in Reynardian matter in Britain at both adult and young people's levels. It is perhaps worth recalling here that both poet and painter had, indirectly, links with that most influential of late medieval and illustrated texts, the 1498 Lübeck *Reynke de Vos* (directly descended from the Dutch *Reynaerts Historie*, as was Caxton's text). Goethe's immediate literary source was Gottsched's 1752 High German translation (via a Wolfenbüttel 1711 reprint) of the Low German Lübeck text. Kaulbach's models for his pictures included the seventeenth-century Dutch artist Allart van Everdingen (mentioned above in connection with an early English children's version of Caxton; and whose illustrations were published for the first time in Gottsched's 1752 *Reineke Fuchs*), as well as one or more of the several woodcut cycles published in Germany such as the Rostock versions (1517, 1539, 1549) and the Frankfurt versions (1550, 1556, etc.) all of which go back to the woodcut cycle in the 1498 Lübeck edition (Menke 1992: 256–355). The earliest translation of Goethe's *Reineke Fuchs* into English seems to have been the one by Soltau in 1803. Others followed in Queen Victoria's reign, probably in part through the influence of Prince Albert who inspired much admiration for German culture, though Goethe's reputation was by then immense. Among the more important translations were Naylor's in 1844; Holloway's in 1852; Arnold's in 1855; a fine, folio, Kaulbach-illustrated reprinting of this in New York in 1872; Ainslie's in 1886; and Rogers's in 1888. A selection of Kaulbach's Reynardian illustrations first appeared in England as early as 1851 in a rather unusual book which celebrated and commemorated an unusual aspect of the Great Exhibition held in the Crystal Palace in 1850 (all also Prince Albert inspired). This book's title is: *The Comical Creatures from Wurtemberg, Including the Story of Reynard the Fox with Twenty Illustrations Drawn from the Stuffed Animals Contributed by Hermann Ploucquet of Stuttgart to the Great Exhibition* (London: Bogue, 1851). One reads in the Preface that 'the famous painter Kaulbach has recently illustrated Goethe's version [of the Reynard story] with perhaps the finest series of pictures with which a book was ever adorned'. Ploucquet selected six of Kaulbach's etchings to illustrate the thirty-three-page abbreviated (censored, expurgated) version of *The Story of Reynard the Fox* with which this strange little book (clearly intended for both mature and young people as a kind of souvenir of their visit to the Stuffed Animals Section of the Great Exhibition) concludes. 'Everyone,' says the anonymous author in his Preface, 'from her Majesty the Queen down to the charity boys, hastens to see the Stuffed Animals from the Zollverein'. Exaggerated though this claim may seem, it is at least supported by the sober Professor J.A. Froude who, in *Fraser's Magazine*, 1882, in an essay entitled 'Reynard the Fox', writes: 'The appearance of the Wurtemberg animals at the Exhibition came fortunately *apropos* to our assistance: a few years ago it was rare to find a person who had read the Fox Epic... but now the charming figures of Reineke himself, and King Lion, and Isegrim, and Bruin... had set all the world asking who and what they were, and the story began to get itself known. The old editions, which had long slept unbound in reams upon the shelves, begun to descend and to clothe themselves in green and crimson. Mr Dickens sent a summary of it around the households of England. Everybody began to talk of Reineke...' This is a fascinating tribute to the power of illustration, even in the form of stuffed animals from Noble's court, to stimulate interest in a story.

But as the twentieth century grew older, even translations and adaptations of Goethe's *Reineke Fuchs* faded from view, as did those based on Caxton. Translations and adaptations of the Beast Epic from other languages and cultures have recently appeared in English but, in spite of their excellence, they show no sign of bringing about a revival in its fortunes in Britain or in other anglophone cultures. One thinks in particular of Adriaan Barnouw's 1967 fine translation from the Dutch ; Patricia Terry's 1983 lively verse translation of a few of the early branches from the *Roman de Renart*, reprinted in 1992; Roy Owen's 1994 highly readable, scholarly prose translation of most of the branches; and the especially well written, beautifully illustrated children's 1986 retelling by Anderson,

Bradby and Dewar. Although the name Reynard will probably make many Britons think of the fox, and that of Bruin will be associated with the bear, and Tibby or Tabby are names they give to cats, they have forgotten Noble and his animal-courtiers, they have lost sight of Reynard and of his descendants, unless one of them is Beatrix Potter's Mr Tod, or Roald Dahl's (and many another's) Mr Fox.

CHAPTER 10

HARTMANN SCHOPPER'S
LATIN *REINIKE* OF 1567

Wilfried Schouwink

We are in the midst of the sixteenth century. Shakespeare has already been born and Elizabeth I is Queen of England, Mary Stuart Queen of Scotland. In England as well as in Germany the Reformation has put an end to the Christian Universe as it had been known throughout the Middle Ages. Its various new factions are engaged in bloody warfare. Among the fighting armies we find a countless crowd of adventurers and mercenaries, one of them being Hartmann Schopper, the author of the 1567 Latin *Reinike*.[1]

Reinike's exploits, arranged by several Flemish editors in several stages, resulting in the now familiar double cycle of two court procedures against the fox[2] had been translated into English by Caxton in 1481 and, with great public success, into Low German in the anonymous Lübeck edition of 1498.[3] The invention of printing had obviously given wings to the stories of the wily fox. A vulgate version of the Renardian cycles, established in the preceding centuries, was now circulating successfully in the vernaculars of the sixteenth century. Since it was the time of ecclesiastic unrest with the ensuing Reformation and Counter-Reformation, the pranks and wiles of Reinike, as well as those of his beastly antagonists, had been capitalised on in every version as an instrument to disparage the lamentable state of affairs in the established

Church. In particular, Reinike's half-hearted confessions to the badger and to Martin, the monkey,[4] had been a most welcome opportunity to crack down on the hypocrisy, greed and rapacity of all sorts of ecclesiastics. Moreover, since the Lübeck edition of 1498, Reinike's adventures were accompanied by a gloss, a largely moralist commentary on specific details of the action. When the Reformation had taken effect in Germany a new gloss was published in 1539,[5] now specifically attacking Catholic abuse and extolling good examples of Protestant behaviour. This is nowadays referred to as the 'protestant' or the 'younger gloss' as opposed to the 'older' or 'catholic gloss' of 1498. In 1544 the Low German *Reynke de Vos* and protestant gloss was translated into High German.[6] The translator, obviously having in mind a largely Catholic public, modified the gloss though he did not completely eliminate its anti-Catholic innuendos. This work of 1544 supplied the direct source for Schopper's Latin *Opus Poeticum*. It seems to be somewhat surprising that after all these vernacular versions and commentaries somebody should have the idea of creating a new Latin *Reinike*. We may well ask: What on earth could have made Schopper deem a translation of a well-established vernacular epic into the antiquated idiom of the learned and the privileged a worthwhile undertaking? The sixteenth-century reader, however, must have thought differently about this project. Schopper's Latin *Reinike* enjoyed great esteem not only in Germany but also in other European countries. At that time communication in Latin still proved to be more reliable to assure general and widespread understanding than any vernacular.

Schopper follows closely the familiar structure of the plot as to be found in *Reynke de Vos* and its High German translation of 1544. He maintained its division into four books and the respective chapters. The most striking differences, apart from unavoidable alterations as necessitated by the Latin idiom, may be summarised under three different aspects: firstly, the tremendous impact of classical Roman literature on the representation of all animal characters, in particular the fox; secondly, literal adaptations of liturgical language, especially in the episodes of the fox's confession and penance; thirdly, the world of the mercenary, Schopper's own world, in the representation of specific details of the fox's exploits and, more openly, in various prologues and epilogues with biographical digressions. A brief look at the posterity of this sixteenth-century Latin *Reinike* will conclude this essay.

1. A Virgilian *Reinike* – Schopper's Humanist Ambitions

Schopper's narrative starts with a significant alteration to the old first line *Id gheschach vp eynen pynxstedach* (It happened the day of Pentecost). The presentation of a typical Arthurian situation, the festive ambience of a major religious holiday, does not seem to have caught the imagination of the sixteenth-century neolatinist. He just omits the line and continues, now in accordance with his model, with a description of springtime:

> An amazing thing once happened in the mellow time of spring,
> when pleasant groves deck themselves in luscious colours of flowers ...
> King Lion, ruler of all beasts,
> called them from all parts of the earth
> to come to a sumptuous feast. (*Op. Poet.* I, i,13–16)

Since they are written in humanist Latin, the introductory lines almost inevitably conjure up a classical *locus amoenus* (place of pleasance) and are certainly closer to the spirit of Virgil's *Bucolics* than to a medieval court scene. We may safely assume that Schopper was well aware of the artistic dilemma implied in a project that was to transfer medieval roques into the world of the Roman classics, a world considered to be the model of perfection by all humanist writers. After all, translating this medieval Beast Epic had not been a project of his own choice and decision, but a commission given to him by the very successful Frankfurt publisher, Sigmund Feyerabend. Schopper's reservations are reflected in the very first lines of his epic:

> The fate of those who have to serve, enormous hardships produced by the courts of kings, I write them down almost against my will. Kindly assist me, Delius-Apollo, and grant guidance to your poet. Let pungent Iambics, shunned by me at other times, suffice for this work without green bile getting in the way, so I may pronounce stupendous feats of the fraudulent fox to all this earth's inhabitants. (*Op. Poet.*, I, i, 1–12)

A good portion of this *exordium* may be considered rhetorical commonplace: modesty as the traditional poetic device to gain the public's affection. Nevertheless, the poet's awareness of a very unusual task for a lover of classical Latin is clearly noticeable. 'Pungent iambics', the iambic quadrimeter, frequently used in medieval Latin, but rarely in the time of humanist classicism, seem to drive up the green bile in him. And yet he chose them as if picking a formal bracket to hold together what otherwise would fall apart: the idealised world of the classical hero and the world of beastly rogues trying to outdo each other in whatever fraud, cunning or mindless brutality can be conceived. Translating the medieval Beast Epic into the language of Virgil thus meant for Schopper squeezing material into a form which he considered basically unsuitable. The artistic consequences of this outlook can be observed in many episodes of the Latin *Reinike*. The following examples may demonstrate how this mismatch of form and content produced rhetorical constructions which cannot help drawing a good laugh from the reader.

At the beginning of the ninth chapter of the second book we see the fox and the badger for the second time on their way to the royal court. The fox has just confessed another series of misdeeds, with as little disposition to mend his ways as ever. Instead he has decried the lamentable state of the Church and its clergy (*Op. Poet.* II, vi – viii). Now they meet up with Martin, the ape, who happens to be on his way to Rome (*Op. Poet.* II, ix, 1–4). Whereas in the German versions of the episode the ape greets the fox with a simple 'Cheer up and be confident' (*Reynke de Vos*, II, ix, 5; *Von Reinicken Fuchs*, II, ix, 5), Schopper lets him start a solemn Horatian discourse on the virtues of composure and equanimity:

> O most welcome friend, keep your equanimity and know to endure in the most arduous situations just the way when in success and convenience for your brave soul you don't lower the high bowsprit but turn the billowed sails into propitious winds. (*Op. Poet.* II, ix, 8–15).[7]

When it comes to the old chicken-thief with billowed sails to reply, he does not just 'talk' (*Reinike sprach*) as in the German versions, but 'draws a deep sigh from the innermost abode of his heart' (*Op. Poet.* II, ix, 18f.).

He does not just hope to be admitted to the king and to remain a respected person (*unnd woell noch bleiben ein geachter Man*), but is prepared 'to protect the pristine dignity and good reputation of his name with his brave heart' (*Op. Poet.* II, ix, 37–39). The ape's intimate knowledge of the wicked ways of the high Roman clergy, as expounded in detail in the ninth chapter of the second book, offers a welcome intermezzo for the fox and his friend, the badger. But when approaching the royal court the old sinner all of a sudden feels a little bit queasy. Nevertheless, he manages to 'conceal his bitter pain in his high-spirited heart'. The reader's imagination is inevitably caught by another hero's sorrows: Aeneas, when leaving the ashes of Troy in order to set out for a new world, looks back once more: 'His face's appearance seems to indicate hope, but in his heart he conceals the deep-felt pain' *(Op. Poet.* III, i, 15f).[8] As opposed to the emotions of the classical hero of ancient Rome, the fox's uneasiness is only the air of a brief moment. The badger, as versed in classical literature as he himself, cheers him up with the all too well known 'Fortune favours the brave' *(Op. Poet.* III, i, 27).[9]

A definite humanist touch may also be noticed in episodes which do not involve the fox directly. In the ninth chapter of the first book the bear, beguiled by the fox, is trapped in a trunk and bashed by a mob of angry peasants. Both the version of 1498 and its High German translation present us with a cabinet piece of rural chaos with bodies hurled around and flung into the mud without achieving anything, a scene already to be found in the *Ysengrimus*[10] and repeated many times since. Schopper seems to have had little appreciation for the bizarreness of a rustic mob wielding household equipment and garden tools. He reduces the passage to little more than half its original length, deletes most of the bizarre names which characterise the actors and introduces instead a oneeyed Acon and a red-haired Tityrus, a name taken from Virgil's *Bucolics*.[11] Schopper's presentation of the angry peasants thus no longer features names like *Abelquack* and *Ruckelsrey* (*Von Reinicken Fuchs,* fol. xxi), but somewhat decadent representatives of the bucolic world of Virgil. This humanist touch in fashioning details of the narrative may be observed on many more occasions. For example, in the thirty-sixth chapter of the first book Bellinus, the gullible ram, carries a sealed bag with the hare's head in it to the lion-king, believing Reinike's letters and not the gruesome evidence of a murder to be the contents of his pack. He presents it with the words: 'Sire, Reinike has beseeched me to deliver these letters which bear the fragrance of Attic eloquence' *(Op. Poet.* I, xxxvi, 59–62). Resorting to comparisons with the epitome of classical rhetorics of course does not help the ram at all and he is handed over to the wolf and the bear for them to do with him whatever they like *(Op. Poet.* I, xxxvii).

Schopper's ambition to capitalise on his knowledge of classical authors wherever possible left its mark also on the commentaries. The gloss of 1539 had already made use of many classical commonplaces, even though its main sources are supplied by medieval German moralists like Hugo of Trimberg's *Renner*, Freidank's *Bescheidenhait* and Sebastian Brandt's *Ship of Fools*.[12] This gloss was then substantially abridged and modified by the High German translator. Schopper, however, expands this abridged version by inserting many examples taken from the classics. His method can be demonstrated by a brief look at his commentary on chapter I, xxv (I, xxvi in the German version). In this part of the narrative we see Reinike talking his way out of the imminent execution of his death sentence. He tells lies about a treasure discovered by his father and invents a conspiracy, planning to finance the hiring of soldiers who would implement the planned rebellion against the king. The old fox had already recruited a large number of mercenaries (*Op. Poet.*, I, xxv, 27–30) when Reinike managed to steal the funds for the insurrection, thereby saving the king. The respective gloss follows the version of 1544 and reads: 'Mercenaries are paid daredevils who would do anything for money which they worship as *altera anima*, as another part of themselves. They would even help Satan to conquer heaven if it were possible' (*Op. Poet.*, I, xxv, *Commentaria*). The mention of money as the driving force to get mercenaries to assail the obviously impossible prompts the Latin author to a major digression on the vicissitudes of *pecunia* as exemplified by classical authors such as Euripides, Aristophanes, Horace and Seneca.[13]

2. The Language of the Latin Liturgy

Schopper's poetic personality certainly displays the typical characteristics of a Latin humanist of that time, e. g., ample use of classical imagery and mythology, contempt for the common crowd, particularly for the *rusticus quadratus*, the 'blockheaded peasant', to whom he denies the right to criticise ecclesiastic authorities, however corrupt they may be (*Op. Poet.* II, viii, *Commentaria)*, and above all a very pronounced poetic self-assurance. Nevertheless, he cannot conceal his debt to the Latin of the medieval liturgy. The narrative itself with its various episodes involving a fox-monk or a wolf-monk[14] inevitably requires expressions of ecclesiastic Latin. This is particularly evident in all the passages which deal with the fox's phony promises to mend his ways and to do penance. In chapter I, xvi, for example, the fox beseeches the badger to hear his confession since he expects that such an act 'will be wholesome atonement for ruthless cruelty and a wretched life' (*Op. Poet.* I, xvi, 16-19). Schopper's German model speaks only of an improvement of his affairs as a possible result of his confession (*Von Reinicken Fuchs*, I, xvi, fol. xxxii[verso]). Compared with this rather vague notion the Latin text is more precise. Here, the fox expects *salubris expiatio* (wholesome atonement), a terminology which can be traced in a number of liturgical texts, particularly in formulas for the days of Lent, the annual time of penance before Easter.[15] The badger, in his admonition of the rueful sinner, uses typical New Testament phraseology, as opposed to the German version (*Von Reinicken Fuchs*, I, xvi, fol. xxxiii) where he only suggests feeling truly sorry for every deed of evil:

> Now is the time to put off the old skin, to put on new habits and to do penance (*Op. Poet.* I, xvi, 24-27).

The primary source for the old self to be stripped and clothed in a new garment is found in Eph. 4: 22ff. 'Put off the old man and put on the new man who is created in righteousness.' The same concept is, however, present in a variety of other New Testament passages. The term 'do penance' (*poenitentiam agere*) clearly reflects the call of John the Baptist to the multitudes in Matthew 3: 2. Biblical imagery and contemporary penitential terminology may also be recognised in the badger's promise: 'I shall free you of the thousand worms of a bad conscience' as opposed to 'A good penance will certainly do you good' in the German version (*Op. Poet.* I, xvi, 36f.).[16] The typical style of liturgical prayers, the formulation of a request by means of an infinitive construction depending on the devout expression *dignari* (to deem worthy), may be found in the lines with which the fox begins his phony confession: 'I beseech these beasts that they may deem me worthy of forgiveness and have mercy on the penitent' (*Op. Poet.* I, xvi, 43-45). In chapter I, 17 which contains the continuation of the fox's confession, the author reveals intimate knowledge of precise monastic terminology. When it comes to the passages where the wolf intends to become a monk Schopper expresses this as 'assuming the rule of the celibate cenobite' and 'ascending to the dignity of this rank' (*Op. Poet.*, I, xvii, 13f., 17f.).[17] The fox´s confession terminates, as customary in the respective ritual, with an assertion of his disposition to mend his ways and to do penance as imposed by his confessor. Without any hesitation Schopper's Reinike promises a 'life of unblemished integrity and perfect moderation' (*Op. Poet.* I, xvii, 73–75). His confessor, the badger, then grants remission and absolution of all his trespasses provided that the fox completes a *poenitentia utilis*, a 'useful penance'. The choice of the word *utilis* is odd in itself. Whereas the other key words in this mock confession have a perfect equivalent in the Roman ritual of penance, the expression *utilis* is a misfit. In a way it seems to unmask the true nature of the ritual in process: the fox's *poenitentia* is neither *vera* (truthful), nor *fructuosa* (fruitful, productive) nor *salubris* (wholesome),[18] but *utilis*, useful to get him out of a momentary predicament. The details of the penitential action underline this perspective, and this more so than can be noted in Schopper's German model. The badger breaks a *virgula*, a minute twig, from the *ramusculis*, the smallest branches of a wayside tree, hands it over to the fox and orders him to castigate himself by three strong blows on his skin. After the completion of this penance the badger pronounces his confessant 'acquitted of all ruthless misdeeds and the whole burden of his crimes' (*Op. Poet.* I, xvii, 103–05)[19] and admonishes him again to lead henceforth a true Christian life of moderation. The quality of the fox's penance is put to a test immediately afterwards when the two travellers come past the chicken-yard of a monastery and Reinike can't help taking a flying leap for the nearest prey (*Op. Poet.* I, xviii).[20] The badger's reproach presents an ingenious assemblage of ecclesiastic and classical rhetorics: 'O you uncouth bandit', he exclaims, 'more voracious than any wolf, how long do you put off the useful penance (*poenitentia utilis*) which I give you? You think constantly of illicit ways of poaching as being fruitful (*praedae fructuosae*)' (*Op. Poet.* I, xviii, 40–48). We have to compare the Latin wording with Cicero's Catilina-invective to appreciate how close the badger comes to the Roman classic:

Quousque differs vtilem Quam trado poenitentiam (*Op.Poet.* I, xviii, 43–44)
Quousque tandem Catilina abutere patientia nostra (Cicero *In Catilinam* I).

However, the labelling of a *praeda*, a prey, as *fructuosa* might well be a terminological pun on the uselessness of the fox's penance since *fructuosa*[21] is a liturgical term to qualify a good penance.

Apart from these obvious adaptations of liturgial phraseology there is another, more formal aspect that may demonstrate

Schopper's debt to the medieval Latin liturgy. In the dedication to Maximilian II which precedes Book I, in the first lines of the first chapter, and in the refutation of his critics (*In Zoilum*) at the end of Book IV he justifies his choice of the iambic meter. He refers to his lines as *Iambos pugnaces* or *Iambus acer* (*Op. Poet.*, *Epistola Dedicatoria* and *In Zoilum*, p. 400). Iambic quadrimeters are, as mentioned above, not the typical choice of a Latin poet of that time. Schopper himself and his friends use a variety of classical models, frequently the elegiac distichon. The verses about life at court, however, are meant to be pungent and with a beat. In the context of a reflection on the wiles of courtly life we may consider such a choice reasonable and almost self-explanatory. We must, however, bear in mind that this particular verse, the iambic quadrimeter, has a very long ecclesiastic tradition. Many hymns of the office of the hours are fashioned in this way. Among them there are such dignified poetic productions as Venantius Fortunatus' *Vexilla regis prodeunt* (The banner of the King comes forth) of the sixth century, but also the daily hymn *Te lucis ante terminum* (Before this day comes to a close, to Thee, Creator, all we turn), well known and translated into several vernaculars. The iambic quadrimeter is also present in many later productions, not only in hymns but also in liturgical texts of the narrative type, particularly in the solemn antiphones of festive days.[22] Such liturgical texts were produced throughout the Middle Ages and it is simply not feasible that a learned Catholic of the middle of the sixteenth century was not thoroughly familiar with both iambic hymns and also narrative iambic antiphones.

The presence of liturgical Latin in a production by a sixteenth-century humanist thus demonstrates the pertinacity of speech patterns acquired in the medieval liturgy, in spite of the repeated claims of the author to produce a poetic work in the style of Ovid and Virgil. And if we consider Schopper's personal situation with the publisher's pressure on him to finally complete the overdue translation, we may suspect something different still when reading his repeated justifications of the iambic meter: The iambic quadrimeter must have come in handy because it was easy to wield. He was well versed in it – in a literal sense – because of his intellectual heritage from a Catholic institute of higher education.[23] In a more generalised perspective we may observe that neolatin poets of the sixteenth century, in their efforts to resurrect classical Latinism, cannot conceal their indebtedness to medieval Latinism, however hard they may try.

3. Hartmann Schopper, the *Landsknecht:* the World of the Mercenary

Our author is representative of a particular type of German mercenary, called *Landsknecht*. This military institution had its great days between the end of the Middle Ages and the Thirty Years War. The Habsburg Emperors Maximilian I, Charles V, and Maximilian II relied on it in their numerous campaigns, and in the first decades of the sixteenth century we may observe the spontaneous formation of a veritable order of the *Landknechte* with rituals not unlike the ones of the traditional military orders of the Middle Ages.[24] It was a respectable institution in the days of its prime, and we know of several members who also excelled in the field of literature, amongst them Hartmann Schopper.[25] On various occasions he gives us detailed insight into the world where he lived as a young man in his early twenties, and whenever it seemed suitable he had the characters of his Latin *Reinike* act as if they were *Landsknechte* themselves. For example, in chapter I, xxv Reinike lies about a conspiracy against the king which was led by his father. Schopper's High German model and also the respective lines in *Reynke de Vos* speak of mercenaries recruited by Reinike's father. The *Landsknecht* poet, however, goes one step further. He has the old fox pride himself on the large number of soldiers he managed to recruit so they could all pillage the secret hoard: 'More than a thousand soldiers ready for war had sworn the oath of military glory' (*Op. Poet.* I, xxv, 24–29). The glamour of military glory together with plenty of loot, this is what any *Landsknecht* would have dreamt of.

The *Landsknecht's* imagination is also kindled by the various episodes where the king feels that he has finally had enough of Reinike's tricks and pranks and now wants an all-out war against him. Unlike his German model, Schopper goes into detail. The potential war would be furnished with hidden war machines, secret arms, so to speak, iron machineries, missiles joined together, in fact, equipment of the very worst kind (*Op. Poet.* I, xxxvii, 63f.; II, iii, 69–72; II, iv, 13f., 41f.). The author certainly knew what he was talking about, whereas we can only guess what these wondrous machines would have looked like and must resort to contemporary manuals of war equipment, like the one produced by Schopper himself, the ΠΑΝΟΠΛΙΑ *omnium illiberalium artium*,[26] an illustrated compendium of crafts and trades of the day, with emphasis on the military.

While the Latin *Reinike* is full of beastly *Landsknechts* wielding mysterious weapons and swearing oaths of military glory, its author's career in this field seems to have been a veritable disaster. When examining the few documents which illustrate episodes of his life, we get the impression that Schopper was a very talented, but also highly impulsive young man who found it difficult to decide between a poetic and a military career. Expelled from both Heidelberg and Freiburg Universities, he ends up in the army of Maximilian II on a campaign against the Turks in 1565. The young poet is no match for the older and more experienced mercenaries and becomes the victim of their uncouth jokes. Having fallen violently ill and just about to die in a filthy barrel, he is picked up by a compassionate man who gets him out of his absolute misery and into medical care (*Op. Poet.* III, *Prol.*, 73–85). After several more mishaps he finally manages to make his way back to Frankfurt where he had left the unfinished work on his Latin *Reinike*. With warm affection he describes how he was received with food and drink by a certain Cnipius, whom he remembers as *vir humanissimus*, as a 'true humanist'. This man had known our poet from his first stay in Frankfurt and may be identified by his publications as a contemporary teacher of Catholic theology. He encourages the totally destitute mercenary poet to resume his original vocation and complete the translation of *Reinike*. In fact Schopper manages to collect the already completed pages from wherever they had been scattered and finishes the *Opus Poeticum* within one year by the end of 1566. Judging by the circumstances, we have every reason to admire the impressive achievement of a complete Latin versification of the text, a translation and modification of the gloss, and several prologues with autobiographical passages and discussions about critics and contemporary literary activities. It seems highly improbable that Schopper enjoyed a long life and was able to see much of the revenues of his evidently successful literary production. It seems to be more likely that he died as a young man, a short time after his last publication, the *Panoplia*. After this book of 1568 there is no more evidence relating to any event of his life. Long-term effects of his sufferings during his brief mercenary career, as well as his precarious economic situation, may well be the reason for his vanishing from the literary scene at the age of only twenty-six.

4. The Posterity of the Latin *Reinike* – the English Translation of 1706

Schopper's Latin *Reinike*, addressed to a specific public, was a literary success of considerable dimension. The existence of a High German *Reinike*, an even greater success with its twenty-one subsequent editions within a century, does not seem to have been an impediment to marketing the Latin version.[27] The quantity of extant copies indicates that this book must have circulated in large numbers. Several thousand copies as the total figure for the five sixteenth-century editions would not seem to be an exaggeration. Schopper's work also provided most of the Latin text for an abridged bilingual *Reinike* which was published in 1588 under the title *Technae Aulicae / Weltlauf und Hofleben* (Courtly Crafts / This is the Way of the World at Court). The Latin *Reinike* was, of course, not limited to the German market. Since Latin was still understood everywhere in Europe many copies found their way to the learned readers of other countries, particularly in northern Europe. This can be documented not only by the number of copies in Scandinavian and English libraries, but also by direct influence on Reinike translations into the respective vernacular. In 1747 a versified Danish Reinike was published under the title: *Speculum Vitae Aulicae, Eller Den Fordanskede Reynike Fosz*[28] (A Mirror of Courtly Life, or the Danish Reinike). The author's versification is based mainly on another Danish translation already in existence at that time. But the title suggests that he must at least have known of the Latin version. There is, however, one version which must be considered a direct descendant of the Latin *Reinike*. Its title page reads: *The Crafty Courtier or the Fable of Reinard the Fox, newly done into English Verse, from the Antient Latin Iambics of Hartm. Schopperus*, London, printed for John Nutt, near Stationers-Hall, *1706*. It would be misleading to call this work a translation in the proper sense. Many details have been adapted to the tastes of an English public of the eighteenth century. Specific places, known only to contemporary local readers, are alluded to, and the spirit prevailing in this Beast Epic is that of a life at court in the eighteenth century. Nevertheless the author did not fail to draw attention to the artistic model of his source. In fact Schopper had made it more than clear that he was aiming at a project comparable with the masters of classical antiquity. The initial lines of *The Crafty Courtier* seem to be designed to deflate these pretentions in a slightly sarcastic manner:

> Nor arms I sing, nor of Adventurous Deeds,
> Nor Shepherds playing on their Oaten Reeds,
> But civil Fury, and invidious Strife.
> With the false Pleasures of a Courtiers Life.

These lines conjure up at once the world of the *Aeneid* and the *Bucolics* and at the same time dispatch the notion that the material dealt with merits such a comparison. Once informed in such a manner the reader will not expect noble characters and imitable deeds of honour, but all sorts of wicked ways and hilarious pranks presented in a burlesque fashion. The reader will not be disappointed. If, for instance, we compare the different versions of the fox's conversation with the royal messenger, the bear Bruno, we notice that Schopper already had the fox list up more dishes than are mentioned in his source:

> If we cannot have meat and other palatable food, then we have to live on milk, bread, cheese or even yellow honey (*Op. Poet.* I, 47–50).

The English author, sensing the comic potential of the scene, wrote:

> My Stomach's weak, and I'm prescribed to eat
> Gruels and Sallads, and abstain from meat;
> Safe in my Cupboard, I've a hollow bit,
> As fine a chick as ever turn'd on Spit,
> This my grave Doctor who's a Graduate Owl,
> Forbids me to dispatch, because 'tis Fowl (I, 7: 26f.).

A few lines afterwards the bear praises the qualities of honey. Again the Latin version goes beyond its model and cites several more dishes than the latter:

> Golden honeys, I would gladly prefer them to meat and fish and all sorts of dishes (*Op. Poet.* I, vii, 64–68).

And again The Crafty Courtier presents even more specific culinary details:

> Gods! says the BEAR good Honey is a Dish,
> Nice Feeders wou'd prefer to Flesh or Fish,
> To Venison, Lobsters, or to Sturgeon's Spawn,
> To Gellies by PONTACK, or Soups by BRAWN (I, 7: 28).

He who presents a gourmet bear with intimate knowledge of caviar and contemporary delicatessen shops and who rhymes a *Graduate Owl* with the ominous sounding phoneme *foul/fowl* which can denote both an edible bird and moral decadence, is, of course, capable of many other good puns and original witticisms. However, to illustrate these is beyond the scope of this essay. Once again the story of Reinike and his band proves its extreme versatility, and in this case it was a version in the language of classical Rome which had set the tone for a modernised up-to-date version of the ancient story.

Notes

1. Hartmann Schopper, *Opus poeticum de admirabili fallacia et astutia vulpeculae Reinikes,* Frankfurt (Sigismund Feyrabend), 1567 (five editions by the same publisher up to 1595). The quotations in this essay as given in the endnotes are based on the edition of 1584 and appear under the abbreviation '*Op. Poet.*'
2. See Wackers's essay, Chapter Five.
3. *Reynke de Vos,* Lübeck 1498, reprint of the only completely preserved copy edited by Sodmann (1996).
4. See *Reynke de Vos* I, chapters XVI–XVIII; II, chapters VI–IX (to be found in the same order in Schopper's version).
5. The gloss of 1539 was edited by Brandes in 1891. A comparative evaluation of the different glosses was established by Richards (1987).
6. The High German version of 1544 was reedited in facsimile, together with an introduction, by Menke (1981).
7. Cf. Horace, *Odes* II, 3, 1.
8. Cf. Virgil, *Aeneid,* I, 209.
9. Cf. Terence, *Phormio,* I, 204, and Virgil, *Aeneid,* X, 284.
10. Cf. the calamities of Ysengrimus when he fishes with his tail (*Ysengrimus* I,600ff.).
11. Tityrus is one of the two speakers in the first *Eclogue.* The name also occurs in *Eclogues* V, VI, VIII and IX.
12. See H. Brandes, *Die jüngere Glosse zum Reinke de Vos* (1891), p. xx–xlv of the introduction (*Die Quellen der Glosse).*
13. *Op. Poet.* I, xxv, *Commentaria:* 'Nothing is dearer to mortals than money' (Euripides, *The Phoenicians.* 'What a misery it is that you never find anything which is completely healthy. In one way or another everybody slaves for his selfish gains' (Aristophanes, *Ploutos* <On Wealth>). 'Queen money hands out everything: a wife with dowry, reliable friends, a family title and a handsome appearance' (Horace, *Epistles* I, 7). 'I neither wish to live rich nor to die poor. Everybody who dies while he is working on his profit dies well. Money is an enormous asset to the human race' (Seneca, *Epistles,* 3). This one example taken from the gloss must suffice since it is way beyond the scope of this essay to present in detail Schopper's humanist remodelling of the commentaries.
14. See, for example, chapter I, iv (a cowled Reinike tricks the rooster); chapter I, xvii (the fox, now inhabitant of a monastery, fools the wolf who is anxious to become a monk); chapter II, ix (Reinike relates an episode wherein he helps the monk Isengrim to quit his Order).
15. Cf. Ash Wednesday (blessing of the ashes); Wednesday after the third Sunday of Lent (Postcommunio); Tuesday after Passion Sunday (Collect); For

further examples see A. Pflieger, *Liturgicae Orationis Concordantia Verbalia*, Freiburg, 1963, pp. 213ff. and 600.
16. For '*worms*' cf. Ecclesiasticus 7,19: 'The flesh of the ungodly will fall victim to fire and worms.' Isaiah 66,24 and Mark 9,55: 'Their worm shall not die.' The German text reads here: 'Doing penance for sins of the past and abstaining from future ones: this will certainly do you a lot of good.' (*Von Reinicken Fuchs* I, xvi, fol. 33).
17. As a proper monk, Isengrim, now a 'little saint' *(sanctulus)*, lives with 'shoes removed, donning a cowl and with a rope girding his loins' (*Op. Poet.* I, xxviii, 75–77). A monastic public with some sense of humour must have appreciated these lines.
18. The expressions *vera, fructuosa* and *salubris* are frequently used in ecclesiastic Latin for emphasising the authenticity of a penance. Cf. *paenitentia* in Thesaurus Linguae Latinae, vol. 10, fasc. 1, Leipzig, 1982, cl. 50–57.
19. The procedure reflects more clearly than the German model the three steps of the traditional ritual of penance as it was applied since the early days of Christianity: (1) Confession, (2) Imposition of Penance, (3) Absolution.
20. Schopper's publisher commented on this episode by a marginal note containing Horace's *Naturam expellas furca tamen usque recurret* (You may try to drive out nature by a pitchfork and yet it will come back) (*Epistles* I, x, 24).
21. The term *paenitentia fructuosa* (fruitful penance) also occurs in the Latin formula of the papal blessing as it is still used today: *...spatium verae et fructuosae paenitentiae contribuat vobis omnipotens et misericors Dominus* (...may the almighty and merciful Lord grant you time and opportunity for a true and fruitful penance). The biblical foundation for this term is found in Matthew 3: 8 and Luke 3: 8.
22. The latter type, often containing a brief versified life of a saint, was often called *historia* or *historia rhymata*. This liturgical practice was still in use during Schopper's youth. Only the Tridentine Council abolished this tradition and replaced the versified *historia* antiphones by fragments of Bible prose.
23. For the biography of Hartmann Schopper see Schouwink (1995).
24. See Baumann (1994: 109–28).
25. The best known among these authors is a certain Jörg Gräff who describes the order of the *Landsknechte* in a song still printed in modern songbooks: *Und unser lieben frauen vom kalten bronnen / Sie geb uns armen Landsknecht eine warme sonnen* (Our Lady of the cold well, may she let the sun shine warmly on us poor mercenaries).
26. ΠΑΝΟΠΛΙΑ *omnium illiberalium mechanicarum... artium genera continens per Hartman. Schopperum...*, Frankfurt: S. Feyrabend 1568 (2nd edition: 1574 with modified title: *De omnibus illiberalibus... sive mechanicis artibus... succinctus liber*). For more information on contemporary equipment see L. Fronsperger, *Kriegßbuch*, vol. 1–3, Frankfurt, 1565–73; D. Wintzenberger, *Beschreibung einer Kriegs-Ordnung zu Roß und zu Fueß sampt der Artalery und zugehörigen Munition*, Dresden. 1588.
27. Menke (1992) lists 295 copies as still in existence. They may be found in most major libraries and also in a number of private collections. Thirty-four more copies seem to have been still available when F. Prien published the first bibliography of printed Reinike editions in 1887. See Menke (1992: 50–59); also the introduction to the edition of *Reinke de Vos* by Fr. Prien, Halle/Saale, 1887.
28. *Speculum vitae aulicae, eller den fordanskede Reynike Fosz*, Kopenhagen (Ch. G. Glasing), 1747. The first three words are an obvious adaptation of the title of Schopper's *Opus*, whereas the text itself is based on an earlier Danish translation of Hermen Weigere of 1555.

≈ CHAPTER 11 ≈

THE POLITICAL IMPORT OF GOETHE'S *REINEKE FUCHS*

Roger H. Stephenson

Given the often appalling nature of his experience in the winter of 1792, during the campaign against the Revolution in France, it is perhaps hardly surprising that Goethe should have found solace and delight in reading *Reineke der Fuchs*. This he did in J.C. Gottsched's 1752 High German prose translation of the 1498 Low German verse-epic, *Reynke de Vos* – on which, in combination with the recent (1788) reprint of the 1485 Low German 'Delft prose' edition, he drew heavily for his own 1794 version, in hexameters. In the short interval back in Weimar before his (equally reluctant) participation in the 1793 Siege of Mainz, Goethe made a start on his own treatment of the Beast Epic, inspired by the 'good humour' of what he calls 'the truly delicious import' of *Reineke* (Goethe, *Hamburger Ausgabe*, volume X, p. 360).[1] Both his reading and his writing about the crafty and self-seeking, yet curiously sympathetic, fox seems to have provided some relief from the impressions made on him in France and, later, in Mainz. Not only were the physical conditions that he had to endure utterly disgusting (*H.A.*, X: 195): he felt 'an outcast in a chaotic, filthy world' (269). Goethe was also dismayed by the incompetence and fecklessness of the aristocracy at the head of the counter-revolutionary forces. Confusion in the High Command (199), bred by the Royalists' ill-informed and irresolute leadership (215), is seen as symptomatic of a general 'irresponsibility', a point tellingly made by Goethe's citing the indignant protestations of an old hussar officer (288). In particular, Goethe is haunted by two overriding impressions, vividly expressed in the memoirs he published almost thirty years later. On the one hand, he is struck by the high valuation placed in times of war on hypocrisy and 'guile and cunning' (214 and 275). On the other hand, he finds it difficult at times to hide his (wry) amusement at the often grotesquely comical situations he is witness to (229, 242 and 266).

The uncompromisingly realistic depiction of corruption, violence and general degradation, in high places and low, that the reader finds in the versions of Reynard that Goethe knew, clearly helped him come to terms with this his most recent, and most emphatic, direct experience of the deplorable ways of this world. The traditional satire on the ruthlessly egotistical world in which Reynard plays his part, central to the cycle of the *Roman de Renart*, is taken over in Gottsched's translation of *Reynke de Vos*, as it is in Goethe's own version. The medieval feudalism of the source-material functions in both eighteenth-century versions as a mirror of the aristocratic culture of the *ancien régime*, with its (shaky) social and political hierarchy. All of the main motifs of the Beast Epic reappear in Goethe's text. The rapacity of the animals is compounded, as in Gottsched, by the portrayal of an identical desire to kill and eat on the part of humans (II, 146 and 161; Gottsched in Bieling's edition, page 26).[2] Thoughtlessness and credulity characterise the behaviour of the characters (Gottsched, 22; II, 47 and 52); and near-anarchy, Society as a whole (Gottsched, 100; IX, 330ff. Money is all-powerful (Gottsched, 84; VIII, 188); while two 'principles' regulate the characters' doings and intentions: the motivation of revenge (Gottsched, 32 and 61; III, 304 and III, 304 and VI, 208–9), and shame at failure exposed and the desire to save face (Gottsched, 17 and 23; II, 187 and III, 72–3). In a world in which good examples have little effect (Gottsched, 85; VIII, 195–6) the Court is the epitome of society's depravity: 'We all know that the King is as much a thief as anyone else', declares Reineke (Gottsched, 82; VIII, 109). Neither King nor Queen can hide their lust for the treasure that Reineke has conjured up as a fictitious ploy (Gottsched, 50; V, 150–1); and, in considering how to handle the convicted Reineke, the King has recourse to political calculation of the support Reineke enjoys at Court by virtue of his connections (Gottsched, 40 and 74; IV, 105–10 and VII, 122–3).

Here, as in Goethe's play, *Der Groß-Kophta* of 1791, in which he pilloried the Necklace Affair of 1785 as symbolising the corruption of the *ancien régime*, the Court is a pit of financial greed, cynicism and self-indulgence.

In a late essay (of 1823) Goethe commented on the definitive shape the Reynard-figure had taken in the development of 'the political fable' and on the central role he played in its social satire:

> Reineke Fuchs plays the great role, in that he decisively understands his own interests and pursues them with utter ruthlessness (*H.A.* XII, 321).

His own Reineke has all the by-now established qualities associated with the fox's legendary tactical and strategic sense and self-serving purposive rationality. All of the negative aspects that Goethe found in his immediate sources he appropriated as characterising Reineke. The Lion-King's condemnation of him as 'false, wicked, full of cunning, a flattering liar and deceiver' (I, 279–81; Gottsched, 11) is born out in the action faithfully reproduced by Goethe (e.g., VI, 119–20; 59). Indeed, the King's later judgement, that Reineke is 'one of the worst liars on the face of the earth' (Gottsched, 51) is made even more trenchant in Goethe: 'Truly there has never been a greater liar' (V, 171). The apparent amorality of this creature, who lies even to his own wife (VI, 185–6; Gottsched, 61), is, as is traditional, something that Reineke freely acknowledges: he professes himself indifferent to the sinfulness of theft, adultery, treachery and murder (III, 87–88 and 126; Gottsched, 24–5). It is, for Reineke, an article of faith that one cannot remain pure in this world (VIII, 92–4; Gottsched, 82). And, again, Goethe heightens the impact of this piece of practical wisdom by adding to the text he found in Gottsched a proverb which he took from the 1485 Low German edition: 'If you handle honey, you have to lick your fingers' (VIII, 94) – a belief in the incompatibility of action and conscience which Goethe himself endorsed in one of his most-quoted aphorisms: 'the person engaged in action is always unconscionable; no one except the contemplative has a conscience' (Stopp 1998: 27). In Goethe's version, likewise (as in his sources) the positive characterisation of Reineke by the badger is borne out by elements of the action. Grimbart's praise of the fox as 'learned, wise, and clever' (III, 199–200; Gottsched, 28), like his encomium to Reineke's great knowledge of the world (VIII, 239–53; Gottsched, 86), is incontrovertible. In Reineke's favour, too, it is said, and shown to be the case, that he keeps his side of a bargain (I, 113–4 and IV, 220–3; Gottsched, 43); that he has a tender regard for the well-being of his wife and children (III, 244–53 and VII, 200–1 and 245; Gottsched, 30 and 77–8); and that, for all his bragging about his moral indifference, both his wish to confess and his (double) confession itself are sincere (III, 255–65; Gottsched, 30): the reader, after all, knows what he reports at this point to be true. Furthermore, Reineke has friends, as well as enemies (IV, 96; Gottsched, 39). Indeed, his friend, the badger, so loves him that, despite being put at risk by Reineke's calumny against him, he holds no grudge but continues to provide warm support (IV, 96; V, 5 and VII, 157–60; Gottsched, 39, 46 and 75); and even Merkenau, the crow, mourns (or, at least, reports that he mourns) Reineke's supposed death (VII, 61–62; Gottsched, 72). Moreover, Reineke also recommends himself by dint of his clear-headed intellectual virtues (despite their lack of obvious effect on his conduct): he is perceptive (II, 92; Gottsched, 14) – he sees clear through the Lion-King, for example (IX, 161 and 361; Gottsched, 95); he is contemptuous of pretence in others (IX, 24–25; Gottsched, 91); he is indifferent to the snobberies of birth, considering Vice and Virtue the only appropriate categories for the judgement of others (VIII, 203–5; Gottsched, 85); he is honest with himself at least (XII, 95–6; Gottsched, 135); and he has higher values than the attraction of money (XII, 183–4 and 345; Gottsched, 137 and 143). There is, then, rather more to the Reynard-figure Goethe took over than the mere trickster-figure of picaresque tradition (Schwab 1971: 26). He is certainly *désabusé* with regard to the World; but he is not entirely cynical: he knows that Virtue can exist (even if it is rare), and he has a conscience (even if he seems rarely to obey it). In a world in which the wisdom, and wit, of good counsel are at a premium, Reineke has significance, indeed stature. His feelings of superiority (VII, 191–3; Gottsched, 76) – which he vividly expresses in the (at first blush, apparently immoderate) boast that the Court could not sustain itself without him: '[I am] Counsel personified, and … those sitting in the King's *Council* have no *counsel* (III, 218–43; Gottsched, 29) – turn out to be justified, as the King laconically acknowledges: 'Could he not in the end bring a country down?' (VII, 149; Gottsched, 75). As the Queen neatly observes, despite his outrageous conduct, Reineke's advice is invaluable (VII, 121–22; Gottsched, 74). Since he lacks power (XII, 119; Gottsched, 135), Reineke makes his courageous way (IX, 5–6; Gottsched, 90) by his admirably sharp wits, triumphing with craft over brute strength.

Such commendable qualities notwithstanding, it is somewhat disconcerting, at least at first blush, to note Goethe's evident self-identification with this brilliant, unprincipled pragmatist. A hint of Goethe's identification with the unscrupulous fox is contained in the dedication of a copy of *Reineke Fuchs* that he sent to Lichtenberg on 9 June 1794, where he speaks of his Reineke as 'the primeval worldling ... in his rebirth'. For the word *Weltkind* ('worldling', literally 'world-child') is one that Goethe often used of himself, particularly to emphasise his impatience with would-be sophisticates who, in his view, mistook the mere means of thinking for its true object (a clearer understanding of reality), as in his 1774 poem, 'Between Lavater and Basedow', which ends with the couplet:

> Prophet to the right, prophet to the left,
> The *Weltkind* [i.e., Goethe] in the middle (*H.A.*, I: 90).

In that part of his Autobiography published in 1822 (The *Campaign in France*) this identification with the *Weltkind* Reineke is developed to a very high degree. Goethe compares himself with the wily Ulysses (*H.A.*, X: 236 and 290), of whom A.N. Whitehead famously remarked that he shared Reason 'with the foxes'; and he speaks of his own 'roguish spirit' (250), using the word he found in Gottsched (e.g., 73) which he then consistently uses of Reineke, *Schalk* (as in II, 81 and IX, 341), commenting on his inability to resist the satirical thoughts that came to him about the Royalist diplomatic corps (270). Using of himself, as both he and Gottsched had of Reineke (III, 79; Gottsched, 23), that most untranslatable of German words, *Schadenfreude* (which he and Schiller had called the 'original womb-sin of all Adam's children'; *H.A.*, XII: 91), he reports on the glee he felt at seeing a certain Count Haugewitz caught up in the chaos of war (*H.A.*, X: 273). His identification with Reineke is complete when Goethe avers that, under the conditions of a campaign, 'we had to think of ourselves' (264), thus endorsing that principle of self-preservation that informs all of Reineke's actions (e.g., IV, 147 and VI, 191 and 220; cf. *H.A.*, X: 272); though perhaps the most striking expression of Goethe's assimilation of Reineke's outlook is the almost word-for-word repetition in his war-memoirs (259) of the maxim, added by Goethe and enunciated by the snake in the story-within-the-story narrated by the monkey: 'hunger knows no laws' (IX, 263–4).

One of the elements in the Reynard material that clearly entranced Goethe was that 'idyllic-homeric' domesticity that he longed for during the French campaign (256) and which he prized so highly in his contemporary J.H. Voß's epic idylls. Over and over again in the *Campaign in France* he touches nostalgically on the peace of domestic bliss (e.g., 217, 236, 289, 309); and in his *Reineke* he powerfully evokes the warmth and intimacy of the home-life enjoyed by Reineke and his family (e.g., VI, 251; Gottsched, 63) in language that is much more pregnant than Gottsched's, implying the profound satisfaction of irresistible motive or instinct. But this aspect of the fable does not explain, of itself, Goethe's assimilation of Reineke's character. Nor again does Goethe's well-known love of irony, which, he insisted, is a necessary condition of intelligent, flexible, interaction with the world:

> Every time we attentively look into the world ... [we need to do so] with clarity of mind, with self-awareness, in a free way and (if I may hazard a difficult word) with irony (*H.A.*, XIII: 317).

While this statement from the preface to his *Theory of Colour* provides a very accurate account of Reineke's mental attitude; and while it is the case that the *Campaign in France* is replete with a sardonic irony – in particular, a self-irony – that is distinctly reminiscent of Reineke (e.g., *H.A.*, X: 227, 239, 247, 249, 306), it does not explain, any more than Reineke's and Goethe's shared love of the domestic idyll, the degree of self-identification with the artful fox that informs Goethe's war-memoirs of 1822. His sardonic comment on the Royalists' war-council being 'a council without counsel' ('dieser ratlose Rat', 244) is typical, in that it continues, in exactly the same terms, Reineke's irony about the Lion-King's incompetent council (III, 218–31). Such emphatic identities clearly go beyond shared ironies or an overlapping taste for domestic comfort.

It is a commonplace of the scholarship on *Reineke Fuchs* that, besides his introduction of a classicising versification, Goethe's only contribution to his Gottschedian model consists in his seventeen invented lines. This is seriously misleading. Seen from the perspective of content, it is true enough that almost nothing appears to have been changed; but a line-by-line comparison with Goethe's immediate source reveals that, seen from the perspective of form, almost everything has been transformed. For hardly a sentence of Gottsched's is left unmodified. It is not just that Goethe's employment of (rather loose and irregular) hexameters acts as a distancing device, heightening both the irony and the atemporal, typical characteristics of his original. More important is the fact that the often small, but nonetheless highly significant, alterations that Goethe made to the linguistic texture do more than occasionally tone down blasphemies and erotic or scatological crudities. Singly, and as a whole, they constitute a deep transformation of the import of his inherited cultural material. It is, for example, typical of Goethe's treatment that an established theme of the Reynard cycle is given particular emphasis, as in the case of '(In)justice'. In the opening canto, justice and injustice are highlighted where, in Gottsched, they are simply not mentioned: in I, 135, Isegrim is labelled 'unjust', whereas Reineke (I, 168) is described as 'just'. Equally characteristic is the way in which a simple pun found in Gottsched (29) – the play on *Rat* ('council'/'counsel') – becomes in Goethe's hands a complex, and sustained, poetic playfulness. In Canto III, the word-element *rat-* is emphatically repeated in lines 218, 226, 228, and 229, culminating in Reineke's conceptual, and alliterative, identification of himself with both 'counsel' and 'council' in line 231.

Of particular importance in respect of the political import of Goethe's epic is the way in which he subtly heightens and modifies certain traits of Reineke's character which in Gottsched remain latent and merely implicit. Without ever losing sight of the sinful *ego* – indeed Goethe emphasises early on (II, 26) Reineke's 'treacherous heart' and explicitly names Reineke repeatedly as 'the hypocrite' (e.g., V, 230 and VI, 67) – he shifts the depiction of Reineke towards a more definite characterisation of his essentially good *self*. Goethe's changes make clear that Reineke's superiority over the other animals consists in being better, and not just cleverer. For by means of a welter of easily-overlooked emendations Goethe develops certain traits of Reynard in the direction of nobility. Emphasising right from the outset (I, 109–10) Reineke's bravery and intelligence (a combination absent in Gottsched), Goethe consistently represents Reineke's behaviour as more noble and more responsible to others. In Canto IV (125), for instance, Goethe substitutes for Gottsched's *List* ('low cunning'), the more dignified, and richer, connotations of *Witz* (in its widest sense of *esprit*). And he adds to the account of Reineke's special contempt for Isegrim and Braun an explanation: unlike the cat Hinze, the wolf and the bear lack judgement and wit; their desire for cruelty and vengeance lacks all measure; and they cannot finish him (Reineke) off, because they are carried away by their hatred – not that, as in Gottsched (41), Reineke is simply bemused by their inability to bring about the intended execution. By contrast (in particular to the King and Queen's lack of measure, VI, 367) Reineke's aggression is mitigated by enlightened self-interest: he usually gives his victims a (slim!) fighting-chance (III, 160–161 and 275–6). His commitment to self-preservation is raised to a higher level, throughout Goethe's version, by virtue of the fact that this drive is invariably articulated as 'self-salvation' or 'self-rescue' (*Selbstrettung*: e.g., IV, 147; VI, 191 and 220; VII, 75–6; and VIII, 100–1). Just as in the very opening lines where Goethe's deft introduction of the antithesis (I, 5) 'heaven and earth' provides a cosmic framework that is wholly lacking in Gottsched (1), so here, too, and throughout, the narrow connotations of mere (continued) existence that self-preservation carries in Goethe's sources are transmuted into those of a broader scheme of things in which life is not merely sustained, but can (it is implied) also be enhanced, possibly by atonement for past error and certainly by exhilaration at deliverance from danger. In this way, Reineke's sheer *attrativa* (emphasised by Goethe in Canto II, 94–95, and not thematised by Gottsched) becomes, as zest for enhanced life, more plausible, and more comprehensible, than in those versions Goethe drew on. Goethe's Reineke is very clearly a 'lovable rogue' (a *Schalk*, II, 81), perhaps most evidently in the final Canto (XII, 169) where 'der Lose' ('dissolute', 'mischievous' certainly, but also 'loose' and 'relaxed') wins his duel with the physically superior wolf – and 'saves himself' for honour and wealth – by gripping very tightly indeed Isegrim's tenderest parts. We can hardly help sympathising with a triumphant underdog, especially one who combines courage, intelligence and nonchalant charm.

This crucial refinement of Reineke's progressive character is insisted on throughout Goethe's version: the fox does not simply negotiate, diplomatically, agreements, but – unlike Gottsched's Reineke – agreements with his *enemies* (III, 243); he is, again unlike his counterpart in Gottsched, said to be only half-responsible for the misfortunes into which he seems to encourage the other animals to fall: Isegrim, we are told for instance, does what his own inner drives (his 'desire') urge him on to do (III, 313). Nor is he himself wholly responsible for his own, regrettable, actions: his 'all-too-human' and almost instantaneous reversion to his 'old game' after his first confession (III, 425) is given by Goethe (as it is not by Gottsched) the gloss of 'regression', once more invoking the pervasive, inherently optimistic and psychologically realistic schema of fall and redemption, of 'dying and becoming': Reineke's yen for mischief-making is a well-nigh irresistible instinct in Goethe's epic (VI, 143) which he nonetheless manages, just about, to keep from degenerating into the rapacious and ultimately self-destructive compulsions that define his enemies. In Goethe's version, the contrast between Reineke's moderation (VIII, 255, again missing in Gottsched) and Isegrim's insatiable appetite (XI, 170–1; Gottsched, 87) is one of the work's most striking motifs: even in triumph at the end (XII, 300), Reineke is restrained. And in Goethe, though not in Gottsched, there is explicit reference to Reineke's (albeit rare) good actions (IV, 179). It is, therefore, only fitting that, in Goethe, the Lion-King's recognition of Reineke's superiority (IX, 343) should be both much stronger and more encompassing than Gottsched's narrowly focused 'he is too sly [for some of the animals]' (101). The incomparably more generous tribute in Goethe's version, 'Who is his equal?' indicates, like the description of Reineke (not found in Gottsched) as 'the man of experience' (XI, 281), that Reineke has raised (unconscious, instinctive) existence to the higher level of life lived with self-awareness.

Goethe's thoroughgoing transformation of his inherited material is of particular interest in respect of Reineke's use of rhetoric. In a discussion of *Le Misanthrope*, in a review written in 1828 of a new edition of Molière's Life and Works, Goethe noted (*H.A.*, XII: 354) that 'the social world' requires *Verstellung* ('pretence', 'hypocrisy'), by which he means the necessary fictions of presenting one's own unique, particular self in generally acceptable terms; and, in a review a few months earlier of Niebuhr's *Roman History*, he remarked that nowhere was this necessary assumption of a persona or mask (*Verstellung*, 'pretence') more marked than in that quintesssentially public discourse, formal rhetoric (347). The veracity of these comments is powerfully corroborated by the Reynard fable as Goethe received and assimilated it. Traditionally Reynard is a brilliant orator; and he appears as such in Gottsched's translation (e.g., 39, 42, 60). His lies are said to be powerfully effective (45; IV, 270); so effective that, as the leopard puts it (67), 'if he gets to speak, they'll never hang him' (VI, 394–5). The world Reineke inhabits prizes rhetoric highly, particularly at Court where hypocrisy is diligently cultivated. Tricked by Reineke into mistaking Lampe's head in a sack for a diplomatic bag of good counsel composed by Reineke for the King, Bellyn the ram jumps for joy at the prospect of his cutting a (bogus) prestigious figure as a fine speaker by reading out at Court these putative despatches as if they were his own invention:

> Now I shall be the recipient of high praise from all the gentlemen at Court, once they see that I can conceive of something so clever, in fine and clear words (Gottsched, 65).

Reineke's world requires pretence, and in its most strictly codified form, that of rhetoric.

Goethe retains all of these motifs, but adjusts them to produce a significantly different effect. As in his subtle transformation of Reynard's character, Goethe gives greater prominence to Reineke's rhetorical gifts from the very start (I, 89), replacing Gottsched's simple verb 'speak' (4) with the more formal noun 'speech'; in Canto III, 212–6, Goethe introduces Reineke's ability with 'turns of speech', an element lacking in Gottsched's account; in Cantos V (6) and X (441), we learn in Goethe's version of Reineke's talent for narrative which, again, Gottsched does not mention. Likewise Goethe foregrounds everyone's eagerness to listen to Reineke's speech (IX, 33–5) and emphasises his status as a rhetor (X, 1), neither of which appears in Gottsched's text at this point. In order to heighten Reineke's sophisticated play with social pretence Goethe also stresses the obtuseness of the other animals in ways that are not part of Gottsched's account. In Canto VIII, 170, Goethe's text suggests that it is precisely their lack of discrimination that causes so much appalling damage. His displacement of Gottsched's 'stupid' (14) by 'glutton' in Braun's question in anticipation of the feast of honey promised by Reineke, 'What do you think I am, a glutton?' (II, 97), accentuates the bear's ridiculous lack of self-knowledge and the depth of his unconscious hypocrisy. Similarly, Goethe highlights, as Gottsched does not, Isegrim's folly (III, 352–3) and also his lack of self-awareness (IV, 45). It is only against such a background of unreflective existence that the plea implicit in Reineke's self-defensive question (not found in Gottsched), 'Do I deserve to be punished because they have acted foolishly?' (IV, 45), rings true. Unlike Reineke, the other animals believe that what they do is right and proper (e.g., VIII, 185–6 and IX, 324), thus confirming the truth of that maxim of La Rochefoucauld's that caused Rousseau such offence: 'Hypocrisy is the homage that vice pays to virtue'. (By contrast, Reineke's self-conscious, self-ironic hypocrisy is a parody of this true hypocrisy which has become the norm: VIII, 138.) An inability to distinguish clearly between Appearance and Reality, with its concomitant mistaking of the former for the latter, is consistently thrown into relief in Goethe's work: the Lion-King believes (the liar's) *words* (V, 92), whereas in Gottsched, it is the (lying) man he puts his trust in (Gottsched, 51). Goethe offers a psychological explanation of this general obtuseness by linking it to the other animals' inability to distinguish between what gives them pleasure and what really ought to be done – a confusion of inclination and duty that lies at the very heart of the corrupting self-indulgence of this society: the leopard's advice, for example, is taken, not because of its objective merit, but merely because it 'pleases' (in Goethe's addition) the King.

What heightens Reineke's rhetoric (and behaviour) is not so much the erotic undertones that are a long standing motif of the traditional Beast Epic, but rather his aesthetic impulse. His exuberant and crafted lying is undertaken with that 'good conscience' that Nietzsche claimed, in Book V of his *Gay Science*, defined the true artist. By skilful amendments to his sources, in which only desultory mention is made of Reynard's arts, Goethe consistently creates the impression that everything that his Reineke does is not just more acutely intelligent than the beliefs and behaviour of his fellow-animals but is, in some sense, artistic. He adds, for instance (I, 24), the adjective *künstlich* ('artificial', but retaining, too, especially in late eighteenth-century usage, connotations, as in VI, 324, of 'skill-as-art') to Gottsched's description of Reineke's well-fortified home, Malpertus; in Canto VIII (12–13) the aesthetic connotations of Reineke's self-confessed duping of the king are far stronger than in Gottsched's much plainer formulation (79); in Goethe's version Reineke's zestful playing of the game for the sheer aesthetic pleasure of it contrasts tellingly with the crabbed self-serving, utilitarian motivations of the other characters (exemplified in Goethe's addition in X, 320); Reineke's speech (X, 422) is believed by all who hear it, not simply because of his feigned gravitas (as in Gottsched, 17), but because of the beauty of his description of the fictitious treasure; his audience is beguiled in Goethe's account (but not in Gottsched's, 118) by the art of Reineke's tissue of lies (X, 460–2); and the 'knot tied with art' that seals both the sack containing Lampe's head and Bellyn's fate (VI, 323–4) is Goethe's supplementation of Gottsched (65), and applies to Reineke's way of doing everything. It is this aesthetic flair of Reineke's which, in Goethe's text, lends authority to the monkey's description (added by Goethe) of Reineke's kind as 'noble' (IX, 350).

Reineke's rhetoric deploys the traditional topoi of argumentation, such as the appeal to kinship (III, 284–5) and the *argumentum ad pecuniam* (IV, 237–40), that Goethe found in his sources. But Goethe's Reineke is an artist, a spell-binding teller of tales which give pleasure to the imagination by means of the delights of aesthetic discourse. In Gottsched (39) the adroitness and skill of Reineke's oratory is duly noted; but his uncannny ability to lend to what he says 'the appearance of truth' (IV, 78–81) and to project good-natured warmth (VI, 153–4) is not a feature of Gottsched's account (60). Just as, in their various escapades involving Reineke, the other animals are foolishly taken in by his ruses, so, as listeners, they lack that ironic distance Goethe's hexameters invite his own readers to maintain, in order to be in a position to distinguish fantasy from fact, aesthetic illusion from truth-telling. And so, they bear witness to the principle, enunciated by Goethe, very much in the sober spirit of La Rochefoucauld, in an aphorism: 'One is never deceived, one deceives oneself' (Stopp 1998: 92). Yet, in spite of his listeners' obtuse confusion of fact and aesthetic fantasy, Reineke's rhetoric has the great virtue of restoring to them that 'belief in humanity' (*H.A.*, X: 203) of which the stress of the social struggle robs them. If the story-within-the-story about the snake, driven by hunger to kill and eat its rescuer (IX, 221ff) articulates a pessimistic view of humanity's lot, Reineke's rhetoric fills his auditor with hope for an alternative, fairer, way of being. This is the burden of Goethe's addition of Reineke's sincere hopefulness even on the scaffold (IV, 183 and 198) – which contrasts tellingly with his feigned pious hope of God's grace in the afterlife (IV, 193); and it is also implicit in the Queen's judgement of Reineke's suggestion of how his shoes and satchel for his 'pilgrimage' might be provided: 'right and fair' (*billig*) is her prompt response (VI, 54). Above all, the positive, life-giving, indeed *enlightening*, influence of Reineke's words (and behaviour) is made manifest in Goethe's rendition by the much greater emphasis he places on laughter which, in this text, functions, as social anthropologists like Mary Douglas have argued, as a real or imagined shared social phenomenon. Goethe often adds the motif of laughter (e.g., II, 192 and III, 338–40). Laughter, like that provoked by Reineke in Canto XI (377), is linked to exposure, not of weakness or failure as such, but of the social secret, namely hypocrisy. In Goethe's text, shame derives from believing a falsehood (e.g., VI, 382–3); and shame is something that can be *learned* (X, 375), for it is essentially awareness of the (invariably embarrassing) discrepancy between one's own behaviour and the beliefs one holds. Shortly before his death in 1832, Goethe assured a young poet that 'the Muses like to accompany prudent circumspection' (*H.A.*, XII: 359). This is certainly shown to hold in respect of his Reineke, who, in the freedom with which he conducts himself ('the free man', III, 180; not in Gottsched), symbolises the liberation that flows from courageous self-awareness.

In one of the only two short passages in the epic that constitute Goethe's own free invention, Reineke deplores the lack of discretion of corrupt clerics, and the blatant way in which they naively flaunt their misconduct, which is indistinguishable from that of the average sinner:

> ... they spare us, the laiety, nothing, and they do whatever they like before our very eyes, as if we were struck blind. But *we see all too clearly* that their vows please the good gentlemen as little as they appeal to the sinful friend of worldly affairs (VIII, 173–77; my emphasis).

These lines provide, then, a succinct summary of the socio-ethical attitude that Goethe has, by means of a myriad of stylistic transformations, imported into the material that he has appropriated. For what his Reineke is doing here is demanding, not any self-righteously imposed purity, but rather a responsible awareness of regulative values. And in the only other extended passage that is wholly of Goethe's own making, the hopeful, idealising strain running through all of Reineke's rhetoric blossoms, in the midst of trenchant social criticism, into a vivid Utopian vision of the good society:

> But worst of all, I find, is the sheer conceit involved in the erroneous illusion that grips people, namely that each one of us, in the delirium of violent desire, could govern and rule the world. If only everyone would maintain his wife and children well, knew how to manage those refractory souls who are subordinate to him, and could, by contrast with wasteful fools, enjoy himself and his life with moderation. But how can the world be improved? Every single individual denies himself nothing, and wants to subdue all others with violence. And thus we sink ever deeper into the worst of states (VIII, 152–60).

The consensus view amongst commentators, that this passage – often dubbed Reineke's 'political credo' – represents an attack on the French Revolution and all its works, has really very little to commend it if it is read, as it should be, in its immediate context. After all, in Goethe's epic, the eminent exponents of the kind of individualistic social egotism that Reineke is attacking are, not the lower orders (VIII, 134–5), but the ruling aristocracy at Court, principally the wilful, self-indulgent Lion-King himself, for whom Reineke privately, and publicly, expresses his contempt (IX, 361). It is the rulers who seek to suppress all others with violence, and who live in an unbroken state of illusion that they are the rightful masters of their world, when in fact they are prey to both internal and external pressures. And the only glimpse the reader catches of anyone consistently taking good care of his family, managing with any success the fortunes of his close associates, and living with a modicum of good sense and moderation is that apparently most anarchic of figures, Reineke (who, in Goethe's version, does not acknowledge the King's authority, unlike Gottsched's fox, who does: 42). The most that might be claimed is that Reineke's speech is not supportive of revolutionary values. Yet, if we distinguish properly between 'rebellion', as replacement of one irrational authority by another, and 'revolution', as replacement of irrational by rational authority, then Reineke's tenacious entertainment of the validity of rationality in the face of powerful, life-threatening pressures to act irrationally may, in his world at least, be fairly seen as profoundly revolutionary.

Read in context, Reineke's 'political credo' does corroborate at least that part of the critical consensus that holds that Reineke is here functioning as Goethe's spokesman. For there is much to suggest that Reineke's radical moderation comes very close indeed to Goethe's own view of the Revolution, and of political affairs in general. While there is abundant evidence, in contemporary letters and conversation, of Goethe's initial, violent reaction against the events in France from 1789 onwards, and while rejection of some aspects, particularly the violence, of the Revolution is vented in his *Venetian Epigrams* of 1790, there is also a great deal of counter-evidence that indicates that Georg Lukács was not wrong to ascribe to Goethe an affinity with revolutionary ideas (Lukács 1967: 336). Though he is obviously fearful of, and at times vituperative about, the possibility of the Revolution's importation into Germany (*H.A.*, X: 289), Goethe is equally venomous about aristocratic arrogance and irresponsibility, particularly with regard to the misery caused by the French émigrés' forged *assignats* (278), which he sees as symptomatic of the depravity of the aristocracy as a whole (270), as is made quite clear in his peppering his *Campaign in France* with authoritative and bitter complaints about the appalling ways of the privileged nobility (e.g., 296, 299, 303, 320, 348). Nor does Goethe in any way qualify the admiration he, by contrast, felt for members of the Revolutionary army, remarking on the principled behaviour of the French commander at Verdun (210) and on 'the exemplary conduct' of the French soldiers in general (*H.A.*, X: 276) – an admiration that finds its way into Canto VI of his *Hermann und Dorothea* of 1796–7.

As Thomas Mann shrewdly perceived, what we encounter in Goethe's political thinking is a lively, sophisticated debate going on within him, between the claims and values of democracy on the one hand and aristocracy on the other (between, that is, the fundamental constituents of Aristotle's *polis*). Goethe's repugnance for revolutionary (or any other kind of political) violence reflects his despair at the breakdown of the on-going political process which such violence entails (Reiss 1993: 226–90). We simply cannot infer from Goethe's initial, personal (over-)reaction that he was opposed to the principles of the Revolution; and we certainly cannot infer that he deemed these principles inherently invalid just because of his pragmatic, political judgement that the principles of the Revolution were inapplicable to the Germany of his day. There is, above all, convincing evidence that Goethe viewed revolution in a positive light. In conversation with Eckermann, 4 January 1824, he speaks of the French Revolution as a 'great necessity' with 'beneficial effects' – a positive evaluation that accords well with the place assigned in the 'Classical Walpurgisnight' of his *Faust* to eruptions from below. In his scientific work, similarly, Goethe was aware of the sudden leaps and bounds which result from a growing organism's passing over one or more stages in reaching maturity. In fact, Goethe's commitment to a polaristic natural philosophy entails acceptance of recurrent discontinuity – of 'regression' – as energy switches from one pole back to the other. As he had learnt from the teacher of his youth, Herder, revolution is a process of rejuvenation, of 'dying and becoming', a conviction perhaps most memorably expressed in the great poem, 'Blessed Longing', from the *West-East-Divan*, of 1814. In the present context it is perhaps sufficient to consider Goethe's aphoristic formulation of the poem's central *pointe*: 'Our whole achievement is to give up our existence in order to exist' (Stopp 1998: 36). His dialectical political utterances, like such political poetic works as *Reineke Fuchs*, bear witness to the centrality in his sociopolitical thinking of this essentially revolutionary sentiment.

'The world', remarks Goethe, 'has always been divided into parties' (Stopp 1998: 126):

> But the poet, who by nature must always be impartial, seeks to assimilate the conditioning factors of both elements in conflict; and, if mediation should prove impossible, must decide to give the work a tragic conclusion (*H.A.*, X: 361).

Despair at ever reconciling the forces he saw at war with each other in the counter-revolutionary campaign of 1792 led him to 'declare the whole world to be worthless' – just at the moment when Gottsched's *Reineke der Fuchs* came to hand (359). What Goethe clearly saw in the Beast Epic was the hopeful possibility of creating a fictional world in which, in spite of horrifying violence and political decadence, an individual could, with enough good fortune, intelligence and, above all, imagination, enjoy life. The world of Goethe's *Reineke Fuchs* is an unambiguously post-revolutionary world, reflecting the 'new epoch in world history' that Goethe declared had begun with the Battle of Valmy in 1792 (235). It is the active, self-reliant individual who plays the crucial role: liberated by enlightenment of mind, such an individual is free, to an unprecedented degree, to play a role that offers maximum scope for self-expression and 'self-salvation'. The repeated reflections of action and theme that play to and fro between the two halves of Goethe's carefully constructed symmetrical structure (of Cantos VII–XII echoing recurrent motifs of Cantos I–VI), like the fact that Reineke's offspring continue his 'ferocious game' (VII, 233; Gottsched, 78), are exploited by Goethe to underline the fundamentally untragic, anti-pessimistic point, that the enhanced, quintessentially human vitality that Reineke personifies will, in all probability, find a way of establishing itself in a wicked world. Perhaps the impetus that the French Revolution gave to the opening up of such (albeit limited) opportunities 'to all the talents' is one of those 'beneficial consequences' Goethe had in mind when he looked back on what, initially at least, had been a traumatic experience for him.

Notes

1. With the exception of *Reineke Fuchs*, which is referred to by canto and line number, all textual references to Goethe are to the widely available 'Ham-

burger Ausgabe' (C.H. Beck, Munich, originally edited by Erich Trunz in 1948, but with critical apparatus regularly revised). Henceforth cited in the text as *H.A.*, plus (Roman) volume and (Arabic) page number. There is a useful introduction to, and helpful commentary on, *Reineke Fuchs* in the 'Münchener Ausgabe' of Goethe's works, vol. 4.1, edited by Reiner Wild (Carl Hauser, Munich, 1988), while the 'Frankfurter Ausgabe', edited by Waltraud Wiethälter in collaboration with Christoph Brecht (Deutscher Klassiker Verlag, Frankfurt am Main, 1994) provides a stimulating general interpretation of Goethe's epics (including *Reineke Fuchs*, pp. 1135–55) and a short bibliography. All translations into English, unless otherwise indicated, are my own.
2. Bieling, (ed.), *Gottscheds Reineke Fuchs,* 1886. Henceforth referred to in the text as 'Gottsched'.

≈ CHAPTER 12 ≈

PAUL WEBER'S SATIRICAL USE OF REINEKE IN CARTOON FORM

Kenneth Varty

Andreas Paul Weber (1893–1980) was one of Germany's finest book-illustrators and political cartoonists, and the only one we can prove beyond any reasonable doubt to have taken the Beast Epic fox out of his printed History, out of his fictional world, and into the real world of living history where his actions speak as loud as anything he said or did in fiction. Not once in his cartoons did Weber label him 'Reynard the Fox' or, rather, since he was German, 'Reineke Fuchs'. Not once did his fox quote from Goethe or any other text of his fictional History. So how do we know Weber's cartoon fox was Reineke?

Weber studied art in Erfurt, and began his career there as a commercial artist. Conscripted in 1914, he did work of national importance on the railways. During the war years he made comic and satiric cartoons for an Army newspaper and for the *Leipziger Illustrierte Zeitung*. He also began to illustrate books at this time, and by the end of his life he had illustrated more than sixty books. Among the first significant books he illustrated was Hans Sachs's *Fastnachtspiele* (1920–21); Meyer's *Till Eulenspiegel* (1921); and then, important for us, Goethe's *Reineke Fuchs* (1924). From 1928 to 1934 he played an active role in fighting fascism, and made his living partly by drawing satirical political cartoons. He illustrated, with six clearly critical drawings, Niekisch's *Hitler: ein deutsches Verhängnis* [Hitler:

A Disaster For Germany] of which 50,000 copies sold before Hitler came to power. Eventually he was arrested by the Gestapo (1937) and imprisoned in concentration camps, first at Fuhlsbüttel, Hamburg; then to Berlin; then to yet another, in Nuremberg. Just after a year in concentration camps he was released (summer of 1938). One of the first artistic results of his new-found freedom was to illustrated a selection of *Ballades* by François Villon with drawings which reveal his immense sympathy for the underdog, the misunderstood, imprisoned artist (here, of course, a poet), victim of so-called justice (even if, in Villon's case, being sentenced to prison was not entirely undeserved!). In 1944, aged 51, Weber was once more conscripted. After the war he continued to make a living by his talent for illustrating books and for making socially critical, political cartoons. From 1954 to 1967 he drew for *Simplicissimus*, one of Germany's longest-lived socially and politically aggressive periodicals, heavily dependent on illustrations, akin to *Punch* and to *Private Eye*. Then, in 1959, he published his first *Kritischer Kalender* [Critical Calendar], a collection of lithographs which satirically attack contemporary people and events, profiteers and people in power or with authority not always used in the best interest of the public. These Calendars, lavishly produced, bibliophile treasures, became annual events. It is here, in particular in the 1960 Calendar, that Reineke, freed from the fictional History which had imprisoned him, was let loose to practise his cunning and to reveal the truth about what Weber saw as confidence tricks and tricksters.

Before looking at some examples of the cartoon Reineke, let us briefly return to Meyer's *Till Eulenspiegel* (1920–21) and to Goethe's *Reineke Fuchs* (1924), each of which Weber illustrated with a substantial cycle of drawings (forty-six for *Reineke*) within a period of three years. It is clear that these two trickster figures had, in Weber's mind, the freedom of the fool, the wise fool, to say what he liked about anybody or anything (especially in high places), and get away with it. There is, of course, a long literary-didactic tradition of wise fools, especially active in the Middle Ages and at the Renaissance (one thinks of some of Rabelais's characters, and of Erasmus's *In Praise of Folly*). Weber makes Reineke more of a wise fool than he really was in the Beast Epic. There he is more of the calculating, cunning trickster, out to get what he wants by practising any kind of deceit; but this does involve his exploiting the culpable weaknesses, even vices, in his victims, be it the simple vanity of the cock, the stupidity, lying and slander of the wolf, the greediness and readiness to accept bribes of the lion. In failing to get what he wants, as happens on a number of occasions, Reineke more readily reveals his own blameworthy character and evil designs. In the Beast Epic, our villainous hero often wins our sympathy for the way he, the little man, gets the better of the big and selfish ones; but at times we join in the pleasure of the others at his failures, especially when his intended victims are weaker than he is. Weber clearly saw both these sides of Reineke's character and roles as depicted by Goethe.

In one of his most admirable and memorable earlier lithographs, Weber brings together the two almost mythical tricksters whose trickery he so obviously admired (Figure 12.1). He shows Eulenspiegel wearing the traditional dress of the professional fool, in particular the headgear with long ears like those of an ass (but here they droop), little bells attached to their tips, sitting, leaning back along the sloping trunk of a willow tree, cuddling a little fox. The level of the river by which the willow grows has risen very high and flows fast on either side of the tree trunk. These two tricksters are clearly sheltering from the effects of a prolonged storm, still raging around them. The picture is painted in very dark colours. Given its date, 1935, there can be no doubt that it is from the rising tide and stormy weather of Hitler's national socialism that they seek shelter. To judge by their gentle smiles, they shelter with

Figure 12.1 *Eulenspiegel cuddles Reineke.* Die Geduldigen. *Lithograph, 1935, by Paul Weber.*

confidence. Weber calls this lithograph *Die Geduldigen* [The Patient Ones]. Was he, one wonders, counselling his fellow citizens to be patient in the hope that the storm would pass and the floods subside? Or himself, and his urge to give expression to his criticism of fascism? Much later, in his 1960 *Kritische Kalendar* [Critical Calendar], Weber recalled the Eulenspiegel-Reineke alliance with a drawing of these two characters (Eulenspiegel now depicted quite simply as an owl), facing each other with knowing smiles. He titled this *Schabernack* [The Hoax, or, The Practical Joke]. This drawing is number two in an anthology of Weber's Reineke drawings and lithographs mostly made for his 1960 Calendar and published by him in 1966 (Weber 1966). The one he called *Die Geduldigen* appears as number eleven in that anthology. (From this point on, to simplify matters, all references to the numbers of other Weber cartoons appearing in that anthology will be given in square brackets preceded by the letter W. Thus, the two lithographs on which we have just dwelt are [W 2] and [W 11]).

On the cover of that anthology, Weber depicts Reineke wearing the traditional fool's headgear with multiple ass-ears to which are attached little bells (Figure 12.2). However, instead of carrying the traditional fool's wand with a miniature fool's cap and bells at its tips, he holds a tightly-bound

Figure 12.2 *Reineke as jester. Drawing for the cover of a book, 1966, by Paul Weber.*

bunch of birch twigs with which to flog his victims, and he dances, prances over a sea of heads; bespectacled asses' heads, stiff-collared bulls' heads, pigs' heads...parrots'...dogs'.

But to return to the question: how do we know for sure that the fox in these cartoons is Reineke? First, there is the title of the anthology (Weber 1966): *Mit Allen Wassern...Neue Geschichten Vom Alten Fuchs*. [...New Stories About The Old Fox]. The old fox is surely the fox of the long Beast Epic tradition. Secondly, a number of the 1960 cartoons bear a striking resemblance to the illustrations made for the 1924 *Reineke Fuchs* (illustrations which reappeared in a 1970 reprint of the 1924 volume, and again in a 1986 edition of a Low German version of the Beast Epic by Mähl). In one of these 1924 *Reineke Fuchs* drawings, the fox and the owl face each other in a way which immediately brings to mind a 1960 *Kritischer Kalender* lithograph: [cf. Mähl p. 72, and W 2]. There is also a striking similarity between pictures of Reineke's apparently imminent execution on the gallows [cf Mähl p. 60, W 40]; and of Reineke preaching [cf Mähl p. 108, and W 24]. And there are others which resemble each other. Thirdly, there is the use of a single word from the German Beast Epic in a title of one of the 1960 lithographs which confirms the link. This picture [W 7] shows the fox comfortably installed on the balcony of his fortress home and is titled *Malpartus*. This is the German version of the name given to Renart's castle-den in the *Roman de Renart* (Maupertuis), and to Reinaert's in *Reinaert de Vos* (Maupertuus).

It is perhaps worth pausing over the two pictures of the preaching fox. In both pictures Reineke has climbed to his pulpit up steps decorated with scenes which depict his usual victims: a duck, a cock or a goose. In 1924 he is clearly shown seizing a goose by its neck (Figure 12.3). Reineke has reached his high position by killing creatures weaker than himself. From that eminence he uses his office and the trust normally accorded to it, and his rhetoric, to deceive those who listen, trust, and allow themselves to be persuaded. The 1924 congregation is made up of anthropomorphised animals who appear, on the whole, quite interested in what they hear, but probably unlikely to be persuaded to do anything out of inertia. They are largely a mixture of asses, pigs and dogs. Here there is a female cat (she wears a necklace) more interested in a book than in Reineke's sermon; there is a hare who seems momentarily distracted from his book; there is a grinning hedgehog (who will, presumably, stupidly roll up on the spot when danger approaches); there is a vacant-looking mouse. In

Figure 12.3 *Reineke preaches. Drawing from J. Mähl's* Reineke Voss, *1986, p. 108. Made by Paul Weber, 1924.*

1960, this congregation has become one of entirely cowed, really-alarmed dogs (that is, apart from the two or three who have nodded off) (Figure 12.4). The title *Busspredigt* means the preacher who admonishes his listeners to be penitent, to make penance. The earlier picture reflects the cunning, ruthless Reineke's way with words and the dangers which could be incurred by the complacent; the later one reflects the powerful effects of the false prophet and rhetorician, while the background mural painting depicting a pilgrim-dog wearing a halo, says more about the possible consequences of being taken in, of being persuaded to pursue paths which the unholy, charismatic rhetorician would have the gullible follow. The later picture is altogether more frightening than the earlier one.

Most of Weber's Reineke cartoons warn his viewers to take nothing at face value, to be independent-minded, to question everything they see, hear or read, as is suggested by *Der Nonkonformist* [W 50] and *Im Parterre* [W 51]. In the former a group of ten animals sit before a television set, eyes almost popping out of their heads, glued to the screen with evident

Figure 12.4 *Reineke preaches.* Busspredigt. Drawing, 1960, by Paul Weber.

wonderment and pleasure. Behind the seated group, facing away from the television screen, is a diminutive Reineke intent on the open pages of a book. In the latter (*Im Parterre* [W 51]), row upon row of wide-eyed, brutish creatures are spellbound by what they see on a theatre stage. But in the very centre of the picture, lost in the crowd, sits an elegant Reineke, note-pad on his knee, pencil in hand. He squints fiercely at the spectacle unfolding before him, ready to note down his critical reactions. Elsewhere, Weber's viewers are warned to be careful that the information they receive has not been tampered with, as when he has Reineke slip the reading glasses of his choice on to an ass as he reads in a newspaper (Figure 12.5), the ass's own glasses lying broken on the floor beside his chair [W 35]. One is also warned to watch out for what goes on behind one's back by a delightfully comic drawing of Reineke sneaking up behind a seated hunter's back, peering through his binoculars into the distance, and snatching a dead hare the hunter had bagged [W 17].

Many another cartoon shows Reineke mastering, by his skills and his ability to assess other animals' weaknesses, much more sizeable, physically powerful adversaries. An enormous enthroned lion sits mesmerised by a soap-bubble-blowing fox [W 32]; then he skips, apparently happily, as Reineke

Figure 12.5 *Reineke offers reading glasses to an ass.* Die bessere Brille. *Lithograph, 1960, by Paul Weber.*

and fox-friend turn the skipping rope between them [W 33]; another two large lions seated on drums within a circus ring watch him lash his whip and hold up a hoop through which they are obviously going to jump when ordered to do so [W 29]; and a tiny figure, rapier in hand, he stands triumphantly atop a dead bull [W 53]. Sometimes he brings the powerful to heel by granting them rewards they very much prize. This is shown in a picture of a palace-like interior where a pompous ceremony takes place [W 34]. Here a line of bulls not only kneel to receive their medal, but crawl away on their knees, goggle-eyed with pride (Figure 12.6). Elsewhere, Reineke keeps powerfully-built animals in their place by the power of his office and the dazzling use of language. This seems to be the case when he presides over a meeting of the Cabinet. Only he talks in such a manner that his ministers, all eyes on him, pay attention entirely to him and not once to the documents lying on the table before them. [W 36].

But most cartoons show Reineke deluding little, defenceless creatures, creatures he wants to make his own, as when he plays a concertina and has a circle of happy hens dancing around him (Figure 12.7) [W25]. Or when he offers help to a drowning rabbit by reaching out to him from a swollen river-

Figure 12.6 *Reineke awards medals.* Dekoration. *Drawing, 1960, by Paul Weber.*

Figure 12.7 *Reineke and dancing hens.* Tanz der Hennen. *Lithograph, 1960, by Paul Weber.*

bank with a long stick [W 12]. On other occasions he is seen offering to guide the unwary and unthinking, as when he acts as cox to a team of rowing hens [W 14] or ferryman to a large and laughing party of little rabbits (Figure 12.8) [W 43]. Sometimes he deceives from quite a distance, almost unseen by his intended victims. A trail of luscious cabbage-leaves leads some sheep across a meadow towards their distributor, Reineke, about to disappear over the horizon [W 22].

Perhaps some of the most telling of his cartoons are those in which he has Reineke give voice to his anti-militarist, anti-war feelings, though the role played by the fox is not always entirely consistent. In one of these drawings, Reineke is shown dressed like the conductor of an orchestra, raised baton in his hand (Figure 12.9). He is conducting three helmeted geese, each with a sword at its side, along a tight-rope. The helmets, typical German helmets, are so big that they slip over the geese's eyes and, in effect, blind them. This apparently cynical 'general' is clearly unconcerned about the 'music' his troops may play, and is especially unconcerned about their fate [W 37]. Contrasting with this is the Reineke who tries, in vain, to break up an old-fashioned, First-World-War cannon, with a sledge-hammer (Figure 12.10). The cannon stands on top of a

Figure 12.8 *Reineke ferries a boatload of rabbits.* Die Überfahrt. *Lithograph, 1960, by Paul Weber.*

Figure 12.9 *Reineke the conductor.* Gänse... marsch. *Lithograph, 1960, by Paul Weber.*

heap of dead, brutish animal bodies [W 38]. And then there is the 1976 lithograph depicting an elegantly attired little Reineke, all alone to one side of the picture, a briefcase under his arm, facing an advancing horde of brutish, helmeted

Figure 12.10 *Reineke the cannon-breaker.* Schluss! *Lithograph, 1960, by Paul Weber.*

beasts, flags held high, bayonets fixed and at the ready (Figure 12.11) (*Kritische Kalendar*, 1976). The title: *Entscheidung* (Decision). To fight, or to find a political solution by discussion?

Figure 12.11 *Reineke confronts an armed horde.* Die Entscheidung. *Lithograph, 1976, by Paul Weber.*

≈ CHAPTER 13 ≈

THE DEATH AND RESURRECTION OF THE ROMAN DE RENART

Kenneth Varty and Jean Dufournet

Part One (by Kenneth Varty)

To judge by the number of surviving manuscripts, the *Roman de Renart* was one of medieval France's most popular collections of comic stories. Created in the later twelfth and early thirteenth centuries, it survives in fourteen extensive manuscript anthologies, in a few shorter ones, and in numerous fragments all of which date from the end of the thirteenth to the later fifteenth century. The extensive anthologies show that their compilers were, from time to time, moved to reorganise the stories, or the branches into which they were grouped, partly to reflect their popularity, partly to make them tell in a more logical way the life-story of its villainous hero. Scholars have long seen in the manuscripts three major groups or families, alpha, beta and gamma, which reflect something of the growth (in particular the amplification) and the reorganisation (in particular in the ordering) of the branches. It is the gamma family which is, in several ways, the most logically ordered to reflect the birth, life and near-deaths of the fox. And this is the family which first appeared in print; but not till the nineteenth century!

Death

Perhaps the most extraordinary thing about the *Roman de Renart* is that, in spite of its immense popularity in medieval

France, and in spite of the fact that it provided the Alsatian Heinrich der Glichezaere and the Flemish author of the first Dutch-language Beast Epic with the raw material for their literary masterpieces (the Dutch then going on to spawn all the other major European Beast Epics), it failed to survive into the age of the printed book. This is difficult to understand because the kind of comic, satiric, critical spirit which animated it also animated so much of the literature of the French Renaissance, in particular Rabelais. Perhaps its death had something to do with the fact that the branches were not turned into prose, as were many of the great medieval French verse romances and epics in the mid and later Middle Ages; for quite a few of these prose renderings often did cross the gap from manuscript to printed page, and survived for a decade or two. But even these soon disappointed changing public tastes, and hardly any survived into the seventeenth century. It may be that the *Roman de Renart* was so loved in its verse form that there was resistance to its being turned into prose; prose which would also modernise the language. Thus, by the fifteenth century, the language of its verses was probably no longer easily understood. As the Middle Ages grew older the French language evolved rapidly, and the petrifying syntax of the branches may have become a rope which slowly strangled the liveliness out of them. It is also probable that the political and religious problems reflected in the branches were more accessible in some of the continuations of the *Roman de Renart*, such as the *Couronnement de Renart, Renart le Nouvel* and *Renart le Contrefait*, for it is a later prose version of one of these, *Renart le Nouvel*, which was put into print during the first half of the sixteenth century, in 1516, 1534, 1550 and 1551 (Suomela-Härmä 1998, x).

Resurrection

The *Roman de Renart* seems to have been resurrected by Legrand d'Aussy in 1800. His article 'Le *Renard*: poème héroïco-comique, burlesque et facétieux' is briefly described as entry 117 in Varty (1998). (From this point on, to avoid cluttering the Bibliography to this volume of essays, full bibliographical details of the texts referred to in this essay will be found in my 1998 Guide to scholarly work on the *Roman de Renart*. References to it will be made in square brackets with the prefix V followed by the entry number.) Legrand d'Aussy's article begins with a literary-historical description of the *Roman de Renart* (from now on abbreviated here to *RdR*) and then gives examples of (or from) about twenty of the branches. In what seems to him a more logical order than he finds in the manuscripts, Legrand d'Aussy presents a mixture of prose translations, adaptations and summaries based on four of the extensive anthologies of branches. On the whole his summaries are good and fairly full, but one or two are brief and garbled. Here and there he comments adversely on what he considers to be vulgarity, and one branch is passed over because he considers it too vulgar even to summarise.

Inspired by this article, Méon published in three volumes, in 1826, the first edition of the *RdR* [V 8]. It was to be the only edition till the 1880s, and the one most commonly cited in articles and studies well into the twentieth century. Some of its shortcomings were rectified by the publication of some omissions, variants and corrections by Chabaille 1835 [V 9]. Since few of the well-educated were able to read Old French in those days, the way was open for translations and adaptations in modern French. The first of these appeared in 1843: an expurgated adaptation in prose by Collin de Plancy [V 100]. Expurgation was to be expected not only because of the Victorian-style reserve felt in polite society even in France at this time, but because the publisher was the Printer to the Archbishop of Malines. The date of publication is significant for, until 1843, the *RdR* had been on the Index (*Index librorum prohibitorum*: the list of books forbidden to Roman Catholics, or to be read only in expurgated editions), and this since the sixteenth century. There were several reprints of this adaptation, sometimes with different titles, for example (third, 1854 edition): *'Le Roman du Renart: version épurée par Collin de Plancy'* (The Romance of the Fox: 'purified' by...). Hot on the heels of Collin de Plancy's first edition came, in 1845, a collection of fabliaux, comic short stories in verse, to which was added, using Collin de Plancy's text, the *Roman de Renard* [V 119]. On the page facing the title-page there is a statement by the Bishop of Châlons to the effect that he had examined the contents of this book and had noted that the author had successfully removed all the bad doctrine and other reprehensible matter normally found in the poetry of the distant past. Encouraged perhaps by the Church's new tolerance of the *RdR* in the form Collin de Plancy had presented it, others felt bold enough to bring it into the bourgeois drawing-room. This was a time when home entertainment included father's reading aloud to the family gathered round the fireplace in the evening. To cater for this there were a number of periodical publications including *Le Musée des Familles: Lectures du Soir* (The Museum for Families: Readings for the Evening). In 1850–51, and composed by Amiel [V 89], there appeared in this magazine a series of summaries, translations and adaptations in prose of many branches of the *RdR*. It is interesting to note that Amiel used Méon's edition, and not Collin de Plancy's adaptation.

Evidently dissatisfied with the forms of the Beast Epic thus far available in French, Potvin published in 1861what he considered to be a good verse translation in modern French of the truly original Reynardian texts: *Le Roman de Renard mis en vers d'après les textes originaux...* (The *RdR* put into verse following the original texts...). The title is misleading for this is primarily a translation of the first half of the Dutch *Reynaerts Historie*, to which some additions are made from the *RdR* (called *les branches gauloises*: the gallic branches). He begins, in fact, with Branch XXIV (Reynard's Birth), then follows the Dutch to the point where Renart-Reinaert is released after making his 'confession' from the gallows. This French version of the Dutch Beast Epic was moderately successful since it had at least two further reprints, one in 1862 and the other in 1891. [V 126].

The year 1861 was also the year in which Paulin Paris published his translation-adaptation in prose [V 122]. With twenty different reappearances in one form or another between 1921 and 1991, this was to prove to be one of the most successful modernisations ever of the *RdR*. He too used Méon's text as his base but, just like Legrand d'Aussy, Collin de Plancy, Amiel and Potvin, reordered the branches and created yet another story-line. But more of this later.

The way was now clear for the publication of a truly fine, scholarly edition of the *RdR*, and this was provided by Martin in three volumes, 1882, 1885 and 1887 [V 1], an edition which was to inspire two of the most important and influential critical studies of the *RdR*, the one by Sudre in 1893 [V 611] and the other by Foulet in 1914 [V 331], sometimes described with ample justification (along with Martin) as the founding fathers of *RdR* studies. Martin published the whole of the alpha family's branches, to which he added what he thought to be the best version of all the other branches then known which were not in the alpha family. It is his system of numbering the branches and of titling them that has been accepted by most Renardians. During the twentieth century quite a number of paperback, low-price, scholarly editions of the *RdR* have appeared following, with certain reservations and amendments, Martin's text. Most of them present only a few branches, but three present a fair number. These include Dufournet (1970) with eight branches [V 14]; Combarieu du Grès and Subrenat (1981), reprinted 1985, with all or most of seven branches [V 12]; and Dufournet and Méline (1985) with fourteen branches [V15]. The less-extensive anthologies include Breuer (1929) with all or part of four branches [V 11]; Jauss-Meyer (1965) with five branches [V 16]; and Cortes Vázquez (1979) with two branches [V 13].

Until 1948, Martin's was the only truly scholarly edition available, yet it was not reprinted till 1973. But in 1948 Roques published the first of six slim volumes which, between them, and by 1963, made available in a scholarly way most of the beta family of manuscripts. These appeared in 1948 (volume I, reprints 1963, 1971, 1978, 1982), 1951 (volume II, reprints 1972, 1982), 1955 (volume III, reprint 1973), 1958 (volume IV, reprint 1983), 1960 (volume V), and 1963 (volume VI) [V 2–7]. So far these have given birth to only one paperback, low-price, scholarly anthology, namely Finoli (1957) which presents most of Branches II–Va [V 18]. The gamma family, the most extensive of them all, was edited in two volumes by Fukumoto, Harano and Suzuki in 1983 (volume I) and 1985 (volume II) [V 10]. They used MS C as their base (Paris, Bibliothèque Nationale, f fr 371) while Lodge and Varty used, in 1989, MS M (Turin, Biblioteca Reale, Varia 151), the other main manuscript in this family, for their edition of Branches II–Va [V 48]; and Harano published, betwen 1987 and 1989, n (Rome, Vatican Library, Reg. Lat. 1699), the only substantial part of a manuscript containing gamma-family material, thereby completing the publication of the whole of this family and completely replacing Méon's early, pioneering edition of 1826. In the run-up to the publication of their 1983 and 1985 volumes, Fukumoto, Harano and Suzuki published, mostly in learned journals, mostly in Japan, many an edition of just part of one, or just the whole of one branch, but sometimes two branches [V 20–38, 50], but as yet there has been no paperback, low-price edition based on their work. Recently, the most important of the independent, non-family manuscripts, MS H (Paris, Bibliothèque de l'Arsenal, 3334) has been edited in its entirety under the direction of Armand Strubel, aided by Roger Bellon, Dominique Boutet and Sylvie Lefèvre (Paris: NRF Gallimard, Bibliothèque de la Pléiade, 1998). Apart from the four major scholarly editions of Martin, Roques, Fukumoto et al, Strubel et al., and the important partial editions listed above (all but one based ultimately on Martin), there have been fifty-one editions of single branches in the period 1972–1994 [V 20–38, 40, 42–58, 66–68] as well as seventeen editions of fragments of branches [V 55A, 59–65, 69–78], the large majority by Fukumoto and Harano. Almost all have appeared in not-easily consulted, learned journals, or in unpublished university dissertations, or in almost unobtainable electronic, 'desk-top' publications. Even so, *RdR* scholars now have at their disposal far more well edited branches than ever before.

The cultured general reader is also very well catered for. Good-quality adaptations have appeared from time to time, though none has been quite as successful as Paulin Paris's. Curiously, the authors of many of these adaptations do as Paulin Paris did and rearrange the order of the branches they present, each in his own way. We draw attention in particular to one of the earliest, and one which remained in demand over quite a long period of time: Robert-Busquet (1935) [V 129]. He follows Méon's text, of which he claims to have made a literal translation (into prose). But for literary or moral reasons, he felt obliged to omit or summarise some parts of the original. The first edition was illustrated by numerous black-and-white drawings and one coloured (outside cover) drawing. The second edition, published in the same year [V 129a] is extended by about thirty pages, chiefly to accommodate the illustrations which are all now in colour. Fine paper is used and the book is very finely bound. By contrast, the third edition, also published in 1935, has no illustrations at all and is over fifty pages shorter than the first edition. A fourth appeared in 1960, and a fifth in 1966, each shorter than the previous one by the omission of more and more branches [V 129ab–129c]. Quite different in character is Genevoix 1958 [V 105]. This is a lively prose retelling of most of the branches and episodes in a completely original order, occasionally expurgated (still!), illustrated by André Pec. For collectors, 150 copies were numbered. There have been at least two edited paperback versions of Genevoix's text with additions of various kinds, but without Pec's illustrations. Both of these were by Dufournet, the one in 1986, the other in 1991 [V 105c and 105d]. There have also been two de luxe, collector's reprints, the one in 1958–59, the other in 1968 [V 105a and 105b]. One of the more recent, high-quality retellings for the cultured general reader, deserving to be better known, is Schmidt 1963 [V132]. Intriguingly entitled *Le Roman de Renart, transcrit dans le respect de sa verdeur originale pour la récréation des tristes et la tristesse des cafards* [transcribed with respect for its original vigour for the amusement of sad people and the sadness of people with the blues], this is a loose prose translation-adaptation based, it seems, on Martin's text, but the branches are arranged differently, into three books, each containing ten branches, and illustrated with black-and-white reproductions of miniatures from a *RdR* and a *Renart le Nouvel* manuscript. A limited edition (only 800 copies), printed on good-quality paper and finely bound, followed one year later to house twenty watercolour illustrations by Yvette Alde [V 312a]; while a simple reprint of the first edition was made in 1992. We return to this below, with Jean Dufournet. Parallel with Schmidt's retelling is Toesca's, (1962) [V 136], more of a translation (albeit often a loose one) into prose of thirteen branches based on Roques's edition and illustrated by Philippe Gentil. A boxed, de luxe edition limited to 276 copies, came out in 1970 [V 136a], now illustrated with seventeen copperplate engravings by Gaston Barret; and a paperback version of the first edition was published in 1979 [V 136b]. In this group of high-quality translation-adaptations, we draw particular attention to one of the most recent: Bonnot 1975 [V 88]. This is a beautifully presented and illustrated part-translation, part-adaptation in prose which, by and large, follows the gamma family collection. The text is, however, presented in two parts with separately-numbered pages within one volume. Part I begins with the branch which tells of Reynard's birth (Branch XXIV), and continues with tales from those branches that do not involve quests for justice, all under the heading *Les Renardies*. [Foxy Adventures]. Part II contains most of the branches that contain quests for justice under the heading *Le Procès* (The Trial). There are numerous black-and-white illustrations and vignettes made by the Compagnons de Saint Georges. To conclude this section about good-quality retellings and *rearrangements*, we should recall the entirely scholarly prose translation by Combarieu du Grès and Subrenat [V 12] in which the branches have been grouped according to the nature, interrelationship and intentions of the protagonists: for example, the animals among themselves; satiric and parodic animals; animals with men, etc.

A special feature of these modern translation-adaptations is their relatively frequent use as vehicles for the drawings, etchings, watercolours or lithographs by accomplished artists. Combined with fine bindings, elegant fonts and the use of high-quality paper, these illustrated books have often been designed as artefacts for the bookcollector. Several such books have been mentioned in passing in the preceding paragraph, in particular the ones by Robert-Busquet [V 129a]; Genevoix [V 105a and 105b]; Schmidt [V 132a]; Toesca [V 136a]; and Bonnot [V 88]. In addition to them we mention: Larrieu (1925), illustrated with watercolours by Lorioux [V 114]; Curvers (1930) illustrated with sixty-eight woodcuts by Stuvaert and limited to 400 copies [V 101]; Richard-Mounet (1930) illustrated with forty fine etchings by Maurice de Becque, limited to 200 copies [V 128]; Arnaud (1952) illustrated with twenty original lithographs and limited to 262 copies [V 90A]; and Hecht (1950), a set of fourteen engravings without text and limited to 275 copies [V 111].

Young people have also been well catered for in the renewal of interest in the *RdR*. Translations and adaptations for teenagers, and especially for schoolchildren, as well as the very young, are numerous. Here we mention only a few of the more interesting and typical. One of the earliest, best and long-lived, is that by Chauveau (1924) [V 99]. It is mostly a set of summaries based on Méon's text, presenting the *RdR* in three parts (the urge to rearrange the branches is just as prevalent in these children's versions as it is in adult versions). Four years later (1928) a new, illustrated edition appeared, illustrated with Chauveau's own drawings [V 99a]. A year after this (1929) saw a reprint of the first edition, without illustrations. Then new illustrated versions appeared in 1936, 1956, 1964 and 1980 [V 99c and 99d]. The quality of Chauveau's text was sufficiently impressive for an English two-volume schoolroom version to be made with it: Clarke (1931, I, and 1932, II). These reproduce both the text and its illustrations which are interrupted, from time to time, by classroom exercises. They conclude with a French-English glossary [V 99b]. Chauveau's text was even translated into Japanese: Mizutani (1941) [V 144]. Early appearances on the schoolroom scene were: Verron (1927), complete with coloured illustrations [V 139]; Giraud (1933) [107]; and Vallerey (1936) [V 138]. Giraud's is a simple adaptation which was first reprinted in 1956 and again in 1982. These reprints were expanded by twenty-six pages to include numerous, pleasing engravings in two colours by Bailly. A shorter selection of the 1933 text was made in 1955, to which are joined pen-and-ink illustrations by Touchet [V 107a]. Vallerey adapts from seventeen branches (sometimes only parts) and includes four coloured plates and numerous black-and-white illustrations. By 1946 her book had reached its fifth reprinting, and went on to further reprintings, less the coloured plates, in 1976, 1988 and 1990. Two other very successful and widely used translation-adaptations for the young are the ones by Frappier and Boyon (1937) [V104], and Cadot (1960) [V 95]. The former appeared in the famous Classiques Larousse series with reprints in 1941, 1966, 1972 and 1984. The last two reprints are expanded versions of the original edition due to the inclusion of several illustrations and some classroom exercises. The text consists chiefly of summaries and prose translation, occasionally interrupted by quotations in the old French. The latter, Cadot (1960), appeared in the Classiques Hatier series, reprinted in 1972. It contains translations and adaptations from seven branches, following fairly closely the order they appear in Martin's edition, and there are a few quotations in the old French. Edited by Chappon (1968) it passed into Hatier's Classiques Illustrés series in 1968 with reprints in 1972 and 1987 [V 97], and a new version in 1991 aimed at 'classes de 6e et 5e' [V 97b]. Chappon also reproduced Cadot's text to which illustrations by Roger Guy Charman were joined in another Hatier volume in 1970 [V 97a]. Among the more scholarly schoolroom offerings, and clearly meant for older schoolchildren are: Hacquard (1978), reprints in 1982 and 1993, with good translations of part or all of three of the best, earlier branches, illustrated with some fine reproductions of miniatures [V110]; Notz (1986) with good prose translation extracts from Martin's text [V 121]; and Charbonnier (1987) with good prose translations interrupted by narrative summaries, also based, ultimately, on Martin's text. For younger schoolchildren there is Verron's selection described above, published in a 'Collection des Fleurs et des Fruits: Bibliothèque pour les Jeunes'; and the anonymous *Roman de Renart: illustrations de André Verret* 1985, a simple prose adaptation with lively, cartoon-like illustrations [V 87]. For the very young there is an *embarras de richesse*. One of the most popular and long-lived is Samivel (1936), the forty pages of which offer little text and many pictures. Concentrating on the fox, here called Goupil, this was reprinted in 1945, 1981 and 1989. A parallel, similarly-constructed volume featuring the wolf, Ysengrin, first appeared in 1939 and reappeared in 1945 and 1981; and another featuring the bear, Brun, in 1939, 1945, 1980 and 1984 [V 130]. François (1960), with attractive illustrations, retells in simple prose three of Reynard's tricks (all from Branch III) aimed at seven- to twelve-year olds [V 103A]. Simon (1986) [V 134] and Danika (1993) [V 101A] offer simple prose retellings of the main events, all well and abundantly illustrated, from several branches. Lastly we mention Beaumont (1964) for his *Roman de Renart: adaptation en français facile* which was first reprinted in 1971 but had reached its ninth reprinting in 1994. Beaumont adapts thirty episodes from numerous branches whilst using fewer than five hundred different words. In addition, the eighty pages contain sixty-eight simple illustrations [V 91]. A rather different way of bringing the *RdR*, much modified and simplified, to children is by way of recorded readings, sometimes accompanied by printed texts. For example, in 1991, Michel Hindenach published six half-hour cassette recordings accompanied by illustrated booklets, each of which features one of the protagonists of the *RdR*: Chantecler, Renart, Isengrin, Tibert, Brun, and Roënel the hound [V 93]. Other recordings have been made with both adult and young listeners in mind. These range from a 33-rpm record made in 1954 through to a compact disc in 1995 [V 93]. And there have been adaptations for the theatre for both adults and children. The text of one of these, Grau-Stef and Terensier (1977), dramatises the text in three acts, presenting first Reynard's early adventures and misdemeanours away from the court, then his brushes at court and with courtiers, then his trial [V 108]. Poslaniec (1988) dramatises a number of events in octosyllabic lines clearly meant for schoolchildren. His text is accompanied by suggestions for sets and numerous illustrations [V 125].

Alongside these translations and adaptations of varying quality and standards, there have been a number of serious, scholarly translations into modern French. Among the most wide-ranging, offering careful translations of many branches, are the ones by Combarieu du Grès and Subrenat (1980), reprinted 1985 [V 12]; and Dufournet and Méline (1985) [V 15], both of which have been mentioned above in the survey of modern editions based ultimately on Martin's text. Offering a careful translation only, and of one branch only, are three outstanding examples: Rey-Flaud and Eskénazi (1972), reprinted in 1981, who translate Roques's edition of Reynard's Trial (Martin's Branch I) [V 127]; Dufournet (1989) who translates Roques's edition of Tibert's Vespers (Martin's Branch XII) [V102]; and Dufournet (1989) who translates Roques's edition of Reynard and Liétart (Martin's Branch IX) [V 103].

Finally, translations and adaptations of many kinds have appeared in languages other than French: in Dutch [V 79–80]; English [V81–85]; German [V 141–42]; Italian [V 142A];

Japanese [V 143–46]; Portuguese [V 146A]; Romanian [V 147]; Russian [V 148]; and Spanish [V 13].

Paulin Paris's *Les Aventures de maître Renart de d'Ysengrin son compère*, 1861

The first edition of Paulin Paris's translation-adaptation and re-ordering of many of the branches and individual episodes found in Méon's edition was published in 1861. It begins with a prologue that is a conflation of Branches II and XXIV (Martin's numbering; branches which tell of Reynard's birth and his earliest adventures); it continues with thirty miscellaneous adventures grouped as Book I (various tricks played by Reynard, all away from the royal court, but culminating in encounters with Noble); then with another thirty entitled *Le Procès* (The Trial) grouped as Book II (centred, to begin with, on events at Noble's court, and culminating in Reynard's duel with Ysengrin). The book's full title is: *Les Aventures de maître Renart et d'Ysengrin son compère, mises en nouveau langage, racontée dans un nouvel ordre et suivies de nouvelles recherches sur le 'Roman de Renart'* [The Adventures of Master Reynard and of his companion Ysengrin, put into a new language, told in a new order, and followed by new research on the *Roman de Renart*]. It was published in Paris by Techener and ran to xi + 372 pages [V 122]. Most later editions omit the pages (from 323 onwards) devoted to scholarly argument (the *nouvelles recherches*), and considerably shorten the title. However, in the first re-edition (Paris: Georges Crès, 1921, lviii + 333 pages) the scholarly arguments are made to precede the text, and the work is enhanced by a series of woodcuts made in late medieval or early Renaissance style by Jean Lébédeff [V 122a]. In a way, Paris's first edition came as the climax of a short series of half-hearted modernisations; his second as a prelude to the very many that have appeared since.

Meanwhile, the first of many appropriations of Paris's text to produce a truly beautiful book had taken place. In 1909 J. Leroy-Allais published a prose adaptation of the *RdR* based, but very loosely, on Paris's adaptation. He selected just twenty-four tales (or 'aventures' as Paris called them) which are accompanied by 305 illustrations, of which forty-one are 'hors texte', twenty-five in colour, and sixteen in black and white. The paper used is of good quality, the font elegant, the binding sumptuous: red cloth, bevelled covers decorated in black and gold with, at the centre of the front cover, in a shallow sunken frame, a coloured illustration. A highly prized collector's item, this was reprinted in 1983 and again in 1990 [V 118]. The next in time of this kind of de luxe book (but less lavishly so) was published in Switzerland by Jean Graven in 1946. Here the original sixty tales have been reduced to forty, and they are presented in yet another new order, and are illustrated with eleven colour plates and forty woodcut vignettes by Robert Halnard [V 122e]. Only one year later, in 1947, A.F. Cosijns published two editions of the whole of Paris's text as he had first published it. Both were richly illustrated with woodcuts made by Cosijns, but one of them was very finely bound, printed on good-quality paper, and limited to 400 copies [V 122f]. The last of these highly-crafted, artistic versions of Paris's work appeared only three years later, in 1950. For this, only twenty of his 'aventures' were selected. Printed on good-quality paper and beautifully bound, they were illustrated with forty fine copperplate engravings by Jean Frélaut. This edition was limited to 175 copies [V 122h].

Other relatively ordinary but nevertheless attractively produced editions have also been made. For example, there is Jean de Foucault's (prefaced by Henri Poulaille) 1949 edition which contains numerous black-and-white drawings [V 122g]; and there are two book-club editions, the one made for the Club des Jeunes Amis du Livre in 1958 [V 122j], and the other for the Club des Librairies de France in 1963 [V 122k]. This is bound in red cloth, printed on good paper, and contains eight high-quality colour plates of miniatures, actual size, from MS f fr 12584 of the Bibliothèque Nationale. Jacques Haumont's 1966 edition, prefaced by Matthieu Galey, contains numerous woodcuts by Jost Amman and Virgil Solis from Hartmann Schopper's *De admirabile fallacia et astutia vulpeculae Reinikes libros quator*, a Latin version of the Beast Epic published in Frankfurt in 1567 [V 122l].

Besides these de luxe and quality editions of Paris's text, quite a few simple, paperback and cheap versions have been printed, aimed, it seems, at the curious, cultured adult reader. Among these are Poulaille's in 1949 [V 122g], the Gallimard Collection 1000 Soleils in 1982, reprinted in 1991 [V 122o]; and Gallimard Collection Folio in 1986, reprinted in 1991 [V 122p].

Paris's text has also been put to use in schools and colleges for young people. The earliest example of this appears to be the Jean Crès version of 1936. Compared with later schoolroom versions, this is of superior quality (it contains one illustration and many decorated initial letters by Guy Dollian), and it is one of the few which present the entire text [V 122c].

In 1977, Arnaldi and Anglade presented just thirteen episodes, based on Paris's text, in a way thought to be appealing to secondary-school children, and likely to encourage discussion and group activity. It contains fifteen illustrations, and was reprinted in 1990 and 1993 [V 90]. Neveu, Lemaître and Bauchart took, in 1991, just ten short extracts from Paris in their *Le Roman de Renart, Lecture Suivie pour les Collèges*, on which they based numerous comprehension and grammar exercises [V 120]. Much the most ambitious schoolroom versions have been devised by Biet, Brighelli and Rispail. In their first volume (1997) they reproduce the first thirty of Paris's 'aventures', and in their second (1986), the last thirty. To each volume they added a supplement with questions and suggested group activities to be supervised by the teacher. Each volume is illustrated. The first was reprinted in 1987 and 1995; the second in 1991 and 1994 [V 122n and 122q]. Paris's text has also made its way in specially edited forms into foreign schools. In 1945 Brotherton published, in Glasgow, *Les Aventures de Maître Renart et de ses compères: A Reader Specially Prepared for Second Year Pupils According to Vander Beke's Word Frequency Lists*. Only a few 'aventures' were selected, and they were rendered into very simple French [V 94].

In one form or another, Paulin Paris's text, first published in 1861, has appeared at least twenty-four times during the twentieth century: 1909, 1921, 1936, 1946, 1947, 1949, 1950, 1957, 1958, 1963, 1964, 1966, 1977 (twice), 1982, 1983, 1984, 1986 (twice), 1990 (twice), 1991 (twice) and 1993.

Part Two (by Jean Dufournet)

Albert-Marie Schmidt's *Le Roman de Renart, transcrit dans le respect de sa verdeur originale pour la récréation des tristes et la tristesse des cafards* (1963); and some comparisons with the adaptations by Paulin Paris and Maurice Genevoix.

Schmidt (1901–66), a distinguished Professor of French in the Universities of Caen (1941–44) and Lille (1945–66) and an eminent critic who contributed regularly to the weekly *Réforme*, combined in a masterly fashion the often quite distinct approaches and qualities of the literary historian, the scholar and the critic. Although he was primarily a specialist in different aspects of sixteenth-century French literature and thought (for example, the alchemist Paracelsus, scientific poetry,

Calvin), he was also an authority on authors and subjects from later centuries (for example, the seventeenth-century humanist Saint-Evremond; minor eighteenth-century thinkers; Maupassant; modern symbolist poetry; and emerging modern writers: he collaborated with Raymond Queneau on *Oulipo* < l'*Ou*vroir de la *litt*érature *po*tentielle = [The Workshop for Potential Literature] and he spent many a long year working on the *Roman de Renart*. This culminated in his adaptation published in 1963 (Paris: Albin Michel, reprinted 1992; and, as mentioned above, a new edition appeared in 1964 (Marseille: Lacydon) chiefly, it would seem, to house twenty watercolour illustrations by Yvette Alde). Nothing of Schmidt's preparatory work on his *Roman de Renart* has survived: no notes, no document whatsoever, not even a rough draft. This has been confirmed in writing (letter to Jean Dufournet, 1 April 1986) by his son, the critic Joël Schmidt: 'At his death my father left no written material relating to his earlier researches, nor on research currently in progress, nor on planned research. Nor did he keep any letters. This attitude [to written material] was part and parcel of his instinctive Protestant ethic which demanded that one should set little store by the things of this world even if, for a while, he was keenly interested in them. In fact, what was past was definitely past, and he would never return to it'.

In rewriting the *Roman de Renart*, it is obvious that Schmidt wanted to take up a position totally opposed to that of Paulin Paris and to what he called his tame fables and his vain pseudo-classical elegance. Schmidt aimed to restore to adult readers and not to 'some still naïve children' a *Roman de Renart* which astonishes by its scandalous spirit, its avenging bitterness, its ribald audacity, its vitality and vigour, all qualities to be kept, of course, in his adaptation into modern French. This he made very clear in his truly bold and especially closely-argued Preface (pp. 7–14).

For Schmidt, the medieval animal epic (which he saw as a sumptuous and scandalous festival), is characterised by its prodigious freedom of expression. Far from being a vast animal epic knowingly conceived as such, he saw it as a collection of short tales which display an amusing incoherence which could not help but entertain every social group within the French nation. For him the authors of this collection of tales have a double and difficult objective. Their first aim 'is to represent the qualities and behaviour of the wild and domesticated animals whose mobile portraits they elaborate, always paying particular attention to minute detail. Beyond this, they want, by dressing them rather unexpectedly in human beings' cast-offs, to make them into emblematic representations of people typical of French society in their day. But they (the authors) take exquisite precautions so that we do not forget that they never intend these quadrupeds and these winged creatures to be totally transformed into men and women' (Preface, p. 8). These animals, which suddenly wear masks without losing their identity, allow the authors of the branches to give way to flights of satiric and parodic fantasy which they use to denounce the favouritism and bias of Capetian kings, judges' duplicity, crusader excesses and deviations, Church abuses, the ungodly use of holy sacraments, the grotesque aspects of religious ceremony whose splendours they caricature as if they were popular festivals. Intertextual effects also have to be taken into account, effects which turn the *Roman de Renart* into a subtle parody of Breton (Celtic) romances and adventure stories. Behind the portrayal of Hersent (the she-wolf) and Fière (the lioness) are the mythical figures of Isolda and Guinevere: 'Fière and Hersent symbolize those great medieval ladies, infatuated by themselves, who put themselves beyond good and bad so that they may claim the privileges of absolute autonomy' (Preface, pp. 11–12). On the other hand, the authors of the branches have made capital out of the narrative processes of the *chansons de geste* (epics about great wars and great warriors); processes such as the enumeration of the combatants, warning dreams, accounts of diplomatic missions, funerary laments, descriptions of drawn-out sieges and never-ending military engagements, etc.

Less obvious is the fact that Schmidt aimed to compete with Maurice Genevoix's *Roman de Renart* (Genevoix 1991) although his adaptation dates from 1958 and had been in wide circulation. While Genevoix proclaimed his determination to keep fully his writer's freedom (Genevoix 1991: 25–26), Schmidt wanted to be rigorously faithful to both the letter and the spirit of the branches, even if he reshapes its structure and its architecture. To allow scholars and medievalists to appreciate the judiciousness of his undertaking, he set out, at the end of his Preface, a Table of Concordance between the branches of his version and those of the Old French *Roman de Renart*. Schmidt used as his base the Old French texts established by Martin in 1882, 1885 and 1887, whereas Genevoix (as his work-notes show) used chiefly Paulin Paris's adaptation together with, on occasions, the lexicon established by Gaston Reynaud and Henri Lemaître for their edition of *Renart le Con-*

trefait (Paris: 1914). In the same spirit (of authenticity) Schmidt had his text illustrated with nine drawings taken from Renardian manuscripts kept in Paris at the Bibliothèque Nationale (f. fr. 1580 and 1581).

The tripartite structure of both Genevoix's and Schmidt's versions of the *Roman de Renart* is inspired directly by Léopold Chauveau's (1924). (Schmidt sometimes attended the meetings organised by Paul Desjardins at Pontigny Abbey, where he almost certainly met Léopold Chauveau, a frequent participant in Desjardin's colloquia.) The chapters in Genevoix's version of the *Roman de Renart* were unevenly divided between the three parts: nine in the first (entitled *Les Écoles de Renard* = Reynard's Schools); sixteen in the second (*Les Gabets de maître Renard* = Reynard's Tricks); ten in the third (*Le Plaid Renard* = Reynard's Trial). This contrasts with Schmidt's adaptation which consists of ten chapters in each of the three parts, or books, as he called them.

What is new and unique to Schmidt is his insistence that his prose rendering of the branches 'should always be supported by unobtrusive octonary cadences (we recall that the branches are built on octosyllabic couplets), discreet enough for the attentive non-specialist to perceive their beat, supressed enough so as not to deflect his attention from the meaning and not to spoil his pleasure' (Preface, p. 13). One has only to open his adaptation anywhere to prove that these unobtrusive octonary cadences are indeed to be found everywhere.

As for the vocabulary, if Genevoix, with his joy in the creative and narrative processes, plays with words which he borrows from various linguistic registers such as the regional *bahuler* or *groumer*, and the technical *linaire* or *se raser* (referring to game which stretches itself out flush with the ground), and produces extraordinary verbal flourishes as when hens *cotecottent, coclorent, glossent* (cluck); Schmidt prefers to use old or aging words (revealing his close familiarity with Old and Middle French), but always judiciously so that the reader does not need to consult a dictionary. They are mostly the kind of word which a good, comprehensive French dictionary labels either *vieux* (old, and out of use), or *vielli*, (aging, and rarely used), or *régional* (regional, not used in standard French), or *littéraire* (literary, used only in elegant, written texts). Here are a few examples, all drawn from Schmidt's Book I, Branch I: *bourdes* (lies, or jests), *oyoit* (he heard, from *oïr*, to hear), *hoir* (heir), *huis* (door or gate), and *dolent* (wretched, or pained or angry). Other words, not in even a good, comprehensive dictionary of modern French, are taken directly from the *Roman de Renart* (Martin's edition), or from Old French, but in context are usually fairly easily understood by a native speaker of French. For example, again from his Book I, Branch I, *dextre* (right), *cortil* (courtyard or garden), *oisel* (bird), *cil* (= *celui*, this one, he, she, it, the), *s'accoise* (calm down, remain silent). While remaining faithful to the medieval text, Schmidt uses a very rich and colourful vocabulary, especially to describe male genitals, e.g.: *garniture* (normally 'fittings', etc.); *breloques*, normally 'charms' or 'trinkets'; *ripon*; *olive*, etc.; and to describe the sexual act, making love, e.g.: *biscotter*, derived from *biscotte*, a dry finger-sponge; *bricoler*, to put the breast harness on a horse; *hutiner*; *sabouler*, to jump on somebody; *tracasser*, to fuss or potter about; *beluter*, to pass something through a sieve; *acclamper*; *fouler la vendange*, to tread grapes; *se dépenser sur vos arçons*, to spend oneself in the saddle; *gravir la croupe*, to climb up the rump; *battre l'écu*, to batter the shield, etc.

In conclusion: if Genevoix's *Roman de Renard* is a recreation like Joseph Bédier's *Roman de Tristan et Iseut*, Schmidt's is without doubt the most faithful to the text, the spirit and the rhythm of the branches of the Old French animal epic while being, at the same time, extraordinarily vivacious and richly worded. It is the only one of the great adaptations which have not been edited. For the pleasure of the reading public, it would be good if it were indeed edited and again made easily available.

Jean-Gérard Imbar's and Jean-Louis Hubert's *Le Polar de Renard*, 1979

The year 1979 marks a turning-point in the history of the French detective story. So much so that one may speak of the detective story's Springtime: the creation of some new series of books such as *Engrenage*, *Sanguine* or the *Miroir obscur*; the appearance of new authors; the development of specialised journals such as *Enigmatika*, *Les Amis du crime*, *Gang* and *Polar*; the detective film festival at Royan from 6 to 9 April; the exhibition of tough thrillers which began on 15 April at the Centre Beaubourg; the first festival for detective novels and films held in the Maison de la Culture at Rheims from 2 to 13 May; but, above all, the French tough thriller, soon baptised *néo-polar*, neo-detective story, assumed a paramount place in the development of the genre. For the authors of these stories, some of whom were known (for example, Bastid-Martens, Errer, Varoux, Siniac, Vautrin, A.D.G...) and others who were new (for example, Alain Dubrieu, Fajardie, Delacorta, Hervé Jaouen, C.

Camara), each new work had to call into question both writing and the author himself, to sweep aside by a constant creative and critical attitude, received ideas; and to break the moulds which tend to form as a tradition develops. In this way the tough thriller was to become a true literary genre which would go beyond simple entertainment and for which, according to Jean Vautrin, what really mattered were the glimpses one had of men, and of contemporary political and social scenes.

In this very same year of 1979 the *Polar de Renard* [Reynard Detective] was published by Éditions du Square, Paris. Jean-Gérard Imbar wrote the script, Jean-Louis Hubert drew the pictures (Figures 13.1–13.3). Imbar, born 1944 in the Contrescarpe quarter (Paris 5), had published several novels which contain descriptions of some professional milieux which he knew well through having been part of them (he had been, among other things, a press photographer and a private detective). He joined the newspaper photographers in *Scoop* (*Série noire*, no. 1477, 1968) and in *Ah! ça IRA* (*Série noire*, no. 1656, 1974) which contains a kind of report on the confrontations in Ireland; also on long-distance lorry-drivers in *Les Lignards* (*Super Noire*, 1977) and on private detective agencies in *Cocu and Co.* (*Engrenage*, 1980). The last-named novel tells of the ruthless struggle for market supremacy between two private detective agencies. Young Freddy, employed by Rapidos, decides to play a double game to get higher fees. But can one swindle an employer who is himself a swindler? The book begins with a comic sequence: a company director frolics with his secretary in a little wood, unaware that the surrounding bushes are alive with detectives and that a bailiff describes in detail everything he sees. We should add that Imbar was also the script-writer for the television series *L'Inspecteur mène l'enqête* [The Inspector Investigates], and where cartoon strips are concerned, he is to be credited with *L'Encyclopédie en bandes dessinées* [The Strip Cartoon Encyclopedia] as well as our *Polar de Renard*.

Under the patronage of Jean-Patrick Manchette, the *Polar de Renard* is a kind of fusion between the *Roman de Renart*, the strip-cartoon story and the tough thriller. It is, as Manchette has written, 'to inform humanized animal tales with brutal realism; to tell stories about MPs, coppers, bandits; and to tell (or to draw) who in all this is the fox, the wolf, the dogs and the dirty rats'. *Le Polar de Renard* is in a direct line of descent from George Orwell's *Animal Farm*. Against a background of current slang and the politcs of the day, it is set in Paris's Fifth District, around the Contrescarpe, Rue Mouffetard and the *Artouses*

Figure 13.1 *Three pages of drawings, 1976, by Jean-Louis Hubert for* Le Polar de Renard.

(slang for the *Arènes de Lutèce*, Paris's Roman Arena), with occasional stop-overs at the Irish Bar run by O'Ready the Dog.

On the whole, Imbar has kept the names and characters from the *Roman de Renart*, and these often determine both their profession and their social status. Goupil the Fox is a dealer in second-hand things with a shop-sign displaying the Maupertuis coat of arms. He lives with his wife Hermeline and son Percehaie. One notes that, inverting the situation in the

Figure 13.2

medieval epic, Goupil is the Christian name, Renart the family name. Isengrin the wolf is a shady character who owns a bar-restaurant specialising in Burgundian fondue. He is the strong man at the service of Tibert the cat, a candidate for a seat in Parliament. Tibert recalls the name of the Parisian MP

Figure 13.3

Jean Tiberi, and this doubtless explains the role given to the cat, who makes common cause with the wolf. Mouflart the vulture is a journalist-reporter who, through his articles in *Le Serpent* [The Snake], throws oil on the fire. Chantecler the cock is, of course, a policeman, even a commissioner. Noble the lion makes a fleeting appearance on television as President of the Republic. Patous the bear is a knock-about comedian on Contrescarpe Square, and his friend Roenel the dog is a tramp who knows the sewers of Paris like the back of his hand. Baudouin the ass is the owner of a Billiard Hall where Goupil and Patous go for a game, while Raisant the mare is an old prostitute, and Pelé the rat often patronises Isengrin's bar.

Besides making use of the animal-characters' names, Imbar takes up the old rivalry between the wolf and the fox who rapes his enemy's wife, Hersent. The two who enact their closely-related roles are given the physical appearance of the animals they typify, but they wear men's clothes, and act and behave like men living in the second half of the twentieth century. It is as he drives his old car, his *tas de boue* (literally, a pile of mud) that Goupil first meets Isengrin; and he often goes to a sports hall to practise foot-boxing, just as he often watches television with his family. It is this double view of things which is ever-present, and subtly so, in the story which unfolds in two games and seven rounds (three in the first game, four in the second):

Game One

Round One. In the course of a squabble between poster-stickers, caused by Isengrin, Goupil witnesses a murder. Mouflart inflames the situation by writing a series of articles for *Le Serpent*. Isengrin tries to intimidate or bribe Goupil in a variety of ways.

Round Two. While playing billiards with Patous, Goupil is attacked by members of Isengrin's gang. After having his wound dressed at a chemist's, Goupil goes home, only to discover that his son has been kidnapped.

Round Three. On finding out that Isengrin was responsible for the kidnap, Goupil arms himself to the teeth and takes Isengrin by surprise at the Thai Massage Parlour. He forces him to take him to his home where he finds and succeeds in releasing his son. This is when he seizes his opportunity to rape Hersent in full view of her captive husband. Soon afterwards he learns that his name is writ large on every notice-board in town: 'Rabies: Goupil wanted dead rather than alive', and that a real hunt has begun to get him. The first game goes, in effect, to his enemies.

Game Two

Round Four. On the run, and with the help of Patous, Goupil tries to recover his war booty, one hundred *briques* (from 1945 a *brique*, literally a brick, was slang for a million old francs).

However, he is taken by surprise by the police and flees over the roof-tops. Eventually the old prostitute Raisant shelters him.

Round Five. On the point of being arrested, he is rescued by Roenel, Patous's friend, who carries him off through the sewers. Here they come face to face with rats who, recognising him, flee because (warned by the message broadcast by so many posters), they are afraid of contracting rabies. Back home, Goupil discovers that his home has been searched and all his money has been stolen. Through a tunnel dug by rats he gets, with them, into Tibert's house and then loots it. There he takes possession of some confidential papers which implicate Isengrin, Chantecler and Tibert.

Round Six. By shooting O'Ready in the knee, Goupil settles an account with him, having discovered that this landlord of the Irish Bar is a police-informer. Then, disguised as a tramp, he mingles with some old folk at a banquet organised for them by Tibert at La Mutualité. There he creates indescribable chaos, and forces Tibert's wife, Fala Duna, to undress in public. He then joins a street demonstration against Tibert.

Round Seven. In order to recover the confidential papers, Isengrin plots to capture Goupil, beat him up and then torture him in the presence of Chantecler. But in the end, Goupil comes to an understanding with Tibert, and he forces Isengrin to flee. From this point on, he is the one to call the tunes in the Mouffetard area. The new slogan is: 'Tibert, Goupil, the same ticket: vote Tibert'. Goupil finally wins by default.

This most recent rewriting of the *Roman de Renart* is thoroughly political in character, set at the time of an election campaign which involves violence, corruption and debauchery. All means are justified if they lead to victory at the polls. Political opponents are killed; Goupil takes revenge for the breaking of his shop window by blowing up the editorial offices of *Le Serpent*. People are made to 'sing', and their 'singing' is used to compile secret dossiers which are then fought over. People are tortured, raped, and a child is kidnapped. Tibert, a candidate for election, organises a great banquet and feast at La Mutualité on the very eve of the poll in order to rally the votes of the district's senior citizens. Then there is the matter of the services provided by an organisation called the *Sympathiques Animateurs du Club* [the Friendly Promotors of the Club] whose initials, SAC, are identical with those of a real organization, the *Service d'Action Civique* [the Civil Action Group] which had come into conflict with the law because of its readiness to use violence. Tibert traffics in housing, while Commissioner Chantecler levies taxes on prostitutes, and Isengrin runs a racket involving bars and a night club. At one point he is found in the Thai Massage Parlour with a Minister of State, a Senator and an Abbot. Newspapers exist only to stir up antagonisms, and to unleash pent-up feelings and ferment violence.

Finally, these adventures are related in an incisive, very colourful style in which, besides a rich panoply of onomatopoaeic words dear to cartoon narratives such as *Smop...Uuh!...Slaec...ouarf, ouarf...gniar, gniar...*, one finds all the ingredients of that kind of popular speech typical of the tough thriller: apocope or abbreviations such as *du mat* = du matin, a.m.; *la Mouf* = la rue Mouffetard, Mouffetard Street; *le broc* = le brocanteur, dealer in second-hand goods, etc.). There is also much use of slang such as *je t'arrose* (literally, 'I water you', in slang 'I stand you a drink'), *on se casse* (let's go), *les joyeuses* (in slang 'testicles, balls'), *chouraver* (to steal), *lardon* (kid), *trouille* (funk), *rapidos* (very quick), *bonnard* ('cool'), all of which may be found in the *Dictionnaire de l'argot* [Dictionary of Slang] by Jean-Paul Colin, Jean-Pierre Mével and Christian Leclère (Paris: Larousse, 1990). There is many a swear-word and insult of the kind *cette grande salope d'Isengrin* = that big bitch of Isengrin's; *mange-merde* = shit-eater. There is many a disparaging comparison and metaphor: Goupil threatens to change the people he speaks to *en anus d'hémorroïdaires* = into haemorrhoid-ridden arses, and when, with a gun in his hand, he goes off in search of Isengrin, he declares that 'with my stradivarius under my arm, I am prepared to play a concerto for wolf-bowels *obus douz*, words meant to recall 'opus twelve' but literally 'with twelve shells'. Finally, there is a constant play on words. Goupil is armed with a *tumpamarrant*, an allusion to the Tupamaros guerrillas; and he becomes a *Ratcula* (built on Dracula) to the startled rats.

This latest renewal of the *Roman de Renart* is a subtle and original re-creation as well as an entertaining recreation which addresses several kinds of reading public; in particular the kind which usually reads narrative cartoons with its usual share of squabbles, insults and slang woven into a police story. It also addresses people who readily pick up and decode allusions to political intrigue and to literary texts. An entertaining example of this is when Goupil falls asleep after reading two pages of his favourite novel, a novel which one later discovers is entitled *Le Voleur* [The Thief]. Although the script-writer does not name the author, his name, Georges Darien, would come into the mind of every member of the novel-reading public.

CHAPTER 14

THE FOX AND THE WOLF IN THE WELL:
THE METAMORPHOSES OF A COMIC MOTIF

Kenneth Varty

The motif of the fox and the wolf in the well has often been treated in fable, short story, sermon-exemplum and folklore. In his *The Types of the Folktale*, Aarne lists it as Type 32 under the descriptive heading 'The Wolf descends into the well in one bucket and rescues the fox in the other' (Aarne and Thompson 1961). The all-important mechanism on which this motif and much of the ensuing comedy depend is a pulley suspended above the well – a pulley around which runs a rope with a bucket attached to either end so that, as one bucket descends to the bottom of the well to gather water, the other, filled with water, is hauled to the surface. In most accounts, the wolf is induced into the upper bucket by the prospect of food to be had at the bottom of the well. In early versions, that food is said to be a round cheese – in fact, a reflection of the full moon (this links them to Aarne's Type 34: 'The Wolf dives into water for reflected cheese'). Versions of Aarne's Type 32 abound in different regions and cultures, from ancient to modern times. This is in part confirmed by the information Aarne provides about its distribution, but it is far from complete. The relevant entry in Dicke's and Grubmüller's 1987 catalogue of medieval and Renaissance fables in German and Latin reveals something of the limitations of Aarne's list; and the German scholars' work is for a limited period and confined to German-speaking regions. A similar, up-to-date catalogue for every other European language-area would doubtless reveal further limitations to Aarne's entry concerning Type 32.

The aim of this essay is to trace the way the comic qualities of this motif in oft-retold tales occasionally reflects the culture and period of its retelling, in particular in its Beast Epic and related forms.

A few scholars have treated the likely evolution of this motif, either on its way to the *Roman de Renart*, and (or) thence to its Middle English relation, *Vox and Wolf*. Lucien Foulet contributed to this as he studied the best-known *Roman de Renart* treatment of the motif and a variant Renardian form, dating the former c.1178 and the latter somewhat later (Foulet 1914: 290–307). Haim Schwarzbaum re-examined this matter as he studied the Rabbi Berechiah Ha-Nakdan's 117th fable of the *Mishlé Shu'Alim* (Fox Fables), dated by him mid thirteenth-century (Schwarzbaum 1979: 550–58). J.A.W. Bennett and G.V. Smithers have also considered this bit of literary history in their edition of *The Fox and the Wolf*, generally dated late thirteenth- or early fourteenth-century (Bennett and Smithers 1966: 65–76). All these scholars agree that the immediate forerunners and most likely sources of the *Roman de Renart* versions were, firstly, Rabbi Rashi (c.1070); secondly, Petrus Alphonsus, a converted Spanish Jew (between 1109 and 1114). According to Schwarzbaum, these two medieval Hebrew sources may, in their turn, have been influenced by (a) Rabbi Meir, who flourished c.135–170 A.D.; and (b) Rabbi Hai Gam who died 1038. Schwarzbaum also thinks Berechiah Ha-Nakdan's 117th fable may have been available to the *Roman de Renart* authors. In short, there seems to have been a strong Jewish link in the evolutionary chain of our fable motif before it appears first in the *Roman de Renart*, then, eventually, in *Vox and Wolf*.

The better-known of the two *Roman de Renart* treatments of our motif – indeed, by and large the only one generally known – is presented as Branch IV in volume I (1882) of Martin's edition and in all those editions and translations which follow in this Alsatian scholar's footsteps (e.g., Combarieu du Grès and Subrenat 1981; Dufournet and Méline 1985; and Owen 1994). In what follows this is referred to as the standard version. The other *Roman de Renart* treatment occurs just once in all the many surviving manuscripts – in MS 3334 of the Bibliothèque de l'Arsenal, Paris. It has been published only three times: by Chabaille 1835, and (following Chabaille), by Varty 1991a, then by Strubel et al 1998. This is referred to as the variant version, though I feel this does it a serious injustice. As is well known by specialists, Foulet argued that the standard version was composed in c.1178, and the variant version at a later date. I have argued that the variant version must have been composed before the standard version, and could be as early as c.1120, and I will return later to this question of precedence. In the readily-available Introduction to their edition of *The Fox and the Wolf at the Well*, Bennett and Smithers summarise the main reasons why they think this poem derives ultimately, in part, from the *Roman de Renart* tradition, including both the standard *and* the variant versions, so they are not repeated here.

Rabbi Rashi's version is a two-part fable-exemplum which serves as a commentary on three Talmudic passages: (a) the fathers have eaten sour grapes, and the teeth of the children have become blunt (*Ezek.*, 18: 2); (b) just balances, just weights (*Lev.*, 19: 36); (c) the righteous man is delivered out of trouble, and the wicked person comes in his stead (*Prov.* 11: 8). In the first part of Rabbi Rashi's fable, a fox inveigles a wolf into entering the Jews' courtyard on a Friday evening with a view to joining them in their Sabbath banquets: but, on the wolf's approach, the Jews fall on him with sticks and give him a terrible thrashing. He intends to wreak vengeance on the fox, but the fox defends himself by telling the wolf that the Jews have a grudge against his father who once helped them prepare their meals, but then consumed all the choice morsels. The fox then quotes *Ezekiel* 18: 2 (as above). In the second part of this fable, the fox, at night, under a full moon, leads the wolf to a well, then quite deliberately gets into the upper bucket, causing it to descend and to raise the lower one. The wolf asks the fox why he has done this. Now at the bottom of the well, the fox calls up, 'Look here', and points to the reflection of the moon: 'Here's a big cheese'. The wolf then asks how he can join the fox to get at the cheese. The fox points to the other bucket, and invites the wolf to get in it, which he does. When down, he asks the fox how he is to get back up. The fox replies by quoting first from *Leviticus*, then from *Proverbs* (as above).

Such comedy as there is in this fable depends chiefly on seeing the wolf duped twice in rapid succession, and by the linking of three Talmudic texts to these events. As it can hardly be said that the buckets are just, or that the fox is a righteous man, there is clearly much irony here. This, and the totally unexpected association of holy texts with the unholy events of this fable, were no doubt largely responsible for the great success it seems to have enjoyed over a long period.

Petrus Alphonsus's version (Hermes 1977: 143–44) is embedded in an exemplum-fable, the amoral moral of which is 'take what is on offer at any given moment, and do not refuse it in the hope of better in the future' (rather like the English saying 'a bird in the hand is worth two in the bush'). In the first part, a fox offers to settle a dispute between a farmer and a wolf over the ownership of oxen. The fox asks for two hens as his fee from the farmer, and offers the wolf an enormous round cheese to replace the oxen he will forego (a poor bargain, one might think, but the wolf agrees). In the second part, the fox takes the wolf on a moonlit night to a well, and there points to the reflection of the moon, telling the wolf that it is a cheese. He urges the wolf to go down and get it. The wolf refuses, and tells the fox to go down and bring it up to him. However, should it prove to be too heavy, he says he will come down and help. The fox descends in the the upper bucket, then pretends the cheese is too heavy for him to carry alone; so the wolf goes down in the other bucket, thereby raising the fox, by his greater weight, to safety. The fox then abandons the wolf at the bottom of the well.

This does not strike us as being a particularly funny fable. Such comic qualities as it has depend chiefly on the fox's way of exacting food from the farmer, and on his way of duping the wolf – another case of the clever little man outwitting stupid big men. There is also some humour in the success of the calculated risk taken by the fox.

Both these fable-exempla depend on the well's mechanism, the fox's quick-witted exploitation of it, and of the reflection of the moon in the well-water. Renart's quick-wittedness coupled with his imaginativeness are made much of in most branches of the *Roman de Renart*, and they play a major role in the two *Renart* versions of Branch IV to which we now turn.

The comic qualities of the variant version of Branch IV depend chiefly on the way the fox (Renart) dupes the wolf (Ysengrin) into believing he is dead, that he is a spirit, and in paradise, with all the food and drink he could wish for. Comic irony abounds in the depiction of such a notoriously wicked creature being admitted to paradise, and in situating paradise down below and not up above. This image of the fox in paradise is, of course, at the heart of both the standard *Renart* version, and of the Middle English version. It is the chief innovation in this motif's long history, and it first occurs, it seems, in the *Roman de Renart*. Important to the way the fox dupes the wolf is the killing of three hens, and in particular the fate of the third hen. It is in the discovery by the wolf of this third hen at the well wall that convinces the wolf that the fox is telling the truth when he claims to be a spirit in paradise. (The fox had eaten two of the three hens he had killed. Desperately thirsty, he sought water, came upon a well, dropped the third dead hen by the well wall, and accidentally plunged, in the upper bucket, to the bottom of the well. When the wolf came to the well Renart pretended he was a spirit, in paradise, with all the food and drink he could ever want. At first the wolf did not believe him, but the fox insisted, and said to the wolf that if he wanted proof that he (Renart) was telling the truth, he (Ysengrin) had only to look on the ground, and he would find the carcass of a hen. Ysengrin did so, ate it, and was convinced.) In the standard *Renart* version, the third hen is abandoned where the fox dropped it, and is heard of no more. Unfortunately the Middle English version is unclear here. It is possible to deduce that, in its preliminary section, the fox killed three hens, but nothing is made of them in the poem's later sections. To my mind this is one of a number of significant factors which show that the authors of both the standard *Renart* and the Middle English poems based on our motif knew the variant *Renart* poem in one form or another, but were too preoccupied with their own innovations to weave the fate of the third hen into their work in a satisfactory way. There are numerous other comic qualities (other, that is, than the paradise image) in the detail of the variant *Renart* version. One that seems to be unique to it is the fox's use of the popular belief that the soul of the good is, at the moment of death, carried off to paradise by God's angels. Here (line 341) the fox tells the wolf to jump for the rope above the upper bucket when 'angels will carry (him) off'.

The chief comic qualities of the standard form of Branch IV arise from the way the notorious affairs between the fox and the she-wolf (first told in the *Ysengrimus*, then in Branch II) are drawn into the narrative, and especially on the way the wolf mistakes his own reflection in the well water for his wife who, he presumes, is enjoying yet another round of sex with the fox. This comic element is enriched when the fox tells the wolf that his suspicions about being cuckolded are ill-founded, and that he must accept that he was mistaken, and wrong to harbour such suspicions, especially if he wants to join him (Renart) in paradise. The wolf admits having thought the worst, and says he was indeed wrong, providing us with the comic spectacle of the cuckold grovelling before the cuckolder. There is also much comedy in the detail too, but the entertaining image of the buckets as the scales of divine justice is not new: it comes, as we have seen, from the Jewish versions of our motif. The miracle of the candles which light up in paradise to celebrate the wolf's forgiving nature and his imminent admission to that holy place is, it seems, a tellingly comic and original development of the way the moon is reflected in the water of the well. Here we guess it now reflects the stars. The denouement concerning the wolf's escape from the well is much longer than in the variant *Renart* version, and the comedy here is of the violent (Tom and Jerry cartoon-like) kind as we see the monks beat him up, even with candelabra from the monastery altar. And there is a further development stemming from the fox's adultery with the she-wolf with the arrival on the scene of one of the wolf's cubs who discovers his distressed father. This is one of the cubs over whom the fox urinated and branded a bastard just after witnessing his mother commit adultery. In these ways the standard *Renart* version of our motif is made to counterbalance that part of Branch II in which the she-wolf first seduced the fox and was then raped by him. In the one, the she-wolf is victim; in the other, the wolf himself.

The comic qualities of the Middle English poem depend in large measure on (though perhaps at several removes) both *Renart* versions, standard and variant. At the heart of it, to be sure, is the paradise image, and the duping of the wolf. From the *Renart* variant version, the English poem draws especially on the way the wolf discovers the fox in the well – by overhearing the invisible fox (whose voice he recognises) talking to himself. Their subsequent conversation is developed in a masterfully comic way. All three Renardian versions include lively and entertaining direct speech, but the best is in the English poem. It is easily the funniest, with the psychologically best battle of wits, beginning with the wolf pretending not to recognise the fox's voice, and clearly relishing the knowledge that his old enemy is down a well. This heightens the comic effect when, finally, the wolf is duped. The way the fox's adultery with the she-wolf is drawn into the narrative is admirably ironic. From totally rejecting the fox's claim to be dead, to be a spirit, and in paradise, the wolf is, it seems, gradually convinced this is so – or, rather, he lets his greed convince him that it is so. Before he too may enter paradise, he must confess his sins. But there is nobody to confess to – except the fox. And the fox makes him go on and on with his catalogue of sins until he gets him to admit that he had believed tales about an affair between the fox and his wife, the she-wolf. He had actually, and stupidly, believed what he had seen with his own eyes! In the variant *Renart* version, the fox tells the wolf he has to forgive everybody everything before he can enter paradise; forgiving the fox is, of course, implied, and in particular forgiving the adultery with the she-wolf, but it is only implied. In the standard *Renart* version the fox tells the wolf he must confess as well as forgive. The wolf says he has already confessed – to an old hare and to a she-goat. No details are reported. It is only in the English poem that the wolf confesses to the fox, and brings in the notorious affair between the 'confessor' and the she-wolf. In this way it is all the more comically outrageous, comically dramatic – in particular the wolf's repudiating the evidence of his own eyes. Here, as Bennett and Smithers say: 'we have uninhibited relish for the scandalous triumphs of the brazen reprobate'. There are, of course, uniquely comic traits in the details of the Middle English poem. These include, early on, the comic metaphor on which the fox founds his blandly insolent claim to have done Chauntecler's hens good by letting their blood, and by offering to do the same for the cock.

This glance at just a segment or two of the many segments that make up the history of this motif as far as the Middle Ages inhibits one from drawing many conclusions, and even these must be tentative.

Once again the *Renart* authors are seen to exploit popular material – in this case as re-interpreted by European Jewish culture. *Roman de Renart* authors are also seen to expand the fable by fleshing out the protagonists; and, especially in the standard *Renart* version, by fitting it into the sexually motivated war between the fox and the wolf, the foundation of so much else in the French Beast Epic.

It seems to me that each of these Renardian treatments of our motif advances up the ladder of comic literary achievement in the order I have commented on them – the variant form of Branch IV, then the standard form, then *Vox and Wolf*. I do not believe that a new or reworked version of a tale necessarily improves on its model, but this does seem to me to be the case here, both in narrative detail and in comic quality. That is, if the variant *Renart* version preceded the standard one. Among specialists it is generally known that Foulet argued that the variant version was a later rewriting of the standard version, and his view has generally prevailed (Foulet 1914). Relatively recently I have argued that the variant version was the original French Renardian poem, that the standard version is a reworking of it. What is so intriguing is the fact that the first 148 lines of both versions are, to all intents and purposes, identical. The reworking is from line 149 on. I have set forth elsewhere, and at some length, my arguments in this debate (Varty in Rossi et al. 1996: 451–63). These involve a detailed analysis of the rhymes and various aspects of the grammar, as well as certain ideas and images. Whoever is right in this matter, it is clear that the author of one of the *Renart* versions knew the other's, and they probably both knew one or more of the Jewish versions. The author of the Middle English poem seems to have known something of both French poems (though the proper name Reneward for Renart, and Sigrim for Ysengrin suggest a rather distant knowledge). Did the people who heard or read the Middle English poem also know some of these earlier versions of this motif? And was their appreciation of the comic qualities of *Vox and Wolf* heightened thereby? I guess they did know other versions, and did appreciate the originality of the Middle English poet; but this cannot be proved. One can only point to the evidence of the numerous versions which seem to have been in circulation, in particular to Odo of Cheriton's Latin prose fable (c.1219) and, later, Bozon's fable in Anglo-Norman (c.1340), and John of Sheppey's fable (before 1360).

We conclude with one of the remoter, more modern and more metamorphosed versions of our motif, but still clearly recognisable as our motif: the tale Joel Chandler Harris published in 1880 under the title *Old Mr Rabbit He's A Good Fisherman*. So titled, it appeared as Chapter Twenty-Six in his *Legends Of The Old Plantation*, part of his *Uncle Remus* stories. Uncle Remus is an old negro slave house servant, and his stories about Brer Fox, Brer Rabbit and Brer Terrapin are told to a white seven-year-old boy of the family he serves. The thirty-four tales, one per chapter, that make up the *Legends Of The Old Plantation*, form a modern folk-lore Beast Epic in which Brer Fox plays an important and very frequent role, but the main role goes to

Brer Rabbit. And in the tale with which we are now concerned, Brer Rabbit plays the part given to Renart in the fourth branch of the *Roman de Renart*, and Renart plays the part given to Ysengrin the wolf.

The two *Roman de Renart* versions we have looked at, as well as the Middle English version, all contain six main sections which may be summarised thus: 1. Renart at the well; 2. Renart alone in the well; 3. Ysengrin at the well; 4. Renart and Ysengrin converse; 5. Renart and Ysengrin change places; and 6. Ysengrin's fate. By comparing the details in each of these six sections in each of these three versions one soon sees how different comic effects were achieved, and how individual each version is. But this is not the place to make that detailed comparison, especially as it has been made elsewhere (Varty 1997: 26–30). Instead, we continue to concentrate on Joel Chandler Harris's tale which may also be divided into six similar sections, thus:

1. Brer Rabbit, Brer Fox, Brer Coon and Brer B'ar are working on the plantation, clearing a new piece of ground. It is very hot, and Brer Rabbit is almost overcome by the heat. Pretending to have got a thorn in his hand, he takes a break from work. Then, hoping nobody has seen him, he wanders off looking for a cool place to rest. It is then that he comes upon the well with one empty, hanging bucket.

2. Brer Rabbit decides that the bucket looks like a good, cool place for a nap. He jumps in, and suddenly finds himself going down. The bucket hits the water, but stays upright. Brer Rabbit sits as still as he can, stiff with fear lest the bucket capsize.

3. Brer Fox, who had seen Brer Rabbit sidle off, has followed him. From a little distance he sees him jump in the bucket and disappear from sight. Puzzled, he wonders if Brer Rabbit is hiding his money down the well, or has discovered the way into a gold mine. He approaches stealthily. Meanwhile Brer Rabbit has taken to saying his prayers over and over again.

4. Brer Fox looks down the well and calls out: 'Heyo, Brer Rabbit! Who you wizzitin' down dar?' On the spur of the moment, Brer Rabbit says he is fishing. 'Who? Me? Oh, I'm des a fishin', Brer Fox, sez Brer Rabbit, sezee'. He goes on to explain that he thought he would surprise his fellow workers with fresh fish for dinner. Brer Fox asks if there are many fish. Brer Rabbit replies that there are scores and scores, and invites Brer Fox to join him to help him haul them in. 'How I gwinter get down, Brer Rabbit?' 'Jump inter de bucket, Brer Fox. Hit'll fetch you down safe en soun'.

5. Brer Fox unhesitatingly jumps into the empty upper bucket and promptly goes down. Brer Rabbit, of course, comes up, and teases Brer Fox as they pass. Immediately on escaping from the well, Brer Rabbit goes back to the field where the others are still at work and he tells them that Brer Fox is down the well muddying up their water. He then returns to the well-top to tease the fox yet more, telling him that a man is coming for him with a gun.

6. We are not told how Brer Fox got out of the well, but get out he did. We may guess that Brer Rabbit helped him out because the very brief conclusion says that about half-an-hour later both companions were back at work in the fields: 'wukkin des like dey never hear'd er no well, ceppin' dat eve'y nour'n den Brer Rabbit'd burst out in er laff, en old Brer Fox, he'd git a spell er de dry grins'.

For the anglophone reader (or listener) the comic qualities of this tale reside largely in the southern United States dialect of the negro slave who is telling it. Comedy also flows from the fact that Brer Rabbit and Brer Fox are fellow slaves on a plantation, a fact that is even funnier if the reader is familiar with these protagonists' Beast Epic roles where they are high-ranking nobles, with the fox depicted as the more powerful and clever one. And instead of taking place at night, in moonlight, the action unfolds during the day, under a hot sun; that the well-bucket is seen, in the first instance, as a place in which to shelter from the heat. It is, on the whole, a gentle comedy. There is no violence, no sex, no hint of justice or injustice, no religious ideas or images, no maliciousness. The fox is just very curious, then silly and obviously greedy in letting himself be duped going to the aid of a fellow slave who claims to be thinking of his fellow slaves' hunger and the pleasure they will have when he turns up with a fish supper. It is, in fact, just about the gentlest version of the very many that belong to Aarne's Type 32.

The source of this negro version of our tale is unknown. Theories are numerous. Chandler Harris thought it came from Africa. 'It would be presumptuous of me to offer an opinion as to the origin of these curious myth-stories; but, if ethnologists should discover that they did not originate with the African, the proof to that effect should be accompanied with a good deal of persuasive eloquence'. Certain touches, in particular the well with its mechanism, may suggest that it had to have passed, at some stage, along European paths. Perhaps via slaves from Anglophone or Francophone West African territories? Or directly from early settlers, most probably French, in the south of the USA? Even along a line which reaches back to the Beast Epic, in a form not too far removed from its Branch IV *Roman de Renart* versions? There are one or two hints and suggestions that this was so. For example, why does Brer Fox begin his conversation with Brer Rabbit down the well by asking him *who* he is visiting when he had thought, according to the text, it might be money or treasure of some kind that made Brer Rabbit seem so eager to go down into the well? In the Branch IV and the Middle English poems, Ysengrin is drawn to the well by the voice he hears coming from it. While the text tells us that it is curiosity which draws Brer Fox to the well, it also tells us that Brer Rabbit was muttering his prayers over and over again, so Brer Fox *may* have heard these mutterings. Even the gentle conclusion of Chandler Harris's version recalls the violent ones of the standard *Roman de Renart* and the Middle English versions where the wolf is in effect fouling the religious's well-water and is severely punished for this. On escaping, Brer Rabbit runs back to the workers on the plantation to tell them that Brer Fox is muddying their drinking water. There is also a return to the well, though here it seems to be by Brer Rabbit alone, though one would have thought his telling the others about Brer Fox in the well would also have brought them along. Even so, his shouting down to Brer Fox that a man was coming with his gun:

> 'Yer come a man wid a great big gun;
> W'en he haul you up, you jump en run'

recalls the threats by the monks (friars in the Middle English) and the violence they perpetrate on the unfortunate, marooned animal when they have hauled him out of the well.

The negro version could have come via one of the many non-Beast-Epic forms, from a fable descended from one like Odo of Cheriton's, told in Latin in England in the first half of the thirteenth century, for in this fable the fox tempts the wolf to get into the empty upper bucket to join him at the bottom because there is an abundance of large fish to be had (Jacobs 1985: 89). And it could have come via non-European fable or folklore. There is, for example, an ancient Arabic fable version which features a fox and a hyena (which plays the role usually given to the wolf). When they pass each other in the well, the hyena asks the fox where he is going, and the fox replies 'I am ascending and you are descending in accordance with the merchants' fashion, one merchant rising high and soaring aloft, while the other goes down and sinks low... The world is likened to a ladder, one ascending it, the other descending it'. (Scharzbaum 1979: 555). This recalls something of Brer Rabbit's words to Brer Fox:

> 'Fer dis is de way de worril (=world) goes
> Some goes up and some goes down'. (Harris 1880).

However, given the many parallels between the tales in *Uncle Remus* and the *Roman de Renart*, some link with the French Beast Epic seems probable. It has been demonstrated that there are sixteen especially close parallels, and five more less-close parallels between these two collections of fox-centred stories (Warren 1890). We leave the last words to Joel Chandler Harris.

> The story of the Rabbit and the Fox, as told by Southern negroes, is artistically dramatic in this: it progresses in an orderly way from a beginning to a well-defined conclusion, and is full of striking episodes that suggest the culmination. It seems to me to be to a certain extent allegorical, albeit such an interpretation may be unreasonable. At least it is a fable thoroughly characteristic of the negro; and it needs no scientific investigation to show why he selects as his hero the weakest and the most harmless of animals, and brings him out victorious in contests with the bear, the wolf, and the fox. It is not virtue that triumphs, but helplessness; it is not malice, but mischievousness (Harris, London: Routledge edition, no date,xviii).

≈ CHAPTER 15 ≈

THE FOX AND THE HARE: AN ODD COUPLE

Elina Suomela-Härmä

In medieval animal epics, some of the protagonists form couples whose conduct is more or less predicatable. The strong ones are liable to attack the weak ones at any time in order to devour them, but they are often outwitted by their would-be victims who, more intelligent, foil their efforts. This state of affairs is subtly modified by likes and dislikes which stem from earlier events or situations in their fictional history: Isengrin cannot forgive Renart for having had an affair with his wife; Chantecler cannot forget that Renart has murdered members of his clan. Family relationships also play their part: Renart is always well served by his first cousin Grimbert the badger. Protagonists who belong to no camp at all are rare. That is why Tibert the cat, whose social links are not fixed once and for all, is so exceptional.

If we leave the domain of literature for that of oral tradition, these things are quite different. The animals' adventures are partly the same, but the distribution of the roles they play is more capricious. Take, for example, the case of one of the most famous episodes, that of the animal who goes fishing with his tail. In this well-known tale a hungry animal follows the apparently well-intended advice of his companion by trying to catch fish in fiercely cold weather with his tail through a hole cut into the ice. But the hole ices over, and the poor fisherman escapes only by sacrificing his tail. In written tradition, the trickster's role is always given to the fox, and that of the tricked, to the wolf. By contrast, in popular tales (in which innumerable variants of this motif occur), even the fox may appear among the tricked. But oral tradition has other surprises in store for us. To a less uniform distribution of roles may be added another fact just as interesting, namely, the presence of couples and groups of animals, or animals and material things, unknown to literary tradition, such as that of *The Needle, the Glove and the Squirrel* (Aarne and Thompson, type AT 90).

Important among these non-literary couples is that of the hare and the fox, the couple on which we will concentrate in this chapter. From one point of view, this couple may be thought of as a variant of the cat-and-fox couple, given that the outcome of their shared adventures is not foreseeable. Even so, as opposed to the hare, the cat has no food value for the fox, and therefore does not risk ending his days between the fox's jaws. The hare makes few appearances in literary texts; nor is his presence in them regularly linked to that of any other animal; nor does he have a specific role (although in a number of episodes his behaviour is characterised by cowardice). But what about his roles in oral tradition? To attempt to answer this question we will concentrate on popular tales of northern European origin, and in particular those from Finland. We make this choice not just because the oral tradition in Finland is especially well documented (thanks to the researches of several generations of professional scholars and educated amateurs) but because the main story-types featuring these two animals are very numerous there. Furthermore, the types AT 72B and 72C are known only in Finnish. Aarne and Thompson (1961) show that, apart from Estonia, no other country offers several variants of the type AT 36. In their catalogue, the tales that concern us are numbered and entitled in this way: AT 2 (*The Tail-Fisher*); AT 36 (*The Fox in Disguise Violates the She-Bear*); AT 47A (*The Fox [Bear, etc] Hangs by his Teeth to the Horse's Tail [Hare's Lip]*); AT 70 (*More Cowardly than the Hare*); AT 72B* (no title); and AT 72C* (*Hare in Trap Complains*). We note straight away that the catalogue titles occasionally mislead because of their approximate nature, for they generally quote only one of the animals which fits the role in question. Thus, in all the Finnish versions of the type AT 36, the protagonists are the hare and the vixen, and not the fox and the bear as the catalogue heading suggests.

The six story-types which constitute our corpus are not homogeneous. Quite the opposite. Two of them (AT 2 and AT 36) are stories about trickery, while all the others have in common a joke ending, or a rejoinder meant to delight their (apparently not very demanding) public. If we try to characterise our little corpus not from the point of view of the action but by the state in which the protagonists find themselves at the end, we discover that four types (AT 2, 36, 47 and 70) often turn out to be aetiologies, that is to say, tales which explain how an animal came to have a particular physical feature; in this case, the hare. He has two features which have caught storytellers' imagination: the cleft in his nose, and his very short tail.

We begin with the two simplest types: AT 72B* and 72C*. The first takes the form of a riddle, and consists of a question (or two) and an answer (or two). The question is always justified, but not so the answer, for it rarely meets the expectations of the questioner.

> The hare and the fox journeyed together. The hare asked the fox, 'Why are you always looking behind you?' The fox replied, 'because I don't have eyes at the end of my tail. But you, why do you cross the road as soon as you hear a noise?' 'Because I can't get underneath it', replied the hare. (Archives, at Raisala, 1935, no.3).

Our translation, we hasten to add, fails to do justice to the comic flavour of the dialect in the original.

This kind of riddle is popular even today, especially among young people, who may be heard to ask 'why is the moon round?' and get the reply 'because it isn't square'. However, because the type 72B* does not result in any change in the status of the protagonist, it is difficult to classify it as a tale. The catalogue of the Archives of the Society for Finnish Literature quotes only eight variants, but their number would be considerably increased if all the ones described as a riddle were added to them. As for the choice of protagonists, one notes that the hare is selected because he is timid, a characteristic generally attributed to him. The fox's presence at his side is less easy to explain. He could be replaced by any animal sporting a fine tail. Apparently the fox is considered to be the hare's most natural 'companion'.

Although listed under the same heading, type 72C* is not a riddle but a conversation or a tale. Its brevity, the few attestations, and the variety of protagonists (wolf, fox, glutton, old man) make analysis difficult. The variant we quote below is the longest of them all. Because there is a change in the hare's status (he loses his freedom), it is to be considered as a tale.

> A fisherman had put his nets out to dry. The hare got caught in them and could not escape. He complained: 'It's unbelievable, I just can't get away. I'm losing my whole day here'. By chance, a fox passed that way. 'You'll not just pass a day here, but the rest of your days', he said. (Archives, at Narvusi,1891, no. 5).

The hare is unable to perceive the reality of his situation, and it is left to the fox to reveal the awful truth to him. The fox's cynicism is obvious: instead of rushing to the victim's aid, he lets it be known that he is in no way concerned about the hare's distress. The story's point rests on the opposition 'a whole day' / 'the rest of your days', pointed out by the fox. In other words, the tale depends on a play on words, and this is its only justification. The choice of protagonists (here, hare and fox; elsewhere fox and wolf) seems to be the result of pure chance.

The tale type 70 illustrates the saying 'one always needs somebody smaller than ones self'. In its simplest form, it features only one character, the hare, who complains about not being feared by anybody. He concludes that he is the most wretched of all creatures. To put an end to this sad situation, he considers exiling himself, even killing himself. What prevents him from doing so is a last-minute meeting with an animal (fish, frog, sheep) which is frightened at the sight of him. This motif, known from Classical Antiquity, appears in two different forms in Aesop, Phaedrus and their medieval counterparts (Chambry 1985: 83; also *Phaedri Fabulae Aesopiae*. 1856: 66; and Hervieux 1893–99, index). These present either a monologue or a general assembly at which all the representatives of the species decide to commit collective suicide. On the other hand, forty-five of the 188 Finnish variants feature a dialogue between the hare and the fox (whose role is played on five further occasions by the wolf). The relationship between the two animals is not antagonistic. Neither threatens the other by his presence, nor does the bringing together of these two automatically give rise to violence. However, the fox ridicules the hare's insignificance. Sometimes he goes even further and boasts that, because of his bushy tail, he is sometimes mistaken for a wolf. Sometimes his words make the hare angry, thereby showing that the hare is less insignificant than he thinks he is. To upset the fox's low opinion of him, he jumps into the middle of a flock of sheep and causes them to flee in all directions. The fox follows suit, but his attempt to demonstrate his superiority fails. In some variants, the fox does not only criticise the hare; he also urges him to do something. In this case, they make a bet (which the hare never fails to win) involving either the hare alone, or both animals:

> The fox and the hare met and began to discuss which of them was best able to make other animals afraid. Each wanted to show that he was the better at doing this. The hare jumped into the middle of a flock of sheep which fled, afraid. When, a little later, the fox came upon these sheep, they took him for a dog, and were not at all put out by him. The hare then laughed so much that ever since he has had a cleft nose (Archives at Mouhijävi, 1936, no. 17).

The majority of the tales of the type AT 70 are aetiologies. In no way does this depend on the number of protagonists. The animals' reaction causes the hare to laugh wildly even when he is alone, but obviously the presence of a witness increases his laughter. The result of this joyful explosion is usually revealed at the end of the story, but some versions tell the events in reverse order and begin, for example, like this:

> The hare was not created with a cleft nose. This happened much later. This is how it came about...(Archives at Rautalampi, 1885, n. 51).

The fox, whom we usually see playing the role of trickster, is even capable of trying to profit from the hare's psychological distress. In the following version, of which we quote only the beginning, his natural wickedness (not particularly emphasised in popular tradition) causes him to offer perfidious advice to the hare:

> The fox tells the hare to go and drown himself in the lake since he is so timid that nobody fears him. He planned to devour him as soon as he was dead. The hare went to the lake shore: 'I'm going to drown myself, for I've had enough of always being afraid.' (Krohn 1886: 89).

The first attestations of the following tale-type, AT 47A, little known in the northern European oral tradition, are (according to Shojaei Kawan 1987, V, col. 511–22) to be found in the *Roman de Renart*, Branch IX, lines 1619–1903, as well as in Steinhöwel's Fables (Österley 1873: 203–05). In these texts, the fox (or wolf) attaches himself to a horse's (or ass's) tail in the hope of capturing the animal. It goes without saying that the stratagem proves to be ill-conceived, and that the story ends badly for the aggressor. The similarities between written and oral traditions, suggested very cautiously by Shojaei Kawan, only half persuade, and do not encourage us to make a detailed comparison of the two tale-types. In fact, the learned tradition (which features only two protagonists) does not involve the fox-and-hare couple. By contrast, this often appears in popular tales where the number of protagonists may be as many as three. In outline, the basic tale goes like this: for one reason or another (hunger, the illusion that it will teach him to run more quickly, to kill bears, etc.) an animal bites the tail of a horse as it lies in a meadow. The horse jumps up and begins to gallop, but the aggressor is unable to free himself. By sheer chance, a third animal witnesses the victim's humiliation, and hurls ironic remarks after him.

Despite its apparent simplicity, this tale-type is the most complex of all those which feature the hare and the fox. This is not due just to the number of the protagonists, but also to the distribution of the roles, which varies from one version to another. Furthermore, this tale sometimes takes the form of a trickster tale in the fullest sense of the words: an ill-intentioned animal persuades his companion to bite the tail of a horse, arguing that he will benefit by this action. In the Finnish tradition, the horse is not apparently dead, as one reads in Aarne and Thompson, and is in fact the case in German versions. Sometimes, however, the protagonist acts alone and becomes the victim of his own miscalculation. The number of protagonists in the initial scene (the animal led into taking the wrong step by a companion, or by himself) could be the primary criterion for classifying the 104 Finnish variants, of which forty lack the trickster agent. However, what is important in this tale-type is not so much the action in itself as the final scene with the exchange between the victim and the one who taunts him. It is not so much a dialogue as a mini-conversation composed of a question and an answer in verse, preferably in kalevalian metre, in which the fox and the hare are given proper names. Among the seventeen names given to the fox we mention Mikko, Mikkeli, Miska, Antti, Antero and Antreas. For the hare one may chose between Jussi, Jussa, Jusu, Juho, Juhana and Johannes. Although there are some variations in the distribution of the roles, the main purpose of this tale seems to be to show that even the fox may be tricked. In fact, he plays the role of the duped sixty-one times while the hare is duped on only seven occasions. On the other hand, the one who asks the final question is almost always (seventy-four times) the hare. How could it be otherwise when the story is an aetiology which explains the hare's cleft lip (the fox's fate causes the hare to laugh so much that...). As one sees, this tale-type is a mixture of heterogeonous elements which make it difficult to classify. To conclude this overview, we offer a variant chosen because of its brevity, although it does not belong entirely to the category we have just described, and is not entirely logical. (Popular tales have their own special 'logic'; their endings do not necessarily follow from their beginnings; their action readily digresses; and the behaviour of their protagonists may be determined by contradictory motives, etc.):

> Once upon a time a fox and a hare were in conversation. The fox asked the hare 'Do you know how the bear manages to kill so many horses?' The hare replies: 'When you see a horse lying down, wind a hair in his tail around your teeth. Pull a little, and the horse will get up. Then pull a second time and the horse will fall down.' However, the fox was disappointed by his experience. The horse, in fact, began to run, and pulled the fox after him. Sitting by the road-side, the hare asked: 'Where are you being taken to, Mikko? The fox replied: 'God only knows, my dear Jussi, where Mikko is being taken. My neck will break before my teeth give way.' Then the hare laughed till his lip was cloven, and it has always remained like that (Archives at Loimaa, 1912, no. 25).

The last two tale-types are known to both the written and oral traditions, although their protagonists are not the same. In the Finnish tradition, the type AT 36, *The Fox in Disguise Violates the She-Bear*, features the vixen (tricked) and the hare (trickster). One recalls that, in the medieval animal epic, the victim's role is given to the she-wolf who had to submit to Renart (e.g., *Ysengrimus*, V, ll.705–818; *Roman de Renart*, Br. II, ll.1238–1296). In the 'tail-fishing' episode (AT 2), the fox plays his nasty trick on the bear or the wolf. In northern Europe, where the tale is widespread, it is often aetiological. If the bear no longer has a tail, it is because he lost it trying to pull it out of the frozen-over fishing-hole in the ice. (There are 183 examples of this tale-type; in ninety-two, the bear is the victim; the wolf in sixty-nine). As the hare's physical appearance lends itself to similar considerations, one understands why he appears sporadically (nine times altogether) in the role of the victim. As this situation remains unknown in written tradition, here is a relatively lengthy example of a popular, oral variant:

The fox [in discussion with the hare]... was wondering how he might be able to arrange for a meal of hare the next morning. He therefore said to the hare: '... I'll teach you a way of getting a right royal prize, but this involves you having to fast till daybreak'. 'It doesn't matter if I have to be patient for a bit provided you give me good advice', replied the hare. 'But what is this advice?' 'Go to the edge of the hole made in the ice covering that pond which you see over there; plunge your tail into the water, and then stay there till day-break. During the night a fish will attach itself to every hair in your tail.' The hare followed this advice. The cold increased during the night and the water began to ice over. The hare felt his tail held firmly in the ice and was greatly pleased because he thought it was the result of more and yet more fish attaching themselves to his tail. He therefore avoided any kind of movement in order to guarantee a more copious meal. In the morning, after having had a good night's rest, the fox was tormented by hunger. When the sun rose, he made for the spot where he was to make a meal of the hare (Archives at Rautalampi, 1883).

A striking aspect of this tale is the fact that the fox plans from the very beginning to eat his victim, not just to trick him. In the medieval animal epics, he is usually well content to get his victim beaten up by peasants, and hopes for nothing more. In popular tales, the fox, less refined, is not given sadistic traits of this kind. By eating his victim, he simply obeys his natural instinct of self-preservation. Obviously, an ending of this kind is not possible when the animal caught in the ice is a wolf or a bear. To substitute for them an edible creature (from the fox's viewpoint) has important repercussions on the tale's structure which, from a simple trickster tale, becomes a tale about a quest for food both for the fisherman and for the one who offers him perfidious advice.

The rape of the she-wolf constitutes a narrative sequence of primary importance because it explains why the wolf harbours an implacable hatred for the fox. It is scarcely an exaggeration to say that it is the founding episode of a myth. One is therefore all the more surprised to note that, firstly, in the popular northern European tradition, the protagonists are not necessarily the fox and the she-wolf (in Finland, this couple is replaced by the hare and the vixen); secondly (still in Finland), the fox has changed both sex and role: from male aggressor he becomes the aggressed-against female. In passing, we point out that Aarne and Thompson found, in Europe, one Lithuanian, one Latvian and one Russian example of the the fox as the aggressor with the she-wolf as the victim. The two French tales they mention (they are really anecdotes) depart too far from the original narrative structure to be included under this heading. They are quoted in full in Tenèze (1976: 43–45). According to Pille Kippar, in the Estonian occurrences of this story-type, the fox plays the trickster's role, while that of the tricked is played either by the she-wolf, or the hare or the vixen.(Kippar 1986: 56). The distribution of the roles in the one Russian example is the same as in Finland (Gerber 1891: 53).

Before comparing the learned, literary tradition with the oral, popular tradition, let us summarise the sequence of events as they occur in the *Roman de Renart*. The wolf justly suspects his wife of having committed adultery. In fact, after having had a sexual encounter with her, Renart dishonours the wolf-cubs (Branch II, 1027–1210). One day, Ysengrin is out in the forest with Hersent when they come across Renart and give pursuit. The she-wolf outstrips her husband, but gets stuck in the entrance to Renart's den from which he emerges by another 'door'. He then rapes her as her husband comes upon the scene (II, 1216–1358).

Of the sixteen Finnish oral versions of this tale, a few begin with the hare's visit to the foxes' den. In our opinion, this is a recollection of the written tradition because the episode is unmotivated. The parents are not at home, but the intruder informs the fox-cubs of his intentions where their mother is concerned. Once she learns what he has said, the vixen gives chase after the hare as soon as she comes upon him. The tales which lack this preparatory scene begin either with a pursuit scene (while the vixen pursues the hare in order to eat him, she gets trapped between two trees) or with the observation that one day the vixen got caught between two trees and could not get free. Whatever the reason for the vixen's immobility, the hare takes advantage of it to rape her. Up to this point the sequence of events has nothing really different about it. It is only in what follows that it takes a direction completely unknown in written tradition. After committing his misdeed, and anxious never to be recognised by the vixen, he dyes himself black. To do this he does not need to have recourse to any kind of magic, as does Renart when he wants to change colour (as in Branch Ib, 2227 and following; Branch V, 95 and following; and Branch XIII, 1011 and following). He rolls in a half-burnt tree stump or in a coal heap. When he later meets the freed vixen, she takes him (because of his black clothing) for a pastor or a professor, and asks him if he had seen a hare go by. The 'prelate' says yes, and gives her to understand that he knows what had happened to her. This upsets the vixen: to her first humiliation is added this second one, that her fate has become common knowledge. In a few versions of this tale-type, she feels so embarrassed that she gives up all ideas of getting her revenge, and goes home. The hare, however, laughs so much that his lip is cloven. One sees that, from the narrative viewpoint, the rape is only a preamble: the story's main point lies elsewhere, in the exchanges between the two protagonists. Here are three passages to illustrate this:

> 1. The vixen asked the hare who he was. 'I am a clergyman' replied the hare. 'Well, have you seen any hares?' 'Yes, I've met one who said he was going to find refuge in Ingermanland because he had just raped a vixen.' 'Oh God!' said the vixen. 'Was he not ashamed to say things like that to a clergyman?' (Archives at Heinolan mlk, 1887, no. 6).
>
> 2. The vixen took the hare for a clergyman and asked him: 'Has the Vicar seen a hare?' 'You mean the one who has just raped a vixen?' The vixen was so ashamed that the vicar had seen her misfortune that she said nothing more about it to anybody. (Archives at Jorovinen, 1886, n. 8).
>
> 3. The vixen takes the hare sitting on a tree stump for a vicar, greets him and asks: 'Vicar, have you seen the hare?' The latter, full of civil-servant-like condescension, asks arrogantly: 'Do you mean the hare who made love with you in the hedgerow?' The vixen could not help but burst into tears. 'Is it possible that that wretched hare has already told you everything?' (Archives at Nilsiä, 1885, no. 10).

As already stated, the distribution of the roles is always the same; it is always the vixen who is raped by the hare. How to explain this fundamental difference between the written and the oral traditions? Is it that the popular storytellers, who did not have to insert this story into a much vaster whole, substituted the hare and the vixen for the original 'literary' couple because these two are so often found together in popular tales, while the she-wolf and fox couple is unknown in that tradition? There is no convincing answer to this question.

From this survey it emerges that, at least in northern Europe, the hare is a partner whom the fox must take seriously. One can never guess how a story (and there are many) which begins 'Once upon a time, the hare and the fox...' will end.

Hans-Jorg Uther's observation (*Enzyklopädie*, V, col. 457) that the companions or chief adversaries of the fox are the bear, the wolf and, in Asia and South America, the tiger, has to be extended to include the hare. As soon as he is involved with him, the fox ceases to be the clever trickster of written tradition, but becomes an animal who may well fall victim to misadventure. The hare of the popular-story tradition is not without real character. In spite of his cowardly nature, he does not avoid conflict, nor does he automatically fall prey to stronger creatures. He is capable of initiating risky actions and of winning the day. His repartee is quick, and he has a great sense of humour. No other animal laughs as much as he does. The fox's misadventures always put him in a good humour. Since the fox is more robust and feared than he is, how could it be otherwise? But his laughter does not express only sadistic mirth; it also expresses pure joy.

A last question. From when does the 'friendship' of these two companions date? For two reasons it is probably relatively recent. Firstly, it is unknown in the written tradition. Secondly (if we set aside the first three tales in Branch II, the ones about Chantecler, the tit-mouse and Tibert), it is from the nineteenth century onwards that the fox begins to be deprived of his age-old characteristics, and to appear in the role of the tricked rather than that of the trickster (Uther 1987, *Enzyklopädie*, V, col. 464). But who would have thought that the hare would play an important role in outfoxing the fox?

THE CONTRIBUTORS

Elaine C Block. Professor Emerita (Education, New York City University, Hunter College), she researches on historiated wood sculptures in choir-stalls, especially on misericords. She has published numerous articles on this pictorial matter, and has completed a book entitled *Miséricordes médiévales: images profanes des lieux sacrés* (Paris: Léopard d'Or). She founded and is President of Misericordia International, founder and editor of its biannual review, *The Profane Arts of the Middle Ages*, and an active member of the Franco-Belgian Groupe International de Recherches sur les Stalles.

Jean Dufournet. Member of the Belgian Royal Academy, now Emeritus, was Professor of Medieval French Literature, Language and Civilisation in the University of Paris, at the Sorbonne Nouvelle. A prolific author of learned articles, editions, translations and books, he is best known to Reynardians for his 1985 two-volumed edition and translation of the *Roman de Renart* (with A. Méline); for his two 1989 translations and studies, the one *Les Vêpres de Tibert*, the other *Renart et le vilain Liétard*; for his two collections of essays, the 1993 *Avatars du 'Roman de Renart'* and the 1990 *Le Goupil et le Paysan*; and for his 1986 and 1991 studies and edition of Maurice Genevoix's *Roman de Renart*.

Jan Goossens. Formerly Professor of Dutch and Low German Philology at the University of Münster, and of Historical Dutch Linguistics in the Katholieke Universiteit, Leuven, he is now Emeritus at Leuven. The author of very many learned articles, editions and books which treat historical, geographic and social linguistics as well as medieval literature, he is especially well known to Reynardians for his editions of *Reynaerts Historie – Reynke de Vos* (1983); *Die Reynaert – Ikonographie* (1983); *De Gecastreerde Neus* (1988); and *Reynke, Reynaert und das europäische Tierepos* (1998).

Jill Mann. A Fellow of the British Academy and formerly Professor of English at the University of Cambridge (U.K.), Dr Mann is now Endowed Professor at the University of Notre Dame. She works on Middle English and medieval Latin literature, and is the author of a dual-text edition of the Latin beast epic *Ysengrimus*. She is currently working on a book on beast literature in medieval England, and preparing a translation of the *Speculum Stultorum*.

Jean-Marc Pastré. Professor of German at the University of Rouen and Deputy Mayor of Clamart (near Paris), he has published numerous articles on *Reinhart Fuchs*, the *Roman de Renart*, the Bestiary and, with Danielle Buschinger, a study and translation into French: *Heinrich der Glichesare: Reinhart Fuchs* (1984).

Wilfried Schouwink. Teaches Latin, German and Catholic Religion at a Gymnasium near Heidelberg. He also does some part-time teaching in Latin of neo-Latin literature in the University of Heidelberg. His main field of research and chief publications are on the boar in medieval art and literature, in particular *Der wilde Eber in Gottes Weinberg* (1985). He is preparing a bilingual edition of Hartmann Schopper's Latin *Reinike*.

Roger Stephenson. Holds the William Jacks Chair of German Language and Literature at the University of Glasgow. His publications include many articles on various aspects of modern German thought and literature, in particular Weimar Classicism, and notably *Goethe's Wisdom Literature* (1983), and *Goethe's Conception of Knowledge and Science* (1995).

Jean Subrenat. Has a Chair of French at the University of Provence (Aix-en-Provence). His chief interests, reflected in many articles and books mainly on the medieval French epic and the *Roman de Renart*, are on the relationship between the text and its public, and on the literary treatment of religious and legal problems. He is the author of a two-volumed edition and translation into modern French of the *Roman de Renart* (1985), and of an *Index des thèmes et des personnages du 'Roman de Renart'* (1987), both with M. de Combarieu. He is the Director of the Centre d'Études et de Recherches Médiévales d'Aix, and the Editor of the series *Senefiance*.

Elina Suomela-Härmä. Has the Chair of Italian Philology at the University of Helsinki, Finland. She has published many articles on the *Roman de Renart* and on later medieval French continuations of the early epic, and is the author of two books in this field: *Les Structure narratives du 'Roman de Renart'* (1981), and *Le Livre de Regnart* (1998).

Rik van Daele. Director of Cultural Affairs in the city of Lokeren, Belgium; Curator of Lokeren's museum; Director of that city's recently-opened Centre for Reynardian Documentation and Reynardian Museum, visiting teacher of Dutch literature at the Hagueschool, Antwerp, Dr van Daele wrote his thesis for the University of Leuven on spaces and names in the Dutch epic, *Van den Vos Reynaerde* (1992). He is one of the founders and is the chief editor of the Reynardian quarterly review *Tiecelijn*, and one of the authors of *Het Land van Reynaert*, a guide to that part of northern Belgium where the legendary fox-hero performed so many of his exploits.

Kenneth Varty. Formerly the Stevenson Professor of French at the University of Glasgow, he is now Emeritus and Honorary Professorial Research Fellow of that University. He founded and was first President of the International Reynard Society. With Brian Levy and Paul Wackers, he also founded that Society's yearbook, *Reinardus*, and is chairman of its editorial board. He has specialised in studies of the text and in the iconography of the *Roman de Renart*, and in the iconography of medieval English fox-centred stories, the latter being the topic of his most recent book, *Reynard, Renart, Reinaert* (Amsterdam University Press, 1999).

Paul Wackers. Recently appointed Professor of Dutch Literature to 1550 at the University of Utrecht, has long been a lecturer in medieval Dutch literature at the Katholieke Universiteit, Nijmegen. His main research fields are the influence of the Latin tradition on vernacular literature and the Middle Dutch Reynaert tradition and its European dimension. Among his many Reynardian publications is his book on *Reynaerts Historie* (*De waarheid als leugen: een interpretatie van Reynaerts historie*, 1986). Since 1987, along with Brian Levy, he edits *Reinardus*, the Yearbook of the International Reynard Society.

BIBLIOGRAPHY

Aarne, A. and S. Thompson. 1961. *The Types of the Folktale*, Helsinki: FF Communications 184.
Altena, E. van. 1979. *Reinaert de Vos, de middeleeuwse satire door Ernst van Altena hertaald en met tekeningen van Bert Bouman geïllustreerd*, Amsterdam: Uitgeverij Ploegsma
Anderson, R., and D. Bradby. 1986. *Renard the Fox* (a retelling by Rachel Anderson and David Bradby, illustrated by Bob Dewar), Oxford: Oxford University Press.
Archives of the Society for Finnish Literature, Helsinki. Flina Suomela-Härmä's study contains several references to oral tales recorded in these Archives by the name of the place where the tale was recorded, its date and number.
Bakhtin, Mikhail. 1968. *Rabelais and His World*, translated from the Russian by Hélène Iswolsky, Cambridge, USA: Massachusetts Institute of Technology Press.
Barnouw, A.J. and E. Colledge. 1967. See Colledge.
Baumann, R. 1994. *Landsknechte. Ihre Geschichte und Kultur vom späten Mittelalter bis zum Dreissigjährigen Krieg*, Munich.
Bennett, J.A.W. and G.V. Smithers (eds). 1966. *Early Middle English Verse and Prose*, Oxford: Clarendon Press.
Berteloot, A. 1988. 'Zur Datierung von *Reynaerts historie*', in *Sprache in Vergangenheit und Gegenwart*, ed. W. Brandt, Marburg: Hitzeroth, 26–31.
———. 1993. 'Een acrostichon in *Reynaerts historie*', in *Reynaert bloemleest Tiecelijn*, VZW Tiecelijn-Reynaert, Sint-Niklaas, 70–3.
Besamusca, B., 1991. 'De Vlaamse opdrachtgevers van Middelnederlandse literatuur: een literair-historisch probleem', *De Nieuwe Taalgids* 84, 154–62.
———. 1996. 'Rewriting the *Roman de Renart*: The Middle Dutch Beast Epic *Van den vos Reynaerde*', in *The Medieval Opus: Imitation,*

Rewriting and Transmission in the French Tradition, ed. D. Kelly, Amsterdam: Rodopi, 387–401.

Bieling, A. (ed.). 1886. *Gottscheds Reineke Fuchs*, Halle: Max Niemeyer.

Blake, N. (ed.). 1973. *Caxton: The History of Reynard the Fox*, London, New York and Toronto: Oxford University Press.

Bouwman, A. 1990. 'On the Place of *Van den vos Reynaerde* in the Old French *Roman de Renart* Tradition', *Reinardus* 3, 15–24.

———. 1991a. '"Na den walschen boucken". Neerlandistiek en romanistiek', in *Misselike tonghe. De Middelnederlandse letterkunde in interdisciplinair verband*, ed. F.P. van Oostrom, Amsterdam: Prometheus, 45–56.

———. 1991b. *Reinaert en Renart. Het dierenepos Van den vos Reynaerde vergeleken met de Oudfranse Roman de Renart*, 2 vols, Amsterdam: Prometheus.

Brandes, H. 1891. *Die jüngere Glosse zum Reinke de Vos*, Halle: Saale.

Brown, R. 1969. *Reynard the Fox Retold by Roy Brown, Illustrated by John Vernon Lord*, London, New York and Toronto: Abelard-Shuman Ltd.

Brucker, C. (ed.). 1991. *Marie de France: Les Fables*, Leuven.

Buschinger, D. and J.-M. Pastré (trans.). 1984. *Heinrich der Glichezare: Reinhart Fuchs* (translation into French), Vienna: Karl M. Halosar, Wiener Arbeiten der germanischen Altertumskunde und Philologie, 25.

Chabaille, P. 1835. *Le Roman de Renart; supplément, variantes et corrections*, Paris: Silvestre.

Chambry, E. (ed. & trans.).1985. *Esope: Fables. Texte établi et traduit par E.C.*, Paris.

Chaucer. See Sisam.

Colledge, E. (ed.). 1967. *Reynard the Fox and Other Medieval Netherlands Secular Literature*, Leyden: Sijthoff & London: Heinemann. See pp. 45–164 for the translation into English of *Van den Vos Reynaerde*.

Combarieu du Grès, M. de. 1991. '*Faire la morte vieille*: la ruse de la mort feinte dans le *Roman de Renart*', in *Bulletin de Liaison de l'Equipe de Recherche sur la Littérature de l'Imagination du Moyen Age* 7, 153–69.

Combarieu du Grès, M. de, and J. Subrenat, (eds & trans.). 1981. *Le Roman de Renart*, 2 vols, Paris: Union Générale des Éditions, repr. 1985.

———. 1987. *Le Roman de Renart. Index des thèmes et des personnages*, Aix-en-Provence: CUERMA, Senefiance 22.

Crafty Courtier, The, See Schopper, 1706.

Decorte, B. 1985. *Reinaard de vos. Tekeningen Dolf De Rudder. Hedendaagse berijming Bert Decorte*, Lokeren: PVBA M. Oelbrandt-Rinla.

Deroy, J. 1979. 'Le Discours du chameau, légat pontifical (branche Va)' in *Third International Beast Epic, Fable and Fabliau Colloquium: Proceedings*, eds. Jan Goossens and T. Sodmann, Niederdeutsche Studien 30, 102–110.

Dicke, G. and K. Grubmüller. 1987. *Die Fabeln des Mittelalters und der frühen Neuzeit: ein Katalog der deutschen Versionen und ihrer lateinischen Entsprechungen*, Munich: Wilhelm Fink.

Dufournet, J. and A. Méline (eds & trans.). 1985. *Le Roman de Renart*, 2 vols, Paris: Flammarion.

Düwel, K. (ed.). 1984. *Der Reinhart Fuchs des Elsässers Heinrich*, Tübingen: Max Niemeyer Verlag.

Flinn, J. 1963. *Le Roman de Renart dans la littérature française et dans les littératures étrangères au Moyen Age*, Toronto: University Press.

Foulet, L. 1914. *Le Roman de Renart*, Paris: Champion, repr. 1968.

Gerber, A. 1891. Great Russian Animal Tales, in *Publications of the Modern Languages Association of America*, 6, 2.

Genevoix, M. 1991. *Le Roman de Renard*, ed. J. Dufournet, Paris: Plon, Presses Pocket, Lire et Voir les Classiques, 6053.

Gielen, W. 1998. Distels... Een vossenstreek na Van Genechten [Thistles. A fox trick after Van Genechten], *Tiecelijn* 11, no. 1, 9–22.

Goethe. See *Goethes Werke*, and editions of *Reineke Fuchs* by Hofmann, Rahn, Wiethälter, and Wild.

Goethes Werke: Hamburger Ausgabe, 14 vols. Hamburg: Christian Wegner Verlag. Band 1 (vol. 1), 1949, ed. by Erich Trunz; later volumes ed. by C.H. Beck.

Goldsmid, E. (ed.). 1884. *The History of Reynard the Fox. Translated and Printed by William Caxton*, Edinburgh: Bibliotheca Curiosa, X.

Goossens, J. 1980. 'Reynaerts und Reynkes Begegnung mit dem Affen Marten', *Niederdeutsches Wort* 20: 73–84.

———. 1983a. *Die Reynaert-Ikonographie*, Darmstadt: Wissenschaftliche Buchgesellschaft.

———. 1983b. *Reynaerts historie. Reynke de Vos. Gegenüberstellung einer Auswahl aus den niederländischen Fassungen und des niederdeutschen Textes von 1498*, Darmstadt: Wissenschaftliche Buchgesellschaft.

———. 1988. *De gecastreerde neus. Taboes en hun verwerking in de geschiedenis van de Reinaert*, Leuven and Amersfoort: Acco.

Göttert, K.H. (ed. & trans.). 1976. *Reinhart Fuchs*, Stuttgart: Reclam 9818 (3).

Goudriaen, K. 1993. *Een drukker zoekt publiek. Gheraert Leeu te Gouda 1477–1484*, Delft: Eburon.

Harris, J.C. (1880). *Uncle Remus and Brer Rabbit*, London: Routledge, no date.

Hastings, S. 1990. *Reynard the Fox, Retold by Selina Hastings, Illustrated by Graham Percy*, London: Walker Books.

Heer, F. 1952. *Die Tragödie des Heiligen Römischen Reichs*, Vienna and Zurich.

Hellinga, W.Gs. (ed.). 1952. *Van den vos Reynaerde. I, Teksten. Diplomatisch uitgegeven naar de bronnen vóór het jaar 1500*, Zwolle: Tjeenk Willink.

Hermes, H. (ed. & trans.). 1977. *The 'Disciplina Clericalis' of Petrus Alfonsi, translated and edited by Eberhard Hermes*, Berkeley and Los Angeles: University of California.

Hervieux, L. 1893-99. *Les Fabulistes latins du siècle d'Auguste jusqu'à la fin du Moyen Age*, vols I-IV, Paris: Firmin Didot.

Hofmann, J. (ed.). 1921. *Reineke Fuchs von Johann Wolfgang von Goethe. Mit Illustrationen nach den 57 Radierungen von Allart van Everdingen. Eingeleitet und herausgegeben von J.H.*, Leipzig.

Hugaerts, F. 1984. *Heel dit valse land, of hoe de Franse hofdichter Eustache Deschamps Vlaanderen zag in de laatste jaren van de veertiende eeuw* [All this false country. Or how the French court poet Eustache Deschamps looked on Flanders in the last years of the fourteenth century], Ghent: Zele.

Hutchinson, P. 1998. See Stopp.

Huysmans, C. 1937. *Quatre Types: le Renard et Ulenspiegel, le démon et le diable*, Antwerp: Ça ira.

Jacobs, J.C. (trans. & ed.). 1985. *The Fables of Odo of Cheriton*, Syracuse: Syracuse University Press.

Janssens, J.D. 1992. 'De "Vlaamse" achtergronden van *Lancelot-compilatie*. Wat onzekerheden op een rijtje: Vlaams, Brabants of Hollands?', in *De onghevallige Lanceloet. Studies over de Lancelot-compilatie*, eds. B. Besamusca and F. Brandsma, Hilversum: Verloren, 21–43.

———. 1994. 'The *Roman van Walewein*, an episodic Arthurian romance', in *Medieval Dutch Literature in its European Context*, ed. E. Kooper, Cambridge: University Press, 113–28.

Jones, M. and C. Tracey. 1994. 'A Medieval Choirstall Desk-End at Haddon Hall: the Fox-Bishop and the Geese-Hangmen', *Journal of the British Archaeological Association*, 144, 107–15 and plates XII–XV.

Kawan. See Shojaei.

Kippar, P. 1986. *Etnische Tiermärchen. Typen- und variantenverzeichnis*, Helsinki.

Klitzing, H. 1989. *Reineke Fuchs, ein europäisches Epos. Eine Ausstellung des Goethe-Museums Düsseldorf. Katalog.* ed. by Jörn Göres.

Knapp, F.P. 1982. 'Über einige Formen der Komik im hochmittelalterlichen Tierepos', in *Wolfram-Studien VII*, ed. W. Schröder, Berlin: Schmidt, 32–54.

Kooyman, R. 1968. *Reinaart de Vos. Getekend en opnieuw verteld door Rie Kooyman*. Groningen O.J.

Krohn, K. 1886. *Suomalaisia kansansatuja 1*, Helsinki.

Lodge, R.A. 1983. 'De Tristan que la chievre fist'', *Romania* 104, 524–33.

Lodge, R.A. and K. Varty, (eds). 1989. *The Earliest Branches of the Roman de Renart*, New Alyth (Perthshire): Lochee Publications Ltd.

Louwe, C. van. 'Uilenspiegel tussen collaboratie en verzet' [Owlglass between collaboration and resistance], *Ulieden Spiegel*, 5–10.

Lukács, G. 1967. *Faust und Faustus*, Hamburg: Rowohlt.

Lulofs, F. (ed.). 1983. *Van den vos Reynaerde*, Groningen: Wolters Noordhoff.

Mähl, J. (ed.). 1986. *Reineke Voss von Joachim Mähl, Bilder von A. Paul Weber, Nachdruck der Ausgabe von 1878*, Kornwestheim: EBG Verlags.

Mann, Jill. 1977. ' "Luditor Illusor": the Cartoon World of the *Ysengrimus*', *Neophilologus* 61, 495–509.
———. (ed. & trans.,). 1987. *Ysengrimus. Text with Translation, Commentary and Introduction*, Leiden: Brill.
Marie de France. See Brucker.
Martin, E. (ed.). 1882–85–87. *Le Roman de Renart*, 3 vols, Strasbourg: Trübner. (Reprint, Berlin: De Gruyter, 1973).
Menke, H. (ed.) 1981. *Von Reinicken Fuchs*, (reprint of the 1544 Frankfurt edition), Heidelberg: privately printed.
———. 1992. *Bibliotheca Reinardiana. Teil I: Die europäischen Reineke-Fuchs-Drucke bis zum Jahre 1800*, Stuttgart: Dr. Ernst Hauswedell & Co. Verlag.
Mont, P. de. 1925. *Reinaert de vos. Volksspel. Dramatische bewerking van het oude dierenverhaal aan de hand van de 2de tekstuitgave door J.F. Willems*.
Morley, H. (ed.). 1889. *The History of Reynard the Fox*, in *Early Prose Romances*, pp. 41–166, London: The Carisbrooke Library, IV.
Muret-Dufourques, ed. *Le Roman de Tristan*, Paris: Champion.
Murray, A. 1978. *Reason and Society in the Middle Ages*, Oxford: Clarendon Press.
Odo of Cheriton. See Jacobs.
Österley, H. (ed.). 1873. *Steinhöwels Äsop*, Tübingen.
Owen, D.D.R. (trans.). 1994. *The Romance of Reynard the Fox*, Oxford: Oxford University Press.
Pastré, J.-M. 1993a. 'La Mort du roi Vrevel: le châtiment d'un crime et son illustration dans le *Reinhart Fuchs*', *Reinardus* 6, 95–104.
———. 1993b. 'Une image de la fin des temps: la mort du roi Vrevel dans le *Reinhart Fuchs*' in *Fin des temps et temps de la fin dans l'univers médiéval*, 343–55, Sénéfiance 33, Aix-en-Provence.
———. 1994a. 'A propos du *Reinhart Fuchs*: la mort du roi Vrevel' in *Tierepik im Mittelalter*, 71–82, Wodan 44, Greifswald.
———. 1994b. 'Héraldique, histoire et littérature: le léopard au cimier du *Reinhart Fuchs*', in *Tierepik im Mittelalter*, 83–93, Wodan 44, Greifswald.
Peeters, L. 1973–74. *Historiciteit en chronologie in 'Van den vos Reynaerde'*, *Spektator* 3, 157–79 and 347–69.
Phaedri Fabulae Aesopiae. (edition). 1856, Leipzig.
Plantijn, Christoffel. 1556. *Reynaert de vos. Een seer ghenouchlicke ende vermakelicke historie: in Franchoyse ende neder Duytsch. Reynier le renard. Histoire tresioyeuse & recreatiue, en François & bas Alleman*, Antwerp: Christoffel Plantijn. Facsimile edition, Brussels: Editions Libro-Sciences, 1989.
Pleij, H. 1987. 'Dutch Literature and the Printing Press: the First Fifty Years', *Gutenberg-Jahrbuch* 62, 47–58.
Rahn, R. and A. Schleich. 1846–47. *Reineke Fuchs von Wolfgang von Goethe. Zeichnungen von Wilhelm von Kaulbach, gestochen von R. Rahn und A. Schleich*, Stuttgart.

Ramberg, J.H. 1826. *Reineke Fuchs. In 30 Blättern gezeichnet und radirt von J.H. Ramberg. Herausgegeben und zu haben bei J.H. Ramberg in Hannover.*
Randall, L. 1966. *Images in the Margins of Gothic Manuscripts*, Berkeley and Los Angeles: University of California Press.
Regalado, N.F. 1976. 'Tristan and Renart, Two Tricksters', *L'Esprit Créateur*, 16, 30–38
Reinhart Fuchs. See Buschinger and Göttert.
Reiss, H. 1993. *Formgestaltung und Politik. Goethe-Studien*, Würzburg: Konigshaus und Neumann.
Richards, E.G. 1987. 'An Examination of the *Reinike Fuchs* Glosses 1498–1650 in the Light of the Cultural History of the Period', unpublished Ph.D. dissertation of the University of British Columbia.
Rodin, K. 1983. *Räven predikar för Gässen: en studie av ett ordsprak i senmedeltida ikonografi* [The Fox Preaches to the Geese: A Study of a Proverb in Late Medieval Iconography], Uppsala: Almquist & Wiksell.
Sands, D.B. (ed.). 1960. *The History of Reynard the Fox Translated and Printed by William Caxton in 1481*, Cambridge, MA and London: Harvard University Press.
Scheidegger, J.R. 1989. *Le Roman de Renart ou le texte de la dérision*, Geneva: Droz.
Schlusemann, R. 1991. *Die hystorie van reynaert die vos* and *The History of Reynard the Fox*, Frankfurt-am-Main: Peter Lang.
Schopper, H. 1567.*Opus poeticum de admirabili fallacia et astutia vulpeculae Reinikes*, Frankfurt: Sigismund Feyrabend.
———. (1706). *The Crafty Courtier or the Fable of Reinhard the Fox, newly done into English Verse, from the Antient Latin Iambics of Hartm. Schopperus*, printed for John Nutt, near Stationers-Hall, London: 1706.
Schouwink, W. 1995. '*Reinike* from the Pen of a Mercenary. Hartmann Schopper's *Opus Poeticum*', *Reinardus* 7, 161–82.
Schwab, L. 1971. *Vom Sünder zum Schelmen. Goethes Bearbeitung des 'Reineke Fuchs'*, Frankfurt am Main: Lang.
Schwab, U. 1967. *Zur Datierung und Interpretation des Reinhart Fuchs, mit einem textkritischen Beitrag von K. Düwel,* Naples: Quaderni della sezione linguistica degli Annali, V.
Schwarzbaum, H. 1979. *The 'Mishlé Shu' alim' (Fox Fables) of the Rabbi Berechiah Ha-Nakdan: A Study in Comparative Folklore and Fable Lore*, Kizon: Institute for Jewish and Arab Folklore Research.
Shojaei, C. Kawan. (1987). 'Fuchs (Bär) am Pferdeschwanz', in vol V of *Enzyklopädie des Märchens*, Berlin and New York.
Sisam, K. (ed.). 1927. *Chaucer's Nun's Priest's Tale*, Oxford: the Clarendon Press.
Slempkes, J.A. 1929. *De zinrijke avonturen van den vos Reinaerde. Zooveel mogelijk tekstgetrouw naverteld door J.A Slempkes*, Zutphen.

Sodmann, T. (ed.). 1976. *Reynke de vos* (facsimile reprint of the unique 1498 Lübeck edition), Hamburg: Kötz.
Sparling, H.H. (ed). 1892. *The History of Reynard the Foxe by William Caxton*, Hammersmith: The Kelmscott Press.
Speculum vitae aulicae, eller den fordanskede Reynike Fosz, Copenhagen: Glasing, 1747.
Spiewok, W. 1964. 'Reinhart Fuchs-Fragen', in *Wissenschaftliche Zeitschrift der Ernst – Arndt – Universität Greifswald* XIII, 281–8.
Stallybrass, W.S. (ed.). 1924. *The Epic of the Beast, Consisting of English Translations of The History of Reynard the Fox and Physiologus*, London and New York: Broadway Translations
Stopp, E. (trans.) and P. Hutchinson (ed.). 1998. *Johann Wolfgang von Goethe: Maxims and Reflections*, Harmondsworth: Penguin.
Strubel, Armand, et al (eds). 1998. *Le Roman de Renart* (Bibliothèque de la Pléiade), Paris : Gallimard.
Stuiveling, G. (ed.). 1965. *Esopet. Facsimile-uitgave naar het enig bewaard gebleven handschrift*, 2 vols, Amsterdam: Hertzberger.
Subrenat, Jean. 1991. 'La Justice dans le *Roman de Renart*', in *A la Recherche du Roman de Renart*, ed K. Varty, New Alyth (Perthshire): Lochee Publications, 239–92.
Suomela-Härmä, E. (ed.). 1998. *Le Livre de Regnart*, Paris: Champion.
Technae aulicae ex apologo astutissimae vulpeculae Latino et Germanico carmine breviter delineatae ... / Weltlauff und Hofleben, jetzt von newem mit kurtzen Versen und kuenstlichen Figuren zugericht..., Frankfurt: Nicolaus Bassaeus, 1588.
Tenèze, M.-L. 1976. *Le Conte populaire français*, Paris: Maisonneuve et Larose.
Terry, P. (trans.). 1992. *Renard the Fox. Translated from the Old French by Patricia Terry*, Berkeley and Los Angeles: University of California Press.
Toeche, Th. 1867. *Kaiser Heinrich VI*, Leipzig.
Trachsler, R. 1994. 'Si le gita / sor son dos, et si l'en porta *(Yvain,* vv. 3445–46) ou: comment porter un cerf si vous êtes un lion', *Reinardus* 7, 183–93.
Uther, H.-J. 1987. 'Fuchs', in *Enzyklopädie des Märchens*, Berlin and New York.
Van Daele, R. 1992. 'Van den vos Reynaerde. De vos die je ziet, ben je zelf' [*VdvR*, The Fox You See, You Are Yourself], in *Brekende spiegels. Beeldveranderingen in de Nederlandse literatuur* [Breaking Mirrors. Changes in the Images of Dutch Literature], eds. D. de Geest and M van Vaeck, Leuven, 19–41.
———. 1994. *Ruimte en naamgeving in Van den vos Reynaerde*, Ghent: Koninklijke Academie voor Nederlandse Taal- en Letterkunde.
———. 1996. 'Het laatste woord is aan Willem. Over het slot van *Van den vos Reynaerde* (A 3390–3469), in *Tegendraads genot. Opstellen over de kwaliteit van middeleeuwse teksten*, eds. K. Porteman, W. Verbeke and F. Willaert, Leuven: Peeters.
Van Genechten, R. 1941. *Van den Vos Reynaerde*, Amsterdam.

Van Oostrom, F.P. 1981. *Lantsloot vander Haghedochte. Onderzoekingen over een Middelnederlandse bewerking van de 'Lancelot en prose'*, Amsterdam: Noord-Hollandse Uitgevers Maatschappij.

———. 1984a. 'Benaderingswijzen van de *Reinaert*', in *Historische letterkunde: facetten van vakbeoefening*, ed. M. Spies, Groningen: Wolters-Noordhoff.

———. 1984b. *Reinaert bij de NSB*, in *Literatuur* 1, 28–33.

———. 1992. *Court and Culture: Dutch Literature, 1350–1450*, trans. by A.J. Pomerans, Berkeley, Los Angeles and Oxford: University of California Press.

Varty, Kenneth. 1967. *Reynard the Fox. A Study of the Fox in Medieval English Art*, Leicester: Leicester University Press.

———. 1980. 'The Earliest Illustrated Editions of 'Reynard the Fox', and their Links With the Earliest Illustrated Continental Editions', in J. Goossens and T. Sodmann (eds.), *Reynaert, Reynard, Reynke: Studien zu einem mittelalterlichen Tierepos*, Cologne and Vienna: Böhlau Verlag, 160–95.

———. 1984. 'Le Viol dans l'*Ysengrimus*, les branches II–Va, et la branche I du *Roman de Renart*', in *Amour, mariage et transgression au Moyen Age*, ed. D. Buschinger and A. Crépin, Göppingen: Kümmerle Verlag, 411–18.

———. 1985. 'Back to the Beginnings of the *Roman de Renart*', *Nottingham Medieval Studies* 29, 44–72.

———. 1986. 'The Giving and Witholding of Consent in Late Twelfth-Century French Literature', *Reading Medieval Studies*, 12, 27–49.

———. 1991a. 'La Datation des contes de Renart le goupil, et la branche IV, *Renart et Ysengrin dans le puits*', in *A la Recherche du Roman de Renart*, New Alyth (Perthshire): Lochee Publications, 330–43.

———. 1991b. 'Le Goupil des bestiaires dans le *Roman de Renart*', in *A la Recherche du Roman de Renart*, New Alyth (Perthshire): Lochee Publications, 344–60.

———. 1996. 'Renart et Ysengrin dans le Puits: la version courte, la version longue, et la version plus longue de la branche IV du *Roman de Renart*', in *'Ensi firent li ancessor': mélanges de philologie médiévale offerts à Marc-René Jung*, ed. by L. Rossi et al, Alessandria: Edizioni dell'Orso, 451–63.

———. 1997. 'On the Comic Qualities of *Vox and Wolf* and Some Related Predecessors', in *Medieval Heritage: Essays in Honour of Tadahiro Ikegami*, Tokyo: Yushodo Press, 17–30.

———.1998. *The Roman de Renart. A Guide to Scholarly Work*, Lanham, Md: Scarecrow Press.

———. 1999. *Reynard, Renart, Reinaert, and Other Foxes in Medieval England. The Iconographic Evidence*. Amsterdam: Amsterdam University Press.

Verzandvoort, E. 1989. 'The Dutch Chapbooks of *Reynaert de Vos* and Their Illustrations', *Reinardus* 2, 176–84.

Verzandvoort, E. and P. Wackers (eds). 1988. *Reynaert den vos oft Der Dieren Oordeel. Facsimile van het rond 1700 in de drukkerij van Hieronymus Verdussen vervaardigde volksboek,* Antwerp and Apeldoorn: Berghmans Uitgevers.
Voigt, Ernst. (ed.). 1884. *Ysengrimus,* Halle a. S.: Waisenhaus; repr. Georg Olms: Hildesheim, 1964.
Wackers, P. 1981. 'The Use of Fables in *Reynaerts historie'*, in *Third International Beast Epic, Fable and Fabliau Colloquium. Münster 1979. Proceedings,* eds. J. Goossens and T. Sodmann, Cologne and Vienna: Böhlau Verlag, 461–83.
———. 1986. *De waarheid als leugen. Een interpretatie van Reynaerts historie,* Utrecht: HES Publishers.
———. 1998. 'Reynard the Fox', in *A Dictionary of Medieval Heroes. Characters in Medieval Narrative Traditions and Their Afterlife in Literature, Theatre and the Visual Arts,* eds. W.P. Gerritsen and A.G. van Melle, trans. from the Dutch by T. Guest, Woodbridge: Boydell Press, 211–19.
Wackers, P. and E. Verzandvoort. 1989. 'Bewerkingstechniek in de Reynaerttraditie', *Tijdschrift voor Nederlandse taal- en letterkunde* 105, 152–81.
Walschap, G. 1941. 'De vos Reynaert is niet amoreel' [Reynard the Fox Is Not Amoral], *Dietsche Warande en Belfort,* 10, 501–506.
Warren, F.M. 1890. '*Uncle Remus* and the *Roman de Renart'*, *Modern Language Notes,* 5, 129–35, cols. 257–70.
Weber, A.P. 1966. *Mit Allen Wassern: Neue Geschichten Vom Alten Fuchs,* Frankfurt am Main: Bärmeier & Nikel.
Wenseleers, L. 1993. *De pels van de vos. Historische achtergronden van de middeleeuwse Reinaert-satire* [The Fur of the Fox. Historical Backgrounds of the Medieval Reynard Satire], Amsterdam and Leuven.
Wiethälter, W. with C. Brecht (eds.). 1994. *Reineke Fuchs* in the Frankfurter Ausgabe of Goethe's Works, Franfurt am Main: Deutscher Klassiker Verlag.
Wild, R. (ed.). 1988. *Reineke Fuchs,* in vol. 4.1 of the Münchener Ausgabe of Goethe's Works, Munich: Carl Hauser.
Willems, J.F. (ed.). 1834. *Reinaert de vos, naar de oudste berijming,* Eeclo. More readily available in more recent editions such as the one entitled *Reinaert de vos, naar de oudste berijming uit de twaalfde eeuw en opnieuw in 1834 berijmd door Jan Frans Willems. Ingelid door W Gs Hellinga.* Den Haag: Bert Bakker, 1958.
———. (ed.) 1836. *Reinaert de vos, episch fabeldicht van de twaalfde en dertiende eeuw, met aenmerkingen en ophelderingen* [*RdV,* Epic Fable Poem of the Twelfth and Thirteenth Century], Ghent.
Witton, N. 1980. 'Die Vorlage des Reineke de Vos', in *Reynaert, Reynard, Reynke: Studien zu einem mittelalterlichen Tierepos,* eds. J. Goossens and T. Sodmann, Cologne and Vienna: Böhlau Verlag, 1–159.

Index of Names and Titles

The names of people, places and events are in plain text, titles are in italics, all in normal alphabetical order.

Titles which contain the name of the fox in one or other of the different languages (e.g., *Reynard, Reineke, Renart*) are all under the letter R.

To help the non-specialist find the animals of the Beast Epic and of closely-related narrative poems by their names, here is a list of them arranged in alphabetical order according to their generic name: the *ape* (or *monkey*), Murten, Martin, Mertijn, Zani; the *ass* (or *donkey*), Baudouin, Bernard, Boudewijn; the *badger*, Brocket, Grimbart, Grimbaert, Grimbert, Krimel; the *bear*, Braun, Bruin, Brun, Bruno, Bruun, Patous; the *boar*, Beaucent; the *bull*, Bruyant; the *camel*, Musart; the *cat*, Dipreht, Hinze, Tibeert, Tibert, Tybaert, Tybeert; the *cockerel*, Cantecleer, Cantekleer, Chantecler, Chaunticleer; the *crow* (or *rook*), Cawood, Corbout, Merkenau, Tiecelin; the *deer* (see also *stag*), Plateau, the *dog* (see also *mastif*), Courtois; the *fox*, Reinardus, Reineke, Reinhart, Reinike, Reneward, Renuard, Reynard, Russell; also Goupil; and his sons are Percehaie, Reynardine and Volpus; the *goose*, Gerard; the *hare*, Couart, Kuwaert, Lampe, Lapeel; *hens*, Coppe, Pertelote, Pinte; the *horse*, Corvigarus; the *leopard*, Firapel; the *lion*, Nobel, Noble, Vrevel (see also, Lion King); the *lioness*, Fière; the *mare*, Raisant; the *mastiff*, Roenel; the *panther*, Sly-Look; the *ram*, Belin, Bellijn, Bellinus, Bellyn, Joseph; the *rat*, Pelé; the *she-wolf*, Eerswijnde, Hersent; the *sow*, Salaura; the *stag*, Brichemer; the *vixen*, Hermeline; the *vulture*, Mouflart; the *wolf*, Isegrim, Isengrin, Sigrim, Ysegrim, Ysengrimus, Ysengrin.

When the name of an author of a chapter in this book is cited in this Index, the reference is to other publications by this author, all of which are listed in the Bibliography.

Aarne, A (and Thompson) 245, 246, 258, 262, 264
Aarschot 144, 159
Abelard 8
Abelquack 179
Abruzzi, Count of 50
Ackerman, F 106
Acon 179
Adam 43
Adenet li Roi 64, 67
Adrian VI 45
Adriatic 48
Aeneas 179
Aeneid 187
Aesop 155, 158, 260
Africa 254
Ah! ça IRA 238
Albert, Prince 172
Alde, Y 227, 234
Aldermary Church Yard 170
Aleide 101, 102
Alexander III, Pope 43–45
Allde, E 164, 165
Alsace 37, 45
Altdorfer, A 116
Altdorfer, E 116
Altener, E 121
America, North 126 (*see also* USA)
Amesbury Psalter 136, 165
Amiel, L 224
Amis du crime, Les 237
Amman, J 116, 232
Amsterdam 109
Amsterdam Oude Kerk 146
*Amsterdamse Keurkamer*109
Ancona, Margrave of 50
Anderson, R 173
Angel of Death 41
Anglade, N 233
Anglo-Norman 252
Animal Farm 238
Anjou, Count of 106
Anselm (Bishop of Tournai) 4–6, 10, 11

Antero, Antreas (folklore fox names) 262
Ants, the Master of the 49
Antti (a folklore fox name) 262
Antwerp 75, 77, 82, 103, 109, 109
Antwerp Cathedral 111
Aosta Abbey Ours 158, 159
Apocalypse 43
Apulia 48, 50, 51
Arber, E 168
Archives of the Society for Finnish Literature 259
Arènes de Lutèce 239
Argolids 5
Aristophanes 180, 188
Aristotle 205
Arnaldi, A 233
Arnaud, G 228
Artevelde statue 111
Arthur, King 18
Arthur, T G 169
Artouses 238
Asia 267
Asti 40
Aventures de Maître Renart et de ses compères... Les: see *Renart*
Aventures de maître Renart et d'Ysengrin son compère, Les: see *Renart*
Avesnes (the) 106
Avesnes, Jan de 106

Babel, Tower of 43
Babylon 43
Backer, W 121
Baels, L 112
Bailly, L 228
Bakhtin, M 12
Ballades (Villon) 210
Ballain, G 32
Barbarossa: see Frederick
Barcelona Cathedral 126, 149, 162
Bardowick 144
Barnouw, A T 108, 173

Index

Barret, G 227
Basedow 195
Basel, bishop of 44
Basel Cathedral 49, 156, 159
Bastid-Martens 237
Battle Poem 110
Bauchart, C 233
Baudouin (the ass) 242
Baumann, R 189
Beaucent (the boar) 22, 23
Beaumont, P de 230
Beck, C H 207
Becque, M de 228
Bédier, J 237
Belgicists 108, 109
Belgium 108, 144, 148, 159, 169
Bellijn (the ram) 74, 75, 97, 98
Bellinus (the ram) 170
Bellon, R 225
Bellyn (the ram) 199, 201
Bennett, J A W (and Smithers) 246, 247, 251
Berard, physician of Henry VI 50
Berlin 106, 158 (the National Gallery), 210
Bernard (the ass) 142
Béroul 32, 33, 35, 58, 59, 65
Berteloot, A 70, 74
Besamusca, B 62, 72
Bescheidenheit 180
Bestiary, the 150
Berthold of Zähringen, Duke 38
Besse-en-Chandesse 162
Beverley Minster 138, 139, 149, 151, 152, 155, 157, 162
Beverley St Mary's 143, 146, 149, 154, 155
Bible, the 15, 64, 189
Bibliotheca Curiosa 168
Biblioteca Reale, Turin 225
Bibliothèque de l'Arsenal 225, 246
Bibliothèque Nationale 129, 225, 232, 236
Bieling, A 192, 207
Biet, C 233
Blackburn Cathedral 144
Blake, N 168
Blanche Lande 32
Blandinium 2
Blauwvoeters 106

Bletterens 144
Bohemia 37, 38, 46, 47
Bolshevik 109
Bolsward, St Martin's 144
Boon, L P 111, 112
Bond, James 102
Bonnot, J de 227, 228
Boston (Lincs), St Botolph's 136, 142, 145, 148, 154, 155
Bozon, N 252
Boudewijn 108
Bouman, B 121
Boutet, D 225
Bouwman, A 61, 62, 68, 72
Boyon, M 229
Brabant, the dukes of 68,
Bradby, D 174
Branches of the *Roman de Renart*
   I *Le Jugement* 18, 28–34, 60–63, 73, 113, 126, 160, 230
   Ia *Le Siège* 51
   Ib *Renart Jongleur* 265
   II *Les Premières Aventures de Renart* 18, 56–59, 105, 134, 139, 163, 164, 231, 249, 250, 263, 265, 267
   II–Va *Premières Aventures + Le Serment* 56–60, 65
   Va *Le Serment* 18, 20–28, 30, 34, 59, 62, 153
   V *Renart, Isengrin et le Jambon* 265
   IV *Le Puits* 163, 245–256
   VIII *Le Pélérinage* 112
   IX *Liétart* 230, 261
   X *Renart Médecin* 49, 156, 157
   XI *Renart Empereur* 46, 51, 52, 158
   XII *Les Vêpres de Tibert* 230
   XIII *Renart teint en noir* 265
   XVII *La Mort et Procession* 152, 159
   XXIV *La Création de Renart* 224, 227, 231
Brandes, H 188
Brandt, Sebastian 180
Braun (the bear) 197, 200
Brawn 187
Brecht, C 207
Brent Knoll, St Michael's 153

Brer B'ar 253
Brer Coon 253
Brer Fox 252–256
Brer Rabbit 252–256
Brer Terrapin 252
Breton Romances 18
Breuer, H 225
Breugel 158
Brewster, E 165, 166, 168, 170
Brichemer (the stag) 23, 24, 26, 27, 33
Brighelli, J-P 233
Bristol Cathedral 114, 126–134, 143, 151, 152, 157
Britain 125, 169
Brocket (the badger) 166
Brothers in Arms 111
Brotherton, F F 233
Brown, R 171
Bruges 106
Bruin (the bear) 108, 111, 126–128, 131, 173, 174
Brun (the bear) 22–24, 29, 44, 126, 229, 230
Bruno (the bear) 6, 187
Bruun (the bear) 61, 62, 74, 97, 98, 108, 111
Bruyant (the bull) 29
Bucolics (Virgil's) 177, 179, 187
Burrell Collection, the (Glasgow) 141, 169
Bury St Edmunds 144
Buschinger, D 38
Busspredigt 214

Cadot, M 229
Caen University 233
Calvin, J 234
Camara, C 238
Campagne in France, The (Goethe) 195, 196, 205
Canon Law 25
Canon Pyon 148
Cantecleer, Cantekleer (the cockerel) 90
Canton, G 171
Cappenburg Castle Chapel 144
Carlisle Cathedral 148
Castle Hedingham, St Nicholas's 139, 143, 147, 159, 161

Catholics (Church, Hierarchy, Theology, Public) 108, 112, 125, 176, 185, 233. *See also,* Church
Cawood (the rook) 167
Caxton's text, translation 60, 126, 127, 153, 156, 168, 172, 175
Celanova, St Sauveur 144
Celestin III, Pope 45
Centre Beaubourg 237
Cesar of Heisterbach 42
Chabaille, P 233, 246
Châlons, Bishop of 223
Champeaux, St Martin 144
Chasons de geste 56–58
Chantecler (the cockerel) 56, 57, 126, 131, 134, 141, 163, 230, 241, 243, 244, 257, 267
Chanteclin (father of Chantecler) 134
Chapel Road 111
Chappon, G 229
Charbonnier, E 229
Charlemagne 18
Charles V (Habsburg) 184
Charles VI (France) 106
Charles the Bald 43
Charmon, R G 229
Château l'Hermitage 144
Chaucer, G 134–136, 138, 140, 163
Chaunticleer (the cockerel) 163, 251
Chauveau, L 228, 236
Cheshire 151
Chester Cathedral 147, 151
Chichester Cathedral 155, 161
Chieri 40
Chrétien de Troyes 67, 139
Christ, Jesus 12, 13, 158
Christchurch Priory 146
Christian, Archbishop of Mayence 44
Chronicle of the Emperors 39
Church, the Catholic 35, 44, 112, 125, 175, 176–178, 234. *See also,* Catholics
Cicero 181
Cîteaux 6
Ciudad Rodrigo 158, 159

Index 287

Claes van Aken 77
Clairvaux 4, 6, 15
Clarke, I H 228
Classical Antiquity 159, 186, 260
Cleomades, *Cleomades* 64
Cleves, Minoriten Church 146
Cley-next-the-Sea, St Mary's 138
Cnipius 187
Coates, W A 169
Cocu and Co. 234
Coghill, N 138, 139
Coimbra 158, 159
Colledge, E 72
Collin de Plancy 223, 224
Colin, J P 244
Cologne, Archbishop of 44
Cologne Cathedral 147, 149
Combarieu du Grès, M de (and Subrenat) 150, 225, 227, 230, 246
Comical Creatures from Wurtemburg...The 173
Compagnons de Saint-Georges 227
Condé, Jean de 153
Conrad II 40
Conrad von Huneburg 45
Constance, the Peace of 41
Constance, wife of Henry VI 41, 42
Continent, the 126, 156, 158
Continuation, Or Second Part Of The Most Pleasant and Delightful History of Reynard the Fox... A: see *Reynard the Fox.*
Contrescarpe quarter of Paris 238, 242
Conyers 170
Coppe (the hen) 74
Corbout (the crow) 75, 94
Cortes Vázquez 225
Corvigarus (the horse) 2
Cosijns, A F 232
Couart (the hare) 159
Counter-Reformation, the 124, 175
Couronnement de Renart, Le 52, 67, 222
Cours d'amour 62
Courtly Crafts / This is the Way of the World at Court 186

Courtois (the dog) 89, 107, 108
Crabron 167
Crafty Courtier, or the Fable of Reynard the Fox... The: see *Reynard the Fox*
Crane, W 169
Crawhall, J 169
Cremona 40
Crès, G 232
Crusade (Second) 5, 14, 15
Critical Calendar 210, 211, 220
Crystal Palace 172
Curvers, A 228

Dag, De 110
Dagsburg: see Hugo von
Dahl, R 174
Damme 106
Dampierres, the 106
Danika 229
Darien, G 244
Death (personnification) 42
De admirabile fallacia et astutia vulpeculae Reinikes libros quator: see *Reinikes libros quator*
De Consideratione (St Bernard's) 14
Decorte, B 121
Decretum (Gratian's) 25
De Dag 110
Delacorta 237
Delft 75, the 1485 prose edition of *Reynke*, 191, 193
Delius-Apollo 177
Demany, F 111
Deroy, J 35
Deschamps, E 106
Desjardins, P 236
Deucalion's flood 15
Devil, the 139, 140, 150: *see also, Satan*
Dewar, B 174
Dicke, G (and Grubmüller) 245
Dickens, C 173
Dietsche Warande en Belfort 109
Diksmuide 70, 74, 111
Dipreht (the cat) 44
Dirix-Van Riet 108
Dollian, G 232
Dominican Order 152
Douglas, M 202

Dubrieu, A 237
Dufournet, J 71, 72, 225–237, 230, 234, 246; Dufournet J (and Méline) 71, 72, 225
Dutch Association for the Promotion of National Socialism 110
Düwel, K 38

Easter 181
Ecbasis eiusdem captivi.. 155
Ecclesiasticus 189
Eckermann 205
Eerswijnde (the she-wolf) 74
Elias, N 96
Elizabeth I of England 175
Ellis, F S 168
Ely Cathedral 135, 140–142
Emmerich, St Martin 149, 159
Encyclopédie en bandes dessinées 238
England 144–148, 151, 155, 157, 158, 161, 162, 172, 173, 175, 255
Engrenage 237, 238
Enigmatika 237
Enlightenment, the 114, 124
Entscheidung, Die 220
Envy (personnification) 52
Ephesians 181
Epistles, Horace's 188, 189
Erasmus, D 210
Erfurt 209
Errer 237
Erstein (abbey, convent, town of) 38, 45–47, 50
Eskénazi, A 230
Esopet (Dutch fable collection) 62, 72
Establishment, the 34
Estavoyer-le-Lac 149
Estonia 258, 265
Etchingham, St Nicholas's 144
Eugenius III, Pope 5, 14, 15
Eulenspiegel: see Till Eulenspiegel
Euripides 180, 188
Europe 126, 159, 186, 264
Everdingen: see Van Everdingen
Evreux Municipal Museum 144
Ezekiel 14, 247

Fabliaux 58
Fajardie 237
Fala Duna (Tibert's wife) 243
False Fox, the 135
Fastnachtspiele 209
Faust 108; *Faust* 205
Faversham, St Mary of Charity's 148, 158
Feraria 166
Feyerabend, S 177, 188, 189
Fière (the lioness) 134, 235
Finland 258, 264, 265
Finoli, A-M, 225
Firapel (the leopard) 166, 167
First World War 108, 110, 214
Flamingants 108
Flämische Kampfgedicht, Das 110
Flanders 52, 66, 68, 103, 106–111; Counts of, 106
Fleerackers, Father E 110
Flemings 106–111
Flemish (language) 67, 68, 108
Flemish Battle Poem 110
Flinn, J 71, 72
Florianus, J 32
Fortuna, Fortune (personnification) 9, 52, 153, 179
Foucault, J de 232
Foulet, L 16, 35, 51, 224, 246, 252
Fox, Mr 174
Fox and the Wolf in the Well, the 163, 246, 247, 249–251
Fox [Bear, etc.] Hangs by his Teeth to the Horse's Tail... 258
Fox in Disguise Violates the She-Bear 258–263
France 5, 50, 68, 89, 144, 148, 157, 161, 167, 169, 171, 204
Fransiscan Order 143
François, P 229
Frankfurt am Main (as a place of publication) 116, 177, 187–189
Frappier, J 229
Frascati 64
Fraser's Magazine 173
Freddy, Young 238
Frederick I 40–42, 50
Frederick II 42

Index 289

Frederick Barbarossa 38, 41, 43, 45–47, 50, 53
Frederick of Bohemia 46, 47
Frederick, son of King Wladislaw 47
Freiburg University 185
Freidank 180
Frélaut, J 232
French (language) 67, 68, 82
Fronsperger, L 189
Froude, J A 173
Fuhlsbüttel 210
Fukumoto, N 225, 226

Galey, M 252
Gamlingay 148
Gang 237
Garstang, St Helen's 162
Gaultier, T 164
Gay Science (Nietzsche) 201
Gecastreerde neus, De 114
Geduldigen, Die 212
Genechten, R van 109–111
Genevoix, M 226, 228, 233–37
Gentil, P 227
Gerard (the goose) 9
Gerber, A 265
German Empire 37
Germany 5, 9, 40, 47, 52, 144, 146, 147, 149, 158, 159, 172, 175, 176
Gesunkenes Kulturgut 101, 107
Gestapo 210
Ghent 1, 2, 5, 106, 111
Gielen, W
Giraud, M H 228
Girbaden 35, 39, 53
Glasgow 141, 233
Glichezaere: see Heinrich der
Glosing, G 189
Gloucester Cathedral 149, 156, 159
God 26, 27, 31, 43, 52, 202, 249
Goethe 60, 118, 119, 172, 173, 191–207, 209, 211
Golden Age 13
Goldsmid, E 168
Goossens, J 72, 94–96, 102, 103, 114, 116
Göttert, K H 38

Gottsched, J C 118, 121, 172, 191–207
Gouda 75, 77, 103, 164
Goupil (the fox) 229, 239, 240, 242–244
Goudriaen, K 102
Gourmont, J de 82
Gräff. J 189
Gratian 25
Grau-Stef, C 230
Graven, J 232
Great Exhibition (Crystal Palace, 1850) 172
Greece, Greeks 5
Gresford, All Saints' 134, 143
Grimbeert (the badger) 74, 75, 94, 107, 257
Grimbert (the badger) 29, 33, 34, 61
Grimm, J 107
Gross-Kophta, Der 193
Grubmüller, K 245
Guinevere 235
Gwide of Dampierre 67, 68

Haarlem Master 82, 118
Habsburg Emperors 184
Hacquard, G 229
Haddon Hall 144, 145
Halnard, R 237
Hamburg 210
Harano, N 225, 226
Hare in Trap Complains 258
Hare, More Cowardly than the 258
Harris, J Chandler 252–256
Hastings, S 171
Haugewitz, Count 195
Haumont, J 232
Hauser, C 207
Haymon 101
Hecht, J 228
Heidelberg University 185
Heinolan 265
Heinrich der Glichesaere 37–53, 222
Heinrich von Horburg 44
Heisterbach: see Cesar of
Helen (of Troy) 58, 91
Hell 4
Hellinga, W Gs 72, 102

Hendrik van Wijn 101, 102
Henry I, Duke of Brabant 106
Henry VI (son of Barbarossa) 38, 41, 42, 44–46, 48, 50–53
Henry the Lion 42
Henry the Lion of Saxony 106
Herder 205
Hereford Cathedral 148
Hermeline (the vixen) 239
Hermes, E 248
Hersent (the she-wolf) 18–34, 60, 235, 242, 265
Hervieux, L 260
High German 116, 118, 171, 176, 179, 180, 184, 186, 188, 198
Historische en letterkunde Avonstonden 101
Hindenach, M 230
Hinze (the cat) 197
Historie van Reynaert de Vos: see *Reinaert, Reynaert*, etc.
History of Reynard the Fox (Caxton): see Caxton and *Reynard the Fox*
Hitler, A 210; *Hitler: ein deutsches Verhängnis* 209
Hohenstaufen 38–41, 44, 47, 48, 51, 53
Holland 74, 110, 169
Holland, J 153
Holloway 172
Holy Roman Empire 37, 38, 41
Holy Land 5, 48, 61, 74, 98
Horace 180, 188, 189
Horburg (the town) 38, 39; Horburg, Heinrich von 44; Horburg, Walther von 44
Hubert, J-L 237
Hugaerts, F 106
Hugo of Trimburg 18
Hugo von Dagsburg 38
Hulsterlo 108
Huysmans, C 109
Hystorie van Reynaert die Vos, Die (Leeu) 164. *See also Reynaert*, etc., and Leeu

Ijzer, River 108; Tower, 111
Ill, River 45
Im Perterre 214, 215

Imbart, J-G 237–239
In Praise of Folly 210
Index, the (*Index librorum prohibitorum*) 76, 223
Ingermanland 266
Inspecteur mène l'enquête, l' 238
Ireland 238
Irish Bar, the 239, 243
Irmgart, wife of Lothar 45
Isaiah 13, 189
Isegrim (the wolf) 98, 105, 112, 173, 197–200
Isengrimmers 106
Isengrin (the wolf) 19–34, 48, 56, 58, 95, 105, 112, 188, 189, 230, 240, 242–244, 257
Isolda 26, 32, 34, 59, 60, 235
Italy 37–53

Jacobs, J C 255
Jacobson van der Meer, J 75
Jacquemart, Gielée 52
Janssens, J D 67
Jaouen, H 237
Japan 225
Jauss-Meyer, H 225
Jena 110
Jeremiah 14
Jerry (the mouse) 249
Jerusalem 5
Jew(s) 109, 110, 247
Jodocus 109, 110
Johannes (folklore name for the hare): see Juhana, etc. 262
John (the evangelist) 63
John the Baptist 181
John Lackland 52
John (of) Sheppey 252
Jones, M 145
Joostens, Renaat: see Punt (111)
Jorovinen 265
Joseph (the ram) 2, 12, 13
Juhana, Juho (folklore names for the hare): see Jussa, etc. (262)
Juno 91
Jussa, Jussi, Jusu (folklore names for the hare) 262, 263

Kampfgedicht 110
Kapellekensbaan, De 111

Kaulbach, W von 119, 124, 172, 173
Kawan, S 261. 262
Keerberghen, P van 75, 77
Kelmscott Press 168, 169
Kempen, St Mary's 144, 146, 158, 159
Kippar, P 265
Klitzing, H 119
Knapp, F P 61
Knowle parish church 154, 161
Kooyman, R 121
Kortrijk 111
Kriekepit, Kriekeputte 93, 108
Krimel (the badger) 44
Kritische Kalender 210, 212, 220
Krohn, K 261
Kuwaert (the hare) 64, 74, 75, 93, 98

La Chièvre 58
La Ferté Beauharnais, Collegiate Church of St Bartélemy 148
La Mutualité 243
La Rochefoucauld 200, 202
Lampe (the hare) 199, 201
Lancelot (prose romance) 66–68
Lanci-Christikruid 108
Landsknecht 184, 185
Lanfert 127
Lantsloot vander Haghedochte 67
Laon 6
Lapeel (the hare) 75, 94
Larrieu, O 228
Last Judgement 12
Latin 42, 43, 63, 82, 86, 107, 112, 116, 145, 171, 173–189, 245, 252, 255
Latvia 264
Lautenbach 144
Lavater 195
Lébédeff, J 231
Leclère, C 244
Leeu, Gheraert 75, 77, 82, 99, 102, 164
Lefèvre, S 225
Legends of the Old Plantation 252
Legnano, Battle of 41
Legrand d'Aussy 222
Leipzig 118

Leipziger Illustrierte Zeitung 209
Lemaître, H 235
Lent 181, 188
Leon Cathedral 148
Leopold III (Belgium) 112
Leopold of Austria 48
Leroy-Allais, J 231
Leviticus 247
Lichtenberg 195
Liège 106, 111; Archbishop of, 51
Liétart 230
Lignards, Les 238
Lille University 233
Lincoln Cathedral 144
Lion, King 97, 177, 193, 194, 196, 199, 201, 204. *See also*: Nobel, Noble
Lithuania 264
Lodge, R A 58, 72, 225
Loimaa 263
Lombardian League 41
Lombardian Republics 40
Lombardy 43, 47, 50, 59
London 153, 170
Lord, J V 171
Lothar 40, 45
Louis of Basel 44
Louis the German 43
Louis the Pious 43
Louvain, St Pierre 148
Low Countries 73, 75, 76, 89, 96, 101, 102, 106
Low German 116, 118, 124, 126, 127, 171, 172, 175, 176, 192 (see Delft, 1485 prose edition), 213 (Mähe)
Lübeck (edition of 1498) 116, 171, 172, 175, 176, 188
Ludlow, St Lawrence's 143, 145
Lukács, G 204
Luke (the evangelist) 62, 189
Lulofs, F 72
Lund Cathedral 158, 159

Machiavellist 109
Maggie 138
Mähl, J 213
Mainz 191
Malines, Archbishop of 223
Malkin (a cat) 171

Malkyn, Dame 138
Malpertus 201
Malpertuus 98, 106, 213
Manchester Cathedral 138, 157, 160
Manchette, J-P 238
Mann, J 15
Mann, T 205
Manton 166
Margharetha of Flanders, Countess 106
Mark (the evangelist) 189
Mark, King 59
Markward von Anweiler 50
Marten (the ape) 94, 95, 97
Martin (the ape or monkey) 176, 178
Martin, E 35, 72, 224–230, 235, 246
Mary, Holy 30
Mary (Stuart), Queen 175
Marxists 108
Mass (the ceremony of) 13
Matthew (the evangelist) 12, 181, 189
Maupassant, G de 234
Maupertuis 28, 29, 51, 110, 213, 239
Maupertuus 110
Maximilian I 184
Maximilian II 183–185
Méline, A (and Dufournet) 71, 72, 225, 230, 246
Menke, H 60, 76, 102, 103, 114, 118, 164, 165, 168, 170, 172, 188, 189
Méon, D M 223–226, 228
Merkenau (the crow) 194
Mertijn (the ape) 75, 94, 97
Messina 41
Metamorphoses 15
Metz, Bishop of 44
Mével, J-P 244
Middle English 163, 246, 249–250, 252, 253
Mikkeli, Mikko (folklore fox names) 262, 263
Milan 38–42, 53
Minster-in-Thanet, St Mary's 137
Minstrel of Rheims 106

Miroir obscur 237
Mirror of Courtly Life, or the Danish Reinike 186
Misanthrope, Le 199
Miska (a folklore fox name) 262
Mishlé Shu'Alim 246
Mit Allen Wassern.. 212
Mizutani, K 228
Moens, W 110
Mohammed 13
Molière, J-B 199
Money, Cardinal 97
Mont, Paul de 109
Montbenoît Abbey 161
Morley, H 168
Monteyne, L 110, 111
Moudon 149
Mouffetard, Rue 238, 243, 244
Mouflart (the vulture) 241, 242
Mouhijavi 261
Moyses Hall Museum, Bury St Edmunds 144
Muret, E (& Dufourques, L-M) 35
Murray, A 70
Musart (the camel) 254
Musée des Familles… Le 224
Muses, the 202
Mussolini, B 109

Nantwich, St Mary's 145, 148, 151
Naples 41, 51
Narvusi 260
Naylor (translator of Goethe) 172
Necklace Affair 192
Nederlands Stichting ter Bevordering van het Nationaal-Socialisme 110
Nederweert 149, 159
Needle (The), the Glove and the Squirrel 258
Netherlands, the 110, 116, 121, 144, 146, 149, 156, 159
New Testament 181
New York 172
Newcastle upon Tyne 170
Niebuhr 199
Niekisch 209
Nietzsche, F 201
Nieuw Vlaanderen 110
Nieuwe Gids, De 109

Nilsiä 266
Nivard 112
Nobel (the lion) 60, 62, 68, 74, 77, 94, 105, 108, 109
Noble (the lion) 18, 19, 25, 26, 29, 30, 32, 34, 46, 50, 52, 56, 105, 109, 126, 129, 134, 157, 167, 173, 174, 230, 241: see also, Lion, King
Nonkonformist, Der 24
Normans 41, 42
North America 126: see also, USA
Norwich Cathedral 137
Notz, M-F 229
Nozeroy 162
Nun's Priest's Tale 134–140, 163; see also, Chaucer
Nuremberg 44, 210
Nutt, J 186

Oakham parish church (All Saints) 136
Octavian, the Anti-Pope 45
Odo of Cheriton 252, 255
Ogrin 33
Oirschot 159
Old Mr Rabbit He's A Good Fisherman 252
Old Testament 14
Onley, W 167, 168
Opus Poeticum (Schopper) 176–189
Orbais Abbey 146
Order of Dominicans 152
Order of the Repented 141
Order of St Francis 143
O'Ready (a dog) 239, 243
Ormesby Psalter 136
Orwell, G 238
Österley, H 261
Otto I 39
Otto of Brunswick 42
Oulipo 234
Ovid 5
Oviedo 158, 159
Owen, D D R 35, 58–60, 72, 105, 173, 246
Oxford, Bodleian Library 136
Oxford, Magdelen College 148

Pallas 91

Panoplia 184, 185, 189
Paracelsus 233
Paris (of Troy) 58, 63, 64, 71, 91
Paris (the city) 82, 108, 129, 238, 242
Paris, P 224, 231–235
Pascal, the Anti-Pope 43
Passion Sunday 188
Pastré, J-M 38, 39, 42, 43, 48
Patous (the bear) 242, 243
Paulus Diaconus 155
Peace Court: see Van Genechten
Peace of Constance 41
Pec, A 226
Pedanto, Dr 166, 167
Peeters, L 106
Pelé (the rat) 242
Penrith 170
Perceval 67
Percehaie (son of the fox) 239
Percy, G 171
Perrot: see Pierre de Saint-Cloud
Pertelote (a hen) 134, 163
Peter of Pavia 44
Peterborough Cathedral 148
Petrus Alphonsus 246, 248
Pflieger, A 189
Pfraumberg, prison of 47
Phaedrus 155, 260
Phaedri Fabulae Aesopiae 260
Philip, Archbishop of Cologne 44, 50, 53
Philip of Alsace 67
Philip of Swabia 42
Philip von Heinsberg, Archbishop of Cologne 45
Philippe-Auguste (Philip-Augustus) , King 33, 50
Physiologus, The 150
Pierre de Saint-Cloud 18, 28
Pinte (the hen) 134, 163
Plantijn, Christoffel 75 (and Plantijn editions 76–103)
Plasencia Cathedral 144, 147
Plateau (the deer) 22
Pleij, H 82
Ploucquet, H 173
Pocé / Cisse 146
Poitiers, Count of 106
Polar, Le Polar de Renard 237, 238

Pontack 187
Pontigny Abbey 236
Portugal 158
Poslaniec, C 230
Potter, B 174
Potvin, C 224
Poulaille, H
Powell, W 164
Pride (personnification) 52
Prien, F 189
Private Eye 210
Proverbs (Book of, Old Testament) 247
Punch 210
Punt, P 111
Pynson, R 164

Quatre Types 109
Queen Mary Psalter 136
Queneau, R 234

Rabbi Berechiah Ha-Nakdan 246
Rabbi Hai Gam 246
Rabbi Meir 246
Rabbi Rashi 246, 247
Rabelais, F 12, 210, 222
Raga 50
Rainald von Dassel, Arch-Chancellor 44, 45, 50, 53
Raisala 259
Raisant (the mare) 242, 243
Ramberg, J H 119, 120
Rapidos 238
Ratcula 244
Rautalampi 261, 254
Ravenna, Duke of 50
Reason (personnification) 195
Reformation, the 175, 176
Regalado, N 65
Réforme 233
Reinaard de Vos (Decorte) 121
Reinaart de Vos (Kooyman) 121
Reinaart de Vos... (Walters) 108
Reinaerde, De zinrijke avonturen van den vos 120, 121
Reinaert (the fox): see Reynaert
Reinaert (Reynaert) de Vos (=Van den V.R.) 126, 153, 213: *see also Van den Voss Reynaerd*
Reinaert de Vos (Altena) 121

Reinaert de Vos (Willems) 120
Reinaert de Vos aan de pinhelmen.. 108.
Reinaerts (Reynaerts) Historie 55, 63–65, 73–103, 107, 126, 153, 164, 172, 224
Reinaert-saga in der strijd der ideeen, De 110
Reineke (the fox) 173, 191–207, 209–220
Reineke Fuchs (Goethe) 60, 118, 119, 172, 191–207, 209–220
Reineke Fuchs (Gottsched) 172, 191–207
Reinhart Fuchs 1, 37–53, 106
Reinicken Fuchs, Von 178, 179, 189
Reinike (the fox) 175–189
Reinike (Schopper) 175–189
Reinike (High German) 186
Reinikes libros quator; De admirabile fallacia et astutia vulpeculae 175–198, 232
Reinke den vos in de Kempen 110
Reinout 101, 102
Remus, Uncle 252
Renaissance, the 120, 125, 222, 245
Renardie 52; *Les Renardies* 227
Renart (the fox) 44, 51, 52, 56–60, 230, 248–256, 257
Reynaert de Vos (Punt) 111
Reynaerts Historie: see *Reinaerts Historie*
Renart le Contrefait 134, 141, 143, 222, 235, 236
Renart: Le Couronnement de 52, 67, 222
Renart le Nouvel 52, 153, 222, 227
Renart: Les Aventures de maître Renart et de ses compères 233
Renart: Les Aventures de maître Renart et d'Ysengrin son compagnon 231
Reneward (a fox) 163, 252
Renner 180
Renuard (a fox) 163
Revolution, the French 191, 204–206
Rey-Flaud, H 230
Reynaert (the fox) 60–71, 74, 105–110

Reynard (the fox) 1, 2, 4, 5, 8, 10, 11, 18–34, 58–60, 105–110, 126–134, 163–174
Reynard-story in the struggle of ideas, The 110
Reynard the Fox: A Continuation, Or The Second Part Of The Most Pleasant History Of Reynard the Fox 165
Reynard the Fox, The Crafty Courtier, or the Fable of... 171, 186
Reynard the Fox, The History of (Caxton) 60, 126, 163, 169, 171
Reynard the Fox, The History of (chapbooks) 170
Reynard the Fox, His Friends And Enemies... The History of (Ellis) 169
Reynard the Fox, The Most Delectable History of (Allde) 165
Reynard the Fox, The Most Delectable History of (Brewster) 167
Reynard the Fox, The Most Delightful History of...In Heroic Verse (Shurley) 168
Reynard the Fox, The Most Pleasant History of (chapbooks) 170
Reynard the Fox, The Pleasant and Entertaining History of... (Ryland) 170
Reynard the Fox, The Pleasant and Entertaining History of... (Summerly) 171
Reynard the Fox, The Story of (Vedder) 171
Reynard the Fox, The Story of (1851, Great Exhibition) 173
Reynard, Master of the King's Household 153
Reynardine; The Shifts of 156, 166, 167
Reynaud, G 235
Reynike Fosz, Speculum Vitae Aulicae, Eller Den Fordanskede 186
Reynke de Vos 60, 103, 118, 124, 126, 128, 129, 131, 172, 176, 178, 184, 188, 192: see *also*, Lübeck edition, and Low German
Rheims, Maison de la Culture 237; Minstrel of 106
Richard (the Lion-Heart) 47, 48, 52
Richard-Mounet, L 228
Richards, E G 188
Ripon Cathedral 137, 142, 148
Ruwaard, Boudewijn en Joducus 108
Rispail, J-L 233
Robert-Busquet, L 226, 228
Rodin, K 141, 153
Roenel (the dog) 27, 28, 106 (Roeniaus), 242, 243
Roger (a publisher) 172
Roger I 41
Roger (Duke of Sicily) 5
Romagnole, Duke of 50
Roman de Renart, Le 1, 17–34, 37, 44, 46, 48, 51, 55–72, 105, 112, 113, 126, 139, 140, 149, 153, 160, 192, 213, 221–244, 246–256, 263–267: see *also*, Branches
Roman de Renart, adaptation en français facile 230
Roman de Renart, Lecture Suivie pour les Collèges 233
*Roman de Renart, transcrit dans le respect de sa verdure originale...*233
Roman Empire 40, 41
Roman History (Niebuhr) 199
Romance (the language) 43
Rome 4, 45, 75, 94, 97, 98, 142, 178, 187
Rommelpot 111
Roques, M 225, 227, 230
Rossi, L 252
Rostock 116
Rousseau, J-J 200
Royon 237
Ruckelsrey 179
Rudder, D de 121
Rudolf of Strasburg 44
Rukenau, Ruckenau (the she-ape) 64, 75, 92, 153, 154
Rumbling Pot 111
Russell, Don (a fox) 138, 163

Russia 126, 264, 265
Rutland Psalter 145
Ryland, E 170

Sabbath 247
Sachs, H 209
Saint (a publisher) 170
St Amand sur Ozerain 161
St Anastasius (monastery, Rome) 2
St Austell, Holy Trinity Church 144
St Bavo 5
St Bernard (of Clairvaux) 5, 6, 14, 15
St Claude, Cathedral 148
St David's Cathedral 145
Saint-Évremond, C de 234
St Jean-de-Maurienne 149
St Luke (the evangelist) 62, 189
St Mark (the evangelist) 189
St Matthew (the evangelist) 12, 181, 189
Saint-Paul (the town of) 48
St Peter's monastery 2
Saint Pol de Leon, Cathedral 146
Saint-Vincent (monastery, Rome) 6
Salaura (the sow) 2, 5, 12, 13, 15
Salerno 42
Samivel 229
Sanct-Wolfgang 112
Sandon 169
Sands, D B 168
Sanguine 237
Saracens 52
Satan 4, 109, 180: see also, Devil
Schabernack 212
Scheidegger, J-R 66, 72
Schinkel 76–103
Schlusemann, R 85–87
Schmidt, A M 226–228, 233–237
Schopper, H 171, 175–189, 232
Schouwink, W 171, 189
Schwab, U 38, 194
Schwarzbaum, H 246, 256
Scoop 238
Scotland 175
Second Crusade, the: *see* Crusade
Second World War 110, 111, 124, 149, 159
Seneca 63, 180, 188

Serpent, Le 241, 242
Service d'Action Civique 243
Shakespeare, W 175
Sherborne Abbey 153
Shifts of Reynardine... The 156, 157, 166, 167, 170
Ship of Fools, The 180
Shojaei Kawan 261, 262
Shurley (Shirley) J 168
Sibyline prophecies 13
Sicily (the island) 5, 41, 42, 48: Roger, Duke of 5
Sigrim (a wolf) 163, 252
Simon, R 229
Simplicissimus 210
Siniac 237
Sinterwolfgang 112
Sisam, K 163
Slempkes, J A 120, 121
Sly-Look (the panther) 166, 167
Smart (a publisher) 170
Smithers, G V 246, 247, 251
Smithfield Decretals 136, 141, 156
Snoeck-Ducaju en Zoon 85
So did Flanders write 110
Sobieslaw II 46, 47
Sodmann, T 188
Solis, V 116, 232
Soltau 172
Soulby (a publisher) 170
South America 267
Spain 144, 147–149, 155, 159, 162
Sparling, H H 168
Speak Dutch 110
Speculum Vitae Aulicae, Eller Den Fordanskede Reynike Fosz: see *Reynike Fosz*
Spiewok, W 38
Spoleto 40
Spreek Dietsch / Sprecht Flämisch 110
Stallybrass, W S 168
Staufen 106
Steinfeld 144, 159
Steinhöwel's Fables 261
Stephen of Metz, Bishop 38
Sterne, L 121
Stopp, E 202, 205, 206
Strasburg, Bishop of 44–46; the city, 45

Index

Strasburg Oaths 43
Strelen 144
Strubel, A 225, 246
Stuiveling, G 72
Stuttgart 173
Subrenat, J 35, 105, 225, 227, 230
Sudre, L 224
Summerly (a publisher) 171
Suomela-Härmä, E 222
Suzuki, S 225
Swan Knight 101
Switzerland 149, 159, 232
Sympathiques Animateurs du Club 243

Tabby, Tibby 174
Taburiaus 106
Tail Fisher, the 258
Talavera de la Reina 144
Talmud, the 247
Technae Aulicae / Weltlauf und Hofleben 186
Te lucis ante terminum 183
Ténèze, M-L 265
Terensier, J 230
Terrence 188
Terry, P 72, 173
Thai Massage Parlour 242, 244
Theory of Colour, The 196
Thesaurus Linguae Latinae 189
Thirty Years' War 184
Thoms, W J 168
Tibeert, Tybeert (the cat) 74, 89, 95–97
Tiberi, J 241
Tibert (the cat) 44, 48, 56, 57, 126, 128, 129, 165, 230, 240, 243, 244, 257, 267
Ticino 50
Tiecelin (the crow) 56, 57
Till Eulenspiegel 108, 109, 111, 209–212
Timmermans, F 108, 110
Tityrus 179, 188
Todd Mr (a fox) 174
Toeche, Th 42
Toesca, M 227, 228
Toledo Cathedral 149
Tom (and Jerry) 249
Tortone 40

Touchet, L 228
Tournai 4–6, 10, 11
Tower of London 153
Trachsler, R 139
Tridentine Council 189
Trimberg: *see* Hugo
Tristan 58–60
Tristan, Roman de (Bédier) 237; (Béroul) 32, 33, 35, 58, 59, 65
Tristram Shandy 121
Trojan War 71
Troy 179
Trunkiano 50
Trunz, E 207
Tupamaros 244
Turks, the 185
Tuschalan 38, 44, 47
Tusculum 44–46, 50; Counts of, 45
Tuttington parish church 138
Tybaert (the cat) 108
Types of the Folktale, The 245

Uilenspiegel, T: *see* Till Eulenspiegel
Ulysses 195
Uncle Remus Stories 252–256
United States of America 254, 255
Uther, H-J 266
Utrecht 74, 149

Vallerey, G 228
Valmy, Battle of 206
Van Daele, R 61, 68, 72
Van den Vos Reinaerde (Reynaerde) 1, 55, 60–63, 73, 85, 105–110
Van den Vos Reinaerde: Ruwaard, Boudewijn en Jodocus (Genechten) 109
Van Everdingen, A 118, 119, 124, 172
Van Genechten, R 109–111
Van Kampen 109
Van Mierlo, J 110
Van Oostrom, F P 65, 67, 71
Van Wijn, H 101, 102
Varoux 237
Vatican Library 225
Varty, K 35, 56, 59, 72, 116, 135, 136, 138, 141, 150, 153, 157, 164, 222–233, 246, 252, 256

Vautrin, J 237, 238
Vedder, D 171
Venantius Fortunatus 183
Venetian Epigrams 204
Venlo 159
Venus 91
Verdun 205
Verdussen 76–103, 177
Vergil, Virgil 13, 176–179, 188, 189
Veron, J H 228
Verret, A 229
Verzandvoort, E 102, 103
Vexilla regis prodeunt 183
Vice (personnification) 194
Victoria, Queen 172
Villefranche-de-Rouergue, Notre Dame de 148
Villon, F 210
Virgil: *see* Vergil
Virtue (personnification) 194
Vlaamse Beweging 107
Voigt, E 1
Voleur, Le 244
Volkhart 101, 102
Volk en Staat 110
Volpus (son of Reynard) 166
Von Kaulbach: *see* Kaulbach
Vooruit 111
Voss, J H 196
Vox and Wolf 246, 247, 249–251
Vrevel (the lion) 38, 39, 41–46, 49–51, 53

Wackers, P 63, 65, 70, 71, 88, 102, 103, 164, 188
Wales 145
Walther von Horburg 38, 44
Walschap, G 109
Wapenbroeders 111, 112
Weber, A P 209–220
Weigere, H 189
Weimar 191
Welfen 106
Wellingborough 148
Wells Cathedral 136, 139, 141, 142, 148
Wenseleers, L 106
West-East-Divan 205
West Flanders 74, 106

Westminster 163
Westminster Abbey 160
Whalley, St Mary and All Saints' 137
Whitehead, A N 195
Wiethälter, W 207
Wild, R 207
Willems, J F 106, 107, 120
William of Dampierre 67
Winchester Cathedral 140, 148
Winchester College Chapel 140, 148
Windsor, St George's Chapel 140, 144, 147, 148, 153, 157
Wintzenberger, D 189
Wittemberg 108
Witton, N 75
Wladislaw II 46
Wolfenbüttel 172
Wolverhampton 170
Worcester Cathedral 143
Würzburg 14
Wynkyn de Worde (edition and/or picture cycle) 114, 115, 129, 131, 161, 164, 165, 168, 170

York Minster 136
Ysegrim (the wolf) 74, 75, 86
Ysengrimus, The 1–15, 112, 155, 179, 188, 249, 263
Ysengrimus (the wolf) 1–15, 188, 189
Ysengrin (the wolf) 37, 38, 126, 163, 229, 248, 249, 252, 253, 255, 265
Yvain 58, 139

Zähringen: *see* Berthold, Duke
Zalep, Kingdom of 166
Zamora Cathedral 146 155
Zani (the ape) 156
Zinrijke avonturen... See Reinaerde
Zolverein 173
Zoo dichtte Dietschland 110

www.ingramcontent.com/pod-product-compliance
Lightning Source LLC
Chambersburg PA
CBHW071149070526
44584CB00019B/2722